Working With 4th EDITION

THE STUDY OF ECONOMICS
Principles, Concepts & Applications

A Student Study Guide
and Workbook

Working With
THE STUDY OF ECONOMICS
Principles, Concepts & Applications
by Turley Mings

4th EDITION

Prepared by Matthew Marlin, *Duquesne University*,
Diane Swanson, *Robert Morris College*,
and Turley Mings, *formerly San Jose State University*

DPG

The Dushkin Publishing Group, Inc.

Working With The Study of Economics: Principles, Concepts & Applications, 4th Edition

Copyright © 1991 by The Dushkin Publishing Group, Inc. All rights reserved.

Printed in the United States of America

Library of Congress Catalog Card Number 91-071652

International Standard Book Number (ISBN) 0-87967-922-0

First Printing

The Dushkin Publishing Group, Inc., Sluice Dock, Guilford, Connecticut 06437

For further information, please contact the
Sales Service Department: 800-243-6532
from all 50 states and Canada.

To the Student

This workbook is intended to help you get the most out of your text, *The Study of Economics: Principles, Concepts & Applications*, 4th edition. It contains summaries of the text chapters, schematic outlines of each section of the chapters, review exercises in accordance with the learning objectives, additional case applications, practice tests, crossword puzzles to test your understanding of the economic terms, and, at the end of the book, answers to the review exercises, case application questions, practice tests, and crossword puzzles.

As you study economics you will encounter many concepts that are new to you. Your first objective should be to understand what each of these concepts means. Being able to explain a concept is the first step in being able to make use of it. The second step is recognizing how the concept applies to a particular situation. This entails moving from the ability to explain a concept to the ability to use it in analyzing a situation and reaching logical conclusions with the help of the concept. The final step is making the concept a part of your intellectual resources, so that whenever a situation arises in the future that can be better understood with the use of the concept, it will come to mind.

The ability to make use of economic concepts in reasoning about personal, national, and world economic problems is termed economic literacy. The importance of economic literacy has been widely recognized in recent years. There has been a great increase in the amount of attention given in the media to economic matters. The vocabulary of economics has spread from the confines of classrooms, textbooks, and specialized journals to newspapers, magazines, and the six o'clock news on television. Each national network and many a local station has its own economics reporter appearing with an important story almost every day. Economic terms such as cost-of-living index, Gross National Product, budget deficit, and balance of payments regularly appear in news stories. To understand what the news is about, you have to be economically literate. When you have completed *The Study of Economics* you will be more literate in economics than most people; and if you make a diligent attempt to incorporate the economic principles and concepts into your intellectual equipment, you can contribute to the nation's ability to deal with its economic problems.

This supplement, *Working With The Study of Economics*, includes a variety of aids to increase your economic literacy. Each chapter begins with a *Chapter Outline* of the contents in the text and a *Summary of Economic Analysis* of the chapter. The summary is more succinct than the Putting It Together sections at the end of the textbook chapters. It briefly states the main principles in the chapter.

The text chapters are divided into 3 to 4 sections headed by organizing questions, and this workbook is organized similarly. I have included a *Schematic Outline* at the beginning of each section that shows the concept organization of that section. These schematic outlines can be very helpful in your studying. The best way to make use of them is explained as follows, in a format similar to that of the schematic outlines themselves.

How Can You Use Your Study Time Most Efficiently?

SCHEMATIC OUTLINES

The schematic outlines at the beginning of each chapter section in this workbook show the relationships between the different concepts and give a brief explanation of their meaning. These outlines can increase the efficiency of your study time when used as follows:

As a Preview

Studies of how people learn show that you get more out of reading something if you have an idea in advance of what the reading is about. Before you read a section in the textbook, look over the schematic outline of that section. Do not try to understand everything in the outline. Concentrate on the headings and observe how the different concepts relate to each other — which ones are parallel concepts, which are sequential, and which are subordinate concepts of others.

As a Review

After reading the section in the textbook chapter, go over the schematic outline again. This time study it more carefully to reinforce your learning of the concepts and better retain what you read in the text.

In the above outline there are two sequential concepts under the topic of schematic outlines. The first concept is the use of schematic outlines as a preview of the material in the text. It is a well-established principle in learning that you can read a selection with better understanding if you first skim it for content. But skimming complex material is difficult. The schematic outlines provide an easier and more certain way of previewing the reading material. In using the outlines as a preview, focus on the relationships of the different concepts. Note which ones are sequential (listed one after the other, as they are in this case), which ones are parallel (listed side by side, such as the three functions of money—see workbook page 141), and which ones are main and which subordinate concepts. The leading concepts are shown in all capital letters in bold typeface, while secondary concepts are in lowercase letters in bold type. Subordinate concepts appear in boxes within main concept boxes. For example, the attributes of a good medium of exchange are listed in a box contained within the main concept box of "medium of exchange" as one of the functions of money in the example cited above. When using the schematic outlines as a preview, do not try to master the concepts. Just observe their relationships and skip the fine print.

The second function of the schematic outlines is their use as a review after reading the material. Again, it is an accepted principle—one taught in the study methods seminars that have become popular in recent years—that understanding and retention are improved by reviewing material that you have just read. The schematic outlines provide a convenient means for doing this. Study them more carefully this time. Do read the fine print. If you find that you are not certain of the meaning of a concept, go over it again in the text. For longer retention of the material, it would then be helpful for you to review the schematic outlines again the next day.

I have provided a new *Case Application* for each chapter section to give you additional experience in applying the economic concepts to real-world situations. The old adage "practice makes perfect" is particularly true for economic literacy. Repeated experience in applying economics will give you the ability to make use of economic reasoning in the future. The value of the case applications is enhanced by answering the *Economic Reasoning* questions following each one. As in the text, the case applications all have three questions. Answering the first of the three should be relatively easy if you have understood the explanation of the concepts in the text. The second question is generally more difficult, requiring you to use economic analysis in answering it. The third question calls for your opinion and involves value judgments as well as economic reasoning. Suggested answers to the Economic Reasoning questions are also to be found in the back of this book.

Each chapter then concludes with a *Practice Test* consisting of 15 multiple-choice and 5 true/false questions. These questions have been prepared with the same objectives in mind as those provided to teachers for use in testing. The answers to these questions are also in the back part of the book.

Following the last chapter in each of the four units into which the book is divided is a *Crossword Puzzle* that can be solved by using the key ideas introduced in the unit. The solutions to the crossword puzzles are at the end of the book.

Best wishes with your study of economics! I hope this workbook will make it easier and more rewarding.

Contents

To the Student   v

Unit I. FOUNDATIONS

CHAPTER 1 ECONOMIC METHODS   1

Chapter Outline   1
Summary of Economic Analysis   1
Review of the Learning Objectives   2
What Is Economics?   2
1.1.   Explain scarcity as an economic term.   2
1.2.   List the factors of production.   3
1.3.   Describe the steps in the scientific method.   4
Case Application: Famine in Africa   4
What Are the Tools of Economics?   5
1.4.   Describe three types of factual tools used in economics.   5
1.5.   Describe the theoretical tools used in economics.   6
Case Application: Hot or Cold? Cost-Benefit Analysis   6
What Are the Uses of Graphs?   7
1.6.   Give four examples of different types of charts.   8
1.7.   Explain what an analytical diagram is used for.   10
1.8.   Draw and label an analytical diagram showing the relationship between two variables.   10
Case Application: Air Quality in the United States   12
Practice Test   13

CHAPTER 2 ECONOMIC CHOICES   16

Chapter Outline   16
Summary of Economic Analysis   17
Review of the Learning Objectives   17
How Do We Make Economic Choices?   17
2.1.   Define and give examples of economic trade-offs.   18
2.2.   Explain opportunity cost.   18
2.3.   Explain the production possibility frontier and increasing costs.   19
Case Application: A Question of Oil   21
What Are the Basic Economic Questions?   22
2.4.   Give examples of the three basic economic questions.   22
Case Application: Is Coal the Heir to the Energy Throne?   23
What Are Society's Economic Goals?   24
2.5.   List the four primarily economic goals of society.   24
2.6.   Show the effect on output of increasing employment to full employment.   24
2.7.   Show the effect on economic growth of producing more capital goods.   25
2.8.   Give examples of trade-offs between economic and socioeconomic goals.   26
Case Application: A Plastic World   27
Practice Test   27

CHAPTER 3 THE ECONOMIC SYSTEM   30

Chapter Outline   30
Summary of Economic Analysis   31
Review of the Learning Objectives   32
Why Are Economic Systems Needed?   32
3.1.   Distinguish between absolute and comparative advantage.   32
3.2.   Explain why specialization based on absolute or comparative advantage results in greater economic efficiency and interdependence.   33
Case Application: From Farm to City   33
What Are the Principal Types of Economic Systems?   34
3.3.   Identify the three major types of economic systems, and explain how they differ.   34
Case Application: Digging a Subway in Calcutta   35
How Does a Market System Resolve the Three Basic Economic Questions?   36

3.4. Explain how a market system resolves the three basic economic questions. 36
3.5. Distinguish between goods and services sold in product markets and those sold in factor markets. 37
3.6. Diagram the circular flow of a market economy. 37
Case Application: The Shale Age—Not Yet 38
Practice Test 39

CHAPTER 4 MARKET PRICING 41

Chapter Outline 41
Summary of Economic Analysis 42
Review of the Learning Objectives 43
What Forces Determine Prices in the Marketplace? 43
4.1. Explain the laws of demand and supply. 43
4.2. Explain why prices move toward an equilibrium price. 44
Case Application: The Grain Drain 45
What Determines Demand? 46
4.3. List the determinants of demand. 46
Case Application: Upscale Munching 47
What Determines Supply? 48
4.4. List the determinants of supply. 48
4.5. Distinguish between short-run and long-run supply. 48
Case Application: Black Walnut Worth Gold 49
Why Do Prices Change? 50
4.6. Identify the causes of shifts in demand and how they affect market equilibrium. 50
4.7. Identify the causes of shifts in supply and how they affect market equilibrium. 52
4.8. Distinguish between a change in demand and a change in quantity demanded. 53
Case Application: Do Boycotts Work? 54
Practice Test 55

CROSSWORD PUZZLE FOR CHAPTERS 1–4 57

Unit II. MICROECONOMICS

CHAPTER 5 THE CONSUMER 58

Chapter Outline 58
Summary of Economic Analysis 59
Review of the Learning Objectives 60
What Choices Do Consumers Make? 60
5.1. Define elasticity of demand. 60
5.2. Define the terms perfectly elastic, relatively elastic, unitary elastic, relatively inelastic, and perfectly inelastic. 61
5.3. Compute elasticity ratios. 62
5.4. Define consumer sovereignty and show how it is related to the allocation of resources. 62
5.5. Define average propensity to consume and average propensity to save. 63
Case Application: Going to the Movies 63
How Do Consumers Make Choices? 64
5.6. Show the relationship of marginal utility to total utility. 64
5.7. Explain the principle of diminishing marginal utility. 65
5.8. State the conditions necessary for consumer equilibrium. 65
Case Application: Life-style and Consumer Choice 66
How Can Consumers Make Better Choices? 67
5.9. Explain the effects of product information and advertising on consumer choices. 67
Case Application: Do You Have Time for Your Possessions? 68
Practice Test 69

CHAPTER 6 THE BUSINESS FIRM AND MARKET STRUCTURE 71

Chapter Outline 71
Summary of Economic Analysis 71
Review of the Learning Objectives 73
What Are the Forms and Economic Functions of Business Firms? 73
6.1. List the three main forms of business organization and cite the advantages and disadvantages of each. 73
6.2 Describe the four economic functions of business firms. 74

Case Application: The Progressive Bike Shop   74
What Determines a Firm's Profits?   75
6.3.   Distinguish between fixed costs and variable costs.   76
6.4.   Show the relationship of total cost and total revenue to output.   76
6.5.   Locate the break-even point and point of maximum profit.   78
6.6.   Distinguish between normal rate of return and economic profits.   79
Case Application: The Fortunes of the Progressive Bike Shop   80
How Does Industry Market Structure Affect Price and Output Decisions?   80
6.7.   List the characteristics of purely competitive industries.   81
6.8.   Explain the principle of diminishing returns.   81
6.9.   Explain the short-run and long-run adjustments to changes in demand in a purely competitive industry.   82
6.10.   Differentiate between pure monopoly, shared monopoly, and differentiated competition.   83
Case Application: Wheat Farmers in Debt   84
Practice Test   85

CHAPTER 7 INDUSTRY PERFORMANCE   87

Chapter Outline   87
Summary of Economic Analysis   88
Review of the Learning Objectives   89
What Determines Industry Performance?   89
7.1.   Describe four factors that determine industry performance.   89
7.2.   Define productivity and state how it is usually measured.   90
7.3.   Explain why product quality is important and how it can be improved.   90
7.4.   Describe why and how businesses respond to social concerns, and give three examples.   91
Case Application: Academic Theory Put Into Practice   91
How Can Industry Performance Be Improved?   92
7.5.   Explain the importance of investment in capital equipment, why the rate is low in the United States, and how it can be increased.   92
7.6.   Describe investment in human capital and show how it affects the learning curve.   93
7.7.   Explain R&D spending and its importance.   94
7.8.   Describe process innovations and explain how they improve productivity.   94
7.9.   List and give an example of three types of EI teams.   95
Case Application: The Factory of the Future Is Next   95
What Are the Effects of Industry Concentration on Performance?   96
7.10.   Describe market concentration and define the degree of market concentration in terms of the concentration ratio.   96
7.11.   Explain the difference between market concentration and aggregate concentration.   97
7.12.   Describe four consequences of high concentration in industries.   97
Case Application: Rent-A-Kidney Business: Dialysis for Profit?   98
Practice Test   98

CHAPTER 8 GOVERNMENT AND BUSINESS   101

Chapter Outline   101
Summary of Economic Analysis   102
Review of the Learning Objectives   103
What Does the Government Do to Regulate Monopoly?   103
8.1.   Explain the purposes of the Interstate Commerce Act and the Sherman, Clayton, and Celler-Kefauver Acts.   103
8.2.   Explain the purpose of industry R&D consortiums and why they are exempt from the antitrust laws.   104
8.3.   List the causes of natural monopoly and indicate what industries fall under that classification.   104
8.4.   Explain how public policy deals with natural monopolies.   105
8.5.   Discuss the positive and negative aspects of regulation.   105
8.6.   Explain the reasons for and consequences of deregulation.   106
Case Application: Water, Water, Everywhere, And Not a Drop (That's Fit) to Drink   106
Why Does the Government Produce Goods and Services?   107
8.7.   Identify the kinds of goods and services that constitute collective goods, and explain why the government provides them.   107
8.8.   Explain the concepts of external economies and external costs.   108
Case Application: Should the Government Be in the Railroad Business?   110
What Is the Role of Government in Protecting Consumers, Workers, and the Environment?   111

8.9. Explain how the government protects workers and consumers. 111
  8.10. Describe three alternative ways by which the government can reduce pollution by getting firms to internalize the external costs of environmental pollution. 112
  Case Application: Declaration of Air Pollution Emergency 113
  Practice Test 114

CHAPTER 9 LABOR AND INCOME DISTRIBUTION 116

  Chapter Outline 116
  Summary of Economic Analysis 117
  Review of the Learning Objectives 118
  What Determines Wages in a Market Economy? 118
  9.1. Explain what determines the demand for and supply of labor and how demand and supply influence wages. 118
  9.2. Discuss how capital availability affects labor demand and wages. 121
  9.3. Describe the effects of minimum wage laws. 121
  9.4. Explain what labor unions do. 122
  9.5. Explain what "sticky" wages are and discuss their impacts in labor markets. 123
  Case Application: Coal and Black Gold 124
  What Determines Other Incomes? 124
  9.6. Describe the different income sources that make up the functional distribution of income. 125
  9.7. Identify the unique characteristics of the determination of rent compared to the determination of other sources of income. 125
  Case Application: How Much Is a Nose Guard Worth? 126
  What Causes Unequal Distribution of Income? 127
  9.8. Describe how the personal distribution of income is measured, how it has changed over time, and how the distribution is shown on a Lorenz curve. 128
  9.9. Describe the causes of unequal distribution of personal income. 129
  Case Application: The New Poor 130
  What Is the Answer to Poverty? 130
  9.10. Explain how poverty is defined and describe the programs for reducing poverty. 131
  Case Application: Increased Opportunities for the Handicapped 132
  Practice Test 132

CROSSWORD PUZZLE FOR CHAPTERS 5–9 135

Unit III. MACROECONOMICS

CHAPTER 10 MONEY 136

  Chapter Outline 136
  Summary of Economic Analysis 137
  Review of the Learning Objectives 138
  What Is Money? 138
  10.1. Discuss the history of money. 138
  10.2. Define the M1 money supply and describe its components. 139
  10.3. Explain how near money differs from money and discuss how near money relates to the broader money definitions of M2, M3, and L. 139
  Case Application: What Isn't Money? 140
  What Does Money Do? 141
  10.4. List the three functions of money and explain the characteristics money must have in order to be functional. 141
  Case Application: Primitive Money 142
  How Is Money Created? 143
  10.5. Discuss how currency is affected by public demand and explain money creation. 143
  Case Application: How the Government Creates Money 144
  How Is the Supply of Money Controlled? 145
  10.6. Describe the Federal Reserve System. 145
  10.7. Explain how the Federal Reserve System controls the money supply. 146
  Case Application: Who's in Charge Around Here? 149
  Practice Test 149

CHAPTER 11 ECONOMIC INSTABILITY 152

  Chapter Outline 152
  Summary of Economic Analysis 153

Review of the Learning Objectives   154
What Causes Unemployment?   154
11.1.   Describe the three major causes of unemployment.   154
11.2.   Explain why some unemployment is hidden.   155
Case Application: Where the Jobs Went   156
What Causes Inflation?   157
11.3.   State the meaning of inflation and the CPI.   157
11.4.   Describe three causes of inflation and explain the usage of the quantity equation.   158
Case Application: Talk About Inflation . . .   159
Is There a Trade-off Between Unemployment and Inflation?   160
11.5.   Explain the relationship between unemployment and inflation and use the Phillips curve to show this relationship.   160
11.6.   Define stagflation and relate the price level to output and employment levels by use of the aggregate supply and aggregate demand curves.   162
Case Application: Phillips Curve International   164
What Are the Consequences of Unemployment and Inflation?   165
11.7.   Explain the consequences of unemployment and inflation.   165
Case Application: Disinflation Losers   166
Practice Test   167

CHAPTER 12   THE ECONOMY'S OUTPUT   169

Chapter Outline   169
Summary of Economic Analysis   170
Review of the Learning Objectives   171
How Much Does the Economy Produce?   171
12.1.   Define the GNP and explain the two ways of measuring it and why they give the same result.   171
12.2.   Explain the four types of expenditures that make up the total demand for goods and services.   172
12.3.   Define National Income and explain how it differs from GNP.   173
12.4.   Define constant dollar GNP and show how it relates to current dollar GNP   173
Case Application: Helen's Gift City, Inc.   174
What Determines Domestic Output from the Demand-Side Point of View?   176
12.5.   Explain the Keynesian economic model and show under what conditions the output of the economy is at equilibrium.   176
Case Application: Changes in Demand   178
What Determines Domestic Output from the Supply-Side Point of View?   179
12.6.   Describe the meaning of Say's Law.   179
12.7.   Explain how supply-side economics differs from demand-side economics.   180
Case Application: Is War Good for the Economy?   181
Practice Test   182

CHAPTER 13   PUBLIC FINANCE   184

Chapter Outline   184
Summary of Economic Analysis   185
Review of the Learning Objectives   186
On What Do Governments Spend Money?   186
13.1.   Describe the size of government debt and deficits.   186
13.2.   Discuss the relative size of government economic activity.   187
13.3.   List the most important types of federal government spending.   187
13.4.   List the most important types of state and local government spending.   188
Case Application: Renovating America   189
Where Do Governments Get the Money to Spend?   190
13.5.   Identify the principal sources of revenue for the federal, state, and local governments respectively.   190
Case Application: Should the United States Have a Value-Added Tax?   191
Who Pays for Government Spending?   192
13.6.   Explain the criteria for equity in taxation.   192
13.7.   Describe how "bad" taxes decrease economic efficiency.   193
13.8.   Define what is meant by the incidence of a tax.   194
Case Application: A Look at the Flat-Rate Tax   195
Practice Test   195

CHAPTER 14 POLICIES FOR ECONOMIC STABILITY AND GROWTH 198

Chapter Outline 198
Summary of Economic Analysis 199
Review of the Learning Objectives 200
What Can the Government Do About Unemployment and Inflation? 200
14.1.   Discuss economic policies in the 1980s and their consequences. 200
14.2.   Identify the government's two major instruments of stabilization policy. 201
14.3.   Differentiate between annually balanced budgets, cyclically balanced budgets, and functional finance. 202
Case Application: The Balanced Budget Amendment 203
How Does Fiscal Policy Help Stabilize the Economy? 204
14.4.   Explain how discretionary fiscal policy works from the Keynesian and supply-side viewpoints. 204
14.5.   Describe the multiplier effect. 205
14.6.   Define and give examples of automatic stabilizers. 206
Case Application: What Happens to Tax-Cut Dollars? 206
How Can Monetary Policy Help Stabilize the Economy? 207
14.7.   Explain how monetary policy is implemented. 207
Case Application: The Interest Rate Yo-Yo 209
How Can Economic Growth Be Increased? 210
14.8.   Explain the investment/GNP ratio and the capital/output ratio and describe their importance. 211
14.9.   Describe the effects on economic growth of the labor-force participation rate and investment in human capital. 211
Case Application: How to Grow 212
Practice Test 213

CROSSWORD PUZZLE FOR CHAPTERS 10–14 216

Unit IV. WORLD ECONOMICS

CHAPTER 15 INTERNATIONAL TRADE 217

Chapter Outline 217
Summary of Economic Analysis 218
Review of the Learning Objectives 219
Why Do We Trade With Other Countries? 219
15.1.   Explain the difference between absolute and comparative advantage. 219
15.2.   Explain why specialization is sometimes complete but normally is limited. 220
15.3.   Compare the types of goods exported by the United States with the types of goods imported. 220
Case Application: U.S. Farmers Selling Overseas 221
Who Benefits and Who Is Hurt by Foreign Trade? 222
15.4.   Describe the effects of foreign trade on economies. 222
15.5.   Specify who benefits and who loses as a result of foreign trade. 225
Case Application: The Top U.S. Exporters 226
How Do We Restrict Foreign Trade? 227
15.6.   Compare the different types of restrictions imposed on foreign trade. 227
15.7.   Discuss the different vehicles for trade negotiations and define "most-favored nation" treatment. 230
Case Application: Made-in-America Japanese Cars 230
Should Foreign Trade Be Restricted? 231
15.8.   Evaluate the arguments in favor of trade restrictions. 231
Case Application: Politics and Trade 232
Practice Test 233

CHAPTER 16 INTERNATIONAL FINANCE AND THE NATIONAL ECONOMY 236

Chapter Outline 236
Summary of Economic Analysis 236
Review of the Learning Objectives 238
How Do We Pay for Imports? 238
16.1.   Explain how payments are made for imports. 238
16.2.   Distinguish between fixed and freely fluctuating exchange rates and explain how the rate of exchange is determined under each system. 239

16.3. Differentiate between currency depreciation, currency appreciation, devaluation, and revaluation.   242

Case Application: The End of the World Credit Binge   243
What Happens When Exports and Imports Do Not Balance?   244
16.4. Define balance of payments and list the different accounts in the balance of payments.   244
16.5. Distinguish between a favorable and an unfavorable balance of trade.   245
16.6. Explain basic deficit and the role of the residual accounts in the balance of payments.   246

Case Application: U.S. International Trade Position Takes a Nosedive   247
What Is the Relationship Between International Finance and the National Economy?   248
16.7. Explain national economic equilibrium and illustrate with a schematic GNP tank diagram.   248
16.8. Show how an import surplus allows the economy to consume more than it produces.   250
16.9. Describe the role of foreign investment in compensating for insufficient domestic savings and taxes.   251

Case Application: A Penny Saved Is a Rare Occurrence   251
Practice Test   252

CHAPTER 17 ALTERNATIVE ECONOMIC SYSTEMS   255

Chapter Outline   255
Summary of Economic Analysis   257
Review of the Learning Objectives   257
What Are the Alternatives to Capitalism?   257
17.1. Explain the distinctions between capitalism, state socialism, market socialism, and the welfare state.   257

Case Application: Down Argentina Way   258
17.2. Compare the way in which a system of state socialism answers the basic economic questions of what, how, and for whom to produce with the way a market system answers these questions.   260

Case Application: Food Production in the Soviet Union   261
How Does the Performance of Alternative Economic Systems Compare?   262
17.3. Evaluate the relative performance of state socialism and market economies in terms of each of the following: efficiency, price stability, unemployment, and growth.   262
17.4. Compare the alternative economic systems in how well they achieve socioeconomic goals.   264

Case Application: Business Cycle Hits Eastern Europe   264
Practice Test   265

CHAPTER 18 WORLD ECONOMIC DEVELOPMENT   268

Chapter Outline   268
Summary of Economic Analysis   269
Review of the Learning Objectives   270
How Do Standards of Living Compare?   270
18.1. Discuss the ways of comparing living standards among countries and explain how China compares with other less-developed countries.   270
18.2. Name the regions where poverty is most prevalent and list four low-income countries in those regions.   271

Case Application: Report on Africa   272
What Makes Countries Poor?   273
18.3. Explain the problems that cause countries to be poor.   273

Case Application: Do You Like Company? How About 10 Billion?   274
What Are the Prospects for World Economic Development?   275
18.4. Explain the significance of the population growth rate in economic development.   275
18.5. Describe the role of foreign indebtedness with respect to the LDCs.   276
18.6. Discuss the relationship between economic development and environmental pollution.   277

Case Application: Growth Prospects for the LDCs   278
Practice Test   279

CROSSWORD PUZZLE FOR CHAPTERS 15-18   281

ANSWERS TO CHAPTER QUESTIONS   282

Chapter 1

Economic Methods

I. Chapter Outline

The study of economics is the study of how society deals with the existence of **scarcity**—the fact that we cannot produce enough goods and services for everybody to have everything that he or she wants. Economists study this problem with a variety of factual and theoretical tools, with a special "fondness" for the use of charts and graphs.

Introductory Article: There's Something in the Air

Most scientists today agree that the earth's air is growing steadily warmer due to the "greenhouse effect" caused by the use of CFCs and the burning of fossil fuels such as petroleum. The fact that we cannot drive our cars, cool and heat our houses, *and* have a completely safe environment is an illustration of scarcity. Economists therefore study environmental issues, and they do so with their own particular set of tools.

Economic Analysis

This chapter introduces what the study of economics is about and the tools that economists use by addressing the three following questions:

1. What Is Economics?

   Important Concepts: Scarcity, The scientific method, Economic reasoning
   Case Application: The Vanishing Land

2. What Are the Tools of Economics?

   Important Concepts: Factual tools, Theoretical tools
   Important Models: Cost-benefit analysis
   Case Application: Does It Pay to Go to College?

3. What Are the Uses of Graphs?

   Important Concepts: Descriptive charts, Variables, Analytical diagrams
   Case Application: The Energy Gluttons

Perspective: The Master Model Builder
            Biography—Paul Samuelson

II. Summary of Economic Analysis

1. The basic problem economics is concerned with is **scarcity**.
2. Anything that is scarce is an **economic good**.
3. Producing economic goods requires the use of **resources** or **factors of production**, which are also scarce.
4. Economics, like other sciences, makes use of the **scientific method** to analyze facts and draw conclusions.
5. **Economic reasoning** consists of using factual and theoretical tools in a logical manner.

6. Simplified representations of the real world called **economic models** are the most important analytical economic tool.
7. Economists often present descriptive information in **charts** and the relationship between variables in **diagrams**.

III. Review of the Learning Objectives *(Answers begin on p. 282.)*

What Is Economics?

SCARCITY
Economics is the social science concerned with how resources are used to satisfy people's wants. Since there are not sufficient resources to satisfy all wants, economics must overcome the problem of scarcity.

RESOURCES

Land	Labor	Capital
Includes all natural resources — minerals, forests, air, and so forth.	Includes workers, managers, and professionals.	Generally refers to real capital — the machinery, factories, and office buildings used in production.
	Entrepreneurs Individuals who organize resources to produce a good or service.	**Financial Capital** The funds to purchase the resources used in production.

SCIENTIFIC METHOD

The scientific method consists of:
1. Observing an event.
2. Devising an explanation (hypothesis) accounting for event.
3. Testing the hypothesis.
4. Tentatively accepting, rejecting, or revising the hypothesis.

ECONOMIC REASONING
Economic reasoning is the process of applying the tools of economics to a problem in order to understand it and analyze the effects of alternative solutions.

(See page vi in the foreword "To the Student" for how to make the best use of this schematic outline.)

1.1. Explain scarcity as an economic term. *(Write in answers below.)*

(THE CODE 1.1 MEANS CHAPTER 1, LEARNING OBJECTIVE 1, IN THE TEXTBOOK. YOU WILL FIND THIS CODE USED THROUGHOUT THIS WORKBOOK.)

A. The basic problem that economics is concerned with is *scarcity*.

B. Any good that is scarce is called a(n) __economic good__.

C. A rare good or resource is only scarce if someone __wants__ it.

D. Place a check next to the items listed below that are scarce.

1. _X_ Pure air.
2. ___ Radioactive waste.
3. ___ Termites.
4. _X_ Time.
5. _X_ Money.
6. ___ Flu germs.
7. _X_ Economics instructors.

1.2. List the factors of production.

A. Indicate the appropriate resource category of each of the following:

1. Water.
   __land__

2. Entrepreneurs.
   __labor__

3. Economists.
   __labor__

4. Technology.
   __capital__

5. Factories.
   __capital__

6. Topsoil.
   __land__

7. Classrooms.
   __capital__

B. List five specific resources used to produce an economics student.

1. _____
2. _____
3. _____
4. _____
5. _____

1.3. Describe the steps in the scientific method.

A. According to the scientific method, a theory should be accepted if it can accurately

____predict_____.

B. The most difficult step in the scientific method for economists is

____testing hypotheses_____.

C. Indicate which of the steps in the scientific method is indicated by each of the following:

I cough when I stand behind an idling car.

____observation_____

I hold a bottle over an exhaust pipe, close the bottle, and then examine the contents of the bottle.

____gathering data_____

I make an educated guess that car exhausts make me cough.

____make a hypothesis_____

I stand behind another idling car and start coughing again.

____accept the hypothesis_____

Case Application: Famine in Africa

A chorus of forty-five of the hottest pop stars in the business got together on January 28, 1985, to record an album. Bruce Springsteen, Kenny Rogers, Dionne Warwick, Cyndi Lauper, Tina Turner, Billy Joel, Paul Simon, and Kim Carnes were a few of the superstars who rearranged their schedules, laid aside their egos, and donated their talents to produce the "We Are the World" album. The purpose of this unusual effort was to raise money to aid the famine victims in Ethiopia and other African countries.

Even in Africa, where starvation is a chronic problem, the degree of the crisis was so extraordinary that it brought forth extraordinary efforts to provide assistance. At the time the "We Are the World" record was cut, the famine had already taken the lives of approximately 2 million people, half of them in Ethiopia, most of them children. Millions more African children were physically and mentally disabled, many blinded, because of malnutrition and lack of vitamins.

The extent of the starvation in Africa was all the more shocking because it was unexpected, at first almost unbelievable. Many of us asked ourselves, why should people starve when the world's production of food had been increasing at record rates? After all, now there were improved seed varieties that gave higher yields than before and were more resistant to diseases, there were new irrigation developments, there was greater use of fertilizers, and there was additional land brought under cultivation, making more food available to more people than ever before in history.

The apparent cause of the African famine was a severe drought. But the underlying causes were less obvious. The drought itself may not be entirely the responsibility of Mother Nature. Some analysts believe it was partly the fault of man's treatment of the land. To obtain wood for fuel and construction, Africa's forests have been cut down at an alarming rate. In the last century, nearly half of Ethiopia was carpeted by woodlands. Today, there are thick forests on only 4% of the land. This deforestation caused rapid water runoff, which reduced the amount of moisture evaporated into the atmosphere to fall as rain. It also caused erosion of the topsoil that resulted in a reduction of agricultural output. The U.S. embassy in Ethiopia reported that the country lost over 1 billion tons of topsoil a year as a result of erosion. The only region in the world where the amount of food produced per person has actually decreased in the past 20 years is the part of Africa south of the Sahara desert.

In late 1985 the drought broke, with the most plentiful African rainfall in 10 years. But now the famine is back, and the United Nations' World Food Program estimates that 27 million people on the African continent are in danger of starving to death. So far, no pop groups have stepped forward to publicise the pending disaster. The starvation problems today are blamed on African governments' policies as much as on the vagaries of nature (see the case application "Report on Africa" in chapter 18 of this book, page 272).

Economic Reasoning *(Write your responses on a separate sheet. Answers begin on p. 283.)*

1. What resources are scarce in Ethiopia, according to this case application?
2. On the basis of the information in this case application, what would be a reasonable hypothesis explaining the recurrent famines in Africa? How would you test the hypothesis?
3. Should the Ethiopian government prevent its citizens from cutting down trees for firewood? Why or why not?

What Are the Tools of Economics?

FACTUAL TOOLS	THEORETICAL TOOLS
Statistics — Data, Methods	**Economic Concepts** — Words or phrases that convey a specific meaning in economics.
History — Economic history	**Economic Models** — Simplified representations of the real world. Words, Mathematical equations, Graphs
Institutions — Organizations, Customs, Patterns of behavior	

(See page vi in the foreword "To the Student" for how to make the best use of this schematic outline.)

1.4. Describe three types of factual tools used in economics.

A. The three types of factual tools used by economists are:

1. _history_
2. _statistics_
3. _institutions_

B. Indicate which factual tool is represented in the list below:

1. The cost of the Savings and Loan "bailout" to taxpayers.

    statistics

2. Savings and Loan Associations.

    institutions

3. The "bank runs" of the 1930s.

    history

4. Federal deposit insurance for banks.

    institutions

5. The amount of unemployment caused by Savings and Loan failures.

    statistics

C. Two uses of statistics are to _describe_ data and to _analyze_ data.

1.5. Describe the theoretical tools used in economics.

A. Economic _concepts_ are ideas that convey specific meanings in economics, and economic _models_ are simplified representations of the real world.

B. Indicate whether the following are concepts (C) or models (M).
1. _C_ Unemployment.
2. _C_ Scarcity.
3. _M_ Cost-benefit analysis.
4. _C_ Equity.
5. _M_ Diagrams.
6. _M_ Y = a + b(X) (the equation of a line).
7. _M_ Weight increases with height.

C. In what three ways can models be presented?
1. _diagrams_
2. _words_
3. _mathematical equations_

Case Application: Hot or Cold? Cost-Benefit Analysis

A small publishing company was having trouble controlling the temperature in its editorial offices. Because of poor insulation and the exposed location of the building, the offices were difficult and expensive to heat on winter mornings. During the summer, they were equally difficult to cool. The company engaged an engineer to study the situation. He recommended the following improvements and estimated their costs:

Additional air conditioning	$1,200
Additional insulation	2,500
Storm windows and screens	700
Total cost of improvements	$4,400

The engineer also estimated the dollar value of the benefits these improvements would provide. The benefits consisted of:

Reduced heating costs from storm windows, screens, insulation	$600 per year
Minus: Increased electric costs for new air conditioning	−175 per year
Net expected savings (benefits)	$425 per year

The company's controller analyzed these costs and benefits and calculated that the cost of the investment would be fully recovered only after eleven years, ignoring future increases in utility costs. With utility costs expected to increase 10% a year, based on past experience, the investment would be recovered in eight years. But the company's goal was to recover its investment of capital within five years. The controller, therefore, could not justify this investment strictly on financial grounds. In fact, several other investment proposals were likely to pay back their investments in periods of five years or less.

But the president of the company felt that other benefits had to be considered, some of which could not be measured in dollars and cents. He felt the company should provide its employees with reasonably good working conditions. If necessary, the company would have to accept reduced profitability. Actually, he doubted profits would suffer from this investment, because he was confident that improved office facilities would generate less-obvious cost savings to the company than the controller had uncovered, such as increased productivity among its employees.

Economic Reasoning *(Write your responses on a separate sheet. Answers begin on p. 282.)*

1. What type of economic tool is a cost-benefit analysis?
2. Are there examples of three types of factual tools in this analysis? What are they?
3. Should the president of the company make the improvements even if it results in reducing profits? Why or why not?

What Are the Uses of Graphs?

DESCRIPTIVE CHARTS		ANALYTICAL DIAGRAMS
Type of Chart	**Use**	Graphic models showing the relationship between two or more variables. Based on observation and economic reasoning.
Pie chart	Show the relative size of the components of a whole.	
Line graph	Show the statistical relation of two or more variables.	
	Variable — an item whose value changes in relation to changes in the value of another item.	
	Time series — a graph with years measured on the horizontal axis.	
Column chart	Compare the discrete values of one variable with another or the values of a single variable over time.	
Bar chart	Similar to column chart.	
Area chart	Show the way in which the relative components of a variable change over time.	

Direct relationship	Inverse relationship
When two related variables change in the same direction they have a direct relationship.	When two related variables change in opposite directions they have an inverse relationship.

1.6. Give four examples of different types of charts.

A. Present the following (hypothetical) data in a Line Chart:

Year	Tons of Pollutants In the Air
1980	2.0
1981	3.2
1982	4.8
1983	7.3
1984	4.2
1985	4.1

B. Present the following (hypothetical) data that show the tons of pollution in the air in an Area Chart:

Year	Pollution From CFCs	Pollution From Energy Production	Other	Total Pollution
1980	0.6	1.2	0.2	2.0
1981	0.6	2.3	0.3	3.2
1982	0.7	3.5	0.0	4.2
1983	0.5	6.1	0.7	7.3
1984	0.7	3.4	0.1	4.2
1985	0.5	3.4	0.2	4.1

C. Present the following (hypothetical) data comparing the 1980 and 1990 average incomes of high school dropouts, high school graduates, and college graduates in a Column Chart:

	1980	1990
Dropouts	$10,000	$12,000
High School Graduates	14,000	18,000
College Graduates	21,000	27,000

pg. 282

D. Present the following (hypothetical) data describing the weights of rats deserting a sinking ship in a Pie Chart:

Weight	Percentage
0.0 to 2.0 lbs	10%
2.1 to 4.0	45%
4.1 to 6.0	20%
6.1 to 8.0	15%
Over 8.0	10%

pg. 283

1.7. Explain what an analytical diagram is used for.

A. Diagrams are used to show the relationship between two _variables_.

B. A diagram that shows a line sloping down and to the right is showing a(n) _inverse_ relationship.

C. A diagram that shows a line sloping up and to the right is showing a(n) _direct_ relationship.

D. Whereas _charts_ are generally used to describe data, _diagrams_ are generally used to show relationships.

1.8. Draw and label an analytical diagram showing the relationship between two variables.

A. Agnes can read 5 pages of economics in an hour, Bob can read 8 pages in an hour, and Carlos can read 10 pages in an hour. Construct and label a diagram that shows how much each can read in 1, 2, 3, or 4 hours. (Put pages on the vertical axis and hours on the horizontal axis.)

pg. 283

B. The following table shows the number of baby buggies Boris made per week in his first six weeks on the job. Construct and label a diagram that shows this "Learning Curve" by graphing weeks on the horizontal axis and the number of buggies on the vertical axis.

Week	Number
1	5
2	9
3	15
4	23
5	25
6	26

1. What does the diagram tell you about learning curves?

_____

C. The Military Industrial Company (MIC) made 10 cannons this past year. MIC can trade cannons to Dove Industries at a rate of 1 cannon for 2 olive trees. Construct and label a diagram that shows how MIC's number of cannons (on the vertical axis) declines and its number of olive trees increases (on the horizontal axis) as it trades more and more cannons for trees. Indicate on the diagram the number of cannons and trees MIC will have if it trades 2, 5, or 10 cannons.

D. Suppose that a field contains 80 pecks of pickled peppers, and that Peter can pick 8 pecks of pickled peppers per hour. Draw and label a diagram that shows the number of pecks of peppers *remaining in the field* on the vertical axis and the number of hours Peter is busy picking peppers on the horizontal axis. Use the diagram to show how many pecks of peppers Peter has picked after four hours.

Case Application: Air Quality in the United States

The threat of global warming is only one aspect of the problem of air pollution. Another is the quality of the air we breathe. In most respects the air we breathe has gotten worse in the last half-century. The emissions of the majority of air pollutants have increased.

The only pollutants that have decreased since 1940 are particulate matter (solid particles suspended in the air) and carbon monoxide (not to be confused with carbon dioxide, which is bad for global warming).

Particulate matter was the major cause of polluted air in our large cities prior to World War II. The reduction in particulate matter in the air is largely due to less reliance on coal, especially soft coal, as a source of heat and energy, and the regulations imposed on smokestack emissions. Now pollution is mainly due to gases of various types.

The emissions of gases such as sulphur oxides, nitrogen oxide, and volatile organic compounds are greater now than they were in 1940, as shown in Table 1.

Table 1
National Air Pollutant Emissions
Millions of Metric Tons 1940–1987

Year	Particulate matter	Sulphur oxides	Nitrogen oxide	Volatile compounds	Carbon monoxide
1940	23.1	17.6	6.8	18.1	81.5
1950	24.9	19.8	9.3	20.2	86.1
1960	21.6	19.7	12.8	22.6	88.1
1970	18.5	28.3	18.3	26.2	100.2
1980	8.5	23.4	20.4	22.3	77.0
1987	7.0	20.4	19.5	19.6	61.4

Source: U.S. Environmental Protection Agency.

Although the quantity of gaseous emissions is higher now than it was in 1940, it has decreased from its peaks in the 1970–1980 decade. Although residents of Los Angeles and some other areas of pollution concentration have not noticed any improvement yet, the efforts to upgrade our air quality are making some progress.

The most progress has been in reducing the amount of lead in the air. The quantity of lead pollutants is not shown in the table because they are of a different order of magnitude—measured in thousands of metric tons rather than millions of metric tons—and because measures of lead pollutants are not available before 1970. Since then lead pollution has been reduced to less than 4% of what it was. This is credited for the most part to the use of unleaded gasoline. It is a very important victory in the clean air battle because of the great health hazards of lead.

On the other hand, ozone (not in the table because it is measured in parts per million rather than tons emitted), a lung irritant and precursor of smog, has been increasing. It increased 5% in 1987 and 15% in 1988.

Altogether, industry releases over 2 billion pounds of toxic substances into the air each year. Add to this the air pollution from vehicles and households and you have to consider whether or not breathing is hazardous to your health.

Economic Reasoning *(Write your responses on a separate sheet. Answers begin on p. 283.)*

1. What type of chart would be best for showing the data in Table 1? Make a rough sketch of the chart, labeling the vertical and horizontal axes and showing the measurement scales.
2. How would you diagram the relationship between the quantity of gaseous emissions and air quality? Is it a direct relationship or an inverse relationship? Sketch such a diagram, labeling the axes but not including any measurement scales.
3. Should air quality standards be tightened even further, despite the costs to producers and consumers? Why or why not?

IV. Practice Test *(Answers begin on p. 283.)*

Multiple Choice *(Circle the correct answer.)*

(1.1) 1. Economics is the study of which of the following?
    a. how to operate a business.
    b. how to turn resources into economic goods.
    c. how to satisfy human wants with limited resources.
    d. how to eliminate scarcity.

(1.1) 2. In economics, the term **scarcity** means which of the following?
    a. Some things cost more than others.
    b. No society has enough resources to produce everything that people want.
    c. All economic goods are made from resources.
    d. There will be poor people in every society.

(1.2) 3. The development and use of microcomputer chips is considered what type of resource?
    a. land.
    b. labor.
    c. capital.
    d. entrepreneurship.
    e. none of the above.

(1.2) 4. What do entrepreneurs do?
    a. They eliminate (or try to eliminate) scarcity.
    b. They combine resources to make economic goods.
    c. They produce and sell the factors of production.
    d. They work according to the scientific method.

(1.3) 5. The **scientific method** includes each of the following steps EXCEPT:

14 / *Working With The Study of Economics, 4/E*

(1.3) 5. The **scientific method** includes each of the following steps EXCEPT:
    a. assuming the correct conclusion.
    b. gathering data.
    c. rejecting or accepting a hypothesis.
    d. observing an event.

(1.3) 6. **Economic reasoning** includes each of the following EXCEPT:
    a. logical reasoning.
    b. assumptions about human behavior.
    c. critical thinking.
    d. value judgments.

(1.4) 7. Which of the following is a **factual tool** used by economists?
    a. an economic model.
    b. a variable.
    c. statistics.
    d. cost-benefit analysis.

(1.4) 8. Which of the following is considered to be an economic **institution**?
    a. private property.
    b. the unemployment rate.
    c. the greenhouse effect.
    d. pollution.

(1.5) 9. Which of the following is the best one-word definition of an **economic concept**?
    a. an institution.
    b. a model.
    c. an idea.
    d. a relationship.
    e. a definition.

(1.5) 10. Economic models can be presented in which of the following forms?
    a. mathematical equations.
    b. analytical diagrams.
    c. words (verbal descriptions).
    d. all of the above.
    e. none of the above.

(1.6) 11. The relative sizes of the parts that make up a whole are best shown in which of the following?
    a. an analytical diagram.
    b. a bar chart.
    c. a pie chart.
    d. a time series.
    e. a line chart.

(1.6) 12. Time series are best shown by using which kind of charts?
    a. analytical diagrams.
    b. pie charts.
    c. column charts.
    d. line charts.
    e. area charts.

(1.7) 13. Analytical diagrams are usually used to show the relationship between two _____.
    a. concepts
    b. models
    c. charts or graphs
    d. variables

(1.7) 14. An **inverse** relationship between two variables means that:
    a. the variables are analytical.
    b. as one variable increases, the other decreases.

c. the variables increase or decrease at different rates.
d. both variables change at the same rate.

(1.7) 15. Economic models are often presented or shown in graphs that are called:
- a. charts.
- **(b.)** diagrams.
- c. variables.
- d. concepts.
- e. models.

True/False *(Circle T or F.)*

(1.1) 16. In economics, a resource is said to be scarce when the amount available is less than the amount needed to satisfy our wants. **T** or F

(1.2) 17. The three factors of production are land, labor, and technology. T or **F** — *capital*

(1.3) 18. The first step in the scientific method is to devise a hypothesis. T or **F** — *observing an event*

(1.5) 19. The two principal theoretical tools of economics are concepts and models. T or **F**   pg. 15

(1.7) 20. We use analytical diagrams to help us understand how two or more variables relate to one another. **T** or F

Chapter 2
Economic Choices

I. Chapter Outline

Because we cannot have everything we want (because of **scarcity**), we are forced to make choices. An unfortunate reality is that when we make a **choice** to have one thing, we are at the same time choosing to give up (**trade-off**) something else. What we give up is a very real **cost** associated with every choice we make. This relationship—scarcity implies choice implies cost—is the heart and soul of the study of economics. Or, as we economists like to say, "There is no such thing as a free lunch!"

Introductory Article: Swords Into Plowshares

If you, as an individual, received an extra $100, you would need to make some pretty hard choices about what to do with it. Spend it or save it? Buy some clothes or buy some tapes? Making up your mind is sometimes painful because you realize that there are things you **could** have, but will not have if you choose to do something else with your money. (At times like this, you learn what costs really are!) The citizens of the United States have to face a similar set of choices in deciding how to spend (or save) the $100 billion peace dividend that is supposed to result from the end of the cold war.

Economic Analysis

This chapter introduces the heart of the economic problem: the fact that choices always must be made and that everything has a cost. The chapter addresses the problem by asking the following three questions:

1. How Do We Make Economic Choices?

   Important Concepts: Trade-offs, Opportunity cost, Increasing costs

   Important Model: Production possibility frontier

   Case Application: Dieting—The National Pastime

2. What Are the Basic Economic Questions?

   Important Concepts: Infrastructure

   Case Application: What Happened on the Way to the Nuclear Power Future?

3. What Are Society's Economic Goals?

   Important Concepts: Efficiency, Full employment, Price stability, Economic growth, Socioeconomic goals

   Case Application: Replaced by R_2D_2?

Perspective: The Affluent Society
    Biography—John Kenneth Galbraith

16

II. Summary of Economic Analysis

1. Because of **scarcity** we must make **choices** about how to use our scarce resources.
2. Choices involve **trade-offs**.
3. That which is traded-off is the **opportunity cost**—or cost—associated with the choice.
4. In a general sense, we must make choices about **what** we are going to produce, **how** we are going to produce it, and **who** will get it once it is made.
5. In order to make our choices wisely, and to get the most from our scarce resources, we must know what we are trying to achieve: we must agree on certain **economic goals**.
6. Most economists agree on the desirability of these economic goals: **efficiency, full employment, price stability,** and **economic growth**.
7. In contrast to their agreement about economic goals, economists have different **values** and therefore different attitudes toward **socioeconomic goals** such as equity, environmental pollution, and income security.

III. Review of the Learning Objectives *(Answers begin on p. 283.)*

How Do We Make Economic Choices?

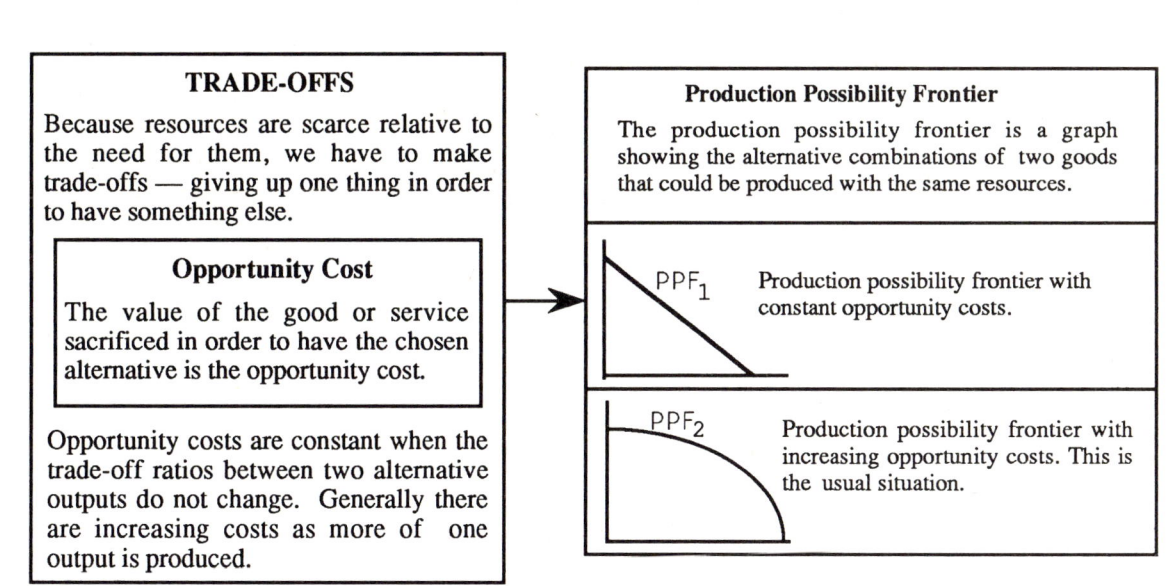

TRADE-OFFS

Because resources are scarce relative to the need for them, we have to make trade-offs — giving up one thing in order to have something else.

Opportunity Cost

The value of the good or service sacrificed in order to have the chosen alternative is the opportunity cost.

Opportunity costs are constant when the trade-off ratios between two alternative outputs do not change. Generally there are increasing costs as more of one output is produced.

Production Possibility Frontier

The production possibility frontier is a graph showing the alternative combinations of two goods that could be produced with the same resources.

PPF_1 Production possibility frontier with constant opportunity costs.

PPF_2 Production possibility frontier with increasing opportunity costs. This is the usual situation.

(See page vi in the foreword "To the Student" for how to make the best use of this schematic outline.)

2.1. Define and give examples of economic trade-offs. *(Write in answers below.)*

A. Having to trade off one thing to get another is sometimes an unpleasant experience. Nonetheless we are forced to make trade-offs because of _scarcity_.

B. Indicate three things that United States citizens have "traded off" in return for their military strength.

better health care,
better roads,
a safer environment.

C. Give three examples of trade-offs that you make with one of your truly scarce resources—your time.

going to college — working full time
studying — family time
working — sleeping

D. Indicate one possible trade-off for each of the following:

1. Increased infrastructure investment.
   more help for the poor

2. Constructing a new shopping mall.
   using the land for a park

3. Sleeping late in the morning.
   eating breakfast

4. Going to a movie.
   going to a concert

2.2. Explain opportunity cost.

A. What is the economic meaning of the expression "There's no such thing as a free lunch"?

Because of scarcity, everything has a cost.

B. Mr. Jones is a health-care worker and Ms. Applegate is a schoolteacher. Would they have the same or different ideas about the opportunity cost of increased military spending? Explain.

Mr. Jones might think of all the hospitals that could be built. Ms. Applegate might think of all the new books or computers that could be bought.

C. Indicate your possible opportunity costs for each of the following:

1. Baking a cake.
   baking brownies

2. Buying a new cassette tape.
   going to a movie

3. Planting a rose garden in your yard.
   planting carrots

4. Going to college.
   the money you could earn on a job

5. Attending economics class.
   doing other homework

6. Paying taxes.
   helping the homeless

D. What is the opportunity cost of eating a big piece of hot apple pie with ice cream?
   any other dessert plus the added calories

2.3. Explain the production possibility frontier and increasing costs.

A. An imaginary economy has the following production possibilities:

	A	B	C	D	E
Guns	0	1	2	3	4
Butter	8	6	4	2	0

Use the grid below to plot each of these points and draw the economy's production possibility frontier.

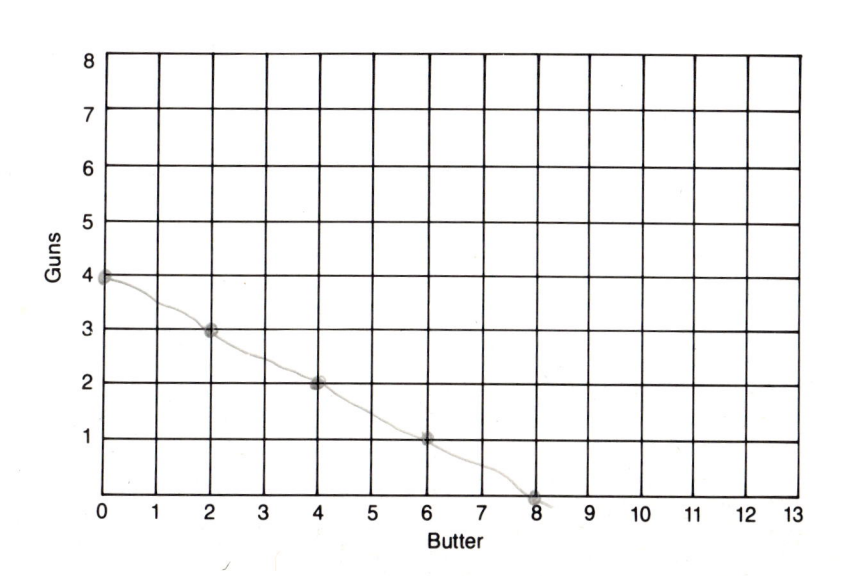

1. What are the opportunity costs of the first, second, third, and fourth units of guns?

   First _2 units of butter_

   Second _"   "   "   "_

   Third _"   "   "   "_

   Fourth _"   "   "   "_

2. The trade-off between guns and butter is an example of

   Constant costs.

B. An imaginary economy has the following production possibilities:

	A	B	C	D	E
Food	0	1	2	3	4
Clothing	10	9	7	4	0

Use the grid below to plot each of these points and draw the economy's production possibility frontier.

1. What are the opportunity costs of the first, second, third, and fourth units of food?

   First _1 units of clothes_

   Second _2 units_

   Third _3 units_

   Fourth _4 units_

2. The trade-off between food and clothing is an example of

   increasing costs.

C. Compare the production possibility frontiers in A and B above. What do the shapes (slopes) of the frontiers imply about the ability to substitute one resource in the economy for another? _Constant costs imply resources are perfect substitutes for one another. Increasing costs imply the more realistic situation where resources are not perfect substitutes._

D. The production possibility curve is an example of an economic _model_. (Hint: the answer is from chapter 1.)

Case Application: A Question of Oil

The increase in fuel prices resulting from the Middle East crisis of 1990–91 reminded us that petroleum is a critical resource in our economy. This country uses over 750 million gallons of refined petroleum products each and every day. Yet even that enormous quantity is not sufficient for all of the uses that we have for petroleum products. We would like to consume more gasoline if we could afford it. We would like the fuel to keep our homes warmer in winter and the electricity to keep them cooler in summer if we could afford the costs of doing so.

Petroleum has many uses: powering vehicles, heating buildings, generating electricity, as a lubricant, and as a raw material for synthetic fibers, among others. The largest part of our petroleum supply is used to make gas for our cars. The next largest use is for fuel oil to heat our homes and power our factories and electric utility plants. Some of the constituent components of crude oil, the lighter parts of the oil, are better suited for making gasoline, while the heavier parts of the oil are better suited for making fuel oil. We have to decide which of the various competing uses are the most vital, to us as individuals and to the economy as a whole. The economy must allocate the available petroleum resources in the way that best meets our needs.

Almost half of our petroleum supplies are imported. In times of extreme shortages, when our normal supplies are interrupted, the government intervenes to allocate the available supply. For emergencies, we have established a strategic crude oil reserve that in mid-1989 amounted to 572 million barrels (a barrel holds 42 gallons). At our normal consumption rate, that is a one-month supply.

There are proposals to increase the domestic sources of petroleum by drilling in the Alaskan National Wildlife Refuge and off our coastal shores. Alternative proposals to decrease our dependence on foreign oil are to undertake energy conservation measures and develop renewable energy sources such as solar power.

Economic Reasoning *(Write your responses on a separate sheet. Answers begin on p. 284.)*

1. What trade-off choices do we need to make in our uses of petroleum?
2. What is the opportunity cost of a gallon of petroleum used to produce gasoline for our automobiles? Sketch a diagram showing the opportunity costs of two alternative uses for petroleum. Do the opportunity costs increase as more of the petroleum is used for one of the two purposes?
3. Should we produce oil in the Alaskan National Wildlife Refuge and off our coastal shores? What are the trade-offs?

What Are the Basic Economic Questions?

WHAT to produce	**HOW** to produce	**FOR WHOM** to produce
The economic system must decide what goods and services to produce with its land, labor, and capital.	The economic system must decide how to produce each good or service — determining what mix of land, labor, and capital to use in production and what production methods to employ.	The economic system must decide which members of society will receive how much of the goods and services produced — the process of allocating income.

(See page vi in the foreword "To the Student" for how to make the best use of this schematic outline.)

2.4. Give examples of the three basic economic questions.

A. Each of the following economic situations presents an example of resolving one of the three basic economic questions. Indicate the correct question (or questions) in each case.

1. Congress debates what to do with the "peace dividend." _what_ and _who_

2. The recreation department of Brownsville, U.S.A., is considering buying automated garbage trucks. _how_

3. An automobile manufacturer is contemplating installing robots on the assembly line. _how_

4. Consumers become more health-conscious and start to eat foods that they think are better for them. _what_

B. An economy's selection of either point A or point B on the production possibility frontier shown on page 23 involves answering which of the three basic economic questions?

what

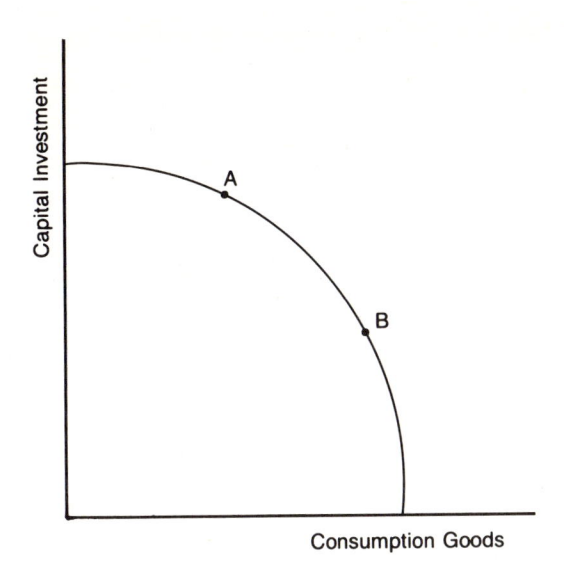

Case Application: **Is Coal the Heir to the Energy Throne?**

Coal, the presumptive heir to the energy throne as petroleum supplies give out in the future and nuclear power becomes more costly and dangerous, doesn't look the part right now. The industry's profits are rather small, often as low as 5 cents a ton after taxes. And despite the fact that coal costs only about one-fourth as much as petroleum per unit of energy produced, utility companies have been slow to embrace coal as a substitute for oil in generating electricity. The air pollution and acid rainwater from burning coal violate environmental standards and are expensive to clean up.

However, coal is regaining some of the respect it had. Long-closed mines are being reopened and new mines are being dug. A lot of the new activity is in underground mines rather than on the surface strip mines. The underground mines of Appalachia produce a higher quality of coal, lower in sulphur content, than the coal from the strip mines of the western states. And the Appalachian coal is closer to eastern industrial centers and to seaports for shipment to European customers.

We should be able to supply European coal needs as well as our own for some time to come. It is estimated that the United States has a 200-year supply of coal reserves. The obstacles to coal regaining its throne as the king of energy are the costs of extracting it and the environmental costs of burning it.

Economic Reasoning *(Write your responses on a separate sheet. Answers begin on p. 284.)*

1. The decision whether to produce coal by underground tunneling or surface strip mining illustrates which type of basic economic decision?
2. What considerations enter into the "what" decision regarding the production of coal?
3. Should coal be substituted for nuclear power in the production of electricity, even if it results in an increase in air and water pollution? Why or why not?

What Are Society's Economic Goals?

GOALS

PRINCIPALLY ECONOMIC GOALS

Efficiency	Price Stability	Full Employment	Growth
Obtaining the largest possible amount of output per unit of input helps to overcome scarcity.	It is important to have the overall level of prices for goods and services remain relatively constant.	It is best to have an unemployment level of not more than 4% or 5%, considered full employment.	Economic growth comes from an increase in the production capacity of the economy.

SOCIOECONOMIC GOALS

| Environmental protection | Financial security | Economic equity | Economic justice | Economic freedom |

(See page vi in the foreword "To the Student" for how to make the best use of this schematic outline.)

2.5. List the four primarily economic goals of society.

A. List the four economic goals.

1. _efficiency_
2. _price stability_
3. _full employment_
4. _growth_

B. Using the numbers to your answers in part A, indicate which goal each of the following statements reflects.

1. _4_ Congress passes a tax act designed to stimulate investment in new capital equipment.
2. _2_ The Federal Reserve Bank announces plans to fight inflation.
3. _1_ Mega Motors Corporation announces plans to install robots on all assembly lines in order to increase productivity.
4. _3_ The president announces a new program designed to find jobs for workers who are replaced by robots.

2.6. Show the effect on output of increasing employment to full employment.

A. Reducing unemployment is an economic goal for two reasons. What are they?

1. household incomes
2. increased output

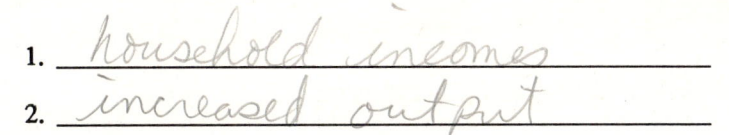

B. Reducing unemployment also contributes to achieving the economic goal of growth.

C. The production possibility frontier below shows the trade-offs involved in producing peanut butter and jelly. Indicate a point on the graph that corresponds to unemployment (A) and a point that implies full employment (B).

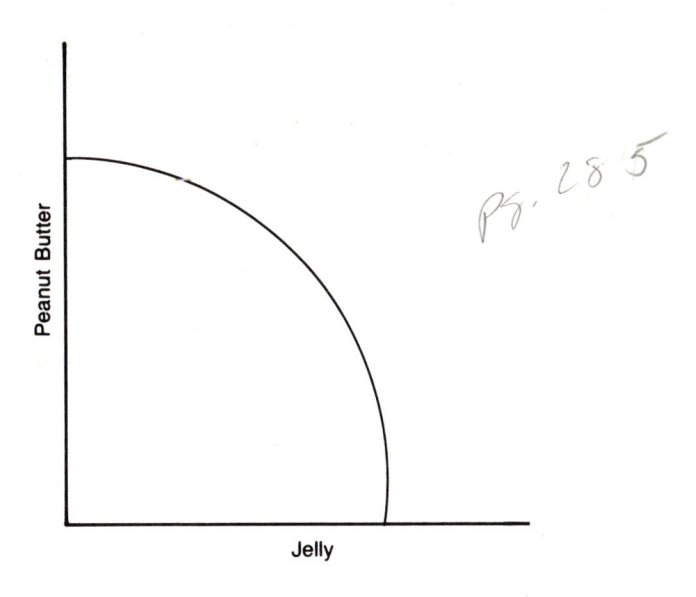

pg. 285

2.7. Show the effect on economic growth of producing more capital goods.

A. The production possibility frontier below shows an economy's trade-off between consumption goods and capital goods.

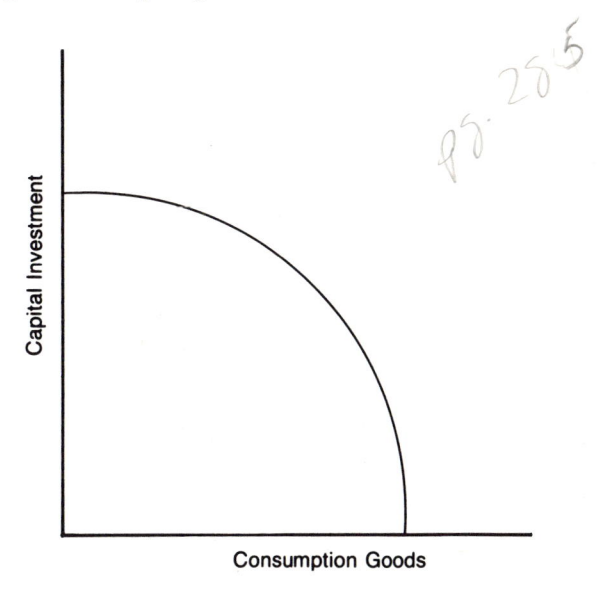

pg. 285

1. Indicate a point on the curve (A) that reflects more capital investment than consumption spending.
2. Draw a new graph that shows what will happen in the future if the economy chooses more capital investment and less consumption spending.

B. Give an example of a productive investment in capital that might be carried out by each of the following:

1. Your school.

   a new auditorium

2. Your local government.

   a new water treatment plant

3. The federal government.

   new highways

4. An automobile manufacturer.

   robots

5. A law office.

   a new computer system

2.8. Give examples of trade-offs between economic and socioeconomic goals.

A. In each of the following situations, indicate an economic goal (or goals) that will be promoted and a socioeconomic goal that will *not* be promoted.

1. A farmer uses insecticides to produce more apples.
   Economic goal:

   efficiency

   Socioeconomic goal:

   safe environment

2. A manufacturer installs robots to produce more goods at lower costs.
   Economic goal:

   efficiency

   Socioeconomic goal:

   job security

3. The government places price controls on the sellers of gasoline (your local gas station).
   Economic goal:

   price stability

   Socioeconomic goal:

   equity

4. Congress passes an act that reduces aid for social programs and increases subsidies for capital investment.
   Economic goal:

   growth

Socioeconomic goal:

equity

Case Application: A Plastic World

Plastics, along with computers and robotics, have become a characteristic of the modern world. The growth of the plastics industry in the past two decades has been three times that of manufacturing in general.

Part of the growth of plastics has been at the expense of other, more traditional materials—steel in automobile production, wood in furniture production, and natural fibers in clothing—depriving workers in those older industries of a livelihood. But some of the growth in the use of plastics has been in entirely new products made possible by this material—foam for floatation and packaging, Gobot toys, and artificial-turf football fields for example.

One of the useful characteristics of plastics, their durability, has also turned out to be one of their drawbacks, a drawback which some environmentalists fear poses a danger to the planet's life forms and ecosystem. Plastic garbage is collecting in the oceans in astonishing quantities. Underwater explorers have come across great "rivers" of plastic garbage carried by currents in the middle of the Atlantic and other oceans. Four biologists who went to Laysan, a small island in a remote area of the Pacific about 1,000 miles northwest of Hawaii, to study the seabirds there were startled to find the beaches strewn with all sorts of plastic trash which had washed ashore.

Other types of garbage tend to decompose under the corrosive action of air, sun, and water. But many plastics are virtually indestructible in the natural environment. They not only despoil nature, but they are taking a heavy toll on marine life that ingest or become entangled in them—especially seals, sea lions, turtles, and various species of seabirds such as albatrosses.

Chemists at a U.S. Department of Agriculture research center and in private laboratories are attempting to develop plastics that will decompose after a period of time in water or under sunlight. But, perversely, plastics that will decompose tend to be more expensive to produce than those that last indefinitely.

Economic Reasoning (Write your responses on a separate sheet. Answers begin on p. 285.)

1. What economic goals has the plastics industry helped in achieving?
2. How has the growth of the plastics industry resulted in a trade-off of some economic or socioeconomic goals which are not being satisfied as well?
3. Should growth of the plastics industry be retarded by restricting the use of plastics that are not biodegradable? Why or why not?

IV. Practice Test (Answers begin on p. 285.)

Multiple Choice (Circle the correct answer.)

(2.1) 1. Why are trade-offs necessary?
   a. because resources are scarce.
   b. because of increasing costs.
   c. because economic goals are not the same.
   d. because of different production possibilities.

(2.2) 2. Which of the following best describes the concept "opportunity cost"?
   a. the money spent to produce goods and services.
   b. the monetary (dollar) value of goods and services.
   c. the value of what must be given up to get something.
   d. the cost of eliminating scarcity.

(2.2) 3. Which of the following is an opportunity cost of a clean and safe environment?
   a. colder houses in the winter because of less heating.
   b. more expensive fruit because of fewer pesticides.
   c. colder food due to less use of foam containers.
   d. all of the above.

(2.3) 4. Production possibility frontiers are usually curved (rather than being straight lines) because of:
   a. economies of scale.
   b. increasing costs.
   c. opportunity costs.
   d. less than full employment.

(2.3) 5. A point lying **outside** of the production possibility frontier represents which of the following?
   a. unemployment.
   b. high prices.
   c. increasing costs.
   d. an unattainable combination of two goods.

(2.4) 6. Which of the following is an example of the "how" question?
   a. deciding upon the mix of public and private goods people will get.
   b. deciding on whether to use labor-intensive or capital-intensive production techniques.
   c. deciding how to divide public goods among different groups.
   d. deciding on how to price different resources for different uses.

(2.4) 7. Which of the following is a TRUE statement about the basic economic question "What to produce?"
   a. It is no longer important in modern post-industrial economies.
   b. It is only important in those few countries where scarcity still exists today.
   c. It is more difficult to answer when costs are increasing than when costs are constant.
   d. The question exists and must be answered because resources are scarce.

(2.5) 8. Which of the following is NOT an economic goal?
   a. equity.
   b. efficiency.
   c. price stability.
   d. full employment.

(2.5) 9. What is the importance (significance) of economic goals?
   a. Each goal provides the answer to one of the basic economic questions.
   b. Economic goals provide a moral or ethical basis for creating an economically fair society.
   c. Economic goals are necessary to help guide us when we make economic choices.
   d. Achieving these economic goals is the only way to overcome the problem of scarcity.

(2.6) 10. "Full employment" is a(n):
   a. economic model.
   b. economic concept.
   c. economic assumption.
   d. factual tool of economic analysis.

(2.6) 11. Which of the following is the best description of "full employment"?
   a. Everyone who wants a job can find a job.
   b. Everyone who is not retired or in school has a job.
   c. Every household has at least one person with a job.
   d. The level of employment necessary to overcome scarcity has been reached.

(2.7) 12. Which of the following is a TRUE statement?
   a. Economic growth cannot be influenced by society's choices about what to produce.
   b. A society's choice to produce consumption goods has no effect on its ability to produce capital goods.
   c. Choosing to produce more capital goods today will result in greater economic growth in the future.
   d. An economy can make choices about which consumption goods to produce, but there are no choices that can influence the level of capital investment.

(2.7) 13. Investment in new plant and equipment creates which of the following?
   a. more capital.
   b. greater productive capacity.
   c. more output.
   d. all of the above.

(2.8) 14. Improving productivity by increasing the use of industrial robots might interfere with which of the following socioeconomic goals?
   a. job security.
   b. equity.
   c. pollution control.
   d. price stability.

(2.9) 15. Cleaning up our environment and keeping it pollution-free will more than likely *directly* conflict with which of the following?
   a. the goal of equity.
   b. the goal of economic growth.
   c. the goal of price stability.
   d. the goal of economic freedom.

True/False (Circle T or F.)

(2.2) 16. Because of scarcity, everything has an opportunity cost. T or F

(2.3) 17. The PPF is curved because of trade-offs. T or F

(2.5) 18. Achieving an equitable distribution of income is an economic goal. T or F

(2.6) 19. The goal "full employment" helps an economy reach the goal "economic growth." T or F

(2.7) 20. Because capital is a resource, investing in more of it leads to economic growth. T or F

Chapter 3

The Economic System

I. Chapter Outline

Every society must resolve the three basic economic questions of what, how, and for whom to produce. Finding satisfactory answers requires the use of some type of economic "system" of organizing and coordinating economic activities. The more advanced and more complex societies become, the more they depend on such systems and the more important the systems become. Similar to most other industrialized countries, the United States depends primarily on the free-market economic system.

Introductory Article: Ranch to Table: A Different Story Now

Changing technology and increasing specialization during the past 100 years have brought about tremendous changes in the way that cattle are produced and brought to market. These changes have contributed to our efforts to deal with scarcity and have resulted in better beef at lower prices. However, one thing that has not changed much during this time is the manner in which the U.S. economic system organizes producers and consumers so that the beef somehow finds its way from the ranch to the table.

Economic Analysis

This chapter introduces economic systems and examines the way that they work by addressing the following three questions:

1. Why Are Economic Systems Needed?

    Important Concepts: Specialization, Interdependence, Absolute and comparative advantage

    Case Application: The Efficiencyburger

2. What Are the Principal Types of Economic Systems?

    Important Concepts: Market economies, Centrally directed economies, Traditional economies, Mixed economies

    Case Application: Capitalists in the U.S.S.R.

3. How does a Market System Resolve the Three Basic Economic Questions?

    Important Concepts: Markets, Product and factor markets, Incentives

    Important Model: The circular flow diagram

    Case Application: What Is the Answer to Power Brownouts?

Perspective: The Industrial Revolution

II. Summary of Economic Analysis

1. **Specialization** in production increases economic efficiency.
2. Specialization can be based on either **comparative advantage**, where different producers are more efficient at producing different things, or **absolute advantage**, where one producer is more efficient at producing both (all) products.
3. Specialization leads to **interdependence**.
4. Because of interdependence, modern societies need some type of **economic system** to organize and coordinate production and thereby find answers to the three basic questions (what, how, and for whom to produce).
5. Three types of economic systems that have been used in the past and continue to be used today are the **market**, **centrally directed**, and **traditional** economic systems.
6. To a greater or lesser extent, all modern economies are **mixed economies**—they contain aspects of all three types of economic systems.
7. **Markets** are either real or abstract places where buyers and sellers meet to buy and sell goods and services.
8. **Factor markets** are where the different factors of production (resources) are bought and sold. These markets represent the inputs into the production process.
9. **Product markets** are where finished goods and services (consumption goods) are sold to their final users. These markets represent the outputs of the production process.
10. In market economies, the **profit motive** is the incentive for businesses to buy resources and sell finished products.
11. The term **households** is used to represent those parts of the economy that own and sell resources and buy finished goods.
12. The term **businesses** is used to represent those parts of the economy that buy resources, undertake production, and sell finished goods.
13. The **circular flow diagram** is an important model that shows the circular nature of a market economy. Households sell resources to businesses and buy finished goods from businesses. Businesses buy resources from households and sell finished goods to households.

32 / Working With The Study of Economics, 4/E

III. Review of the Learning Objectives *(Answers begin on p. 285.)*

Why Are Economic Systems Needed?

SPECIALIZATION

Productive resources, such as labor, can produce more efficiently if they specialize their activities — concentrating on what they do best according to their

Absolute Advantage	or	Comparative Advantage
When one producer can produce a product more efficiently than a second producer and the second producer can produce a different product more efficiently than the first, the two producers benefit when each produces the product in which they have an absolute advantage and trade part of their output for the other product.		When one producer can produce two or more products more efficiently than a second producer, but the ratio of advantage is greater in one of the products than in the other, both producers benefit by the efficient producer producing the product in which he or she has the greatest comparative advantage and the inefficient producer producing the product in which he or she has the smallest disadvantage, each trading for the product they don't produce.

INTERDEPENDENCE

Specialization according to absolute or comparative advantage results in interdependence, each producing unit depending on the other, necessitating an economic system to coordinate their activities.

(See page vi in the foreword "To the Student" for how to make the best use of this schematic outline.)

3.1. Distinguish between absolute and comparative advantage. *(Write in answers below.)*

A. A producer who can produce a good or service at a lower relative cost than another producer has a(n) __comparative__ advantage in the production of that good or service.

B. A producer who can produce both widgets **and** doodads more efficiently than another producer is said to have a(n) __absolute__ advantage in the production of both.

C. If Japan can produce both autos and stereos more efficiently than New Zealand, then New Zealand should specialize in the good in which it has the greatest __comparative__ advantage.

3.2. Explain why specialization based on absolute or comparative advantage results in greater economic efficiency and interdependence.

A. A fast-food company advertises that they do only one thing and that they do it well. An economist would say that they _specialize_ in the production of that good and that this leads to greater _efficiency_ and _lower_ costs in producing it.

B. If every person does only one thing (and does it well, of course), then people will be _interdependent_ on each other in order to get all the different things that they want.

C. List three things that people in the United States at one time did for themselves but depend on specialists for today.

1. _pluck chickens_
2. _make their own clothes_
3. _repair their own roofs_

D. Doing one thing and doing it well has certain advantages for society, but it also involves one major problem. Can you think of what it is?

boredom on the job

Case Application: From Farm to City

At the time of our first census in 1790, the population of the United States was 3.9 million people. Of this number, only 5% was urban—that is, resided in towns or cities of at least 2,500 people. The rural population made up 95% of the total. By 1990 the population had grown to 250 million and three-quarters of it was urban, while only one-quarter was rural.

Most of the rural population is engaged directly or indirectly in agriculture. The dramatic shift of people to the cities implies an enormous rise in the productiveness of agriculture. Formerly, 95 of every 100 Americans were in families whose farms fed the other 5% of the population. Indeed, since the United States has become a major exporter, it is even more productive than these figures suggest.

The concentration of people in cities has resulted in massive urban sprawl in some areas such as BoWash, the nearly uninterrupted urban corridor from Massachusetts to Virginia; ChiPitts, the stretch from Chicago to Pittsburgh; and SoCal, between San Diego and Santa Barbara. The cities continue to grow despite overcrowding, pollution, crime, and other social problems. They grow because they are economically efficient.

Economic Reasoning *(Write your responses on a separate sheet. Answers begin on p. 285.)*

1. Are people more interdependent now than they were in 1790? Why?
2. How does the growth of large metropolitan areas like BoWash, ChiPitts, and SoCal illustrate the principle of comparative advantage?
3. Would the United States be better off if it were still predominantly rural? Why or why not?

What Are the Principal Types of Economic Systems?

MARKET ECONOMIES	**CENTRALLY DIRECTED ECONOMIES**	**TRADITIONAL ECONOMIES**
are economic systems in which the basic questions of what, how, and for whom to produce are resolved primarily by buyers and sellers interacting in markets.	are economic systems in which the basic questions of what, how, and for whom to produce are resolved primarily by governmental authority.	are economic systems in which the basic questions of what, how, and for whom to produce are resolved primarily by custom and tradition.

MIXED ECONOMIES

are economic systems in which the basic questions of what, how, and for whom to produce are resolved by a mixture of market forces with government direction and/or custom and tradition.

(See page vi in the foreword "To the Student" for how to make the best use of this schematic outline.)

3.3. Identify the three major types of economic systems, and explain how they differ.

A. Indicate whether the following are examples of how market (M), centrally directed (C), or traditional (T) economies answer the three basic economic questions.

1. _C_ A pharaoh in ancient Egypt demands that a pyramid be built.
2. _T_ A son takes over his father's business when the father retires.
3. _M_ A person goes to the movies to see a new movie.
4. _C_ Your community provides public schools.
5. _T_ Most nurses in the United States are women and most doctors are men.
6. _M_ Toyota builds a new car factory.

B. List three ways that the government influences the production and sale of beef in the United States.

1. _provides water_
2. _leases land to ranchers_
3. _inspects beef_

C. When the government determines how the three basic questions are answered, the economy is referred to as a _command economy_.

When the government interferes in primarily market economies, the resulting type of economy is called a _mixed economy_.

D. Can you think of one industry or production in the United States that is NOT influenced in some way by government activity?

I can't

Case Application: Digging a Subway in Calcutta

Calcutta is a city with overwhelming problems, even by the standards of other cities in India. A large percentage of its more than 10 million citizens are poor and unemployed, and many are homeless. Its public facilities are totally inadequate for the size of the population. The roads are in very poor condition, and there are not nearly enough of them to accommodate the hordes of pedestrians, carts, rickshaws, ancient and overcrowded buses, and sacred cows that wander the streets. Whereas large American cities have as much as 40% of their surface allocated to streets (and the other major cities of India about 15%), Calcutta's streets cover only 6% of its area. As a result of the congestion, the city is virtually immobilized during peak hours of traffic.

In order to alleviate the traffic problem, work began on a subway in December 1972, the first on the Indian subcontinent. It was scheduled to be completed in 1979. Due to the slow progress of construction, it was not completed before 1990, by which time the population of the city had reached 13.5 million, with the subway accommodating approximately only 13% of the transportation needs of the city's people.

Reasons for the delays in construction included flooding and other geologic difficulties, over-budget costs, and shortages of funds. These are familiar problems for subway projects in the United States as well, but there is one major difference in the way the Calcutta subway was constructed and the way subways are built in most developed countries. In Calcutta there were initially no bulldozers, excavators, or other large earth-moving equipment used. Instead, 3,000 workers, dressed in the traditional garb of the Indian laborer, toiled away with shovels, filling straw baskets with mud from 40-foot-deep trenches. The baskets were carried out of the ditches on the heads of young Indian women to waiting trucks that then carried the mud away to dump sites. In this fashion, 2.25 million cubic feet of earth was removed from the trenches for the subway tunnels. Because the minimum wage was about $1.30 a day, the government planners calculated that digging the subway with Calcutta's hordes of unskilled laborers was cheaper, if slower, than using mechanized equipment. Furthermore, it helped alleviate the unemployment problem.

Economic Reasoning (Write your responses on a separate sheet. Answers begin on p. 286.)

1. The use of manual labor rather than mechanized equipment to dig the Calcutta subway is characteristic of what type of economic system?
2. Manual labor is frequently used in place of machinery by private enterprise in India as well as by government. Why would private enterprise, which is not concerned about the unemployment problem, use manual labor?
3. Do you think the Calcutta government should have used unskilled workers to build the subway even if it slowed down construction and in the end cost more than using mechanized equipment? Why or why not?

36 / *Working With The Study of Economics, 4/E*

How Does a Market System Resolve the Three Basic Economic Questions?

MARKETS
In a market economy the What, How, and For Whom questions are resolved by the interchanges of buyers and sellers in markets.

Factor Markets	Product Markets
Resources and semi-finished products are exchanged in factor markets for the production of final goods.	Finished goods and services are exchanged in product markets where they are supplied to consumers.

INCENTIVES
In a market economy the principal incentive that motivates production is profits.

(See page vi in the foreword "To the Student" for how to make the best use of this schematic outline.)

3.4. Explain how a market system resolves the three basic economic questions.

A. Market economies rely on the __profit__ motive of individuals to answer the three basic economic questions.

B. Higher prices provide incentives for producers to sell __more__ and for consumers to buy __less__.

C. Lower prices provide incentives for producers to sell __less__ and for consumers to buy __more__.

D. The owners of resources (households) provide business firms with __land__, __labor__, and __capital__ in return for income in the form of __wages__, __rent__, and __interest__.

E. Businesses provide households with __finished goods__ in return for __money payments__.

3.5. Distinguish between goods and services sold in product markets and those sold in factor markets.

A. Indicate which of the following are *usually* sold in product markets (P) and which are *usually* sold in factor markets (F).
1. __F__ Tractors.
2. __P__ Automobiles.
3. __P__ Microwave pizzas.
4. __F__ Lawyers.
5. __F__ Farm land.
6. __P__ Refrigerators.
7. __F__ Coal.
8. __P__ Televisions.

B. For each of the following items, give one example of when it would be sold in a factor market and one example of when it would be sold in a product market.
1. A microwave oven.
   factor market __restaurant__
   product market __a household kitchen__
2. A computer.
   factor market __a law office__
   product market __a student's room__
3. A plumber.
   factor market __a construction company__
   product market __fixing a house's leaky pipes__

3.6. Diagram the circular flow of a market economy.

A. Label the circular flow shown below.

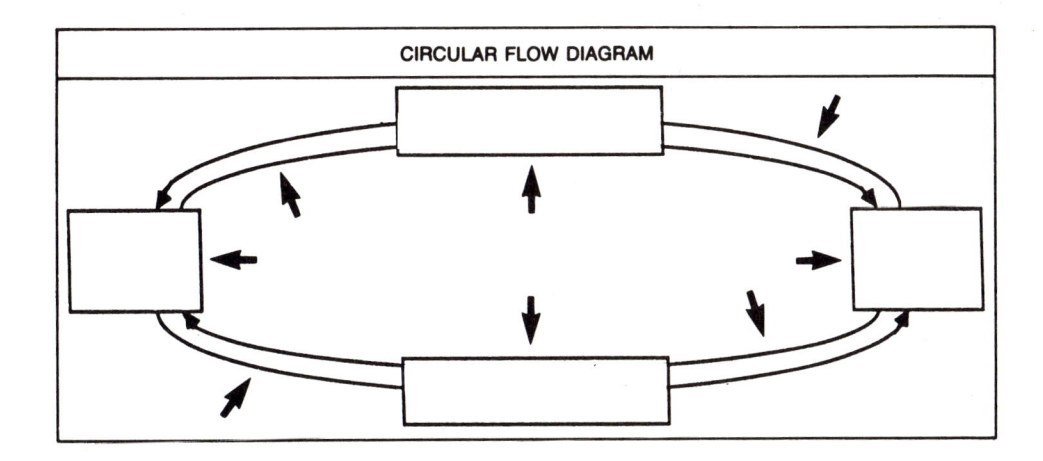

CIRCULAR FLOW DIAGRAM

B. Instead of spending all their income, suppose households **save** some of it by putting it into a **bank**. Suppose then that the bank **lends** the money to businesses for new capital investment. On the circular flow diagram you just filled in, draw a box that might indicate the bank, and draw two new arrows indicating savings and lending.

C. According to this circular flow diagram, the amount that households spend is equal to the amount that they _earn_, and must also be equal to the amount that businesses _earn_.

Case Application: The Shale Age—Not Yet

Under a 16,000-square-mile area in Colorado, Utah, and Wyoming there lie two trillion barrels of oil—three times as much as the rest of the world's petroleum reserves. The problem is the oil is locked up in shale, a laminated rock structure permeated with oil.

Oil from shale rock was actually in use before the discovery and drilling of oil wells in Pennsylvania in 1859. But since petroleum was much easier and cheaper to pump from wells than to extract from the shale, the shale oil deposits remained undeveloped. There were efforts at times to exploit the shale oil fields. In fact, a 1953 headline in the *Denver Post* announced "The Shale Age Has Begun." But the announcement was premature. It was not until the oil price hikes of the 1970s that the large oil companies took a serious interest in shale oil and significant activity began. The deposits are almost entirely on federal government land, and a number of oil companies took leases on various pieces of this property to obtain control of the resources.

A few of the companies undertook experimental processes for extracting the oil from the shale. Exxon, in partnership with Tosco Corporation, invested $5 billion in its Colony Shale Oil Project near Rifle, Colorado, before shutting down the project in May of 1982 due to rising costs and falling oil prices. That project employed a process called "retorting," heating the rock to release the oil after the shale has been brought to the surface. Occidental Petroleum and its partner, Tenneco, experimented with a process that ignites the shale underground, causing the heat to free the oil from the rock so it can be pumped to the surface.

Progress on these and other experimental shale oil projects has been intermittent. The companies have closed down their projects for the present, waiting for increased petroleum shortages and higher prices in the future to justify the high development costs of shale oil technology. In addition to the high costs, there are problems of obtaining adequate water supplies for processing the shale—two to four barrels of water are required for each barrel of oil produced—and disposing of the rock residue from retorting in a way that will not harm the environment. Delayed by high costs and environmental problems, the age of shale has not yet arrived.

Economic Reasoning (Write your responses on a separate sheet. Answers begin on p. 286.)

1. Would shale oil be sold in a product market or a factor market? How can you determine which type of market it will be sold in?
2. If the problems of adequate water supplies and rock waste disposal could be solved, would the oil companies go ahead with their shale oil projects? What would cause them to do so?
3. In view of the country's dependence on imported oil, much of it from the politically unstable Middle East, should the government step in to speed up the development of shale oil production on government lands? Why or why not?

IV. Practice Test *(Answers begin on p. 286.)*

Multiple Choice *(Circle the correct answer.)*

(3.1) 1. Joe Superman is a better plumber **and** a better carpenter than Harry Helpless. This means that Joe has a(n) _____ advantage over Harry in both types of work.
   a. specialized
   b. interdependent
   c. absolute
   d. comparative

(3.1) 2. Based on the information in question 1, which of the following is true if Joe and Harry are on the same construction team?
   a. Joe should do all the carpentry and plumbing.
   b. Harry will still have a comparative advantage in one of the jobs and therefore should do that one.
   c. Harry will have an absolute advantage in one of the two jobs and therefore should do that one.
   d. Specialization cannot occur in this situation because Joe is better at both jobs.

(3.2) 3. Specialization can lead to each of the following EXCEPT:
   a. improved equity.
   b. improved efficiency.
   c. increased interdependence.
   d. lower costs.

(3.2) 4. Specialization deals directly with which of the basic economic questions?
   a. for whom to produce?
   b. how to produce?
   c. what to produce?
   d. how much to produce?

(3.3) 5. Which of the following is the major difference between a market economy and a centrally directed economy?
   a. A market economy relies more on the use of money.
   b. Prices are important in a market economy, but they are not used in a centrally directed economy.
   c. Market economies rely on self-interest and profit incentives to answer the basic economic questions; centrally directed economies rely on agency decisions.
   d. Market economies must find answers to the three basic economic questions; the three questions do not matter in centrally directed economies.

(3.3) 6. Which of the following is an example of how an economic decision is made in a traditional economy?
   a. A community decides to build a new computer center for its residents.
   b. More oat bran is produced after doctors find that it reduces cholesterol.
   c. People go to a concert to see their favorite rock star.
   d. The prince of a country becomes king after his father passes away.

(3.4) 7. Which of the following is most important in determining **what** gets produced in a market economy?
   a. central planning.
   b. efficiency.
   c. comparative advantage.
   d. the profit motive.

(3.4) 8. Which of the following socioeconomic goals is most important to the proper working of a market economy?
    a. price stability.
    b. job security.
    (c.) economic freedom.
    d. equity.

(3.5) 9. Which of the following is most likely to be bought and sold in a factor market?
    a. a television set.
    (b.) a truck.
    c. a can of tuna.
    d. a carpet.

(3.5) 10. Which of the following is most likely to be bought and sold in a product market?
    a. a 40-pound tuna.
    b. 100 acres of farmland.
    (c.) a dozen eggs.
    d. 1,000 feet of copper pipe.

(3.6) 11. In the circular flow diagram, households do each of the following EXCEPT:
    a. buy finished goods.
    b. sell resources.
    c. receive wages.
    (d.) pay interest.

(3.6) 12. Which of the following is NOT shown in the circular flow diagram of the economy?
    a. Everyone's income is someone else's expenditure.
    b. Interest is the payment for the use of capital.
    c. Businesses transform resources into finished products.
    (d.) The prices of finished products depend on the prices of resources.

(3.3) 13. The U.S. economy is best described as being a:
    a. command economy.
    b. traditional economy.
    c. market economy.
    (d.) mixed economy.

(3.4) 14. Market economies rely MOST on which of the following?
    a. accurate planning by the government.
    (b.) the self-interest of individuals.
    c. the interaction between government and individuals.
    d. lessons learned from past economic experiences.

(3.5) 15. Which of the following occurs in factor markets?
    a. businesses earn their profits.
    (b.) individuals earn their incomes.
    c. households obtain their desired goods and services.
    d. consumption spending.

True/False *(Circle T or F.)*

(3.1) 16. If one producer has an absolute advantage over another, there can be no gains from specialization and trade. T or (F)

(3.2) 17. Specialization in production results in increased efficiency. (T) or F

(3.3) 18. Most economies are either purely market, purely command, or purely traditional, with little mixing of the three. T or (F)

(3.4) 19. Prices and profits are key to resource allocation in a market economy. (T) or F

(3.5) 20. There is no market for labor in market economies. T or (F)

Chapter 4
Market Pricing

I. Chapter Outline

In a market economy, prices are determined by the demand for and supply of goods and services. Prices increase to eliminate shortages and decrease to eliminate surpluses. By doing so the price moves to an equilibrium price. Once the market arrives at an equilibrium price, the price will not change unless demand or supply changes. If that should happen, the market will move to a new equilibrium price and the quantity of goods bought and sold will change.

Introductory Article: The Peanut Butter Crunch

Market prices are the result of many influences, including consumer demand, available supplies, and government actions. The prices of agricultural products are especially sensitive to these influences. On the supply side, they are affected by weather conditions, damage from insects and diseases, and government price supports. On the demand side, they are affected by changes in domestic and foreign demand, changes in the prices of related goods, and (of course) government regulation.

Economic Analysis

This chapter examines market pricing by addressing the following four questions:

1. What Forces Determine Prices in the Marketplace?

    Important Concepts: Demand, Supply, Equilibrium

    Important Model: Demand and supply curves

    Case Application: How Much Is a Good Student Worth?

2. What Determines Demand?

    Important Concepts: Consumer tastes and preferences, Income, Substitutes, Complements, Population

    Case Application: Pedal Power

3. What Determines Supply?

    Important Concepts: Short run, Long run

    Case Application: Jojoba: A Desert Weed That Smells Like Money

4. Why Do Prices Change?

    Important Concepts: Shifts in demand, Shifts in supply, Change in quantity demanded

    Case Application: Oat Bran Fettucini?

Perspective: Adam Smith's Marketplace

   Biography—Adam Smith

41

II. Summary of Economic Analysis

1. **Demand** is the amount of a product that consumers are willing to buy at different prices.
2. According to the **law of demand**, a greater quantity of a product is demanded at lower prices (and vice versa).
3. Because of the law of demand, there is an inverse relationship between price and quantity demanded. Consequently, the **demand curve** slopes down and to the right.
4. **Supply** is the amount of a product that sellers are willing to offer for sale at different prices.
5. According to the **law of supply**, a greater quantity of a good is supplied at higher prices (and vice versa).
6. Because of the law of supply, there is a direct relationship between price and quantity supplied. Consequently, the **supply curve** slopes up and to the right.
7. The price of a good and the quantity of it bought and sold are in **equilibrium** when the quantity supplied just equals the quantity demanded.
8. The **determinants of demand** are **consumer tastes and preferences, consumers' income**, the prices of **substitutes** and **complements**, and the size of the **market population**.
9. The **determinants of supply** are the costs of production and the time period being considered—short run or long run.
10. In the **short run**, output can be varied only by changing the amounts of labor or material inputs; the capacity of production (capital) is fixed at some level. In the **long run**, output can be varied by changing the capacity of production as well.
11. A **shift in demand** results from a change in one or more of the determinants of demand and is shown by a shift of the entire demand curve.
12. A **shift in supply** results from a change in the costs of production and is shown by a shift of the entire supply curve.
13. A change in demand changes the price of a good, resulting in a **change in the quantity supplied**. This is shown as *a movement along the supply curve*.
14. A change in supply changes the price of a good, resulting in a **change in the quantity demanded**. This is shown as *a movement along the demand curve*.

… 4 Market Pricing / 43

III. Review of the Learning Objectives (Answers begin on p. 287.)

What Forces Determine Prices in the Marketplace?

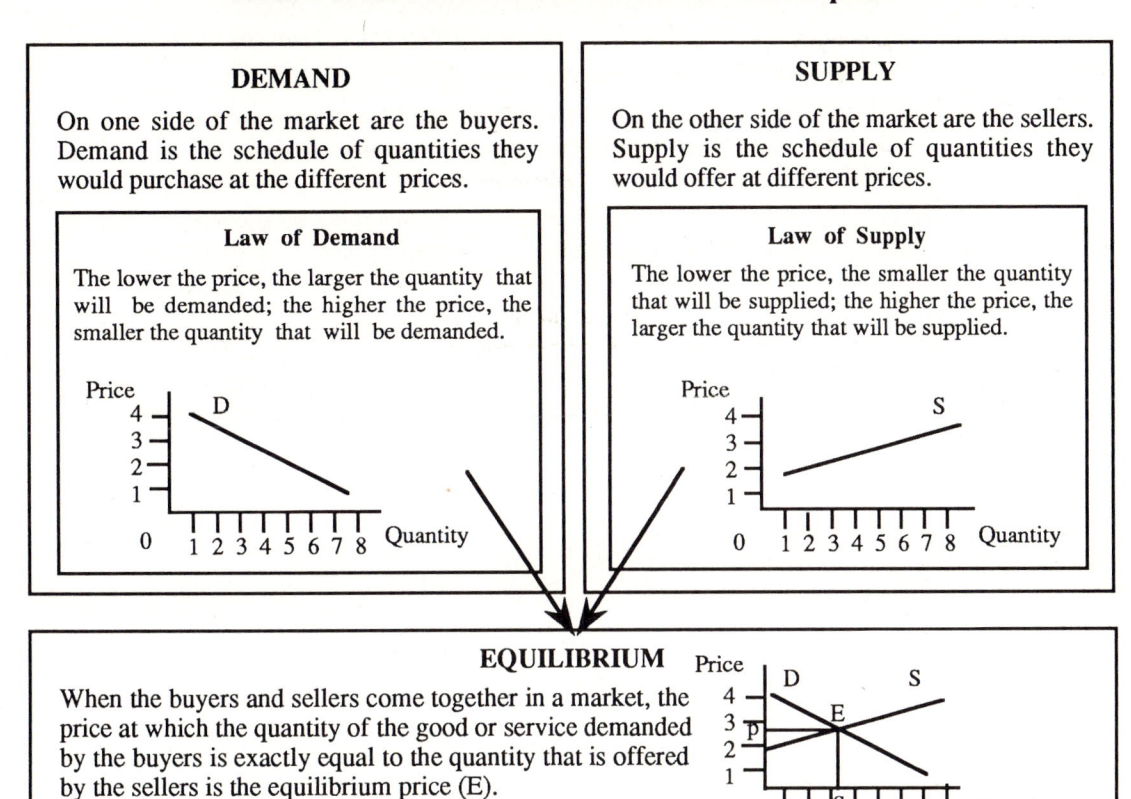

DEMAND

On one side of the market are the buyers. Demand is the schedule of quantities they would purchase at the different prices.

Law of Demand

The lower the price, the larger the quantity that will be demanded; the higher the price, the smaller the quantity that will be demanded.

SUPPLY

On the other side of the market are the sellers. Supply is the schedule of quantities they would offer at different prices.

Law of Supply

The lower the price, the smaller the quantity that will be supplied; the higher the price, the larger the quantity that will be supplied.

EQUILIBRIUM

When the buyers and sellers come together in a market, the price at which the quantity of the good or service demanded by the buyers is exactly equal to the quantity that is offered by the sellers is the equilibrium price (E).

(See page vi in the foreword "To the Student" for how to make the best use of this schematic outline.)

4.1. Explain the laws of demand and supply. *(Write in answers below.)*

A.

1. The law of demand states that lower prices cause a(n) _increase_ in the quantity of a good demanded and higher prices cause a(n) _decrease_ in the quantity demanded.

2. The law of supply states that lower prices cause a(n) _decrease_ in the quantity of a good supplied and higher prices cause a(n) _increase_ in quantity supplied.

B. Indicate whether each of the following is an example of the income (I) or substitution (S) effect on demand:

1. _I_ Because of higher gasoline prices, Ms. Octane cannot afford to drive as much as she once did.

2. _S_ Because of higher pork prices, Ms. Pullet buys more chicken.

3. _S_ When coffee prices increase, Maria drinks tea.

44 / Working With The Study of Economics, 4/E

    4. __I__ When the price of electricity doubled, Mr. Watt had to give up watching television all Saturday night.

C.

    1. Demand curves show the relationship between the two variables, __price__ and __quantity__. Demand curves slope down and to the right, indicating that there is a(n) __inverse__ relationship between the variables.

    2. Supply curves show the relationship between the two variables, __price__ and __quantity__. Supply curves slope up and to the right, indicating that there is a(n) __direct__ relationship between the variables.

D. When the price of chicken, salami, or Krazy Kola increases, people buy a lot less of these products. On the other hand, when the price of electricity, medicine, or salt increases, people still buy about the same amount. Why? __There are fewer direct substitutes for electricity, medicine, & salt__

E. Using the schedules provided, construct a demand curve and a supply curve in the space provided. The schedules show the supply of and demand for jars of jelly.

Price	Quantity Demanded	Price	Quantity Supplied
$1	10	$1	2
$2	8	$2	4
$3	6	$3	6
$4	4	$4	8
$5	2	$5	10

Price

0   Quantity

4.2. Explain why prices move toward an equilibrium price.

A. Use the schedules and graphs from the previous question to answer the following:

    1. If the price of jelly is $1, then there will be a __shortage__ of __8__ jars of jelly.

    2. If the price of jelly is $5, then there will be a __surplus__ of __8__ jars of jelly.

    3. The equilibrium price of jelly is __$3.00__.

4. Show your answers to parts 1, 2, and 3 on the demand and supply graph.

B. Suppose the price of a good is **above** its equilibrium price:
   1. A _surplus_ will exist.
   2. The price will _fall_.
   3. As a result of the price change, the quantity demanded will _increase_ and the quantity supplied will _decrease_.
   4. As a result of your answers in question 3, the _surplus_ caused by the high price will _disappear_.

C. Suppose the price of a good is **below** its equilibrium price:
   1. A _shortage_ will exist.
   2. The price will _rise_.
   3. As a result of the price change, the quantity demanded will _decrease_ and the quantity supplied will _increase_.
   4. As a result of your answers in question 3, the _shortage_ caused by the low price will _disappear_.

D. Only at the _equilibrium_ price will the quantity demanded be equal to the quantity supplied, so that there are no _surpluses_ and no _shortages_.

Case Application: The Grain Drain

Freak spring rainstorms swept across the breadbasket region of the Soviet Union, resulting in the country's worst harvest in half a century. Those storms, which flattened millions of acres of wheat, had a profound impact on towns and cities throughout the United States and Canada as the Soviet Union contracted with North American firms to meet its grain demand.

In Ridgefield, New Jersey, the customers of Palumbo's Bakery were soon paying a few cents more for their bread. Bakery owner Pat Palumbo complained to a customer, "That Russian wheat deal has really hurt. Three weeks ago I was paying $8.10 for a 100-pound bag of flour. Now my suppliers are asking $8.85."

Palumbo's problem was a result of the Soviet Union's sudden need to buy massive amounts of wheat from the United States and Canada. North American farmers were pleased to get top prices for their wheat, but North American consumers were unhappy at paying higher prices. The huge Soviet demand for grain pushed up the prices for all products produced from grain.

Buying and selling on the grain exchanges of the Midwest and prairie provinces was frantic, and for the first time in years the price of wheat broke the $3-per-bushel level. Speculators entered the market from all sides. Millers who processed wheat into flour bid up wheat prices, trying to get what was left of the supply of wheat on the open market after the Soviet contracts were signed. Both bread and nonbread products made with flour were commanding higher prices.

Economic Reasoning *(Write your responses on a separate sheet. Answers begin on p. 287.)*

1. What was the effect of the failure of the Soviet grain harvest on the demand schedule for American wheat?
2. Who caused the price of wheat to rise above $3 per bushel—the farmers, the Soviets, or the American flour millers? Why?
3. After the rise in the prices of flour and bakery products, it was argued that we should not have sold the wheat to the Soviets because doing so raised prices for American consumers. Do you agree or disagree? Why?

What Determines Demand?

DEMAND

Tastes and Preferences	Income	Substitutes and Complements	Population
The desire on the part of consumers for specific goods and services creates a demand for them.	When people have the income to purchase the goods and services they desire, their wants become effective demand. **Effective Demand:** The financial ability as well as the desire to purchase a certain number of units of a good or service at a given price.	The demand for a good or service is decreased whenever there are more or cheaper substitutes for it and demand is increased when there are more or cheaper complements for it.	The larger the population size of the market, the larger will be the demand for the various goods and services.

(See page vi in the foreword "To the Student" for how to make the best use of this schematic outline.)

4.3. List the determinants of demand.

A. Indicate the determinant of demand associated with each of the following:

1. Bicycle sales are up. *tastes + preferences*

2. Jelly sales decreased when peanut butter prices increased. *price of complements*

3. Baloney sales increased when peanut butter prices increased. *price of substitutes*

4. The demand for retirement homes will increase when the "baby boomers" retire. *population*

5. Because of a recession, people buy fewer cars. *income*

B. Indicate whether the following will cause an increase (I) or a decrease (D) in the demand for ketchup in Atlanta.

1. *I* The price of hamburgers decreases.

2. _D_ The price of mustard decreases.
3. _I_ Incomes increase.
4. _D_ A medical report says that ketchup causes baldness.
5. _I_ More people move to Atlanta.

Case Application: Upscale Munching

The sales of super-quality munchies—from ice cream to cookies to popcorn to muffins—have exploded in recent years.

The popularity of so-called super-premium ice creams, containing natural ingredients and an abundance of butterfat, has made familiar names of such foreign-sounding brands as Häagen-Dazs (Pillsbury), Frusen Glädjé (Dart and Kraft), and Alpen Zauber (manufactured in Brooklyn). Famous Amos and Mrs. Fields have made speciality cookie stores almost as common as ice cream shops. Orville Redenbacher and the producers of flavored popcorns elevated the lowly popcorn kernel to the status of a gourmet item. Both the new (to American palates) croissant and the old-fashioned muffin caught on as upscale snack foods.

What explains this upswing in the sales of expensive goodies? It is not always obvious what creates a particular trend, but some of the factors in this trend can be identified.

One of the causes of the surge in snack-food sales in general was the size of the age group that tends to consume such products—teenagers and young adults. The baby boom generation born in the years after World War II created a large market for snack foods. And as the baby boomers obtained jobs and had more disposable income, they indulged their taste for snack foods at a higher level of quality and cost.

The popularity of gourmet munchies may also be a reaction to counterbalance the ascetic diets many of them put themselves on, avoiding meals consisting of fatty, rich foods. They consider a fancy chocolate chip cookie to be a fair reward for sticking to their salad-only lunch diet.

Whatever the causes, the market for upscale munchies has taken off, and the next millionaire is likely to be someone who triples the price of an old snack item and sells it as a new gourmet delicacy.

Economic Reasoning *(Write your responses on a separate sheet. Answers begin on p. 287.)*

1. What determinants of demand have caused the popularity of gourmet snack products?
2. What has caused a change in the effective demand of the baby boom generation, and how has it affected the market for snack foods?
3. Are the super-premium ice creams worth their extra cost? What factors need to be considered in answering this?

What Determines Supply?

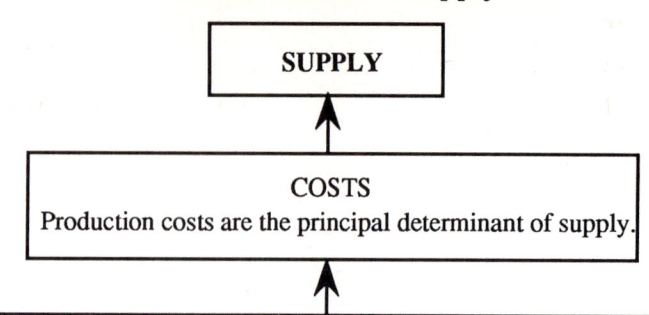

SUPPLY

↑

COSTS
Production costs are the principal determinant of supply.

↑

Short Run
In the short run output can be increased or decreased by changing the amount of labor and materials used in production. The size of the plant and the amount of major equipment cannot be changed in the short run. Production costs depend on the relationship between the amounts of resources used and the amount of output.

↑

Long Run
In the long run all factor inputs can be altered. Production capacity can be increased or decreased by adding to or reducing investment in plant and equipment. It is largely the amount of capital investment that determines long-run supply.

(See page vi in the foreword "To the Student" for how to make the best use of this schematic outline.)

4.4. List the determinants of supply.

A. Indicate which of the following WILL have an impact on determining the supply of orange juice (W) and which WILL NOT have an impact (WN).

1. _W_ A freeze causes orange prices to increase.
2. _W_ Orange pickers get a raise.
3. _WN_ The demand for orange juice increases.
4. _WN_ The price of grapefruit juice decreases.
5. _W_ The government places a tax on orange juice producers.
6. _W_ New orange-squeezing technology is developed.

B. The most important determinant of supply is _production costs_.

4.5. Distinguish between short-run and long-run supply.

A. The difference between the short and long runs depends on how long it takes to expand a firm's _productive capacity_.

B. Increasing production in the short run is usually associated with higher costs because each worker has less _capital_ to work with.

C. For each of the following industries, indicate what you think is the short-run "constraint" that can be changed only in the long run.
   1. A fast-food restaurant. _the dining room capacity_
   2. A hair stylist. _the # of chairs_
   3. A school. _classroom (# of desks)_
   4. An automobile manufacturer. _factory size_

Case Application: Black Walnut Worth Gold

Two rustlers pulled their truck up to the M. W. Leitner house in a comfortable, middle-class section of Des Moines. The family was out of town. The rustlers chopped down the century-old black walnut tree that shaded the house.

The rustlers would get up to $1,000 for the black walnut from a lumber company. Walnut is prized by producers of veneers, thin exterior sheets of wood used for facings on fine furniture. Cut by "shavers" into paper-thinness sometimes only one thirty-sixth of an inch thick, each sheet of veneer brings $25 to $50 at the retail level.

Black walnut trees grow throughout the Midwest. A tree generally takes 60 to 80 years to reach maturity, but with fertilizing and special care, a tree may be brought to maturity in 30 years. Nevertheless, because of growing demand, many conservationists are worried about preserving the species. Competition for wood is fierce—with buyers from the United States, West Germany, Sweden, and Japan bidding up to $1,000 per thousand board feet or higher. In the mid-1960s, the price was about $350 per thousand board feet.

The high demand has more than doubled the value of the wood marketed since the 1960s, while supplies have dwindled. A spokesman for a conservation group said, "In the mid-1960s, nearly half the hardwood veneers from domestic firms were black walnut. But that figure is way down now."

Missouri is the only state requiring the log buyer to know where the wood was cut, but that regulation is rarely enforced. A town marshall in Illinois commented, "Some buyers don't know the wood is stolen. Some don't care. But the law produces few convictions. The stuff is so valuable they're even stealing it from the national parks."

Economic Reasoning *(Write your responses on a separate sheet. Answers begin on p. 288.)*

1. How does the rustling of black walnut trees affect the short-run supply of black walnut veneer?
2. What effect does the length of time required for black walnut trees to mature have on the long-run supply of black walnut veneer?
3. Should laws be enacted in other states to prosecute log buyers who purchase black walnut without knowing where it came from?

Why Do Prices Change?

SHIFTS IN DEMAND	SHIFTS IN SUPPLY
If there is a change in any one or more of the four determinants of demand — tastes, incomes, prices and availability of substitutes and complements, population size — there will be a shift in the demand schedule. A decrease in demand means that at each and every price less would be purchased than previously.	A change in production costs results in a shift in the supply schedule. If production costs increase less will be supplied at each and every price.

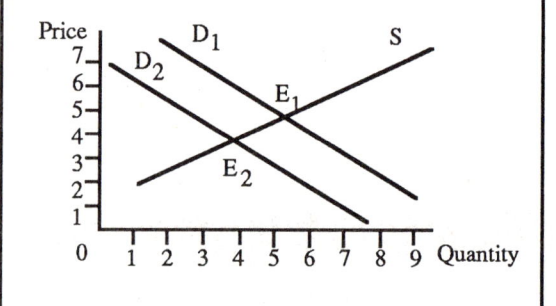

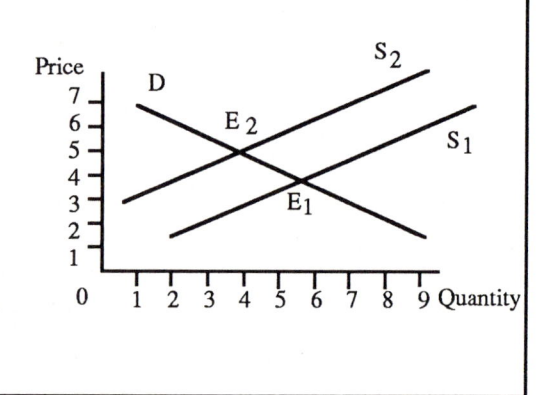

(See page vi in the foreword "To the Student" for how to make the best use of this schematic outline.)

4.6. Identify the causes of shifts in demand and how they affect market equilibrium.

A. List the five things that can cause a shift in the demand curve.

1. *income*
2. *price of substitutes*
3. *price of complements*
4. *tastes & preferences*
5. *size of the market population*

B. Circle the correct answer within the parentheses.

1. Other things being the same, an increase in the price of jelly will cause (**a decrease**/an increase) in the price of peanut butter and (**a decrease**/an increase) in the quantity of peanut butter sold.

2. Other things being the same, an increase in the price of chicken will cause (a decrease/**an increase**) in the price of pork and (a decrease/**an increase**) in the quantity of pork sold.

3. Other things being the same, an increase in the average age of the population will cause (a decrease/**an increase**) in the price of hospitals and (a decrease/**an increase**) in the quantity of hospitals built.

4. Macaroni and cheese is sometimes referred to as being an **inferior** good because when peoples' incomes go up, they buy less of it and when their

incomes go down they buy more of it. This being the case, an increase in incomes will cause (a decrease/an increase) in the price of macaroni and cheese and (a decrease/an increase) in the quantity of macaroni and cheese sold.

C. The demand and supply graphs below represent the market for pepperoni. Graphically show what will happen if:

1. the price of pizza increases.
2. the price of sausage increases.

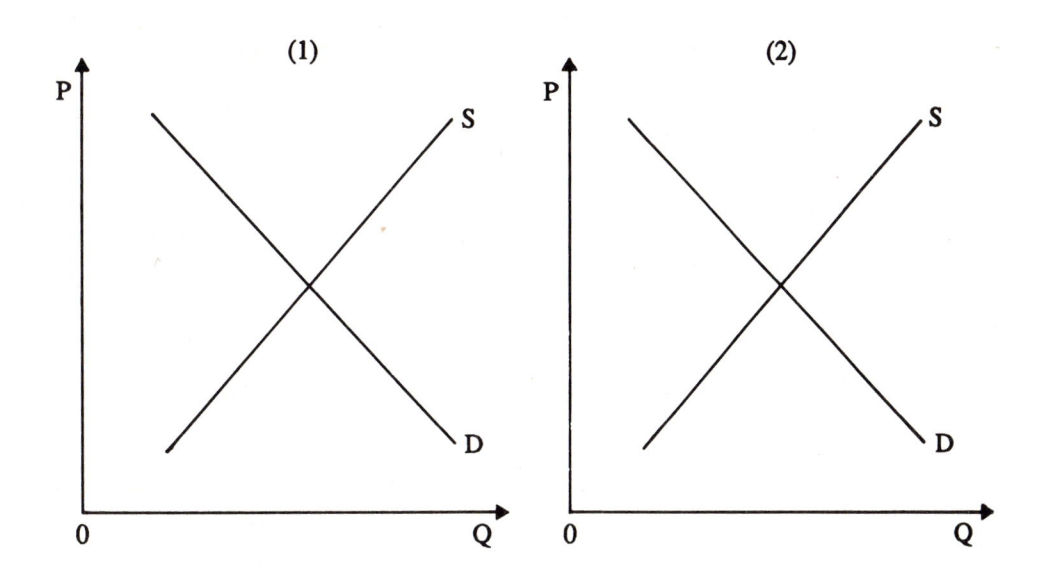

(1)

(2)

D. For each of the above cases, indicate what happens to the equilibrium price and quantity of pepperoni.
   1. Price _decreases_ Quantity _decreases_
   2. Price _increases_ Quantity _increases_

E. Using the schedules provided, construct the two demand curves indicated in the space provided and indicate which one represents an increase in demand.

Price	Quantity Demanded	Price	Quantity Demanded
$1	5	$1	7
$2	4	$2	6
$3	3	$3	5
$4	2	$4	4
$5	1	$5	3

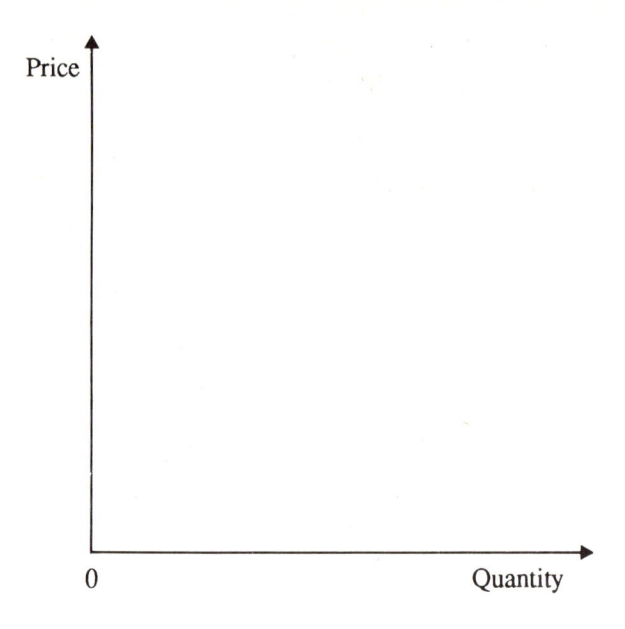

[Empty graph with Price on vertical axis and Quantity on horizontal axis]

4.7. Identify the causes of shifts in supply and how they affect market equilibrium.

A. Circle the correct answer within the parentheses.

1. Other things being the same, an increase in pilots' wages would cause (a decrease/**an increase**) in the price of flying and (**a decrease**/an increase) in the quantity of airplane trips taken.

2. Other things being the same, the use of robots in manufacturing cars will cause (**a decrease**/an increase) in the price of cars and (a decrease/**an increase**) in the quantity of cars sold.

3. Other things being the same, increased specialization will cause (**a decrease**/an increase) in prices and (a decrease/**an increase**) in the quantity of goods and services sold.

4. Other things being the same, increased oil prices will cause (a decrease/**an increase**) in prices and (**a decrease**/an increase) in the quantity of goods and services sold.

B. In 1980, when Ronald Reagan campaigned for president of the United States, he talked about the benefits of supply-side economics—using policies to shift supply curves to the *right*. What would U.S. voters like about the consequences of shifting all the economy's supply curves to the right?

lower prices, and more goods & services

C. The demand and supply graphs shown on the following page represent the market for apple juice. Graphically depict what happens if:

1. Environmentalists force apple growers to use fewer chemical fertilizers and insecticides.

2. Good weather results in an especially good apple harvest.

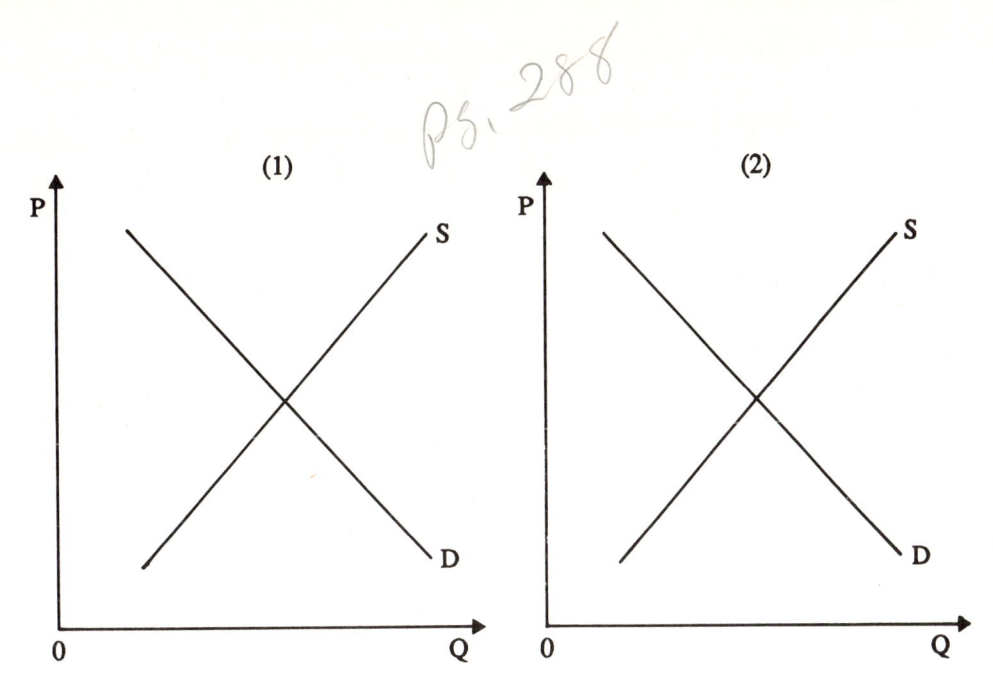

(1) and (2): [supply and demand graphs, both showing S and D curves crossing]

pg. 288

D. For each of the above cases, indicate what happens to the equilibrium price and quantity of apple juice.

1. Price *increase* Quantity *decrease*
2. Price *decrease* Quantity *increase*

4.8. Distinguish between a change in demand and a change in quantity demanded.

A. In each of the following, indicate whether there will be an increase or a decrease in the quantity demanded or supplied.

1. The demand curve shifts to the right.

   quantity supplied increases

2. The demand curve shifts to the left.

   quantity supplied decreases

3. The supply curve shifts to the right.

   quantity demanded increases

4. The supply curve shifts to the left.

   quantity demanded decreases

B. In each of the following, indicate whether there will be an increase or a decrease in the quantity demanded or supplied in the market for **tennis balls**. (Drawing a graph will be helpful.)

1. The price of tennis rackets increases.

   quantity supplied decreases

2. Tennis becomes more popular.

54 / *Working With The Study of Economics, 4/E*

3. Tennis ball workers get a raise.

quantity supplied increases

4. New technology makes tennis ball production cheaper.

quantity demanded decreases

quantity demanded increases

C. Using the supply schedules below, construct the two supply curves in the space provided and indicate which one represents an increase in supply.

Price	Quantity Supplied	Price	Quantity Supplied
$1	1	$1	3
$2	2	$2	4
$3	3	$3	5
$4	4	$4	6
$5	5	$5	7

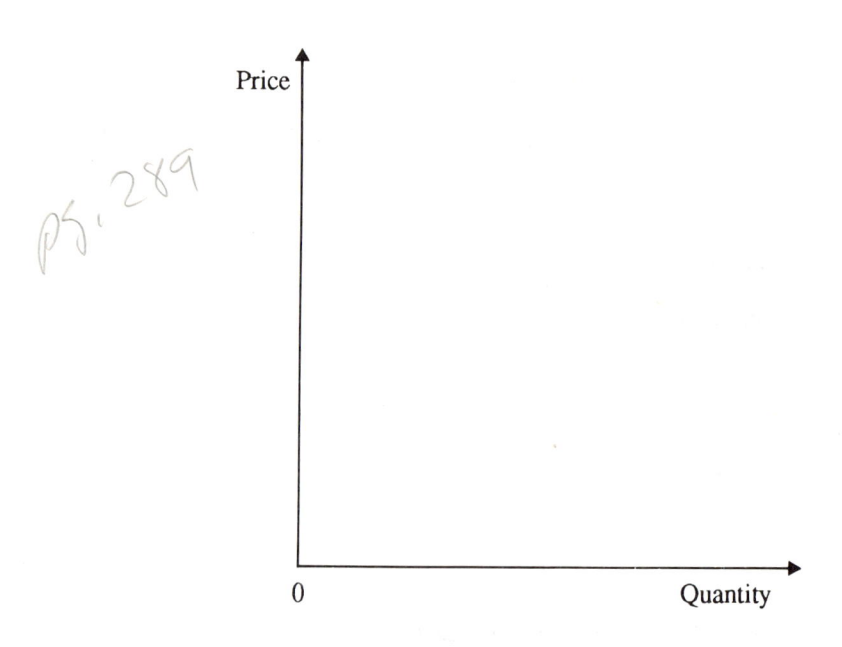

pg. 289

Case Application: Do Boycotts Work?

Some years ago consumers in the United States were faced with very rapid increases in beef prices. Homemakers, restaurant owners, and fast-food operators were outraged. Many organized spontaneous consumer boycotts aimed at supermarkets. People refused to buy or eat beef.

Meanwhile, back in the feedlots, cattlemen complained bitterly about the high cost of grain, the primary food for cattle. They wondered why they should be blamed for high retail prices. After all, cattlemen were not responsible for the high costs of feed for their cattle.

Do consumer boycotts really have an impact on prices? Most consumers do not boycott—they merely reduce quantities purchased as prices rise. They do not change their demand schedules. If the boycotts actually grow large enough to change market demand (to move the whole curve), there may be a reduction in market prices.

Economic Reasoning *(Write your responses on a separate sheet. Answers begin on p. 289.)*

1. Does a boycott cause a shift in the demand curve or a movement along the demand curve?
2. Does a boycott result in lower prices? Why or why not?
3. Are boycotts such as the one described in this application fair? Why or why not?

IV. Practice Test *(Answers begin on p. 289.)*

Multiple Choice *(Circle the correct answer.)*

(4.1) 1. The law of supply indicates that as prices increase:
   a. the quantity supplied increases.
   b. the quantity supplied decreases.
   c. surpluses increase.
   d. shortages increase.

(4.1) 2. Which of the following is an example of the "substitution effect" on demand?
   a. Advertising by a cola company causes you to switch to their brand.
   b. Higher tuition causes you to work longer hours.
   c. An increase in the price of movie theater tickets causes you to rent more home videos.
   d. If the price of corn increases, more farmers will grow corn instead of wheat.

(4.2) 3. Prices above the market equilibrium price result in which of the following?
   a. excess profits.
   b. surpluses.
   c. shifts in supply.
   d. shifts in demand.

(4.2) 4. An equilibrium price will not change unless:
   a. demand changes.
   b. supply changes.
   c. both demand and supply change.
   d. All of the above will cause the price to change.

(4.3) 5. Which of the following will cause the demand for compact laser discs to **increase**?
   a. an increase in the price of audio cassettes.
   b. a decrease in the cost of producing compact discs.
   c. an increase in the price of laser disc players.
   d. a decrease in consumers' income.

(4.3) 6. Good Y is a "substitute" for Good X if:
   a. the demand for Y increases when the price of X increases.
   b. the demand for Y increases when the supply of X decreases.
   c. the supply of Y increases when the demand for X increases.
   d. the supply of Y increases when the supply of X increases.

(4.4) 7. The most important determinant of supply is:
   a. demand.
   b. income.
   c. costs of production.
   d. the equilibrium price.

(4.5) 8. Which of the following best describes the "short run"?
   a. the time period during which demand is fixed.
   b. one accounting period.
   c. the time it takes demand changes to adjust to supply changes.

d. the time period in which at least one factor of production cannot be changed.

(4.5) 9. As output levels increase in the short run, workers will be less and less productive because:
a. demand always increases faster than output.
b. the amount of the fixed factor changes when output changes.
c. each worker has less capital to work with.
d. the equilibrium price is higher in the short run.

(4.6) 10. Which of the following will NOT cause the demand curve to shift?
a. a change in production costs.
b. a change in the size of the population.
c. a change in the price of a complement.
d. fads.

(4.6) 11. Other things being the same, what will happen if consumer incomes decrease?
a. demand and prices will decrease.
b. demand and prices will increase.
c. demand will decrease and prices will increase.
d. demand will increase and prices will increase.

(4.7) 12. Which of the following will NOT cause the supply curve to shift?
a. a change in demand.
b. a change in taxes.
c. a change in wage rates.
d. a change in interest rates.

(4.7) 13. A decrease in supply will result in which of the following?
a. increased prices and equilibrium quantities.
b. decreased prices and equilibrium quantities.
c. increased prices and decreased equilibrium quantities.
d. decreased prices and increased equilibrium quantities.

(4.8) 14. Which of the following describes a "decrease in quantity supplied"?
a. a leftward shift of the supply curve.
b. a rightward shift of the supply curve.
c. a leftward movement along a given supply curve.
d. a rightward movement along a given supply curve.

(4.8) 15. An increase in production costs results in which of the following?
a. a decrease in supply and a decrease in quantity supplied.
b. an increase in supply and a decrease in quantity supplied.
c. a decrease in supply and a decrease in quantity demanded.
d. a decrease in supply and an increase in quantity demanded.

True/False *(Circle T or F.)*

(4.1) 16. Demand represents the buyers' side of the market, and supply represents the sellers' side of the market. T or F

(4.2) 17. In market economies, surpluses are usually eliminated by an increase in prices. T or F

(4.4) 18. Supply depends upon demand. T or F

(4.5) 19. The short and long runs are different in different industries (markets). T or F

(4.8) 20. Changes in demand result in shifts of a demand curve, and changes in quantity demanded result in movement along a demand curve. T or F

Foundations Crossword Puzzle

(Chapters 1–4)

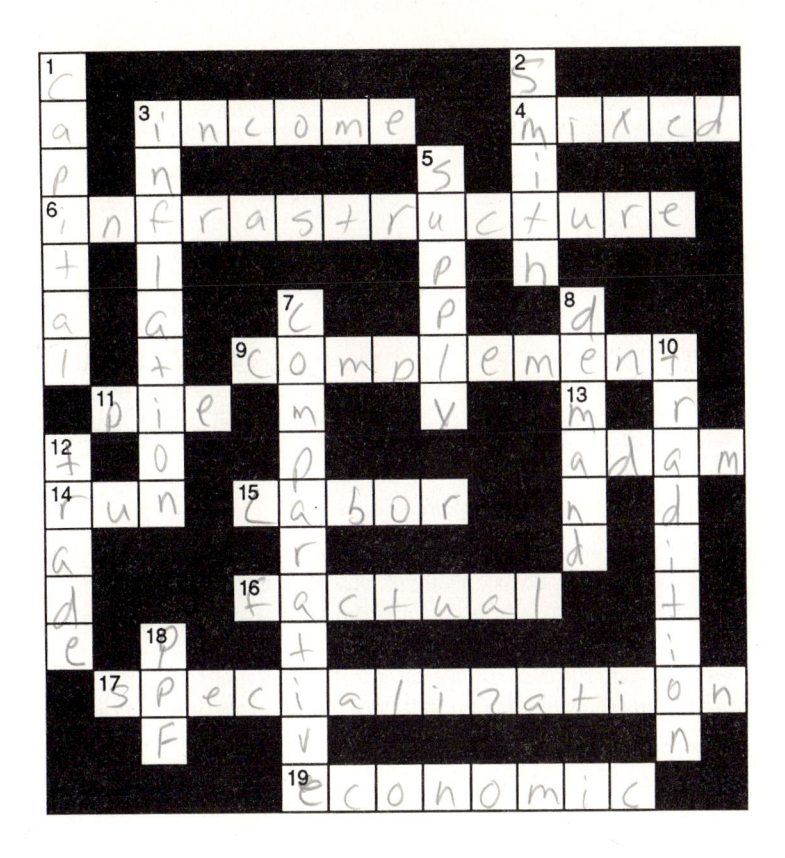

Across

3. This determining effect explains why demand fluctuates when price fluctuates.
4. A description of the type of economy that is prevalent throughout the world.
6. The highways, bridges, airports, and public transportation facilities of an economy.
9. What grape jelly is to Bif peanut butter.
11. The type of chart used to show the relative size of the components of a whole.
13. Smith who wrote *The Wealth of Nations*.
14. Increasing output in the short _____ generally increases the cost of producing each unit.
15. Human resources.
16. These "tools" for an economist are statistics, history, and how institutions operate.
17. The rancher Bill Hayden found a profitable opportunity in it.
19. What to produce is this type of question.

Down

1. Refers to the machinery, factories, and office buildings used in production for an economy.
2. Associated with the "invisible hand."
3. The continual rise of the general price level.
5. This curve shows the relationship between the price of Bif peanut butter and the number of jars the Bif company would like to sell.
7. The western states' advantage over New Jersey in beef production.
8. This curve represents the relationship between the price of a product and the quantity demanded.
10. An economy which produces and distributes goods without the function of a market or the command of a centralized authority usually does so by _____.
12. A _____ off usually must occur when choosing between allocating a nation's production to military use or to civilian use.
18. The type of graph showing the different maximum output combinations of goods or services that can be obtained from a fixed amount of resources.

Chapter 5

The Consumer

I. Chapter Outline

In a market economy, producers supply what consumers demand: the consumer is sovereign. Understanding more about how consumers act, and react, as they attempt to get the most from their limited incomes is therefore important if we are to understand the workings of a market economy better.

Introductory Article: Blowing Smoke Rings

Consumers of cigarettes, like the consumers of any product, make use of any available information when making their decisions about what they will spend their money for. Sometimes the information comes from the government in the form of required product labeling, but mostly it comes from advertisers who have a vested interest in selling their products. Sometimes, as in the case of cigarettes, information alone cannot influence consumer choice because consumers find that they have no substitute product to turn to.

Economic Analysis

This chapter examines the issue of consumer choice by addressing the following three questions:

1. What Choices Do Consumers Make?

    Important Concepts: Price elasticity of demand, Elasticity ratio, Consumer sovereignty, Average propensities to consume and save

    Case Application: The American Dream

2. How Do Consumers Make Choices?

    Important Concepts: Total utility, Diminishing marginal utility, Consumer equilibrium

    Case Application: The Channel Race

3. How Can Consumers Make Better Choices?

    Important Concepts: Information, Advertising

    Case Application: That's No Alligator; It's a Chameleon

Perspective: Conspicuous Consumption

        Biography—Thorstein Veblen

II. Summary of Economic Analysis

1. People divide their after-tax income between **consumption spending** (on **necessities** and **luxuries**) and **savings**.
2. The law of demand states that price and quantity demanded are inversely related; **price elasticity of demand** indicates *how much* quantity changes when the price changes.
3. If demand is **elastic**, quantity demanded is sensitive to price changes and it changes proportionately more than the change in prices.
4. If demand is **inelastic**, quantity demanded is insensitive to price changes and it changes proportionately less than the change in prices.
5. The **elasticity ratio** is equal to the percentage change in quantity demanded divided by the percentage change in the price of the good or service. If the ratio is less than 1 demand is inelastic; if it is greater than 1 demand is elastic; and if it is equal to 1 elasticity is unitary.
6. The principle of **consumer sovereignty** implies that consumer demand determines what is produced.
7. The **average propensity to consume** is the percentage of after-tax income that is spent on consumer goods and the **average propensity to save** is the percentage that is saved. The two propensities must add to 1, indicating that after-tax income is either spent or saved.
8. The amount of satisfaction obtained from consuming or saving is called **utility**. The objective of consumers is to maximize their **total utility**.
9. The satisfaction obtained from consuming one more unit of a good is the **marginal utility** of consuming the good. Because the consumption of additional units of a product adds less and less to total utility, the additional units have **diminishing marginal utility**.
10. Consumers maximize their total utility when they allocate their income so that the marginal utility per dollar spent is the same for all goods purchased, including savings.
11. Making the best consumption and savings decisions requires adequate **information**.
12. Although **advertising** is the major source of consumer information, it adds to product prices and sometimes is deceptive.

III. Review of the Learning Objectives (Answers begin on p. 290.)

What Choices Do Consumers Make?

SPENDING CHOICES

People continuously make spending decisions in order to satisfy their consumption needs and desires for necessities and luxuries.

Price Elasticity of Demand

The extent to which the quantity demanded of a good varies with small changes in its price is its elasticity of demand.

Measurement of elasticity

$$\text{Elasticity Ratio} = \frac{\%\text{ change in quantity}}{\%\text{ change in price}}$$

Consumer sovereignty

means that the spending decisions of consumers dictate what producers make and how resources are allocated.

SAVINGS CHOICES

The alternative to spending for the after-tax income of consumers is savings.

Average Propensity to Consume

The amount we typically spend on goods and services out of a dollar of income is our average propensity to consume. In this country it tends to be around 95¢ of each dollar or 95%.
The other 5¢ we save. The consumers' average propensity to save is 5%.

(See page vi in the foreword "To the Student" for how to make the best use of this schematic outline.)

5.1. Define elasticity of demand. *(Write in answers below.)*

A. Price elasticity of demand is a measure of how much _*quantity demanded*_ changes when the price of a product changes.

B. If goods are necessities their demand will tend to be _*inelastic*_. If they are luxuries their demand will tend to be _*elastic*_.

C. What are the two most important things that influence the elasticity of demand for a product?

1. _*availability of substitutes*_
2. _*price of the good relative to my budget*_

D. Indicate whether the demand for each of the following is elastic (E) or inelastic (I).

1. _I_ Gasoline.
2. _E_ Texaco gasoline.
3. _E_ Brand X paper towels.
4. _E_ Yachts.
5. _I_ Electricity.
6. _I_ Soap.

5.2. Define the terms perfectly elastic, relatively elastic, unitary elastic, relatively inelastic, and perfectly inelastic.

A. If the demand for good X is perfectly elastic, then what must be true about the substitutes for good X?

There must be perfect substitutes

B. If the demand for good Y is perfectly inelastic, then what must be true about the substitutes for good Y?

There are no substitutes

C. Indicate whether the demand for the following goods is close to being perfectly elastic (PE), relatively elastic (RE), perfectly inelastic (PI), or relatively inelastic (RI).

1. *PI* A life preserver for a drowning person.
2. *PE* Farmer Jones's wheat.
3. *PI* Water.
4. *PE* 3/4 inch bolts from Lundberg's Hardware Store.
5. *RE* Pizza.
6. *RE* Movie tickets.
7. *RI* Tickets for the Game of the Century when it is not televised.
8. *RE* Tickets for the Game of the Century when it is televised.

D. On the graph provided below, draw the demand curve for insulin and label it D1. Next, draw the demand curve for the insulin sold at a specific pharmacy and label it D2.

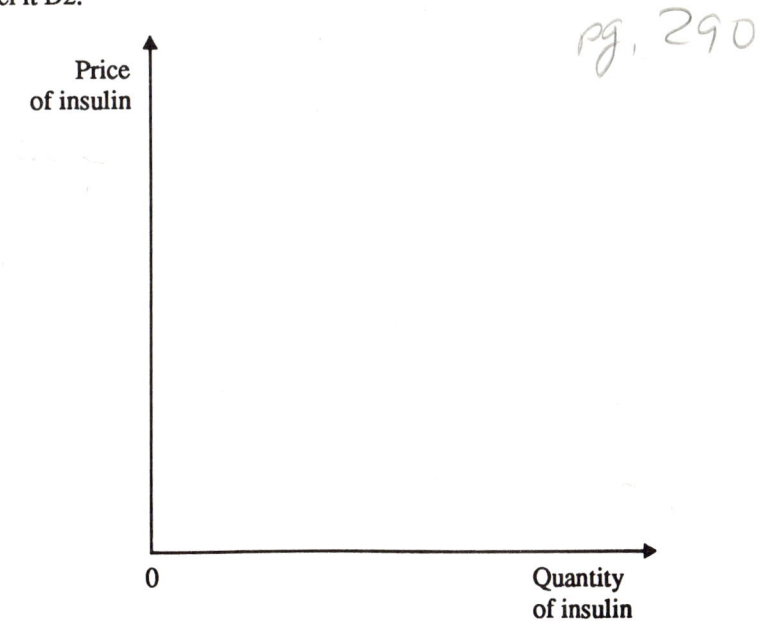

pg. 290

[Graph with vertical axis labeled "Price of insulin" and horizontal axis labeled "Quantity of insulin", origin at 0]

E.

1. On the following page, draw the *relatively inelastic* demand curve for car tires on the graph on the left and draw the *relatively elastic* demand curve for car seat covers on the graph on the right. Draw a supply curve on each graph.

pg. 290

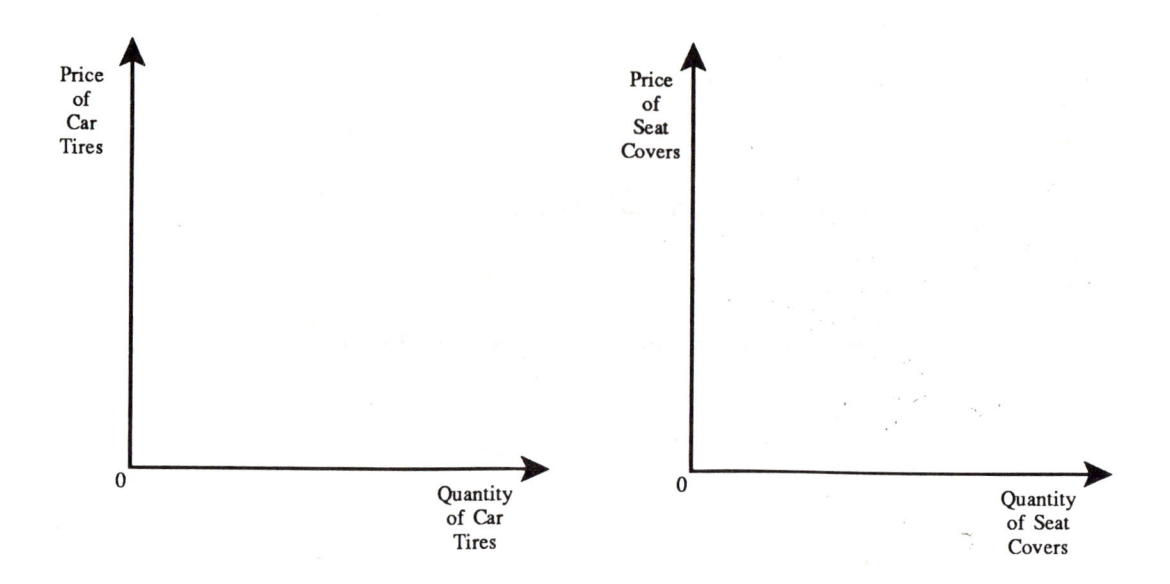

[Two empty graphs: left with axes "Price of Car Tires" (vertical) and "Quantity of Car Tires" (horizontal); right with axes "Price of Seat Covers" (vertical) and "Quantity of Seat Covers" (horizontal).]

2. Draw new supply curves on each of the above graphs that represent equal reductions in supply (the same vertical distance between the supply curves). In which case does the price increase the most, and in which case does the quantity demanded decrease the most?

5.3. Compute elasticity ratios.

A. Compute the elasticity ratio in each of following instances:
1. Price increases 25% and quantity decreases 50%. _2.0_
2. Price decreases 50% and quantity decreases 50%. _1.0_
3. Price decreases 10% and quantity increases 1%. _.10_
4. Price increases 1% and quantity falls to zero. _0.00_
5. Price decreases 15% and quantity does not change. _infinite_

B. For each of the above cases, indicate whether the demand is perfectly elastic (PE), relatively elastic (RE), unitary elastic (UE), relatively inelastic (RI), or perfectly inelastic (PI), and give an example for each.
1. _RE_ _Broccoli_
2. _UE_ _Frozen Veggies_
3. _RI_ _Toothpaste_
4. _PI_ _insulin_
5. _PE_ _Wheat_

5.4. Define consumer sovereignty and show how it is related to the allocation of resources.

A. If consumer sovereignty exists, how does an economy decide what goods to produce?

It produces what consumers want.

5 The Consumer / 63

B. If consumer sovereignty did NOT exist, how would an economy decide what goods to make?

Producers would need to guess, or perhaps tradition or a central administration would answer "what to produce"

C. According to the doctrine of consumer sovereignty, does supply react to demand, or does demand react to supply?

Supply reacts to demand

5.5. Define average propensity to consume and average propensity to save.

A. What are the three things that people can do with their before-tax income?

1. *pay taxes*
2. *spend*
3. *save*

B. If a person's income is $10,000 a year and he or she saves $1,500, then what is that person's:

Average propensity to save? *.15*

Average propensity to consume? *.85*

C. Which of the following would be likely to increase a person's average propensity to consume (C), and which would be likely to increase a person's average propensity to save (S)?

1. *C* An increase in income.
2. *C* A belief that the world will end next week.
3. *S* A decision to go to college.
4. *C* A decrease in the rate of return to savings.

D. Businesses will be both hurt and helped if there is an increase in the average propensity to save. How will they be hurt? *people will be spending & buying less*

How will they be helped? *increased savings leads to more funds available to borrow for investment*

Case Application: Going to the Movies

Carol and Martin Gardner of Little Rock, Arkansas, were avid movie fans and usually saw at least one a week. But recently they have had to make some changes in their choice of entertainment. With ticket prices at $6 or more per person, Carol and Martin have been taking more bicycle rides, having picnics, and watching more television than ever before.

Carol described the situation this way: "Who wants to pay $12 just for tickets? That doesn't even include the price of gas, parking, or snacks. We didn't mind paying $4 or $5 for a ticket, but when the price went up to $6, that was too much. Now we consider more carefully whether we really want to see the film at the theater or whether we can pass it by and wait until it comes out on rental tape or see it on TV."

Movie customers expect certain satisfactions when they pay for their tickets. When admission prices increase to $6 or $7 a ticket people begin to question whether their limited entertainment budgets can handle the higher prices. Many are concerned that as prices of many goods and services continue to rise, they will have to cut into their entertainment budget to buy necessities. As Martin put it, "If the price of food keeps going up the way it has been, pretty soon we'll have to substitute groceries for movies."

64 / *Working With The Study of Economics, 4/E*

The young Arkansas couple, like most people, do not want to stop entertaining themselves, and they do want to see some movies, even at higher prices. That means making choices—deciding how much they want to see a particular film or passing it up altogether in favor of other forms of recreation.

Economic Reasoning *(Write your responses on a separate sheet. Answers begin on p. 290.)*

1. Do the Gardners consider going to the movies a necessity or a luxury?
2. From the application does it appear that the Gardners' demand for theater movies is perfectly elastic, relatively elastic, relatively inelastic, or perfectly inelastic?
3. Is $6 too much to pay for a ticket to the movies? What are your criteria for how much is too much?

How Do Consumers Make Choices?

UTILITY

Consumers decide how much of their income to spend on different purchases depending on how much satisfaction or utility the item has for them.

Total utility
is a measurement of the amount of satisfaction that a consumer receives from all of the purchases of a particular good or service.

Marginal utility
is the additional amount of satisfaction a consumer receives from the purchase of one additional unit of a good or service (or the additional satisfaction from the last unit purchased).

Diminishing Marginal Utility
The more of a particular good or service that a consumer purchases, the less additional satisfaction an additional unit purchased will provide. Nearly everything has diminishing marginal utility.

CONSUMER EQUILIBRIUM

In order to get the maximum satisfaction from the income they spend consumers should allocate their purchases so that the last dollar spent on each good or service provides the same marginal utility as the last dollar spent on every other good or service purchased. When this is true, they are at consumer equilibrium — the allocation of their income that provides them with the maximum total utility possible.

(See page vi in the foreword "To the Student" for how to make the best use of this schematic outline.)

5.6. Show the relationship of marginal utility to total utility.

A. If a consumer's marginal utility for shoes **increased**, what goods would this consumer buy?
   shoes & only shoes

B. Because marginal utility *diminishes* as more of a good is consumed, consumers will pay *less* for additional units of the good.

C.
   1. Which has more total utility for you, diamonds or water?
   water, you'd die w/out it

2. Which has a higher marginal utility for you, (diamonds) or water?

   I value the next diamond more than the next glass of water

3. Explain the apparent paradox in your answers to (1) and (2).

   I have so much water that the marginal utility is small. I have so few diamonds so my marginal utility of the next one is still very high

5.7. Explain the principle of diminishing marginal utility.

A. The figure below represents Andrea's utility for ice cream cones. Use it to answer the questions which follow.

1. Indicate the marginal and total utility for each of the ice cream cones eaten.

	Marginal Utility	Total Utility
First cone.	4	4
Second cone.	3	7
Third cone.	2	9
Fourth cone.	1	10
Fifth cone.	-1	9

2. If each "util" corresponds to one dollar, how many cones will Andrea buy if cones cost $3?

   2

3. What does the marginal utility of the fifth cone imply?

   negative marginal utility — a stomachache

66 / *Working With The Study of Economics, 4/E*

5.8. State the conditions necessary for consumer equilibrium.

A. The table below shows the marginal utility per dollar that Jorge gets from video games, books, and records. For the sake of argument, assume each of the three goods costs $1.

Number	Video games	Books	Records
1	12	14	8
2	7	11	7
3	5	5	5
4	2	4	4
5	1	3	2

1. If Jorge has $9, how much of each good should he buy?

   3 of each

2. According to your answer in (1), what is Jorge's total utility?

   74 utils

3. Is this the most total utility that Jorge can get? How do you know?

   Yes - marginal utilities are equal

4. If Jorge only has $4, what combination of goods will give him the most total utility?

   1 video game, 2 books, & 1 record

Case Application: Life-style and Consumer Choice

Changing life-styles are affecting traditional consumer markets in clothing, food, automobiles, recreational services, and many other areas. No one really knows in what direction consumers are moving, and this uncertainty bothers producers. Are people today embracing values so different from those of the past that they add up to a whole new outlook on life and society?

This question goes to the heart of the future prospects for consumer markets. There may be major shifts in the patterns of expenditure if enough people become antimaterialistic or increasingly environmentalistic. On the other hand, movements like these may be temporary shifts in tastes, reflecting no more than passing fancies. The most dominant new feature, say some observers, is that consumers are trying to express their individuality through their spending patterns. A second important feature is the desire for convenience that has accompanied the new life-styles of the new consumers.

The new consumers' demands for self-expression, uniqueness, and convenience are readily apparent in the clothing market. Many clothing retailers have opened specialized boutiques to meet the new demand for self-expression. Homogenized "uniforms" have given way to individual fashions. Consumers want convenience and easy-to-care-for fashions.

Both the automobile and food markets have also shown great shifts in consumer tastes. Compacts, sports cars, and multipurpose vehicles have taken a large part of the automobile market. Some observers believe consumers reflect their personal life-styles in the cars they purchase. Fast-food chains and frozen dinners have flourished side by side with gourmet cooking schools—reflecting the vitality of consumer behavior. Consumers seem willing to pay for convenience in food preparation and to accept standardization. At the same time, they demand ethnic foods, specialties, wines, and herbs. There is no question that life-style influences consumer choice in the modern market economics.

Economic Reasoning *(Write your responses on a separate sheet. Answers begin on p. 291.)*

1. Large cars can carry more passengers, groceries, baggage, and so forth than compact cars. Does that mean that large cars have greater utility than compact cars? Explain.
2. Does convenience have diminishing marginal utility? How can you be sure?
3. Convenience foods cost more than basic food products. During these hard economic times, can we afford the luxury of convenience foods? Why or why not?

How Can Consumers Make Better Choices?

INFORMATION

In order to allocate their incomes to obtain maximum utility, consumers need to have adequate and accurate information about the availability, characteristics, quality, sources, and prices of the goods and services that they might be interested in buying.

Limits on Information
Ideally, consumers should have as much information as possible about available products, but there are costs to acquiring, disseminating, and evaluating information.

Advertising
The most common source of information about products and services is advertising. Advertising is beneficial when it provides consumers with better information for making choices and when it reduces production costs by expanding the market for a product. But it is detrimental when it is false or misleading and when it adds to costs.

(See page vi in the foreword "To the Student" for how to make the best use of this schematic outline.)

5.9. Explain the effects of product information and advertising on consumer choices.

A. List four products that you have purchased recently where some of your information about the product was provided by the producer because the government required it.

1. *cereal*
2. *advil - asperin*
3. *milk*
4. *bread*

B. List four products that you have purchased recently based on information provided by advertisers.

1. *Triples - cereal*
2. *L.A. Gear tennis shoes*
3. *shower head*

4. *dish detergent*

C. List any cases where false or misleading advertising caused you, or someone you know, to buy a product that might otherwise not have been purchased.

D. What are two sources of consumer information other than that which the government requires and that which is provided through advertisements?

1. *word of mouth*
2. *consumer publications / TV & Radio*
3. Do you feel that the sources indicated above are more or less reliable than advertisements as a source of information? Why?

more reliable because they don't have a vested interest in selling a product like the advertiser does

Case Application: Do You Have Time for Your Possessions?

We consumers are hooked on laborsaving devices and convenience gadgets—coffee makers, programmable VCRs, telephone answering machines, food processors, microwave ovens, remote-control TVs, ice makers, and electronic automobile controls that maintain a set speed, lock doors, and turn lights on and off, all automatically.

There seems to be a limitless market for products that make our lives easier. But the question is now being asked—do all of these new gadgets really save us time, or are they in fact putting more demands on us? Acquiring them takes time. We must evaluate and shop for a new product. Then we must frequently assemble it and learn how to use it. But the problems that most occupy our time and nervous energy are those that arise in servicing, repairing, and replacing items that do not work properly or at all. Another set of problems arises in protecting all of our possessions—VCRs are the favorite target of burglars. Devices to protect the house from burglaries frequently malfunction, sometimes triggering false alarms to the police or private security agencies.

Are our concerns with possessions and our need to own the latest and newest of everything actually adding to our burdens rather than lightening them? By loading ourselves up with gadgets are we cutting into our leisure time and leaving less time for enjoyment?

Our higher incomes have given us the ability to acquire immensely more material possessions than were available to previous generations. As a consequence, studies show we spend a lot more time shopping. And when something goes wrong with one of our personal, household, or automobile convenience devices, we generally have to find someone to fix it and either take it in to be repaired or arrange to be at home for a service call. Even when appliances work properly, many of them require periodic servicing. We have become dependent on the availability and skill of a variety of service technicians to keep our gadget-filled lives functioning smoothly. Every time we buy an additional appliance we assume a new responsibility.

How many more "laborsaving" products do we have time for?

Economic Reasoning *(Write your responses on a separate sheet. Answers begin on p. 291.)*

1. How do consumers normally find out about the availability of new products?
2. What information do consumers need that they do not generally have when purchasing convenience products that would help them make better choices?
3. Should producers be required to provide customers with information about the average number of repairs required on their appliances and the average cost of maintaining them? Why or why not?

IV. Practice Test (Answers begin on p. 291.)

Multiple Choice *(Circle the correct answer.)*

(5.1) 1. Which of the following goods has the most **inelastic** demand?
   a. electricity. *(circled)*
   b. tomatoes.
   c. video games.
   d. going to the movies.

(5.1) 2. Which of the following are the most important in determining the elasticity of demand for a product?
   a. its cost of production and the number of complements.
   b. its price relative to one's income and the number of substitutes. *(circled)*
   c. its price and its cost of production.
   d. the number of available substitutes and complements.

(5.2) 3. If there are very few substitutes for a product, then the demand for the product is likely to be:
   a. relatively inelastic. *(circled)*
   b. relatively elastic.
   c. perfectly elastic.
   d. perfectly inelastic.
   e. unitary elastic.

(5.2) 4. The demand for which of the following types of labor is likely to be the most *elastic*?
   a. heart transplant surgeons.
   b. airline pilots.
   c. basketball players who score 30 points a game.
   d. economics instructors. *(circled)*

(5.3) 5. If the elasticity ratio for a good is 0.1 and its seller wants to make as much money as possible, he or she should:
   a. raise the price. *(circled)*
   b. lower the price.
   c. advertise more.
   d. provide more information.

(5.3) 6. If a 10% price increase leads to a 4% reduction in the quantity of a good sold, then the elasticity ratio is equal to:
   a. 0.40. *(circled)*
   b. 4.00.
   c. 0.25.
   d. 2.50.

(5.4) 7. Which of the following best describes the doctrine of consumer sovereignty?
   a. The average propensity to save plus the average propensity to consume equals 1.
   b. Demand creates supply. *(circled)*
   c. Marginal utility diminishes with additional units of a good.
   d. Consumers respond more to price changes when demand is elastic.

(5.5) 8. The average propensity to save is:
   a. the average number of people in the economy who are net savers.
   b. the percentage change in saving divided by the percentage change in income.
   c. the percentage of after-tax income that is saved. *(circled)*
   d. the quantity of a good not bought when price increases and demand is elastic.

(5.5) 9. Changing the average propensity to consume will result in a change in which of the following?
 a. the position of the demand curve for at least some goods.
 b. the average propensity to save.
 c. the amount of consumer goods and services sold in the economy.
 d. all of the above.

(5.6) 10. Total utility is equal to which of the following?
 a. consumer equilibrium.
 b. marginal utility when marginal utility is equal to zero.
 c. the sum of the marginal utilities for all units of a good consumed.
 d. all of the above.

(5.6) 11. Which of the following occurs when marginal utility is positive but diminishing?
 a. total utility is decreasing at a decreasing rate.
 b. total utility is increasing at a decreasing rate.
 c. total utility is decreasing at an increasing rate.
 d. total utility is increasing at an increasing rate.

(5.6) 12. Individual consumption and savings decisions are made by comparing prices to which of the following?
 a. total utility.
 b. average utility.
 c. marginal utility.
 d. maximum total utility.

(5.7) 13. Which of the following occurs when the consumer reaches consumer equilibrium?
 a. The marginal utility per dollar is equal for all goods consumed.
 b. Total utility is maximized.
 c. A change in the allocation of the consumer's spending will result in less total utility.
 d. all of the above.

(5.8) 14. Which of the following is a result of government programs that provide information to consumers?
 a. lower information costs for consumers.
 b. lower selling prices for producers.
 c. the preservation of firms' reputations.
 d. diminished need for product labeling.

(5.8) 15. In which of the following transactions does the government require the seller to provide information to the consumer?
 a. A bank makes a car loan.
 b. A car dealer sells a new car to a customer.
 c. A person buys a new mattress.
 d. all of the above.

True/False (Circle T or F.)

(5.1) 16. The demand for gasoline will be more elastic than the demand for different brands of gasoline. T or F

(5.2) 17. A good that has a perfectly elastic demand has perfect substitutes. T or F

(5.3) 18. The more elastic the demand for a product, the steeper its demand curve. T or F

(5.5) 19. The average propensity to save is always between zero and one. T or F

(5.6) 20. Total utility always declines as a consumer buys more and more of a given product. T or F

Chapter 6

The Business Firm and Market Structure

I. Chapter Outline

While consumer demand tells businesses **what** consumers want, it is the role of private firms to figure out how to go about producing, pricing, and delivering the goods. In particular, they must determine the best way to organize their firms, how much to produce, and what prices to charge. The answers to these questions depend a great deal on the structure of the industry that the firms are in.

Introductory Article: Let the Good Times Roll Down on the Farm

In a freely competitive market, firms sometimes make a profit and sometimes fail to make a profit. The market system does not guarantee success for everyone. If anything, it guarantees that those that do not make efficient use of an economy's scarce resources will soon be out of business. However, when an industry, such as farming, is considered vital to the national interest, the government will often intervene to prevent the market system from weeding out failing firms.

Economic Analysis

This chapter examines the issue of the business firm and market (industry) structure by addressing the following three questions:

1. What Are the Forms and Economic Functions of Business Firms?

    Important Concepts: Forms of business organization, Economic functions of businesses

    Case Application: Running With the Bulls

2. What Determines a Firm's Profits?

    Important Concepts: Costs, Revenue, Profits

    Important Model: Total revenue and total cost

    Case Application: Aging Rockers Hit the Road One More Time

3. How Does Industry Market Structure Affect Price and Output Decisions?

    Important Concepts: Pure competition, Pure monopoly, Shared monopoly, Differentiated competition

    Case Application: Hard Decisions for the Software Industry

Perspective: The Evolution of the Modern Corporation

II. Summary of Economic Analysis

1. The three main types of business organization are **proprietorships**, **partnerships**, and **corporations**.

2. Each type of organization has its advantages. **Proprietorships** are inexpensive to start and the owner manages the business carefully because the owner gets all the profit. **Partnerships** can take advantage of the human and financial resources of two or more individuals. The main advantages of **corporations** are their **limited liability** and status as legal entities, which enable them to raise large amounts of financial resources.

3. Each type of business organization also has its disadvantages. **Proprietorships** have limited resources and the owner is personally liable for the business's debts. Each partner in a **partnership** is legally liable for the actions of the firm (and the other partner), and the firm must be dissolved if one partner dies. Problems with **corporations** include double taxation, extra regulations, and dispersed ownership that cannot carefully monitor the firm.

4. The principal functions of business firms are to **identify consumer wants, organize production, allocate revenues,** and **increase the amount of real capital**.

5. Production costs consist of **fixed costs** (overhead), such as the depreciation of capital, and **variable costs**, such as labor, raw materials, and other inputs.

6. Economists include the **normal rate of return** on capital invested in a business as a cost of production. This is the opportunity cost of capital. Economists also include the opportunity cost of a proprietor's labor as a cost of production.

7. Net earnings in excess of the normal rate of return are **economic profits**.

8. **Total revenue** is the price times the number of units sold (P × Q).

9. Economic profits are total revenue minus **total cost**. The **break-even point** exists at the level of output where total revenue equals total cost. At the break-even point, the firm earns the normal rate of return, which is the same as **zero economic profit**.

10. The addition to total cost from producing one more unit of output is **marginal cost**. The addition to total revenue from the sale of that unit is **marginal revenue**. Maximum profits are obtained at the level of output that equates marginal revenue to marginal cost.

11. There are four types of **market (or industry) structure: pure competition, differentiated competition, shared monopoly,** and **pure monopoly**.

12. A market is **purely competitive** when it has a large number of firms producing a standardized product and in which there is ease of entry into and out of the industry. As a result of ease of entry, long-run economic profits in purely competitive industries tend to zero.

13. An industry with **differentiated competition** has a large number of sellers, but they produce a nonstandardized product. Production costs are higher because of packaging and advertising, but ease of entry again results in the disappearance of economic profits.

14. A **shared monopoly** is an industry in which there are only a few firms producing either a standardized or nonstandardized product. Because of barriers to entry, economic profits may persist in the long run.

15. A **pure monopoly** is an industry in which there is only one producer—the firm and the industry are one and the same. Pure monopolies are rare, with the best example being regulated **public utilities**.

6 The Business Firm and Market Structure / 73

III. Review of the Learning Objectives (Answers begin on p. 291.)

What Are the Forms and Economic Functions of Business Firms?

```
FORMS OF BUSINESS ORGANIZATION
```

Proprietorships	Partnerships	Corporations	Cooperatives
are owned and operated by one individual or one family.	are the pooling of the capital and the business efforts of two or more people.	are businesses owned by the stockholders and managed by officers of the company.	are business associations of producers or consumers.

```
FUNCTIONS OF BUSINESS FIRMS
```

Identifying consumer wants	Organizing production	Allocating revenues	Real capital investment
The business firms determine what to produce on the basis of consumer wants.	Firms decide what mix of the factors of production will best achieve the desired output.	Firms allocate their revenues to pay company employees, suppliers, and the investors.	Firms increase the stock of real capital by investing in plant and equipment.

(See page vi in the foreword "To the Student" for how to make the best use of this schematic outline.)

6.1. List the three main forms of business organization and cite the advantages and disadvantages of each. *(Write in answers below.)*

A. Indicate whether the following are most likely to be proprietorships (PR), partnerships (PA), or corporations (C).

1. _PR_ The family farm.
2. _C_ A car manufacturer.
3. _PR_ A corner grocery.
4. _C_ A supermarket chain.
5. _PA_ A local real estate development firm.

B. Indicate whether the following are **advantages** of proprietorships (PR), partnerships (PA), or corporations (C).

1. _C_ Ability to raise financial capital.
2. _PR_ Knowledge about actual costs and revenues.
3. _PA_ Combined resources without higher taxes.
4. _PR_ Easy to start.
5. _C_ Limited liability of owners.

74 / Working With The Study of Economics, 4/E

      6. _C_ "Immortality" in the eyes of the law.

C. Indicate whether the following are **disadvantages** of proprietorships (PR), partnerships (PA), or corporations (C).

    1. _C_ Double taxation.
    2. _PA_ Liability for someone else's actions.
    3. _PR_ Difficulty in raising financial capital.
    4. _C_ Regulations.
    5. _PA + PR_ The firm is dissolved when an owner dies.

D. The owners of a corporation are its stockholders, who want the firm making as much money as possible. These owners, however, usually never see or visit the firm which they "own," or have a chance to find out what the firm's managers do all day. What problem can occur in this case that will not occur in a proprietorship?

The managers may be more interested in their own well-being than in the stockholders income.
Ex. big company cars, fancy desks

6.2. Describe the four economic functions of business firms.

A. When a firm makes a decision about how to _organize production_, at the same time they will be making a decision as to how they _allocate resources_ because *what* they buy directly impacts the income of *whom* they buy from.

B. In the two examples below, indicate how each of the following economic functions is represented: identifying consumer wants (I), organizing production (O), allocating resources (A), and real capital investment (C).

    1. A soft-drink company buys new bottling equipment that is designed for using recyclable glass bottles rather than plastic bottles.

      (I) _Consumers are environmentally conscious_
      (O) _Production is geared towards using glass vs plastic_
      (A) _Manufacturers of glass benefit relative to manufacturers of plastic_
      (C) _The bottling machine is new capital._

    2. A farmer buys a harvesting machine that is specialized for harvesting oats.

      (I) _People want oats_
      (O) _Harvesting becomes capital-intensive & specialized_
      (A) _The manufacturer of the harvester earns money_
      (C) _The harvester is new capital_

Case Application: The Progressive Bike Shop

Pat and Jeff, a struggling young married couple attending college on a part-time basis, planned to enter the retail business on a small scale, but they were having difficulty deciding exactly what type of shop to open.

    Pat learned in a marketing course that the percentage of family income spent on recreation and related goods and services had risen from 8% thirty years ago to approximately 13% today. Considering these statistics, they concluded that as society gets more prosperous, people will continue to spend additional money for recreational products. They decided to open a bicycle shop, because bicycles are a product in the recreational category and Jeff had some knowledge of their construction and repair.

After taking a survey at their college to determine what types and brand names of bicycles people demanded most, they formulated an initial purchasing list. Pat's parents agreed to invest $14,000 in the shop for a share of the profits, but running the business was left entirely to Pat and Jeff. The choice of a site was influenced by their limited funds. Rent downtown was unaffordable, so they decided to rent a storefront on the fringe of a decaying inner-city neighborhood near the campus. Here the rent would fall within their budget, and the population of young people was the greatest.

Their chosen site, although affordable and convenient to their target population, needed some renovation. Jeff, who was handy at such endeavors, turned the drab-looking storefront into an attractive, eye-catching shop.

Young and old flocked to the shop on opening day. Nearby community residents praised the couple's attempt to restore retail life to a once-thriving area of proprietorship. Pat and Jeff named their store the "Progressive Bike Shop." To find out what happened to Pat and Jeff's bike shop, see the next case application.

Economic Reasoning *(Write your responses on a separate sheet. Answers begin on p. 292.)*

1. What form of business organization was the Progressive Bike Shop?
2. What economic functions did the Progressive Bike Shop perform?
3. Do you think locating the shop in a deteriorated neighborhood was a good idea? Why or why not?

What Determines a Firm's Profits?

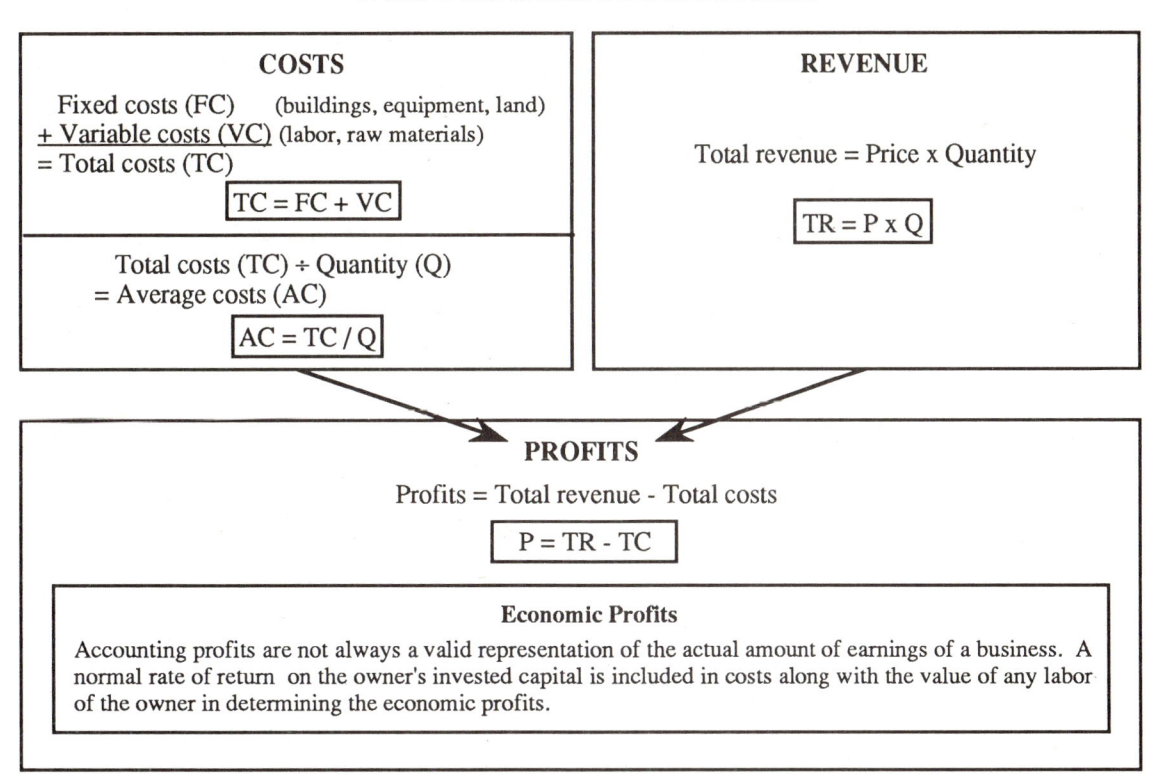

COSTS

Fixed costs (FC)   (buildings, equipment, land)
+ Variable costs (VC) (labor, raw materials)
= Total costs (TC)

$$TC = FC + VC$$

Total costs (TC) ÷ Quantity (Q)
= Average costs (AC)

$$AC = TC / Q$$

REVENUE

Total revenue = Price x Quantity

$$TR = P \times Q$$

PROFITS

Profits = Total revenue - Total costs

$$P = TR - TC$$

Economic Profits

Accounting profits are not always a valid representation of the actual amount of earnings of a business. A normal rate of return on the owner's invested capital is included in costs along with the value of any labor of the owner in determining the economic profits.

(See page vi in the foreword "To the Student" for how to make the best use of this schematic outline.)

76 / Working With The Study of Economics, 4/E

6.3. Distinguish between fixed costs and variable costs.

A. Do fixed costs exist in the **short run** or the **long run**? Explain. (You may want to review the short and long runs in Chapter 4.)

Fixed costs only exist only in the short run because in the long run the firm has time to alter any & all productive capacity.

B. Indicate which of the following are fixed costs (F) and which are variable costs (V).

1. _F_ Mortgage payments on a fast-food restaurant building.
2. _V_ Wages for labor.
3. _V_ Sesame-seed buns.
4. _V_ Electricity to heat the fry kettles.
5. _F_ $30,000 of the owner's money invested in the restaurant.
6. _F_ Depreciation on the grill.
7. _F_ Monthly payments on the delivery truck.

C. The annual fixed costs of capital goods are called _depreciation_. The dollar value of these annual costs depends on the original cost of the capital and its _productive life_. During periods of rapid technological change, capital equipment may need to be replaced earlier because it becomes _obsolete_.

6.4. Show the relationship of total cost and total revenue to output.

A.
1. Total costs equal fixed costs when output equals _zero_.
2. Total costs increase as output increases because _variable_ costs increase.
3. Total costs equal _fixed_ plus _variable_ costs.

B. Complete the following table by entering values for total cost (TC), marginal cost (MC), and average cost (AC).

Quantity	Fixed Costs	Variable Costs	TC	MC	AC
0	$10	$ 0	10		
1	10	12	22	12	22
2	10	22	32	10	16
3	10	30	40	8	13.3
4	10	36	46	6	11.5
5	10	40	50	4	10
6	10	46	56	6	9.3
7	10	56	66	10	9.4
8	10	70	80	14	10
9	10	90	100	20	11.1
10	10	120	130	30	13

C. Complete the following table by computing the amount of total revenue and marginal revenue at each output level.

Quantity	Price	Total Revenue	Marginal Revenue
0	$10	0	10
1	10	10	10
2	10	20	10
3	10	30	10
4	10	40	10
5	10	50	10
6	10	60	10
7	10	70	10
8	10	80	10
9	10	90	10
10	10	100	10

D. The above total and marginal revenue schedules would apply to a firm in what type of industry?

purely competitive

E. Use your answers to parts B and C above to show the amount of profit earned at each level of output.

Quantity	Profit
0	−10
1	−12
2	−12
3	−10
4	−6
5	0
6	4
7	4
8	0
9	−10
10	−30

F.

1. A price increase has both positive and negative impacts on total revenue. A greater price is paid for each unit, but fewer units are sold. If demand is **inelastic,** price increases proportionately more than quantity decreases. Accordingly, what will happen to total revenue if the price increases? Explain.

Total revenue will increase because the effect of increased price dominates the effect of decreased quantity

2. If demand is **elastic,** price increases proportionately less than quantity decreases. Accordingly, what will happen to total revenue if the price increases?

Total revenue will decrease because the effect of increased price is dominated by the effect of decreased quantity

6.5. Locate the break-even point and point of maximum profit.

A.
1. At the break-even point, _total revenue_ equals _total cost_.
2. At the level of output that maximizes profits, _marginal revenue_ equals _marginal cost_.
3. At the level of output that maximizes profits, the distance between _total revenue_ and _total cost_ is maximized.

B. In the exercises B, C, and D in the previous section, you were asked to find different cost and revenue values. Use them to determine the following:
1. The break-even points are __5__ and __8__.
2. At output levels less than __5__ and greater than __8__, the firm loses money.
3. At output levels greater than __5__ and less than __8__, the firm earns a profit.
4. The point of maximum profit (use the marginal cost equals marginal revenue rule) is __7__.

C. Graph the total revenue and total cost curves from exercises B and C in the previous section in the space provided below. Indicate the break-even points.

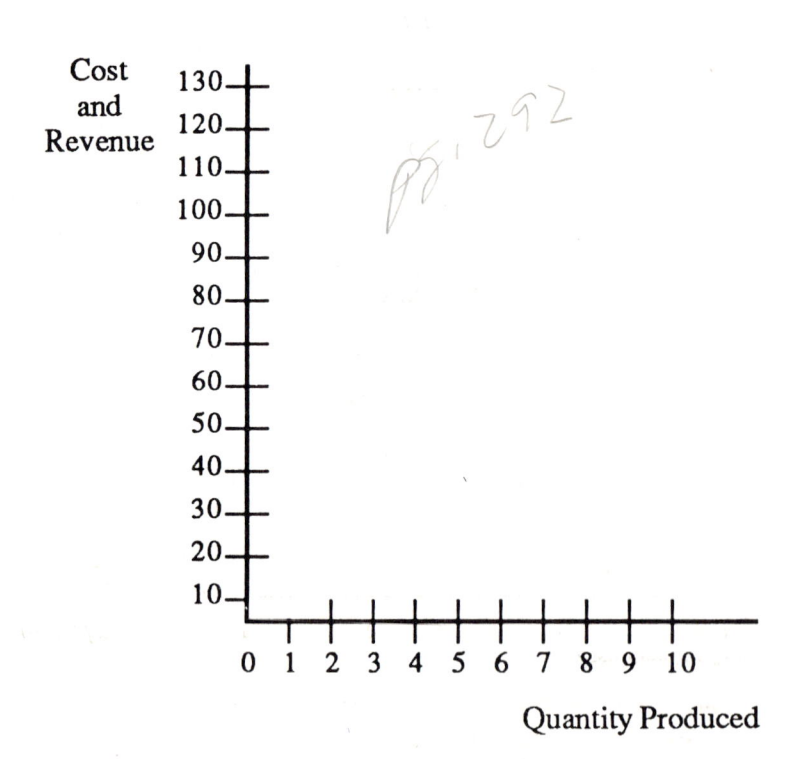

D.
1. On the graph below, TC represents total cost and TR represents total revenue. Draw a new total revenue curve, labeled TR$_2$, that results in only one break-even point. Draw another total revenue curve, labeled TR$_3$, that would indicate that the firm cannot earn a profit at *any* level of output.

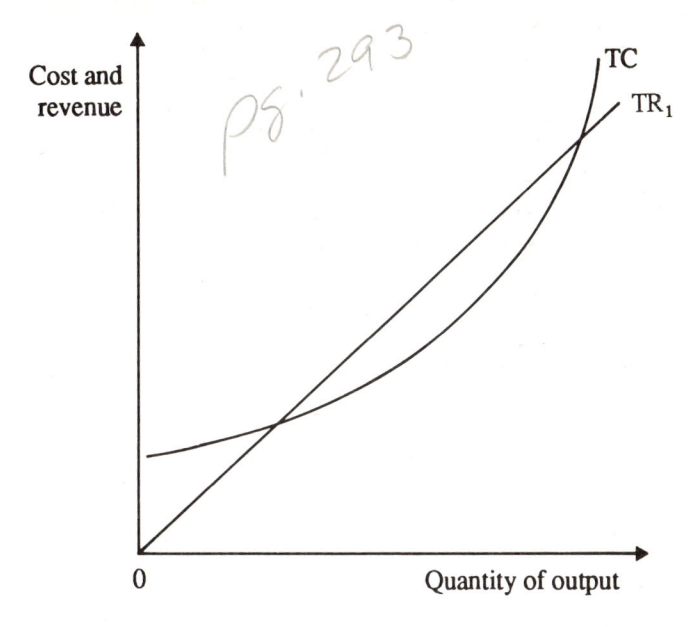

[Graph: Cost and revenue vs. Quantity of output, showing TC curve and TR$_1$ line. Handwritten note: "pg. 293"]

2. What could cause the total revenue curve to "rotate" to TR$_2$ and TR$_3$?
   lower prices

6.6. Distinguish between normal rate of return and economic profits.

A. Suppose that the total costs in the graph above (correctly!) include all opportunity costs and any wages due an owner-operator. Use the graph to answer the following:

1. Between the break-even points along TR$_1$, the firm earns a(n) *economic* profit. At the break-even points, the firm earns a(n) *normal return*.

2. If the firm's total revenue is TR$_2$, the best that the firm can do is to earn a(n) *normal return*.

3. If the firm's total revenue is TR$_3$, the firm will *lose money*.

B. In the above graph, which total revenue curves would be necessary for the firm to stay in business? *TR$_1$ or TR$_2$*

C. Suppose Juanita takes $200,000 from her own bank account, where it was earning 10% per year, and uses the money to start a business. She quits her job, where she was earning $25,000 a year, in order to work the same number of hours in her business. At the end of the first year, her total revenues were $100,000, but she had paid $40,000 in wages to her employees and another $20,000 for rent, supplies, and so on.

1. How much profit did Juanita make? *$100,000 − 60,000 = $40,000 accounting profit*
   see pg 293

2. Should she stay in business for another year? Explain.

p. 293

Case Application: The Fortunes of the Progressive Bike Shop

During their first year of operation, Pat and Jeff sold 144 bicycles at an average price of $310 per bicycle. They sold an additional $9,620 worth of accessories and parts and took in $6,800 for repair work on bicycles brought into the shop for service. Their total revenue during that first year amounted to $61,060. The cost to them of the bicycles and other merchandise they sold was $26,400. Their rent, utilities, and other overhead costs were $16,800. Their total direct costs were thus $43,200 ($26,400 + $16,800).

After subtracting their costs from their revenues, Pat and Jeff were left with a net income of $17,860. According to their agreement with Pat's parents, they paid 20% of this amount to the parents as a return on the money they had invested in the business. This left Pat and Jeff with earnings of $14,288 for the year. Considering all the time they had put into running the shop and the $6,000 of their own money they had invested in it, this did not seem like much. However, business had steadily improved during the year as the Progressive Bike Shop's reputation for charging reasonable prices and standing behind its merchandise spread around the area. Pat and Jeff were confident they would do better during the second year's operations.

Economic Reasoning *(Write your responses on a separate sheet. Answers begin on p. 293.)*

1. Was the $26,400 cost of the merchandise a fixed cost or a variable cost?
2. What economic costs of operating the Progressive Bike Shop were not included in the $43,200 given as the total cost?
3. Was it fair for Pat's parents to get 20% of the net receipts for their $14,000 investment in the business? Why or why not?

How Does Industry Market Structure Affect Price and Output Decisions?

PURE COMPETITION	PURE MONOPOLY	SHARED MONOPOLY	DIFFERENTIATED COMPETITION
An industry in which there are so many producers of a single standardized product that no one firm can affect the market price.	An industry in which there is only one producer.	An industry in which there are only a few producers of a single standardized or of a differentiated product.	An industry in which there are very many producers of a single differentiated product.
Diminishing returns — When one factor input is fixed in supply, an increase in the other inputs results in output increasing at a diminishing rate.	**Maximum profit output** — A monopolist will produce the output at which the revenue from the marginal unit produced just equals the cost of producing it. Marginal Revenue = Marginal Cost [MR = MC]	**Price leadership** — When there only a few firms in a single industry, each one of them is affected by the pricing policies of the other firms. A price cut by one firm to increase sales is likely to start a price war. Consequently, the firms stabilize prices in the industry by means of price leadership.	Firms in the industry attempt to attract new customers by differentiating their product from those of their competitors. This frequently involves spending on advertising and packaging.
In the long run, economic profits in pure competition tend toward zero due to ease of entry into the industry.	Monopolistic firms restrict their output in order to keep the price at the level which will maximize profits.		Ease of entry into the industry causes the profits to tend toward zero.

(See page vi in the foreword "To the Student" for how to make the best use of this schematic outline.)

6.7. List the characteristics of purely competitive industries.

A. Indicate by a check mark which of the following are characteristics of purely competitive firms.
   1. ____ Firms independently determine what prices to charge for their products.
   2. ✓ A firm's total revenue will increase at an increasing rate.
   3. ✓ There are many small firms in the industry.
   4. ✓ It is easy for new firms to enter the industry.
   5. ✓ One firm's product is a perfect substitute for any other firm's product.
   6. ✓ A firm's costs are subject to diminishing returns.

B. Indicate by a check mark which of the following are close to being purely competitive industries.
   1. ✓ Farming.
   2. ✓ The production of nails.
   3. ____ The fast-food industry.
   4. ✓ Different vendors selling peanuts at an outdoor concert.
   5. ____ The snack bar at a movie theater.
   6. ✓ The video tape rental industry.
   7. ✓ Vegetable stands along a highway.

6.8. Explain the principle of diminishing returns.

A. Diminishing returns cause the production costs of additional units of output to _increase_ when one factor input is _fixed_. This reflects the fact that productivity per input is _decreasing_.

B. Suppose Farmer Jones is experiencing diminishing returns in the production of corn. How can Farmer Jones produce more corn at a lower price?

Buy more land & plant corn

C. Do diminishing returns exist in the short run, long run, or both? Explain.

Because one factor of production must be fixed for diminishing returns to exist, they can only exist in the short run

D. Examine the table that you completed in question 6.4 B. At what level of output did diminishing returns set in? _Diminishing returns set in with the 6th unit of output_

E. Draw two total cost curves in the space on the following page: one that indicates diminishing returns after 5 units of output (TC$_1$); and one (TC$_2$) that indicates **constant** returns (no diminishing returns).

_pg. 293_

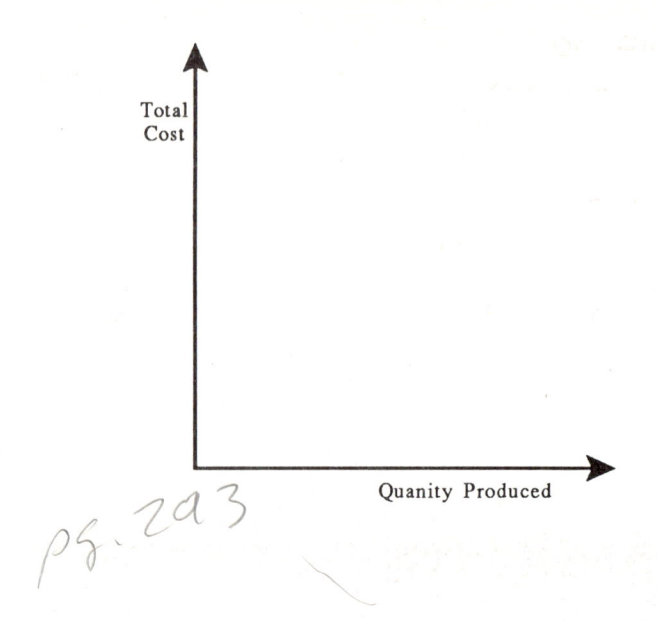

[Graph: Total Cost (y-axis) vs. Quanity Produced (x-axis)]

pg. 293

6.9. Explain the short-run and long-run adjustments to changes in demand in a purely competitive industry.

A. Suppose that oat farming is a purely competitive industry and that all oat farmers are initially in long-run equilibrium (earning a normal rate of return). Now suppose that oat bran becomes very popular because of its health-related benefits. Number the following events in the order in which they will occur.

1. _5_ Market supply increases.
2. _4_ New farmers enter the industry.
3. _2_ The market price increases.
4. _6_ The market price falls.
5. _3_ Economic profits appear.
6. _7_ Economic profits disappear.
7. _1_ Demand increases.

B.

1. In the above exercise, what would have happened if firms could not freely enter the industry?

   Prices + profits would have stayed high for existing firms. Consumers wouldn't have gotten as much oat bran as they wanted.

2. In the above exercise, why was the existence of profit so important?

   Profits induced new firms to enter the industry and allocate their scarce resources to the production of oats — what consumers want.

C. Starting from the same position as in the above exercise, now assume that a new study shows that oat bran is fattening. Number the following events in the order in which they will occur.

1. _3_ Profits become negative (firms lose money).
2. _2_ The market price falls.

3. _6_ The market price increases.
4. _7_ Profits return to the normal rate of return.
5. _5_ Market supply decreases.
6. _1_ Demand decreases.
7. _4_ Some firms leave the industry.

6.10. Differentiate between pure monopoly, shared monopoly, and differentiated competition.

A. Indicate whether each of the following industries is pure monopoly (PM), shared monopoly (SM), or differentiated competition (DC).

1. _PM_ Diamond mining.
2. _DC_ Fast-food hamburgers.
3. _SM_ Automobiles.
4. _SM_ Breakfast cereals.
5. _PM_ First-class mail delivery.
6. _PM_ Cable TV in your neighborhood.
7. _DC_ Retail clothing stores.
8. _DC_ Computer software.
9. _SM_ Airline companies.
10. _PM_ Local bus service.

B. Complete the following table by computing the total revenue and marginal revenue for the firm.

Price	Quantity	Total Revenue	Marginal Revenue
$11	0	0	100
10	10	100	80
9	20	180	60
8	30	240	40
7	40	280	20
6	50	300	0
5	60	300	-20
4	70	280	-40
3	80	240	-60
2	90	180	-80
1	100	100	

C. Use the information from the above exercise to answer the following questions:

1. At what output level is total revenue maximized?

   6 or 7 units

2. If there were no fixed costs, and variable costs were constant at $41 per unit, how many units should the firm produce in order to maximize profits?

   only 3

3. The demand and marginal revenue indicated in the table would be relevant for firms in which type of industry or industries?

   differentied competition, pure monopoly, shared monopoly

84 / *Working With The Study of Economics, 4/E*

D. Which types of market structures have the following characteristics? (PC = pure competition, DC = differentiated competition, PM = pure monopoly, SM = shared monopoly)

1. _____ Above-normal profits in the long run. DC, PM, SM
2. _____ The ability to set prices. PC, PM, SM
3. _____ Efforts to differentiate products from rivals' products. DC, SM
4. _____ A large number of firms in the industry. DC, PC
5. _____ Diminishing returns exist. All
6. _____ The ability to earn short-run economic profits. All
7. _____ Ease of entry into the industry. DC, PC
8. _____ Price leadership. SM
9. _____ Cartels. SM

Case Application: Wheat Farmers in Debt

Gus Bailey, a hardworking wheat farmer, raised his eyes to the hot Kansas sun. He feared the blistering dry spell would reduce his harvest to the point where he could not sell it for enough cash for pay his bills.

The bills for additional seed, gasoline, and fertilizer flashed before him. How would he pay? When he had made the decision to plant more acres, it had seemed such a good idea. Now Gus had doubts. Back then he had reasoned: "I've got to pay taxes on my land whether I use it or not. The mortgage has to be paid, and the hired hand will be on the payroll. My planting and harvesting equipment is already costing me plenty and handling two more acres wouldn't change that." The only additional costs Gus could think of would be some extra wheat seed, the high-yield fertilizer, a few extra gallons of gasoline, and maybe another part-time field hand when harvest time came. "Surely the return on two extra acres will pay those costs," Gus had thought, "and leave some extra money."

Several days later the weather pattern shifted. Rains came in just the right quantities during the remaining growing season, and the warm sun performed its magic. Gus Bailey was blessed with a bountiful harvest, and he eagerly anticipated lucrative market results. His wheat crop was larger and better than Gus had ever obtained before in 20 years of farming.

"Two fifty a bushel," shouted the grain elevator operator. "I can't pay you any more than that." Gus was shocked and saddened by the response. At $2.50 a bushel, Gus could just barely meet his out-of-pocket expenses. He might even have to take out a bank loan to pay his taxes and buy seed for next year. Gus wondered if he should get out of farming altogether. Jake Wilson had offered to buy his land and turn it into house lots. Gus would have to think about the offer, but perhaps prices would be better next year.

Economic Reasoning *(Write your responses on a separate sheet. Answers begin on p. 294.)*

1. What was there in Gus Bailey's experience showing that he is in a purely competitive market?
2. How does the application illustrate that, under purely competitive conditions, economic profits tend toward zero?
3. Do farmers deserve government subsidies or other special assistance not afforded to other industries? Why or why not?

IV. Practice Test (Answers begin on p. 294.)

Multiple Choice (Circle the correct answer.)

(6.1) 1. The concept of "limited liability" applies in which of the following type(s) of business organizations?
   a. proprietorships.
   b. partnerships.
   c. corporations.
   d. all of the above.

(6.1) 2. The firm has a legal identity separate from its owner or owners in which type(s) of business organizations?
   a. proprietorships.
   b. partnerships.
   c. corporations.
   d. all of the above.

(6.2) 3. The answers to which of the following basic economic questions will be influenced by business firms as they undertake their four economic functions?
   a. how to produce?
   b. what to produce?
   c. for whom to produce?
   d. all of the above.

(6.3) 4. Which of the following is a fixed cost for a manufacturer of blue jeans?
   a. denim.
   b. depreciation.
   c. labor.
   d. electricity for running sewing machines.
   e. none of the above.

(6.3) 5. Which of the following is a TRUE statement?
   a. Fixed costs equal total costs when output equals zero.
   b. Fixed costs do not exist in the long run.
   c. Variable costs equal zero when output equals zero.
   d. Fixed costs do change when output levels change.
   e. All of the above are true.

(6.4) 6. Which of the following is a TRUE statement?
   a. Total revenue will always increase as output increases.
   b. The firm's objective will always be to maximize total revenue.
   c. Total revenue is equal to price times quantity sold.
   d. Total revenue always increases faster than total costs as output increases.

(6.4) 7. Total costs are calculated as the sum of:
   a. marginal and average costs.
   b. marginal and fixed costs.
   c. average and variable costs.
   d. fixed and variable costs.

(6.5) 8. If total revenue is equal to total cost at just one level of output, which of the following will be TRUE?
   a. There will be no break-even point.
   b. The break-even point occurs when output equals zero.
   c. The break-even point and profit maximization point will be the same.
   d. The firm will break even at every level of output.

(6.5) 9. The firm will maximize profits at the level of output where:
   a. marginal cost equals marginal revenue.
   b. average cost equals average revenue.

c. total cost equals total revenue.
d. all of the above occur.

(6.6) 10. If a firm is earning zero economic profit:
   a. it will be forced out of business in the long run.
   b. its marginal revenue must be equal to zero.
   c. it is earning the normal rate of return.
   d. it has no marginal revenue.

(6.7) 11. Which of the following is a TRUE statement about purely competitive firms?
   a. They can earn economic profits in the short run, but they are limited to a normal return in the long run.
   b. They can earn economic profits in the long run, but they are limited to a normal return in the short run.
   c. They can earn economic profits in both the long and short runs.
   d. They can never earn an economic profit.

(6.7) 12. Which of the following is NOT typical of firms in a purely competitive industry?
   a. They produce a standardized product.
   b. They set the price that maximizes their profits.
   c. They do not need to worry about what the other firms in the industry are charging for the product.
   d. They can exit and enter the industry easily.

(6.8) 13. Diminishing returns are associated with which of the following?
   a. diminishing prices.
   b. diminishing costs.
   c. diminishing productivity.
   d. diminishing revenues.

(6.8) 14. In the short run, total cost will increase at an increasing rate because of the existence of:
   a. fixed costs.
   b. marginal revenue.
   c. diminishing returns.
   d. increased profits.

(6.10) 15. Price leadership is most often found in which type of industry?
   a. pure competition.
   b. differentiated competition.
   c. shared monopoly.
   d. pure monopoly.

True/False *(Circle T or F.)*

(6.1) 16. Partnerships are subject to double taxation on their profits. T or F

(6.3) 17. Depreciation is a variable cost. T or F

(6.4) 18. Total cost increases at an increasing rate as output increases. T or F

(6.5) 19. A firm maximizes its profits at the break-even point. T or F

(6.6) 20. Economic profit is another name for the normal rate of return. T or F

Chapter 7

Industry Performance

I. Chapter Outline

It is easy, in theory, to discuss how economies need to answer the three basic economic questions as efficiently as possible. In reality, however, the United States has lagged behind others, especially the Japanese, in answering the "how to produce" question efficiently. We first need to understand just exactly what is involved in efficient economic performance, and then we need to learn how to achieve that level of performance.

Introductory Article: Industry Economics as a Martial Art

At one time, the expression "made in Japan" implied cheap, shoddy merchandise that was below the quality of goods produced in the United States. Today, the products imported from Japan are generally accepted as being of superior quality at a competitive price. As a consequence, the Japanese are taking one market after another from U.S. industries. To understand why this has happened, one needs to examine the different ways that economic affairs are conducted in the two countries. Some notable differences are the levels of savings, the production horizon (short- or long-term), the relationship between management and labor, and the managerial emphasis on production rather than on marketing and finance.

Economic Analysis

This chapter examines the relative decline of American industrial leadership by examining the following questions:

1. What Determines Industry Performance?

   Important Concepts: Productivity, Quality, Responsiveness to the market and to social concerns

   Case Application: A Rough Road for the U.S. Auto Industry

2. How Can Industry Performance Be Improved?

   Important Concepts: Investment in capital equipment, Real investment, Investment in human capital, Learning curve, R&D, Process innovation, Employee involvement programs, DFMA, FMS, CIM, Just-in-time manufacturing

   Case Application: The New Industrial Revolution

3. What Are the Effects of Industry Concentration on Performance?

   Important Concepts: Market concentration, Aggregate concentration

   Case Application: Corporate Raiders, LBOs, and the Feeding Frenzy

Perspective: An Imperfect World
      Biography—Joan Violet Robinson

II. Summary of Economic Analysis

1. **Industry performance** is generally measured according to the following criteria: **productivity, product quality, responsiveness to the market,** and **responsiveness to social concerns.**
2. In an effort to stimulate U.S. firms to pay closer attention to improving product quality, the U.S. Congress established the **Malcolm Baldrige National Quality Award** in 1988.
3. Perhaps the most important measure of performance, **productivity**, is measured as the amount of output per unit of input.
4. Increased **real investment in capital equipment** is one necessary condition for increased productivity. However, obtaining the necessary funds for this investment will require an increased **savings rate** in the United States.
5. Another important factor that leads to increased productivity is investment in **human capital**, that is, improvements in worker skills and motivation. Improvements in worker performance over time can be measured by the **learning curve**.
6. Improvements in both capital and human inputs are the result of **research and development (R&D)** that results in new technologies, production techniques, and management techniques.
7. The most productive Japanese innovations have been their **process innovations**, their methods of organizing production. These include **flexible manufacturing systems (FMS), computer-integrated manufacturing (CIM), employee involvement (EI),** and **just-in-time** manufacturing methods.
8. The structure of American businesses may also have an impact on industrial performance. **Market concentration** describes whether an industry is characterized by a few businesses (high concentration) or many separate businesses (low concentration). A commonly used measure of market concentration is the **concentration ratio.**
9. **Aggregate concentration** describes the share of an economy's total output that is accounted for by the nation's largest firms.
10. Concentration can result from a number of factors, including **mergers, barriers to entry,** and **predatory business practices.**
11. The consequences of high concentration include **monopolistic pricing, economic instability,** and a general **misallocation of resources.**

III. Review of the Learning Objectives (Answers begin on p. 294.)

What Determines Industry Performance?

PRODUCTIVITY	QUALITY	RESPONSIVENESS TO THE MARKET	RESPONSIVENESS TO SOCIAL CONCERNS
The low productivity growth growth since 1973 has put industry competitiveness in the United States behind that in Japan and other countries.	The quality of a firm's output begins with the quality of the parts made by its suppliers.	A quick response to changes in consumer preferences and being able to target market niches put producers in a position to better satisfy demand in the marketplace.	Industries are now held accountable for their environmental effects, resource conservation, product and worker safety, and providing equal opportunity in employment practices.

(See page vi in the foreword "To the Student" for how to make the best use of this schematic outline.)

7.1. Describe four factors that determine industry performance. *(Write in answers below.)*

A. The four indicators of industry performance are:

1. _productivity_
2. _quality_
3. _responsiveness to the market_
4. _"   "   social concerns_

B. Using the numbers from the above list, indicate which of the indicators of performance is at issue in each of the following:

1. _2_ MegaMotors, Inc., reports that they are recalling their new cars to repair defects in the steering wheels.
2. _4_ The government fines KO chemicals for dumping waste products that kill whales and dolphins.
3. _3_ Canadian consumers buy more imported stereos because the imports have the features that they want.
4. _2_ American consumers buy more imported personal computers because they break down less frequently.
5. _1_ American shoemakers lobby Congress to restrict foreign shoe imports because the American firms cannot produce shoes as inexpensively.
6. _2_ A washing machine company advertises that its repairmen are lonely.
7. _2_ A product is made with planned obsolescence.

C. Which measures of industry performance are directly related to the "what to produce" question?

1. _responsiveness to the market_

2. _quality_

7.2. Define productivity and state how it is usually measured.

A. Improved productivity directly relates to which of the three basic economic questions?
How to produce

B. An indication of improved productivity would be a _greater_ level of output from a given level of inputs, or a given level of output from a _smaller_ level of inputs.

C. For each of the following, indicate a hypothetical increase in productivity. (For example, increased productivity in car manufacturing might be indicated by fewer labor hours per car.)

1. A fast-food restaurant.
more burgers served per employee

2. A lawyer's office.
more cases litigated per hour

3. Your local electric company.
more electricity from a given amount of coal or oil

7.3. Explain why product quality is important and how it can be improved.

A. Give an example of something that would indicate poor quality in each of the following:
1. Nuclear electric plants. _radiation leaks_
2. Hot dogs. _too much fat_
3. Computer printers. _blurry print_
4. Television sets. _too much snow_

B. List advertisements for three products that you have seen which indicate that the seller is concerned about quality.
1. _"At Ford, quality is job 1"_
2. _Maytag's lonely repairman_
3. _Any American car company that compares to Jap cars_

C. American producers are (rightfully) interested in making profits. Explain why they would also be interested in winning the Malcolm Baldrige Award.
Winning the award will lead to more business & more profits

_____

_____

7.4. Describe why and how businesses respond to social concerns, and give three examples.

A. What are three things that a fast-food restaurant might do that would indicate a **disregard** for social concerns?

1. _descriminate in hiring practices_
2. _use packing made of CFC's_
3. _dump their fry grease in a local stream_

B. What are two **costs** that could be associated with "anti-social" actions by private firms?

1. _boycott by consumers_
2. _fines levied by the government_

C. What are two economic or socioeconomic goals consistent with "responding to social concerns"? (See chapter 2.)

1. _environmental protection_
2. _equity_

Case Application: Academic Theory Put Into Practice

Professor William P. Lyons of Yale, an adjunct professor in both the business and law schools, acquired control of the Duro-Test Corporation in December 1987. He became chairman and president of the country's fourth-largest maker of light bulbs, with 5% of the market. It is the largest maker of specialty bulbs.

Before Lyons obtained control the company had been in decline, with output falling to half the level of the 1960s. It was only operating at 30% of its production capacity.

To reverse the decline, Lyons concentrated on expanding the sales of the company's Vita-Lite bulb. The Vita-Lite bulb has a long life due to its special filament and design. It is said to produce a light closely resembling sunlight. This light is supposed to reduce worker fatigue and error on the job.

The sales force of Duro-Test was consolidated so that sales representatives from different divisions were not competing with each other for the same accounts. Lyons also offered the firm's 1,600 workers an employee stock ownership plan.

Economic Reasoning *(Write your responses on a separate sheet. Answers begin on p. 294.)*

1. Which of the factors determining industry performance do you find in this example of Duro-Test Corporation?
2. What did Professor Lyons hope to accomplish by establishing an employee stock ownership plan?
3. Do you think teachers are likely to make good company presidents? Why or why not?

How Can Industry Performance Be Improved?

INVESTMENT IN CAPITAL EQUIPMENT	INVESTMENT IN HUMAN CAPITAL	RESEARCH AND DEVELOPMENT
Productivity depends greatly on the amount of real investment per worker.	Investment by companies in worker training produces even larger returns than investment in machinery.	The spending on R&D for new products or new production technologies results in greater success of companies in their markets.
Real investment in the U. S. is low because of: 1. a low savings rate and the high cost of financial capital. 2. the diversion of financial capital from real investment into speculative investment in existing assets. 3. short time horizons for corporate objectives.	**Learning Curve** The productivity rate with new equipment and new production processes rises more rapidly when workers are given more training.	

ORGANIZATION OF PRODUCTION
Process innovation is more important than product innovation in achieving a high level of industry performance.

Design for Manufacturability and Assembly (DFMA)	Computer-Integrated Manufacturing (CIM)	Employee Involvement (EI) Programs
	The integration of ordering, scheduling, accounting, and production operations.	1. Self-managing teams. 2. Problem-solving teams. 3. Special-purpose teams.
Flexible Manufacturing Systems (FMS) Makes use of computer-controlled machinery that is adaptable to different products.	**Just-In-Time Manufacturing** The delivery of inputs to production stations.	The use of a flatter rather than a vertical organizational structure results in more efficient communications between different departments.

(See page vi in the foreword "To the Student" for how to make the best use of this schematic outline.)

7.5. Explain the importance of investment in capital equipment, why the rate is low in the United States, and how it can be increased.

   A. Circle the correct answer within the parentheses.

   There is a (**direct**/inverse/constant) relationship between capital equipment per worker and productivity.

   B. If the size of the labor force increases while investment in capital equipment declines, then productivity will _decline_.

   C. Give an example of capital equipment investment that could increase (or has increased) productivity in each of the following industries:

   1. Grocery stores. _use of uniform product codes_
   2. Education. _use of computers_
   3. Auto manufacturing. _use of robots_

D. What are the three reasons why U.S. investment in capital equipment has lagged behind Japanese investment?

1. _short time horizon_
2. _use of investment funds for speculation_
3. _high interest rates_

E. Although the Japanese have been more successful than Americans in investing in capital equipment, they have paid a price. What is an **opportunity cost** of Japan's higher level of investment?

A lower current standard of living because of lower consumption spending, evidence high prices for housing + food

7.6. Describe investment in human capital and show how it affects the learning curve.

A. People will invest in their own human capital as long as they believe that the benefits will outweigh the costs. However, the benefits of such investment (like school) are not achieved all at once or right away. Indicate whether you think the following will be more (M) or less (L) likely to invest in their own human capital.

1. _L_ A 55-year-old laid-off steel worker.
2. _L_ A ghetto teenager with a short time horizon.
3. _M_ A middle-class teenager with a long time horizon.
4. _L_ A prophet of doom who says the world will end tomorrow.

B. In chapter 3 it was argued that specialization based on comparative advantage leads to greater output. Is this consistent or inconsistent with **cross-training** on the job?

inconsistent

C.

1. The learning curves for workers A and B are described in the table below. Graph the curves on the figure provided at the top of the next page.

Total Output	A's Output per Labor Hour	B's Output per Labor Hour
100	40	40
200	50	60
300	60	80
400	65	100
500	70	110
600	70	105
700	70	105

_pg. 295_

94 / *Working With The Study of Economics, 4/E*

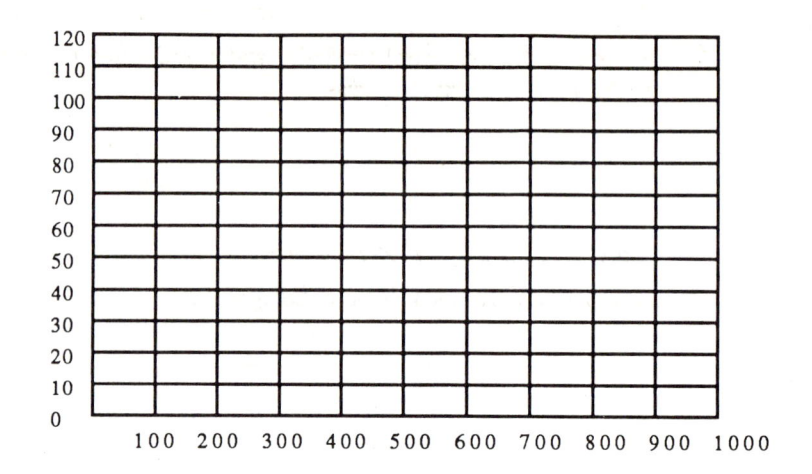

[blank graph with y-axis 0–120 in increments of 10, x-axis 100–1000 in increments of 100]

2. Which of the above workers (A or **B**) learns faster? _____

3. At what level of output do **diminishing returns** to learning set in for A and B? A _300_ B _400_

7.7. Explain R&D spending and its importance.

A. R&D stands for _research & development_.

B. R&D generally enhances the productivity of which factor of production?
capital

C. What are two important sources of R&D in the United States?
1. _the military_
2. _universities_

D. Will a perfectly competitive firm invest in R&D? Why or why not?
No, it earns only a normal profit and has no funds left over for R&D, see pg. 295

7.8. Describe process innovations and explain how they improve productivity.

A. Process innovation is directly related to which of the three basic economic questions?
How to Produce

B. Indicate whether the following would be considered process innovation (PI), investment in capital equipment (EC), or investment in human capital (HC). (More than one response may be appropriate in some instances.)

1. _EC_ A new printing press at the local newspaper.
2. _PI_ A program that includes both design and manufacturing departments in the decision-making process.
3. _PI, EC_ A new computer that monitors assembly-line operations.
4. _PI_ A program that allows labor and management to work together to solve problems.
5. _HC_ On-the-job training for all employees.

C. Process innovation refers to the process of doing what?
producing goods + services

7.9. List and give an example of three types of EI teams.

A. EI stands for _employee Involvement_.

B. Indicate whether each of the following is an example of a self-managing team (SM), a problem-solving team (PS), or a special-purpose team (SP):

1. _SM_ Students and teachers work together to schedule class times, vacation times, and curriculum.
2. _SP_ A special student-teacher committee is organized to study why some students have difficulty reading.
3. _SM_ A team of workers learns each others' tasks so they can fill in if one becomes ill.
4. _PS_ A group of students and teachers meet once a week to discuss mutual concerns about education.

C. The *idea* of using EI teams was first introduced in _the U.S._ but was first used extensively in _Japan_.

D. What are two interest groups that oppose EI groups?

1. _unions_
2. _middle management_

Case Application: The Factory of the Future Is Next

The computer produced by Next is an advanced workstation. And not only is the computer itself state-of-the-art, but so is the factory in which it is produced. Steve Jobs, one of the founders of Apple Computers, determined that his new computer company would be on the cutting edge of technology in its production methods as well as in its product.

In the Next factory, production robots outnumber production workers by more than two to one. The reason for the high degree of automation is not so much to save labor costs—which are only a small part of the production costs of computers in any case—but to maximize quality by eliminating production line defects. The circuit board of a Next computer has 1,700 tiny dots of solder binding its network of hundreds of miniature components. Although these components are attached to the circuitboard at a rate of as much as 150 parts per minute, the solder joint defect rate is only 15 to 17 parts per million. This is less than one-tenth the rate that is typical for the computer industry.

When a circuit board is completed, it does not go to a warehouse; instead it goes directly to the plant's final assembly area. The finished computer, after 24 hours of final testing, is then loaded directly into a truck for shipment.

96 / Working With The Study of Economics, 4/E

The workers at Next must check the operation of the robots for problems, but they are not necessarily engaged on the assembly line. A worker may instead be off using his or her own computer to do a statistical analysis of the defect rate to find any problem.

Economic Reasoning *(Write your responses on a separate sheet. Answers begin on p. 295.)*

1. What operations at Next are examples of just-in-time manufacturing?
2. According to this examination of production at Next, which of the means of improving performance has the company undertaken?
3. Do you think that Next computer will necessarily be a success? What could cause it to fail despite its state-of-the-art manufacturing process?

What Are the Effects of Industry Concentration on Performance?

MARKET CONCENTRATION

Market concentration refers to the number of firms in an industry that are competing for customers. It ranges from pure competition to pure monopoly.

Concentration Ratio

The concentration ratio in an industry is measured by the amount of sales by the largest four firms in the industry as a percentage of the total sales of the industry.

AGGREGATE CONCENTRATION

Aggregate concentration refers to the percentage of the total sales of all industries together that is accounted for by the largest firms. There is no standard measurement for aggregate concentration, but it is increasing.

CONCENTRATION AND INDUSTRY PERFORMANCE

Causes of Concentration
1. mergers
2. barriers to entry
3. predatory business practices
   a. price discrimination
   b. sales below cost
   c. kickbacks

Results of Concentration
1. monopolistic pricing — prices set above costs of production, resulting in monopoly profits.
2. misallocation of resources — supply is limited to keep prices high, resulting in resource misallocation.
3. non-informational advertising expenses and non-utilitarian product differentiation.
4. greater economic instability in the business cycle.

(See page vi in the foreword "To the Student" for how to make the best use of this schematic outline.)

7.10. Describe market concentration and define the degree of market concentration in terms of the concentration ratio.

A. What is the major problem caused by high market concentration?
   high prices

B. Indicate whether each of the following industries is characterized by high (H) or low (L) market concentration.
   1. _H_ Automobile manufacturing.
   2. _L_ Dairies.
   3. _H_ Breakfast cereal producers.

4. _H_ Concentrated lemon juice.
5. _L_ Retail clothes.
6. _H_ Commercial airlines.

C. Which of the four **market structures** is (are) characterized by high market concentration?
monopoly, shared monopoly

D. Calculate the concentration ratios for each of the following three industries:
1. Industry X has 10 firms, each with an equal market share.
_40%_
2. Industry Y has one firm with 37% of the market and 63 firms with 1% each.
_40%_
3. Industry Z has 20 firms with 3% of the market and 20 firms with 2% of the market.
_12%_

E. Which of the above industries is a competitive industry? _industry 3_

7.11. Explain the difference between market concentration and aggregate concentration.

A. The Fortune 500 list of America's largest firms gives an idea of the extent of _aggregate_ concentration.

B. Which of the following mergers would increase both aggregate and market concentration (AM), and which would increase only aggregate concentration (A)?
1. _AM_ General Motors merges with Ford Motor Co.
2. _A_ Alcoa merges with Coca Cola.
3. _AM_ Kelloggs merges with Quaker Oats.
4. _A_ RJ Reynolds merges with Nabisco.
5. _AM_ IBM merges with Apple Computers, Inc.

7.12. Describe four consequences of high concentration in industries.

A. What are three *causes* of high industry concentration?
1. _mergers_
2. _economies of scale_
3. _predatory business practices_

B. Dutch Schultz, a famous gangster in the 1920s, monopolized the New York numbers game by killing his competitors. This is an example of increasing market concentration by
predatory business practices.

C. The four *consequences* of high industry concentration are:
1. _high prices_

2. *inefficient resource allocation*
3. *higher costs*
4. *unnecessary product differentiation*

D. List three products that you use that represent examples of product differentiation by producers:

1. *breakfast cereal*
2. *toothpaste*
3. *perfume*

Case Application: Rent-A-Kidney Business: Dialysis for Profit?

The Rent-A-Kidney business is an industry that provides dialysis—an artificial method of purifying the blood—for people with kidney failure. Those who need dialysis can get it from a dialysis center. If they want dialysis at home, they can buy the machine and its associated supplies from firms like Eric, Inc., or National Medical Care.

In the 1960s the artificial kidney unit was used only in the hospital, and patients had to stay in the hospital for a very long period of intensive care. In the 1970s home dialysis units became affordable and patients were able to dialyze themselves at home. National Medical Care is the largest dialysis business in the United States. They sell all necessary supplies to almost 50% of all home dialysis patients.

Then profit-seeking dialysis centers were established outside hospitals in cities like New York and Boston. National Medical Care is also active in that branch of the rent-a-kidney business. It owns many dialysis centers, where they handle about 16% of those dialysis patients not dialyzing at home.

Congress has enacted legislation under which the government pays the costs for the treatment of kidneys. Even though the cost of dialysis in the centers is 49% higher than that of home dialysis, the percentage of patients in home dialysis has declined steadily since the government program began.

Economic Reasoning *(Write your responses on a separate sheet. Answers begin on p. 295.)*

1. How would you classify the home dialysis equipment industry with respect to the type of market structure in the industry?
2. Does the hospital-based dialysis service industry have the same market structure as the home dialysis equipment industry? How can you judge from the information in the application whether or not the two industries operate in the same type of market?
3. The government dialysis program has increased the profitability of firms such as National Medical Care. Is this justified? Why or why not?

IV. Practice Test *(Answers begin on p. 295.)*

Multiple Choice *(Circle the correct answer.)*

(7.1) 1. Which of the following is NOT one of the four factors that determine industry performance?
 a. responsiveness to markets.
 b. product quality.
 (c.) wages and salaries.
 d. responsiveness to social concerns.

(7.2) 2. Productivity is measured as:
 a. the ratio of wages to outputs.

b. the ratio of quality to quantity.
c. the ratio of inputs to outputs.
d. the ratio of social to market responsiveness.

(7.3) 3. The Malcolm Baldrige Award is a prize awarded for improvements in:
a. productivity.
b. product quality.
c. environmental protection.
d. R&D.

(7.4) 4. Which of the following is true about firms that are NOT responsive to social concerns?
a. They could be fined by the government and/or boycotted by consumers.
b. They will not be as productive as other firms.
c. Product quality will suffer.
d. all of the above.

(7.5) 5. Which of the following is NOT a reason that capital investment has declined in the United States?
a. high interest rates.
b. a relatively flat learning curve.
c. a short-term profit horizon.
d. use of available funds for speculation.

(7.5) 6. The high level of interest rates in the United States is the result of:
a. low productivity.
b. low savings rates.
c. a short time horizon on the part of borrowers.
d. low levels of capital investment.

(7.6) 7. Which of the following is a TRUE statement?
a. Human capital investment has no impact on productivity.
b. Human capital refers to the link between employees and physical capital.
c. Human capital refers to the use of robots in manufacturing.
d. Investment in human capital takes place either in school or on the job.

(7.7) 8. R&D spending is important in order to improve:
a. education.
b. process innovation.
c. technology.
d. responsiveness to markets.

(7.8) 9. Which of the following is NOT an example of **process innovation**?
a. investment in human capital.
b. just-in-time manufacturing.
c. design for manufacturing and assembly (DFMA).
d. flexible manufacturing systems (FMS).

(7.8) 10. Process innovation refers to:
a. the type of capital equipment in a plant.
b. the type of employee training a firm offers.
c. the way a firm organizes production.
d. the management style used by a firm.

(7.9) 11. EI stands for:
a. extra innovation.
b. excess integration.
c. employee involvement.
d. education investment.

(7.9) 12. Which of the following is an example of EI?
a. self-managing teams.
b. investment in capital equipment.
c. responding to consumer wants.

d. eliminating excess labor.

(7.10) 13. Which of the following types of industries has the highest market concentration?
a. pure competition.
b. differentiated competition.
c. shared monopoly.
(d.) pure monopoly.

(7.11) 14. Which of the following is a TRUE statement?
a. Aggregate concentration has increased in the United States since 1940.
b. An industry characterized by high aggregate concentration is either a shared or a pure monopoly.
c. Aggregate concentration refers to the use of capital-intensive production techniques.
d. Aggregate concentration is directly related to the use of process innovation.

(7.12) 15. The most important consequence of high market concentration is:
a. low profits.
b. low productivity.
(c.) high prices.
d. flat learning curves.

True/False *(Circle T or F.)*

(7.1) 16. Industry performance is measured by the concentration ratio. T or **F**

(7.2) 17. Productivity is measured by the ratio of inputs to outputs. **T** or F

(7.6) 18. The steeper the learning curve, the slower labor is in learning new skills. T or **F**

(7.8) 19. Computer-integrated manufacturing is an example of process innovation. **T** or F

(7.11) 20. The concentration ratio measures the level of aggregate concentration in industries. T or **F**

Chapter 8

Government and Business

I. Chapter Outline

Although market economies work well to provide answers to the three basic economic questions, there are instances when the market fails to allocate resources efficiently. These include situations such as a lack of competition (high market concentration), the existence of collective goods, or the existence of external costs and benefits. In these instances, there is a rationale for the government to interfere with the workings of the market in an effort to improve the allocation of resources.

Introductory Article: Reach Out and Swallow Someone

For the 50 years following the beginning of its regulation in 1934, AT&T was just about the only provider of telephone equipment, local service, and long-distance service to the American people. Although "Ma Bell" provided the world's best telephone service, most of her customers were unaware that Ma's monopoly position allowed her to provide a little less than she could, at a price a little higher than she needed to charge. In an effort to introduce competition into the telephone industry, in 1974 the Justice Department filed an antitrust suit against AT&T. The Justice Department's win in this suit has resulted in the current structure of the American phone system: competition in both equipment manufacturing and long-distance service, and regulated local service companies that are no longer affiliated with AT&T.

Economic Analysis

This chapter evaluates the roles played by government in the U.S. economy by examining the following questions:

1. What Does the Government Do to Regulate Monopoly?

    Important Concepts: Antitrust legislation, Industrial consortiums, Natural monopoly, Public utility regulation, Deregulation

    Case Application: Less-Friendly Skies?

2. Why Does the Government Produce Goods and Services?

    Important Concepts: Collective goods, External economies, Merit goods

    Case Application: Private Participation in Public Education

3. What Is the Role of Government in Protecting Consumers, Workers, and the Environment?

    Important Concepts: Consumer protection, Worker protection, External costs, Environmental protection

    Case Application: Environmental Murder

Perspective: The Interstate Highway to Freedom

        Biography—Friedrich August von Hayek

II. Summary of Economic Analysis

1. Concern over the market power of the great American trusts (monopolies) led Congress to enact **antitrust legislation** in an effort to prevent collusion and monopoly abuses.
2. The most important antitrust acts include the **Interstate Commerce Commission Act** (1887), the **Sherman Act** (1890), the **Clayton Act** (1914), and the **Celler-Kefauver Act** (1950).
3. In an effort to help American businesses compete in the global marketplace, Congress now *encourages* collusion through the formation of **industry consortiums**: groups of firms working together in some areas of R&D.
4. The **National Co-operative Research Act of 1984** provides antitrust exemption in some instances where firms collude in their R&D efforts.
5. When **natural monopolies** exist, the market is best served by a single firm. Many public utilities (water, electric, telephone, and gas service) are natural monopolies.
6. When a public utility is a natural monopoly, the firm is allowed to operate as a monopoly, but it is subject to **public utility regulation**, and the regulating agency is often called a **public utility commission.**
7. Growing dissatisfaction with the results of regulation of firms that were not natural monopolies led to a movement toward **deregulation** in these industries.
8. **Collective goods** are goods that are useful and beneficial but are not feasible to produce and sell in a market system. If they are to be produced, they must be produced by the government and consumed "collectively."
9. Goods and services that benefit not only the purchaser and the seller but also third parties are goods that generate **external economies.**
10. Because consumer products have become increasingly complex and difficult for consumers to understand, the government promotes **consumer protection** by testing, regulating, and controlling the products that businesses sell.
11. Because of the dangers involved in some types of work, the government promotes **worker protection** by setting and enforcing standards for worker safety.
12. Goods and services that impose costs not only on the seller of a good but also on third parties are goods that generate **external costs.**
13. **Pollution** is an external cost imposed on the environment.
14. **Environmental protection** laws are enacted and enforced by the government to reduce the external costs associated with pollution.

III. Review of the Learning Objectives *(Answers begin on p. 296.)*

What Does the Government Do to Regulate Monopoly?

ANTITRUST LEGISLATION

Interstate Commerce Act (1887)
The act established the Interstate Commerce Commission (ICC) to regulate the railroads; it abolished rate discrimination.

Sherman Antitrust Act (1890)
Act is the nation's basic antitrust legislation that prohibits monopoly and outlaws attempts to monopolize an industry.

Clayton Antitrust Act (1914)
It reinforced the Sherman Act by specifying specific illegal practices. It exempted unions.

Celler-Kefauver Antimerger Act (1950)
The act prohibits mergers that would lessen competition. It reduced horizontal mergers.

Industrial Consortiums
Recently antitrust policy has been modified to meet foreign competition by permitting firms in an industry to form consortiums for joint R&D projects.

PUBLIC UTILITY REGULATION
If an industry is a natural monopoly because it is more efficient for one firm to serve all of the customers in an area, the government regulates the firm through establishing a public utility commission.

Deregulation
In recent years there has been a move to deregulate industries in order to increase competition.

(See page vi in the foreword "To the Student" for how to make the best use of this schematic outline.)

8.1. Explain the purposes of the Interstate Commerce Act and the Sherman, Clayton, and Celler-Kefauver Acts. *(Write in answers below.)*

A. Indicate which antitrust act would apply in each of the following cases (ICA, SA, CA, CKA):

   1. _ICA_ A railroad charges high prices to one group in order to subsidize low rates to another.
   2. _CKA_ A planned merger between Ford and General Motors would substantially lessen competition in the automobile industry.
   3. _CA_ AT&T attempts to buy a controlling interest of MCI stock.
   4. _CA_ MegaBucks, Inc., is accused of driving the Mom & Pop Company out of business by using price discrimination.
   5. _SA_ Acme Dirtworks, Inc., is accused of attempting to monopolize the market for potting soil.

B. Antitrust laws are designed to limit what two types of activity?

   1. _monopolization_
   2. _collusion_

C. Why are firms in purely and differentiated competitive industries not likely to be accused of violating antitrust laws?

There are too many firms for either effective collusion or attempted monopolization

D. Recall the discussion of the *zaibatsu* from the introductory article in chapter 7. Would this kind of cooperation among businesses be legal in America?

No. It would be prohibited as a form of collusion under either the Sherman or Clayton Act.

8.2. Explain the purpose of industry R&D consortiums and why they are exempt from the antitrust laws.

A. Why does the government grant antitrust exemptions to groups of firms that collude in certain R&D activities?

In order to promote international competitiveness

B. What law permits R&D collusion?

The National Co-operative Research Act of 1984

C. Suppose firms are **not** allowed to collude in their research and development efforts. Give an example of a disadvantage of such policy in the area of automobile safety research.

There might be a duplication of effort. For example 3 different firms might be working on the same brake problem

D. General Motors and Toyota worked together to build the Saturn automobile in Tennessee. What is one possible **disadvantage** of allowing such cooperation?

Collusion between the 2 firms such as price fixing or market sharing schemes

8.3. List the causes of natural monopoly and indicate what industries fall under that classification.

A. The primary cause of natural monopoly is the existence of *economies of scale*.

B. If there are economies of scale in production, why would it be a bad idea for the government to use antitrust laws to break up a natural monopoly?

Average costs would be higher for each of the smaller firms

C. List at least three firms that you know that are natural monopolies.

1. *local electric company*

2. _local phone company_

3. _local cable TV company_

D. In terms of *fixed* and *variable costs*, what do the firms that you listed above have in common? What about their *marginal costs*?

   Fixed costs. _high_

   Variable costs. _low_

   Marginal costs. _low_

8.4. Explain how public policy deals with natural monopolies.

A. What is an alternative to government regulation of natural monopolies? (Hint: this is what is done in most Western European countries.)

   government ownership & operation

B. Public utility commissions are called different things in different states. What is the name of the public utility commission in your state?

   _?_

C. Suppose that you are a public utility commissioner. What kind of real-world problems can you foresee in trying to determine a "fair" price for a giant utility company?

   1. _finding accurate cost information_
   2. _determining a fair rate of return_

D.
   1. Assume that you do not like high electric bills. Have you ever written to a public utility commissioner to complain? _probably not_
   2. Your electric company likes high electric prices. Do you think that they have written to a public utility commissioner? _probably so_

E. According to economists' definitions of profit, what would constitute a "fair" profit for a regulated utility?

   a "normal profit"

8.5. Discuss the positive and negative aspects of regulation.

A.
   1. Look at the three natural monopolies that you listed in Part C of section 8.3 above. What can you guess about the *elasticity of demand* for their products?

      The demand is probably inelastic because of few substitutes

   2. If you were the *owner* of any of these three natural monopolies and no one could tell you how much you could charge for your product, what would be the first thing that you would do tomorrow?

      You would probably raise the price

106 / *Working With The Study of Economics, 4/E*

3. Suppose you are a *customer* of a natural monopoly. Do you think that "free market" prices are fair?

   probably not

4. As a customer, what are your alternatives to allowing natural monopolies to charge "what the market will bear"?

   Regulate their prices or pay the bill

B. List two groups that benefited from the past regulation of potentially competitive industries such as trucking and airlines.

   1. *established companies*
   2. *labor unions*

C. Indicate with a check which of the following industries should be regulated in order to benefit **consumers**:

   1. ___ Long-distance telephone service.
   2. ✓ Local telephone service.
   3. ___ Trash pick-up.
   4. ___ Automobile manufacturing.
   5. ✓ Local electric service.

8.6. Explain the reasons for and consequences of deregulation.

A. Deregulation of an industry will be beneficial to **consumers** only if the industry structure is

   competitive.

B. Indicate which of the following have been **harmed** by the deregulation of the airline industry:

   1. ✓ Labor unions.
   2. ___ Passengers who live in big cities.
   3. ✓ Passengers who live in small towns.
   4. ✓ Established airlines.
   5. ___ Passengers worried about safety.

C. One method used to regulate the trucking industry was the establishment of barriers to entry for potential new firms. After deregulation, what do you think happened to prices and profits in the trucking industry?

   prices & profits fell

Case Application: Water, Water, Everywhere, And Not a Drop (That's Fit) to Drink

The stories are rampant in cities from Massachusetts to California and all over the country between—in New Jersey, Ohio, Oklahoma, Minnesota, Arizona, and at least 15 other states—about drinking water that is not fit to drink.

In the Boston suburbs of Dedham and Westwood, the water flowing from kitchen faucets was so bad—reddish-brown in color, with a sickening smell and taste—that residents of the two towns held a referendum in 1985 on taking over the private water company by condemning it under the power of eminent domain.

Water companies, whether privately owned utilities or municipal utilities, have been confronted with increasing problems of underground water supplies polluted by seepage of toxic waste dumps and surface water supplies poisoned by industrial chemical discharges and runoffs of agricultural pesticides and fertilizers. The public's concern over impure drinking water supplies has resulted in stricter regulation of water systems.

The answer for the citizens of Dedham and Westwood was to acquire the local water company for a price of $17–$20 million and contract with the previous owner, American Water Works Co., to manage it. A new water treatment facility was scheduled for construction. The costs of the new plant would have to be included in the customers' water bills, and rates were expected to increase 20%–25% a year for at least two years. But the 40,000 residents of Dedham and Westwood hope to have clear water running from their faucets at last, water that they can launder their clothes in without ruining them, water that they can drink.

Economic Reasoning *(Write your responses on a separate sheet. Answers begin on p. 296.)*

1. In what way is the move toward stricter regulation of water utilities contrary to the trend in government policies?
2. How did the fact that there was only one company supplying water to Dedham and Westwood result in the problems they were having in obtaining satisfactory water?
3. Should government intervene to ensure the purity of water supplies, whatever the cost? Why or why not?

Why Does the Government Produce Goods and Services?

COLLECTIVE GOODS
Some goods and services that are considered essential to society but are not adequately provided by the private sector are supplied by the government as collective goods (public goods).

External economies
One reason for providing collective goods is the existence of external economies that arise when there are benefits from a good or service that accrue to the public that are in addition to the benefits to the consumer of the good or service. Something that raises the cultural level of society is a merit good.

Collective goods and equity
Another reason for the government to provide goods and services is to achieve the goal of greater equity in real income by providing essential services, such as transportation and housing, to those who cannot afford them.

(See page vi in the foreword "To the Student" for how to make the best use of this schematic outline.)

8.7. Identify the kinds of goods and services that constitute collective goods, and explain why the government provides them.

A. Which of the following goods or services are **collective goods** (CG), and which *could* feasibly be sold for a price by the private sector (PS) in a market economy?

1. _CG_ A fireworks display.

2. _PS_ 200 firecrackers.
3. _CG_ A lighthouse.
4. _CG_ A streetlight.
5. _PS_ Elementary school education.
6. _PS_ Entry to a park.
7. _PS_ Use of an interstate highway.
8. _CG_ Use of a local street.

B. List three goods provided by your local government that *could* be provided by a private company.

1. local schools
2. trash pick-up
3. ~~local~~ libraries

C. Suppose you decided to make some extra money by buying some really great fireworks and charging people to see the fireworks show. Even if everybody loved fireworks displays, why would you have a problem making any money?

you could not exclude non-payers

D. An entrepreneur can determine whether or not to produce a certain good by comparing its cost of production to the amount people will pay for it. What problem does a government agency have in determining whether or not to produce a collective good?

Determining how much the citizens value the good

8.8. Explain the concepts of external economies and external costs.

A. Indicate which of the following activities generate external economies (EE) and which generate external costs (EC):

1. _EC_ Your neighbor's yard is a mess.
2. _EC_ Your neighbor plays loud music all night.
3. _EE_ Parents have their new baby vaccinated against smallpox.
4. _EE_ Everybody in your town learns to read and write.
5. _EE_ You pay to have a telephone installed in your home.
6. _EC_ MegaSlime, Inc., dumps waste products into the air and water.
7. _EC_ A commuter pulls his or her car onto a busy highway at rush hour.
8. _EC_ A full, satisfied diner at a nice restaurant lights up an after-dinner cigar.

B.

1. Total (social) costs are equal to a firm's private costs plus external costs. The graph at the top of the next page shows the demand and supply for a product and the private optimal (Q_{po}) level of production **based on private costs alone**. Draw a new supply curve that represents **total** costs of production and indicate the socially optimal (Q_{so}) level of output.

8 Government and Business / 109

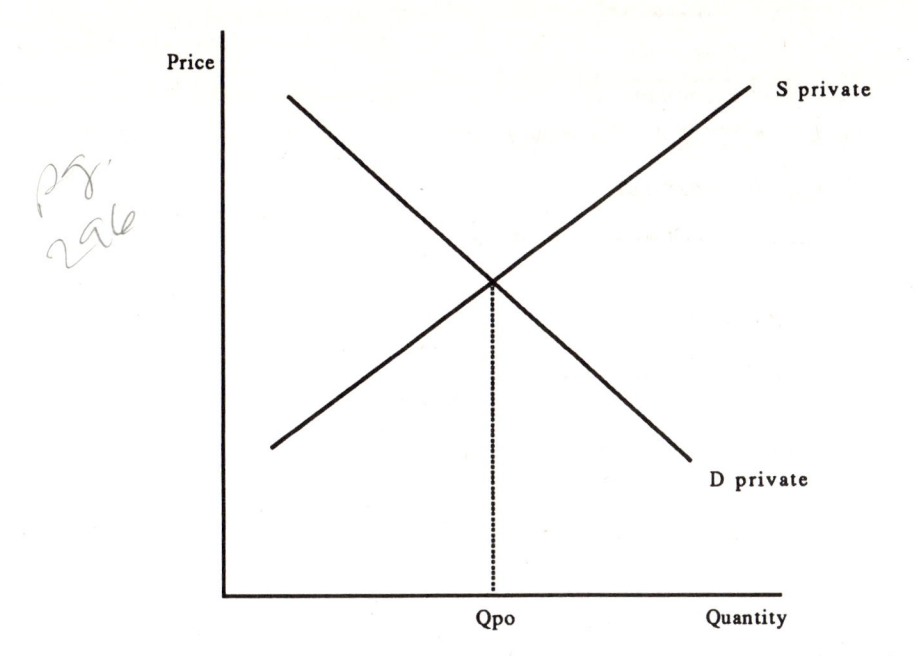

[Graph: Price vs Quantity with S private (upward) and D private (downward) curves intersecting at Qpo]

2. Is the socially optimal level of production greater or less than the amount that would occur if the firm worried only about its private costs?

    less

C.

1. Total (social) benefits are equal to private benefits plus external economies. The graph below shows the demand and supply for a product and the private optimal (Q_{po}) level of production **based on private benefits alone**. Draw a new demand curve that represents the **total** benefits from the good and indicate the socially optimal (Q_{so}) level of output.

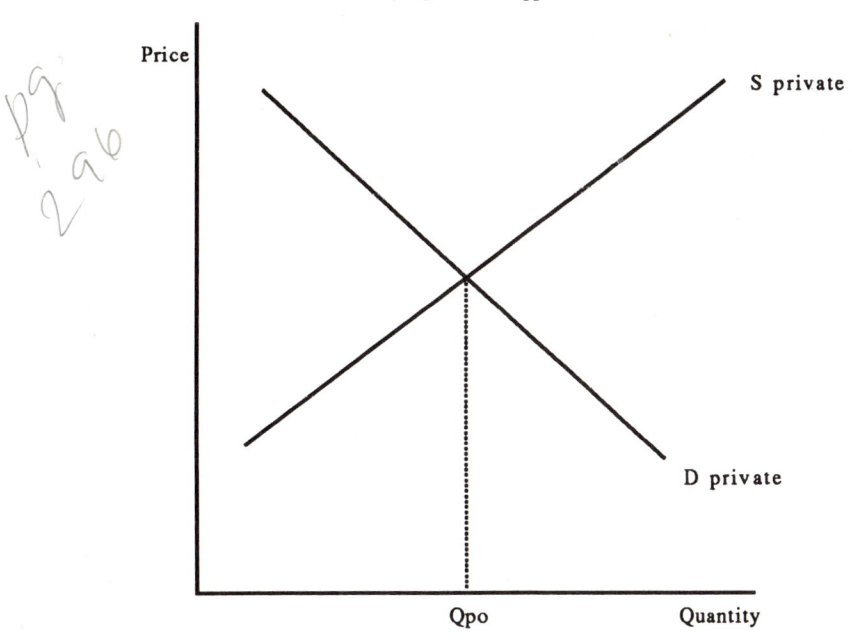

[Graph: Price vs Quantity with S private (upward) and D private (downward) curves intersecting at Qpo]

2. Is the socially optimal level of output greater or less than the amount that would occur if only private benefits were considered?

    greater

110 / *Working With The Study of Economics, 4/E*

D. Based on your answers to parts B and C, what general statement can you make about the amount of goods and services provided by the market when external costs and external economies are present?

Too many goods are produced when external costs are present, and too few are produced when external economies are present

E. What are two external economies associated with a mass transit system in an urban area?

1. *less polution*
2. *less congestion*

Case Application: Should the Government Be in the Railroad Business?

Around the world, the railroads are run by the government—except in the United States, where traditionally railroads have been private enterprises. But two exceptions to the rule of private ownership of the railroads in this country emerged in the 1970s: Amtrak and Conrail.

Amtrak was formed in 1970 as the National Railroad Passenger Corporation. It took over the faltering passenger rail services from the rail lines that no longer found them profitable due to competition from air and bus lines. In 1976 the Consolidated Rail Corporation—Conrail for short—was put together as a government rescue operation from the wreckage of seven failed freight lines.

Conrail lost some $7 billion in its first five years of operation but then began to turn a profit. Amtrak continues to lose money, although less as time goes on and passenger traffic increases. One of the criticisms of the government subsidizing Amtrak is that most of its passengers are middle- and upper-middle-income. A survey of riders in the Northeast, where more than half of Amtrak passenger traffic is, showed that the majority of riders had incomes over $30,000.

In 1987 Conrail, after becoming profitable under government operation, was transformed into a private corporation through the sale of shares. As part of its efforts to deregulate the economy, the Reagan administration also attempted to privatize Amtrak. That would have put an end to Amtrak's long-haul services, if not finish rail passenger service altogether. Congress opposed getting rid of Amtrak because passenger rail service would virtually cease to exist in this country without government subsidy.

Economic Reasoning *(Write your responses on a separate sheet. Answers begin on p. 297.)*

1. Can the government subsidy of Amtrak be justified in terms of equity? Why or why not?
2. Are there external economies associated with passenger rail transportation? With freight rail transportation? If so, what are they?
3. Should the government dispose of Amtrak? Why or why not?

What Is the Role of Government in Protecting Consumers, Workers, and the Environment?

CONSUMER PROTECTION	WORKER PROTECTION	ENVIRONMENTAL PROTECTION
Government agencies that are involved in the protection of the consumer include: • Department of Transportation (DOT) • Food and Drug Administration (FDA) • Consumer Product Safety Commission (CPSC) • Federal Trade Commission (FTC) • Securities and Exchange Commission (SEC)	The principal legislation for government protection of the workers is the Occupational Safety and Health Act. Its provisions are enforced by the Occupational Safety and Health Administration (OSHA).	The principal government agency for protection of the environment is • The Environmental Protection Agency (EPA)
		External costs An economic justification for protecting the environment against pollution is the existence of external costs. Efficiency of resource allocation is improved when producers internalize the external costs.

(See page vi in the foreword "To the Student" for how to make the best use of this schematic outline.)

8.9. Explain how the government protects workers and consumers.

A. Of the following agencies:

DOT (Department of Transportation)
FDA (Food and Drug Administration
CPSC (Consumer Product Safety Commission)
FTC (Federal Trade Commission)
OSHA (Occupational Safety and Health Administration)
SEC (Securities and Exchange Commission)

indicate which one protects consumers in each of the following situations.

1. _SEC_ You were swindled out of your life savings after investing in a bogus stock.
2. _DOT_ Your automobile blew up when a neighbor's kid bounced a baseball off its gas tank.
3. _CPSC_ Your G.I. Joe doll had a live grenade that blew off your big toe.
4. _OSHA_ The product that you handled at work causes cancer.
5. _FDA_ A new cold remedy had side effects that caused your hair to fall out.
6. _FTC_ A deceptive advertisement caused you to pay $100 for a worthless product.

B. Why do we need government to protect us in so many ways? Why can't we figure out for ourselves which products are safe and which products are not safe?

most of us do not have the information to make informed decisions

C. Which industry is the most dangerous in the United States in terms of the number of injuries incurred on the job?

agriculture

D. If workers had complete and perfect information about the dangers of each and every job, how could the job market work efficiently without government regulations?

by paying wage premiums for dangerous work

8.10. Describe three alternative ways by which the government can reduce pollution by getting firms to internalize the external costs of environmental pollution.

A. Pollution occurs because our air and water are treated as *free* goods by producers.

B. What are three ways that firms can be forced to internalize their external costs?

1. *command and control regulations*
2. *eco-taxes*
3. *the sale of emmissions allowances*

C. Suppose that firm X and firm Y each produce 100 tons of hydrocarbons in their production processes. Firm X can reduce its emissions for $5 per ton, and firm Y can reduce its emissions for $10 per ton.

1. What will be the total amount of pollution eliminated and the total cleanup cost if both firms are required to reduce their pollution by half?
100 tons for $*750*

2. What would be a less expensive way to remove the same amount of pollutants?

have firm X clean up 100 tons for only $500

3. What would make Firm X willing to go along with the idea presented in question 2?

Firm X would be willing to clean up 100 tons if firm Y made it worth its while and firm Y would be willing to pay up to $500

D.
1. If firms are not forced to internalize their external costs, who pays for the pollution they generate?

"third parties"

2. If firms are forced to internalize their external costs, who pays for this internalization?

customers

E. Remember that higher costs usually lead to higher prices and a smaller quantity demanded. What are two **opportunity costs** of requiring electric utilities to internalize their externalities?

1. _higher electric prices_
2. _perhaps fewer jobs in the electric industry_

Case Application: Declaration of Air Pollution Emergency

In October 1948, a disaster occurred just 20 miles southeast of Pittsburgh, in Donora, Pennsylvania. Twenty people died. Nearly half of Donora's 14,000 residents became ill. What happened?

Air pollution struck. Some people became sick and others died because of poisonous smog. The huge black cloud was composed of sulphur dioxide, industrial gases, particles of iron oxide, zinc oxide, silicates, and carbon.

In November 1975, in a northeast suburb of Pittsburgh, 30 industrial plants in the Monongahela and Youghiogheny river valleys were forced to curtail operations. The air pollution emergency was declared by the Allegheny county commissioners. In 1974 the residents of Allegheny County had passed a stringent air-pollution law establishing a modern monitoring system. Under the law, the commissioners could take drastic measures. They could close schools and prohibit all commercial activities. As an alternative action, the commissioners decided to cut back the production level of steel output.

According to county public health officials, a pollution index of 15 to 35 is normal. When the index reaches 100, an alert is sent out. When the index reaches the 200 level, a health warning must be issued. One week in November the pollution index in the Allegheny County area was over 250.

The hospitals in the affected area were reporting increased numbers of pollution-related complaints, such as headaches, choking, and stinging eyes. People suffering from asthma, especially asthmatic children, were the most affected. Public health officials warned that the pollution from soot and sulphur dioxide could cause special problems for those with respiratory and heart ailments. The police department reported that the combination of fog and soot caused widespread traffic delays. The Pennsylvania Department of Environmental Resources, a statewide government agency for environmental protection, was also alerted in case the pollution started to spread due to changing weather conditions.

Right after the declaration of the pollution emergency, the U.S. Steel Corporation announced that because of the cutback in production in many of its plants hundreds of workers would be laid off. The situation would be worse by December when the production processes would be required to switch from coal to natural gas. To comply with pollution control requirements, the industry would need to install fabric filters for electric arcs, high-energy wet scrubbers for open-hearth and basic oxygen furnaces, and electrostatic precipitators for smokestacks.

Economic Reasoning *(Write your responses on a separate sheet. Answers begin on p. 297.)*

1. What external costs were associated with steel production in Allegheny County?
2. What would the U.S. Steel Corporation have to do to internalize the external costs of its steel production operations? What would happen to the price and quantity of steel production when external costs are internalized? Explain your answer by a graph of demand and supply.
3. Should U.S. Steel be forced to internalize its external costs even though that would result in increased unemployment in the Pittsburgh area? Why or why not?

IV. Practice Test (Answers begin on p. 297.)

Multiple Choice (Circle the correct answer.)

(8.1) 1. Which of the following acts is designed to reduce the number of mergers that lessen competition?
  a. the Interstate Commerce Act.
  b. the Sherman Act.
  c. the Clayton Act.
  d. the Celler-Kefauver Act.

(8.1) 2. Abuses and monopolistic practices in which industry led Congress to pass the Interstate Commerce Act?
  a. trucking.
  b. agriculture.
  c. the production of military hardware.
  d. railroad shipping.

(8.2) 3. Industry consortiums engaged in R&D are often exempt from antitrust prosecutions as a result of which congressional act?
  a. the Interstate Commerce Act.
  b. the Baker-Hatfield International Competition Act.
  c. the National Co-operative Research Act.
  d. the Industry Consortium Protection Act.

(8.3) 4. Which of the following is the closest to being a natural monopoly?
  a. the U.S. Postal Service.
  b. your local cable TV company.
  c. long-distance telephone service.
  d. public education.

(8.3) 5. The primary economic cause of natural monopolies is:
  a. diminishing returns.
  b. inelastic demand for a good or service.
  c. trade-offs between increased production and environmental damage.
  d. economies of scale.

(8.4) 6. Natural monopolies are usually limited in the prices they can charge by:
  a. congressional acts.
  b. referendums conducted among all voters.
  c. public utility commissions.
  d. their own estimates of consumers' elasticity of demand.

(8.5) 7. Which of the following groups benefited most under the regulation of the airline industry?
  a. passengers.
  b. small, new airline companies.
  c. airline-related labor unions.
  d. all of the above.

(8.6) 8. Deregulation will work best when the deregulated industry:
  a. is monopolistic.
  b. is a shared monopoly.
  c. is competitive.
  d. has high barriers to entry.

(8.6) 9. Most of the industries that were deregulated during the 1980s were originally regulated in order to:
  a. prevent competition.
  b. keep consumer prices low.
  c. ensure consumer safety.

d. reduce foreign competition in American markets.

(8.7) 10. Which of the following is an example of a collective good?
- a. a public school.
- b. a fireworks display.
- c. a barbecue.
- d. a library.

(8.7) 11. Which of the following exists for private goods but does not exist in the case of collective goods?
- a. the ability to charge all those who use the good.
- b. external costs.
- c. a trade-off because of scarcity.
- d. demand and supply.

(8.8) 12. If external costs occur in the production of good X and firms are NOT required to internalize these costs, which of the following will result?
- a. There will be a shortage of good X.
- b. The demand for good X will become more elastic.
- c. Firms making good X will earn economic profits.
- d. There will be too much X produced and used.

(8.8) 13. A good that is provided by governments because it generates external economies is called a(n):
- a. collective good.
- b. external good.
- c. merit good.
- d. positive good.

(8.9) 14. Which of the following agencies was formed to protect the safety of workers?
- a. FDA.
- b. OSHA.
- c. DOT.
- d. FTC.

(8.10) 15. If firms are forced to internalize their external costs, who will pay the resulting higher price for the firms' products?
- a. everybody who bears the external costs.
- b. the government.
- c. the purchaser of the products.
- d. nobody—when costs are internalized they no longer exist.

True/False *(Circle T or F.)*

(8.1) 16. The most important antimerger antitrust act is the Celler-Kefauver Act. **T** or F

(8.3) 17. Elasticity of demand is the most important cause of natural monopolies. T or **F**

(8.5) 18. Deregulation has been especially beneficial to labor unions. T or **F**

(8.7) 19. National defense is an example of a collective good. **T** or F

(8.8) 20. Pollution is an example of an external cost. **T** or F

Chapter 9

Labor and Income Distribution

I. Chapter Outline

Labor is the most important factor of production in any economy. Nearly all businesses use more labor than any other resource in the production of goods and services. As a consequence, the labor market makes up the biggest part of the overall resource market in the circular flow of an economy's income. Although other factors of production are sold in resource markets in order to generate income for their owners (rent, interest, profits), most households depend upon the wages and salaries of family members to keep a roof over their heads and food on the table. The amount of income that a household earns in the resource market depends on a number of things, including labor productivity, opportunities, and the ownership of salable resources. Because these are not distributed equally among all households, income is not distributed equally.

Introductory Article: Immigrants—Part of the Problem or Part of the Solution?

The effects of immigrant labor on the economy are the subject of a great deal of discussion and controversy, not only in everyday conversations, but also among economists. Immigrant workers are an asset to employers who prefer to pay low wages and consumers who prefer to pay low prices. They are not considered an asset by other workers who believe that immigrants depress wages and take jobs away from the local natives. However, a number of recent economic studies have concluded that due to their demand for goods and services, immigrant workers increase the demand for labor as well as the supply.

Economic Analysis

This chapter examines the market for labor in the United States and the role it plays in the distribution of income by examining the following questions:

1. What Determines Wages?

    Important Concepts: Derived demand, Labor supply, Capital availability, Minimum wages, Unions, Sticky wages

    Important Model: Labor demand and supply

    Case Application: "Baby Bust" Generation Replacing "Baby Boom" Generation

2. What Determines Other Incomes?

    Important Concepts: Functional distribution of income, Rent, Interest, Profits

    Case Application: Rent Control

3. What Causes Unequal Distribution of Income?

    Important Concepts: Personal income distribution, Differences in productivity, Differences in opportunity, Differences in asset ownership

    Important Model: Lorenz curve

    Case Application: Created Equal, But…

4. What Is the Answer to Poverty?

Important Concepts: The poverty line, Affirmative action, Entitlement programs, Negative income tax, Workfare

Case Application: The Rich Get Richer and the Poor Get Ketchup

Perspective: The Haymarket Affair

II. Summary of Economic Analysis

1. The demand for labor is a **derived demand** because it depends on the demand for the goods and services that labor produces.
2. The demand for labor is influenced by the amount of available capital that labor works with: labor and capital may be either substitutes or complements.
3. Labor is not a standardized input. The demand for and supplies of skilled and unskilled labor may be much different.
4. Both **minimum wage laws** and **labor unions** are institutions that attempt to keep workers' wages higher than the wages that the market would generate.
5. If wages are too **"sticky"** to fall when the demand for labor falls, then a fall in demand will result in increased unemployment.
6. The **functional distribution of income** shows the relative amounts of household income that come from **wages and salaries, rent, interest,** and **profits**.
7. Unlike other sources of income, **rent** is a payment for resources that have fixed supplies. Increased demand will not result in increased supplies that bring prices and profits back down to a normal rate of return.
8. **Interest** is the payment for the use of financial capital (borrowed money).
9. **Profits** are the payments to entrepreneurs for undertaking risks and organizing production. Much of the profit earned by proprietors should correctly be classified as **implicit wages** and **implicit interest**.
10. The **personal distribution of income** shows the relative size of household incomes. The degree of income inequality can be shown with the **Lorenz curve**.
11. Differences in household incomes are caused by differences in **productivity, opportunity,** and **asset ownership**.
12. Differences in productivity are caused by differences in ability, education, training, and capital availability.
13. In the United States, all citizens have the right to equal employment opportunities. Ensuring this right is the responsibility of the **Equal Opportunity Commission**.
14. The official U.S. **poverty line** varies with the size of the family and is based on the cost of feeding a family of that size.
15. In the United States, the government tries to help families escape poverty by providing equal education and employment opportunities. The government also provides tax-financed **transfer payments** to the poor.
16. Transfer payments can be in the form of either money (**AFDC**) or services (**Medicaid**). The **negative income tax, earned income tax credit,** and **workfare** are transfer programs that are designed to provide incentives for the poor to work for their income.

III. Review of the Learning Objectives (Answers begin on p. 298.)

What Determines Wages in a Market Economy?

WAGES

DEMAND SIDE

Derived demand
The demand for labor services is derived from the demand for the final products labor produces, which is one determinant of the demand for labor.

Productivity
The other determinant of the demand for labor is labor productivity. The more productive labor is, the higher will be the demand for it. A major factor affecting the productivity of labor is the amount of capital available that labor has to work with.

SUPPLY SIDE
The supply of labor in the labor pool depends in part on the population size, which is affected by immigration.

Minimum wage laws
Federal and state minimum wage laws establish a wage floor for workers, with some occupations exempted.

Labor Unions
Unions affect wages by means of their control over the supply of labor. They negotiate wage increases and better working conditions by means of collective bargaining.

Wagner Act
The usual name for the National Labor Relations Act (1935), which established collective bargaining as the basis for labor-management relations.

When labor and management cannot reach an agreement, unions support their demands by job actions such as strikes and boycotts.

(See page vi in the foreword "To the Student" for how to make the best use of this schematic outline.)

9.1. Explain what determines the demand for and supply of labor and how demand and supply influence wages. *(Write in answers below.)*

A.

1. Which is the Simpson-Mazzoli Bill designed to influence, the demand for or supply of labor?

   supply

2. Is it designed to increase it or decrease it?

   decrease

3. What impact do you think the bill has on wages?

   it prevents wages from falling

4. Use the graph below to show the impact of the Simpson-Mazzoli Bill on the labor market.

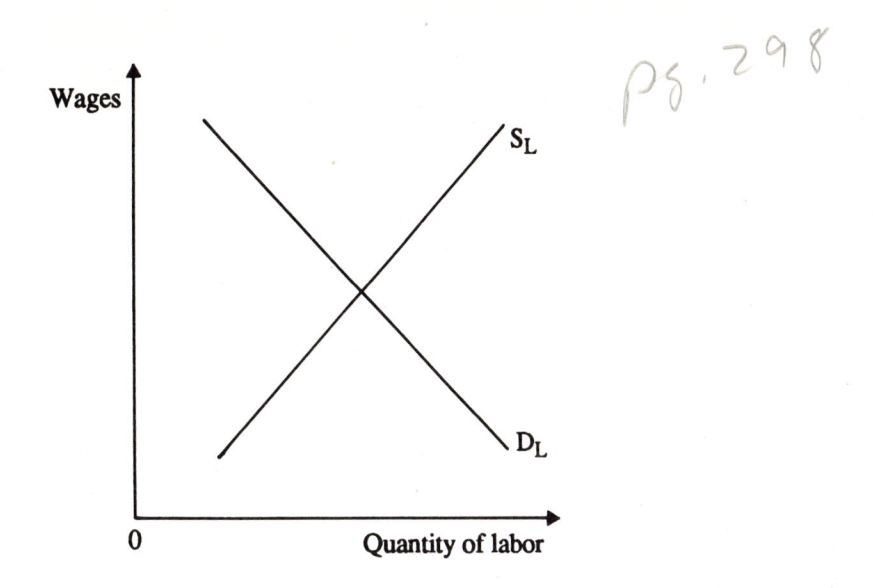

pg. 298

B. Indicate whether each of the following would result in an increase (I) or a decrease (D) in the equilibrium wage rate for workers at fast-food restaurants:

1. __D__ The United States opens its doors to all immigrants.
2. __D__ There is a decrease in the demand for burgers.
3. __I__ There are fewer young people in the population.
4. __I__ There is an increase in the demand for fast food.

C. Use the following four graphs to indicate what happens in each of the above instances.

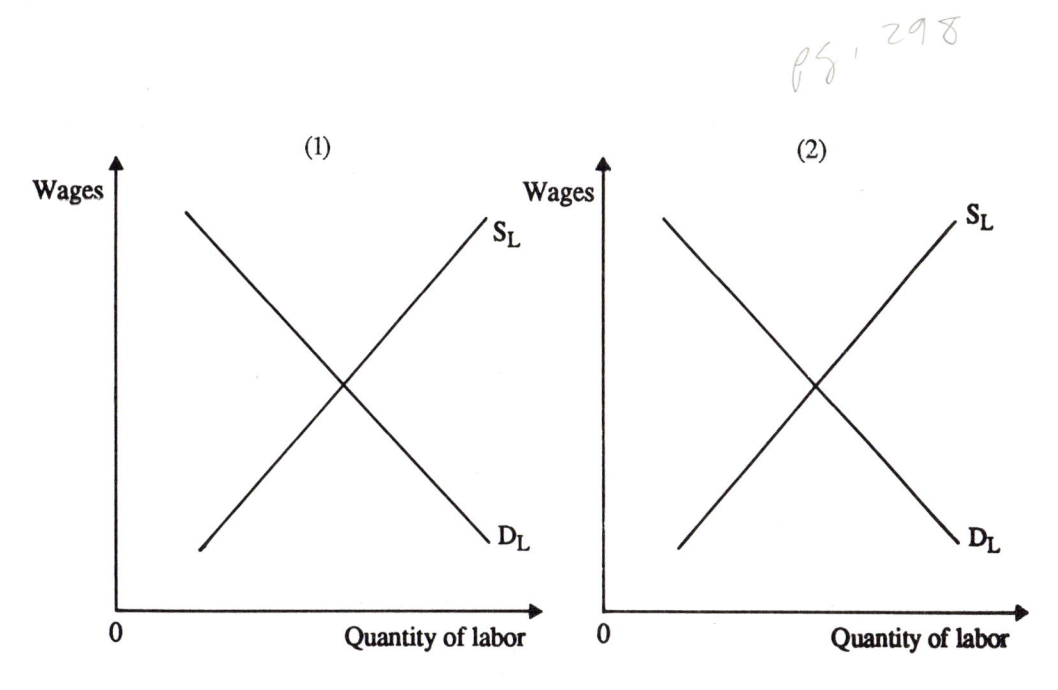

pg. 298

(3) Wages / S_L / D_L / 0 / Quantity of labor

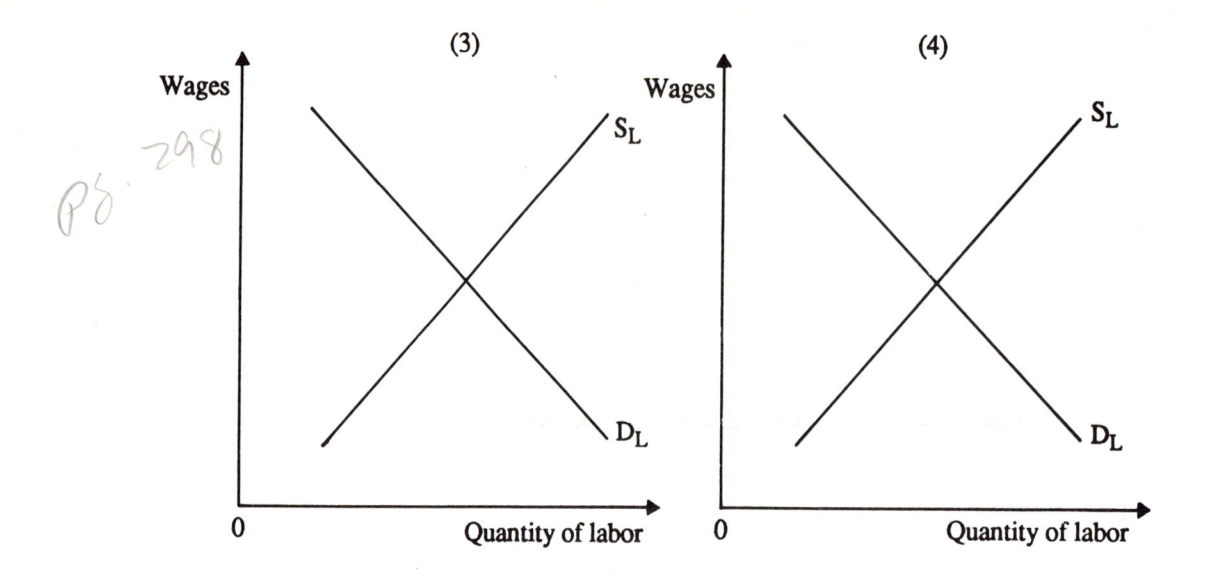

(4) Wages / S_L / D_L / 0 / Quantity of labor

D. Use the graphs below to show what happens to the equilibrium wage in the markets for unskilled and skilled labor when:

1. The number of unskilled high school dropouts increases at the same time that employers have little need for unskilled labor.

2. The number of skilled workers increases only slightly while employers have a greatly increased demand for highly trained technicians.

Unskilled Labor Market (1) Wages / S_L / D_L / 0 / Quantity of labor

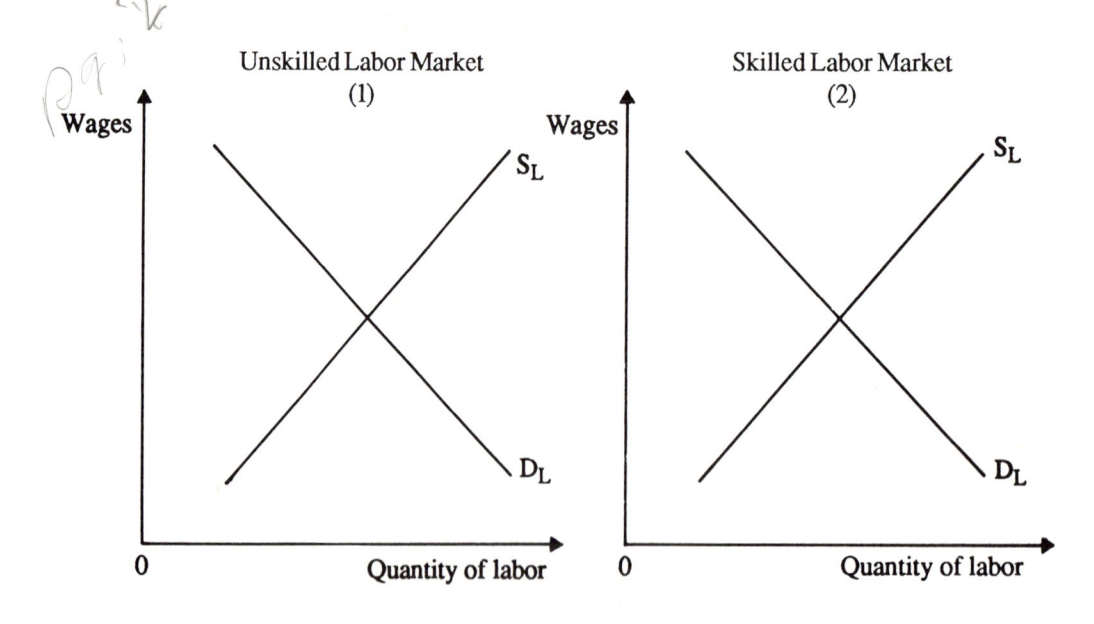

Skilled Labor Market (2) Wages / S_L / D_L / 0 / Quantity of labor

3. Give a real-world example of how two different labor markets, like the ones in the previous question, exist at the same time in the same town.

Dishwashers may earn only minimum wage while computer technicians may earn excellent salaries.

9.2. Discuss how capital availability affects labor demand and wages.

A. If labor and capital are complements, then an increase in capital availability will have what effect on each of the following?
   1. The demand for labor. _will increase_
   2. The wage rate for labor. _will increase_

B. If labor and capital are substitutes, then an increase in capital availability will have what effect on each of the following?
   1. The demand for labor. _will decrease_
   2. The wage rate for labor. _will decrease_

C. Indicate whether each of the following will result in increased (I) or decreased (D) capital investment.
   1. _I_ An increase in the minimum wage.
   2. _D_ Increased numbers of young people in an economy.
   3. _I_ A labor shortage.
   4. _I_ Increased savings rates.
   5. _I_ Increased union power to increase wages.

9.3. Describe the effects of minimum wage laws.

A. Use the following data to construct a demand and supply graph for the labor market in the space provided:

Hourly Wage	Quantity of Labor Demanded (in hundreds)	Quantity of Labor Supplied (in hundreds)
$7	3	9
$6	4	7
$5	5	5
$4	6	3
$3	7	1

pg. 299

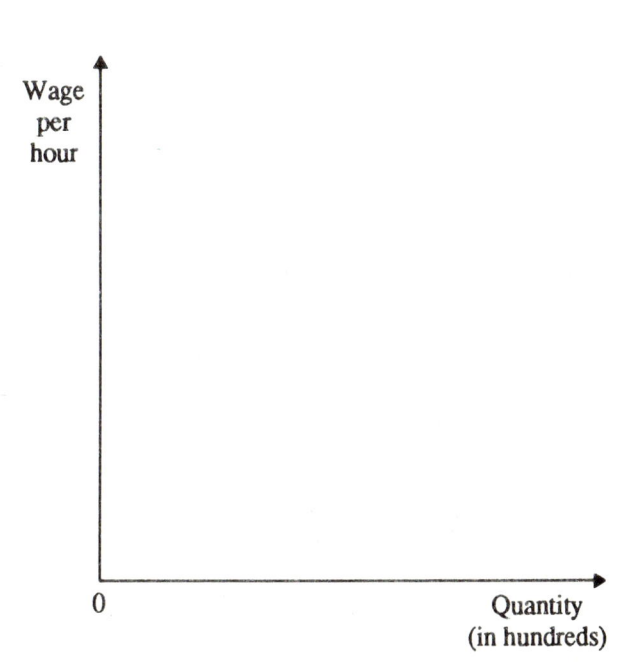

Wage per hour

0 — Quantity (in hundreds)

B. What is the equilibrium wage in the labor market described in the previous question?

   $5

C. Suppose that a minimum wage of $6 is imposed in the labor market shown in Part A above.

   1. Indicate the effect of the minimum wage on the graph.
   2. How many more people will be willing to work now that the minimum wage exists? *200*
   3. How many fewer people will employers be willing to hire? *100*
   4. What has been the effect of the minimum wage?

      a surplus of 300 workers (unemployment)

D. During the late 1980s, the demand for young workers was so much greater than the available supply that the equilibrium wage was much greater than the official minimum wage. What effect do minimum wage laws have in a labor market when the equilibrium wage exceeds the minimum wage?

   they have no effect

9.4. Explain what labor unions do.

A.
   1. The law that first allowed unions to bargain collectively is referred to as the *Wagner Act (National Labor Relations Act)*.
   2. This act established the *National Labor Relations Board* to administer the law and protect union rights.

B. One of the things that makes a labor union strong is when there are few substitutes for union labor such as machines and/or nonunion labor. This makes the demand for union members inelastic. Which of the following do you think have strong (S) or weak (W) unions?

   1. *S* Airline pilots.
   2. *W* Elevator operators.
   3. *W* Airline flight attendants.
   4. *S* The police.
   5. *S* Professional baseball players.
   6. *W* Farm workers.

C. What can unions do to try to force businesses to give them what they want?

   1. *strikes*
   2. *boycotts*

D. What are the two primary things that unions try to obtain for their members?

   1. *higher wages*
   2. *better working conditions*

9.5. Explain what "sticky" wages are and discuss their impacts in labor markets.

A.

1. Economists say that wages are "sticky" when _they do not adjust to decreases in the demand for labor_.

2. Are wages generally sticky in an upward direction? _No (nobody resists a raise!)_

B. The graph below shows the labor market for assembly-line workers.

1. Indicate the equilibrium wage (W₁) and employment (E₁) level.

2. Show what happens if firms begin to replace some workers with robots and **wages are flexible**. Indicate the new equilibrium wage (W_f) and employment (E_f) level.

3. Show what happens if firms begin to replace some workers with robots but **wages are sticky**. Indicate the new equilibrium wage (W_s) and employment (E_s) level.

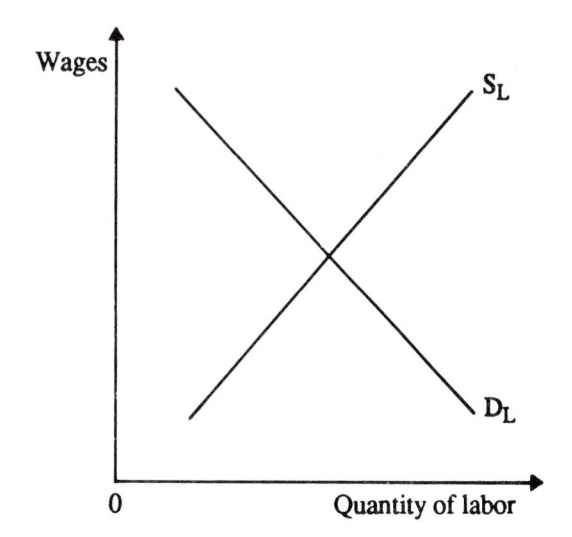

C. What are two things that may cause wages to be sticky?

1. _minimum wage laws_
2. _unions_

D. If you were an assembly-line worker, would you prefer it if wages were sticky or if wages adjusted to market demand and supply?

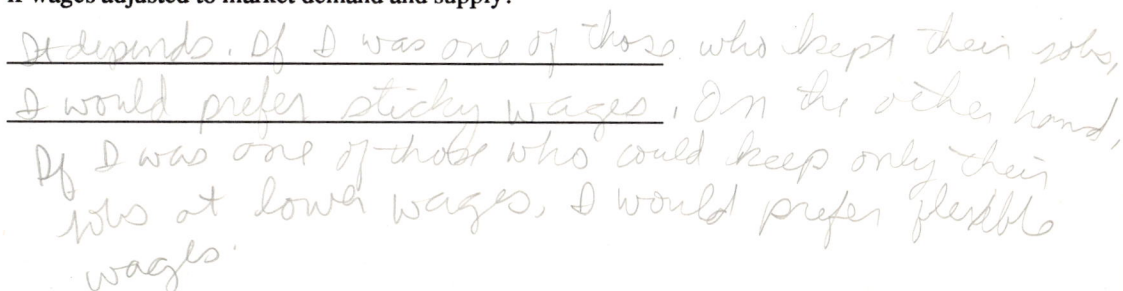

It depends. If I was one of those who kept their jobs, I would prefer sticky wages. On the other hand, if I was one of those who could keep only their jobs at lower wages, I would prefer flexible wages.

Case Application: Coal and Black Gold

During the 1920s, 1930s, and 1940s, the United Mine Workers of America successfully organized the miners in both the soft and hard coal industries. Their president, John L. Lewis, became famous throughout the country for his leadership—not only for his success in the coal fields, but also for providing union money and expertise for organizing the steel, automobile, electrical, and machinery industries.

Lewis supported Franklin Roosevelt's policies of promoting the spread of labor unions through laws requiring employers to bargain with those representatives elected by workers in plants and industries. Perhaps oversimplifying Roosevelt's aims, union organizers went about telling workers, "The President wants you to join the union!"

Following the complete organization of mine workers in 1941, wages for miners rose dramatically, working conditions improved, and a substantial pension plan was negotiated. At the same time, both consumers and industries were shifting away from the use of coal to the use of "black gold"—oil. Consumers found that oil was almost as cheap as coal for home heating, was a cleaner fuel, and was easier to use. Railroads switched from coal-burning steam locomotives to oil-burning diesel engines. Utilities began to favor oil and natural gas to fire the steam boilers that generated electricity.

Employment in the coal mines was cut drastically, and critics of John L. Lewis said he did not seem to care whether or not jobs were lost. He replied by declaring he would rather have smaller numbers of miners work for decent wages than have a larger number work for wages inadequate to feed, clothe, and shelter their families.

Economic Reasoning *(Write your responses on a separate sheet. Answers begin on p. 299.)*

1. In terms of the principle of derived demand, how do you explain the loss of jobs in coal mines after 1941?
2. What was the relationship between the efforts of John L. Lewis to raise the wages of coal miners and the increase in surface strip mining, using giant shovels to scoop out the coal deposits?
3. Do you agree with the attitude of John L. Lewis concerning employment in coal mining? Why or why not?

What Determines Other Incomes?

FUNCTIONAL INCOME DISTRIBUTION

The types of income according to their economic function are:

Wages and salaries (73.7% in 1989)	Rents (0.2% in 1989)	Interest (10.8% in 1989)	Profits (7% in 1989)
Implicit wages — A part of proprietors' income that is actually compensation to the owners for the time that they put into the business should also be included in wages and salaries.	Some other income behaves like rent when there is a fixed supply of the factor. In those cases the price is determined entirely by the demand level.	**Implicit interest** — A part of proprietors' income that is actually a return on the owners' invested capital.	The 7% figure includes corporate profits only. To this should be added a portion of proprietors' income.

Proprietors' income (8.3% in 1989)
The remainder of profits after subtracting the implicit interest and implicit rent are the rewards to entrepreneurs.

(See page vi in the foreword "To the Student" for how to make the best use of this schematic outline.)

9.6. Describe the different income sources that make up the functional distribution of income.

A. List the four types of income that make the functional distribution of income.
1. _wages & salaries_
2. _profits_
3. _interest_
4. _rent_

B. The largest share of income comes from which source?
wages & salaries

C. The smallest share of income comes from which source?
rent

D. Match the following terms with the appropriate description.

a. implicit wages.
b. implicit interest.
c. rent.
d. profit.
e. interest.
f. wages and salaries.

1. _f_ The only type of income earned by most families.
2. _a_ A large part of an entrepreneur's "profit" is actually this.
3. _c_ A large part of Michael Jordan's wages are actually this.
4. _d_ Payment for entrepreneurial risk-taking.
5. _e_ Payments for the use of borrowed funds.
6. _b_ The cost of using your own savings to start a business.

9.7. Identify the unique characteristics of the determination of rent compared to the determination of other sources of income.

A. Indicate with a check which of the following are "rents."
1. _✓_ Michael Jordan's salary.
2. ____ The price of a piece of capital equipment.
3. _✓_ Billy Joel's concert revenues.
4. _✓_ The price of a piece of downtown land.
5. ____ Household income when there is only one wage earner.
6. _✓_ The price of tomatoes immediately after the harvest.

B.
1. What is unique about the determination of rent in terms of demand and supply?
The supply curve is vertical

2. Is the difference between rent and other sources of income more apparent in the short or long run? Why?
long run. pg. 300

C. In the space below, draw a supply curve for a product that earns rent (S_r) and a typical upward-sloping supply curve (S_t). Now draw two demand curves that represent the original demand (D_1) and an increase in demand (D_2).

[Graph with Price on vertical axis and Quantity on horizontal axis; handwritten note "Pg. 300"]

D. Using the graph that you just drew, which price went up more—the price of the good that earns rent (good R) or the price of the typical good (good T)? Why?

The price of good R is increased more because there was no offsetting increase in the quantity supplied to keep the price lower

Case Application: How Much Is a Nose Guard Worth?

As any pro football fan is aware, a nose guard is not a protection device for the nasal extremity, but a football player in the center of the defensive line who protects against trap plays up the middle, among other things. Nose guards are generally anonymous fellows who do not get the cheers and publicity accorded to running backs, wide receivers, cornerbacks, or even defensive ends. As a result of the lack of star status, their salaries are much lower than those of their more renowned teammates. But a good nose guard is as essential to a team's success as players who are always in the limelight.

Although the average salary of players in the National Football League trails the salaries of National Basketball Association players and major league baseball players, it is approaching half a million dollars. (The average is inflated, however, by the multimillion dollar contracts signed by star quarterbacks and Heisman Trophy winners.) Like baseball fans, those football fans who attend the games complain that the inflated players' salaries cause the owners to raise ticket prices, which are already in the $30 range. The players' representatives claim that they oppose raising ticket prices but are unable to convince the fans that increased salaries are not the cause of hikes in ticket prices. If they understood the concept of economic rent, the players' representatives might be successful in placating the fans' concerns. They could explain why the fans do not have to pay higher ticket prices simply because the players receive larger salaries.

The popularity of professional football enables the National Football League owners to fill their stadiums every game and collect billions for the television rights, which are split evenly among the teams. As monopolists, the owners charge the fans and the TV networks prices that maximize their revenues. If they could charge more and get more revenue, they would presumably do so—no matter what they were paying the players. The difference between their costs, including a normal rate of return on their investment, and what they receive in revenue is their economic profits. The level of players' salaries determines how the monopoly profits are divided between owners and players, not how high the ticket prices will be.

Economic Reasoning (Write your responses on a separate sheet. Answers begin on p. 300.)

1. The supply of National Football League games is best represented by which of the supply curves in Figure 8 on page 241 of the textbook?
2. Why is the salary earned by Jim Kelly, star quarterback of the Buffalo Bills, more like a rent payment than a wage payment?
3. One of the contract demands of the Players' Association was the institution of a wage scale that would more nearly equalize the incomes of players at different positions. Was this demand justified? Why or why not?

What Causes Unequal Distribution of Income?

PERSONAL INCOME DISTRIBUTION

The proportion of total income received by different income groups represents personal income distribution.

Lorenz curve

A common way of describing how income is distributed is with the use of the Lorenz curve. Income has been becoming more unequally distributed since 1970.

Differences in productivity

Factors affecting the worker productivity are:
- Education
- Training
- Ability
- Amount of capital equipment per worker

Differences in opportunity

Incomes are affected by lack of educational and job opportunities.

Civil Rights Act of 1964

The act prohibits employers from discriminating in the hiring, firing, promotion, assignment to a job, compensation, or worker training. The EEOC (Equal Employment Opportunity Commission) enforces the provisions of the act.

Differences in asset ownership

The greatest differences in income are the result of differences in the amounts of assets owned by different groups in the population.

Capital gains

is the largest source of income for those with incomes of more than $1 million per year. Their second largest source of income is dividends.

(See page vi in the foreword "To the Student" for how to make the best use of this schematic outline.)

128 / Working With The Study of Economics, 4/E

9.8. Describe how the personal distribution of income is measured, how it has changed over time, and how the distribution is shown on a Lorenz curve.

A. What is the difference between the functional and personal distributions of income?

The functional distribution shows where incomes come from, the personal distribution shows who gets how much of it.

B. Suppose an economy consists of only 15 households with the following household incomes:

Highest Fifth	Fourth Fifth	Third Fifth	Second Fifth	Lowest Fifth
$150,000	80,000	40,000	20,000	15,000
140,000	70,000	30,000	20,000	15,000
110,000	50,000	30,000	20,000	10,000

Total: *400,000 200,000 100,00 60,000 40,000*

Percentage: *50% 25% 12.5% 7.5% 5%*

1. Add up the total income for each "fifth" of the population.
2. Calculate the percentage of total income that goes to each of the fifths.
3. Use the space below to draw a Lorenz curve for the above economy.

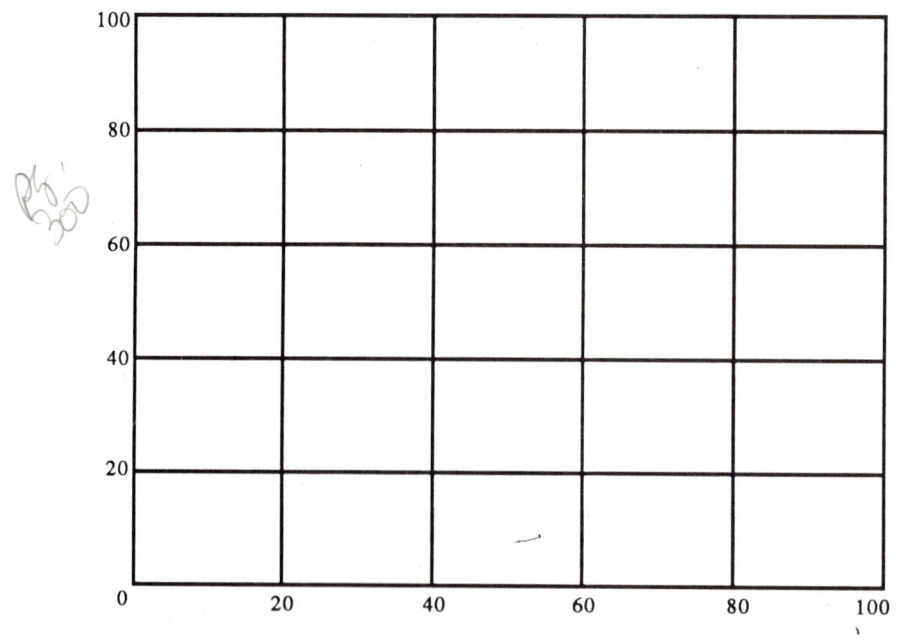

C. Indicate whether each of the following groups increased (I) or decreased (D) their relative share of the nation's income between the years 1970 and 1987 (see Table 2 of the text, p. 246).

1. _D_ Lowest fifth.
2. _D_ Second fifth.
3. _D_ Third fifth.

4. _1_ Fourth fifth.
5. _1_ Highest fifth.

D.
1. A straight-line Lorenz curve indicates _an equal distribution of income_.
2. The more "bowed" the Lorenz curve is, _the less equal is the distribution of income_.

9.9. Describe the causes of unequal distribution of personal income.

A. Three things that contribute to an unequal distribution of income are differences in:
1. _ability_.
2. _opportunity_.
3. _asset ownership_.

B. Use the numbers of your above answers to indicate which is reflected in each of the following:
1. _2_ Ms. Jones earns less than Mr. Smith although their jobs and productivity are the same.
2. _1_ Ms. Schwartz is a skilled tool and die maker.
3. _1_ Darryl Strawberry earns $4 million a year playing baseball for the Los Angeles Dodgers.
4. _2_ The majority of high-paid doctors are men and the majority of low-paid nurses are women.
5. _3_ Ms. Merril earns more from her rental properties and stocks than she does from her law practice.
6. _3_ The Queen of England has a high income although she is not paid a salary for her work.

C. How do the rich and the super-rich in America make most of their money? _by the sale of assets that they own & sell_

D. Indicate three minority groups that have suffered from discrimination in job opportunities in America.
1. _women_
2. _blacks_
3. _hispanics_

Case Application: The New Poor

This country is witnessing the emergence of a new class of poor people. These are families in which the head of the household previously held a well-paying job—former manufacturing, construction, and service industry workers—but lost his or her job because of shrinking markets.

When their unemployment compensation expires and their savings are depleted, many of these people can no longer meet their mortgage or rent payments and have to move out of their homes. Many take to the road, traveling from state to state in search of work. Some families resort to living in tents in national, state, or county parks because it is all they can afford. In many cases, even when they find work, it is only temporary, and they are soon laid off and back on the road again. They are ineligible for welfare, unemployment insurance, and food stamps because they have no permanent address. Also, they are ineligible to vote.

Those who remain in the cities looking for jobs sometimes show up in the soup kitchens of charitable organizations. Previously, those partaking of the free meals had been, for the most part, society's outcasts, the down-and-out denizens of the cities' skid rows. But recently the free food lines include families who previously have been self-sufficient.

Even when economic conditions are stable, there is a constant flow of people into and out of poverty. Studies by James Morgan at the University of Michigan show that only a small minority of those living in poverty remain poor permanently. The majority move in and out of poverty status depending upon changing personal circumstances. According to Professor Morgan, those who do continue to live in poverty are the uneducated, disabled, or very old. These people constituted the hard core of the "old poor." Now they have been joined by the "new poor."

Economic Reasoning (Write your responses on a separate sheet. Answers begin on p. 301.)

1. What are the differences in the causes of poverty between the "old poor" and the "new poor"?
2. Which group is likely to move out of poverty first when economic conditions improve, the "old poor" or the "new poor"? Why?
3. Should private welfare agencies divert part of their resources away from aiding the "old poor" in order to provide assistance to the "new poor"? Why or why not?

What Is the Answer to Poverty?

THE POVERTY LINE

The official designation of who is considered poor in the United States is defined by the poverty line. Initially established in 1964, the poverty line is adjusted each year for changes in the cost of living.

INCREASED OPPORTUNITY	TRANSFER PAYMENTS
One way to achieve more equitable income distribution is to remove obstacles to economic opportunity caused by racial, sexual, or age discrimination. Affirmative action programs are aimed at increasing educational, training, and employment opportunities for minorities and women.	• Money transfers — welfare, Social Security benefits, unemployment income. • Food stamps — food subsidies for low-income households. • Aid to Families With Dependent Children — an entitlement program for families below the poverty line with women heads of household. • Medicaid — federally financed health care for low-income families. • Housing — housing subsidies and public housing.
Workfare Originally established as a requirement for welfare payment recipients to work for government or other non-profit agencies in order to receive transfer payments. In many states it now covers a comprehensive program to move welfare recipients into employment by education, training, work experience, and job placement.	**Negative income tax** A proposal to change the federal income tax laws to provide a tax subsidy to those below the poverty level that is progressive the lower their income. The earned income tax credit (EITC) is a type of negative income tax for the working poor.

(See page vi in the foreword "To the Student" for how to make the best use of this schematic outline.)

9.10. Explain how poverty is defined and describe the programs for reducing poverty.

A. The poverty line (the official definition of poverty) is based on the cost of _food_.

B.
1. Suppose that it costs $4,000 a year to feed a family of four people. Based on food costing 1/3 of a household's budget, what is the "poverty line"?

   $12,000

2. What would be the poverty line if food comprised 1/5 of a household budget?

   $20,000

3. Will the number of people under the poverty line be greater if the correct share is 1/3 or 1/5? _1/5_

4. Which of the two shares, 1/3 or 1/5, is a more accurate measure of food costs in the United States today? _1/5_

5. Which of the two shares, 1/3 or 1/5, is used in calculating the poverty line? _1/3_

6. What can you conclude about the reported versus the actual number of poor people in the United States today?

   the reported numbers understate the true number of people in poverty.

C. What are three examples of transfer payments?
1. AFDC
2. medicaid
3. Food Stamps

D.
1. What types of programs provide the best **long-run** solutions to reducing poverty?

   education and equal opportunities

2. What type of programs provide the best **short-run** solutions to reducing poverty?

   transfer payments

E. What is a "negative income tax," and what is one important advantage of such a plan that is missing from other transfer programs?

   a plan that gives households money when their own income is below a certain guaranteed level instead of taking taxes from the household. The main advantage is it doesn't provide disincentives to work.

Case Application: **Increased Opportunities for the Handicapped**

Since 1973 federal law has forbidden employers who are receiving funds or contracts from the federal government to deny jobs to people with handicaps. Most states now have laws prohibiting discrimination against the handicapped by companies not covered under the federal law. These laws have opened job opportunities to the handicapped—one of the minorities most discriminated against in the past. As a result, overt discrimination by employers has been substantially reduced, and handicapped people who had been excluded from the labor force and forced to live in poverty are now leading productive lives.

However, discrimination still persists, especially toward the "hidden handicapped." The hidden handicapped are those who do not have obvious disabilities such as blindness or crippled limbs and include those with epilepsy, cancer, AIDS, and other hidden health problems. Even though their problems may be under control or in remission, when their health histories are revealed to employers or prospective employers they are not given the same consideration for jobs as other applicants. Employers view them as potential problems either on the job or in costs to the firm's medical coverage program.

Employers who do hire the handicapped often find that such workers are not only productive but also stick with the job longer than other workers. Affirmative action programs to hire the handicapped have usually proved rewarding to the firm as well as to the handicapped workers themselves. Society also benefits from a reduction in the ranks of the poor and the consequent lessening of transfer payments and other costs.

Economic Reasoning *(Write your responses on a separate sheet. Answers begin on p. 301.)*

1. How has the number of handicapped poor been reduced since 1973?
2. Why are affirmative action programs to employ the handicapped needed?
3. Should the government subsidize firms to hire the handicapped? Why or why not?

IV. Practice Test *(Answers begin on p. 301.)*

Multiple Choice *(Circle the correct answer.)*

(9.1) 1. Which of the following is the reason that the demand for labor is referred to as a "derived demand"?
   a. It is derived from the existing technology.
   b. It is derived from the size of the labor force.
   c. It is derived from the amount of capital available.
   d. It is derived from the consumer demand for different goods and services.

(9.1) 2. Which of the following is a determinant of the supply of labor?
   a. the amount of available capital.
   b. the age distribution of the population.
   c. the demand for finished goods and services.
   d. the demand for labor.

(9.2) 3. The amount of capital available can affect wages in which of the following ways?
   a. It can reduce the demand for workers.
   b. It can increase labor productivity.
   c. It can increase the demand for workers.
   d. Any of the above could happen.

(9.3) 4. Which of the following is a TRUE statement?
   a. Minimum wage laws can encourage employers to use more labor and less capital.
   b. Minimum wage laws result in a shortage of workers at the set wage.
   c. Minimum wage laws can result in increased use of capital and less demand for labor.

d. Minimum wage laws are always equal to the equilibrium wage.

(9.4) 5. What are union negotiations with employers called?
    a. collective bargaining.
    b. strike settlements.
    c. boycott discussions.
    d. right-to-work laws.

(9.4) 6. Which of the following is a TRUE statement about the National Labor Relations Act?
    a. The act gives employers the right to use immigrant labor under certain conditions.
    b. The act gives unions the right to negotiate using collective bargaining.
    c. The act forbids discrimination in hiring practices.
    d. The act requires equal pay for equal work.

(9.5) 7. Which of the following will result from a decrease in the demand for labor if wages are "sticky"?
    a. The new equilibrium wage will be higher than before.
    b. There will be fewer workers hired than if wages were flexible.
    c. Employers will have less incentive to substitute capital for labor.
    d. Fewer immigrants will be hired in jobs that native workers want.

(9.5) 8. Wages are referred to as being "sticky" when:
    a. different workers receive different wages for the same work.
    b. they are below the equilibrium wage.
    c. they do not adjust fully to changes in demand and supply.
    d. they are set by the government or unions instead of being set by the market.

(9.6) 9. Which of the following represents the largest portion of the functional distribution of income?
    a. wages and salaries.
    b. profits.
    c. rent.
    d. interest.

(9.6) 10. Which of the following is usually **incorrectly** classified as profit in the functional distribution of income?
    a. corporate earnings.
    b. rents.
    c. profits reported by proprietorships.
    d. profits in excess of the "normal rate of return."

(9.7) 11. Similar to the determination of incomes from other sources, the amount of rent is determined by the interactions of demand and supply. However, unlike other markets, in the rent market:
    a. the demand curve is horizontal.
    b. the demand curve is vertical.
    c. the supply curve is horizontal.
    d. the supply curve is vertical.

(9.8) 12. Which of the following is the most accurate description of what happened to the personal distribution of income during the 1980s?
    a. The rich got richer and the poor got poorer.
    b. The poorer segments of the country increased their relative share of the nation's wealth.
    c. Both the rich and the poor did better at the expense of the middle class.
    d. The middle class did much better while the poorer and richer segments of the economy both did worse.

(9.8) 13. The changes in the personal distribution of income during the 1980s caused the Lorenz curve to:

a. become steeper.
b. become flatter.
c. become more curved.
d. move farther to the left.

(9.9) 14. Which of the following has the greatest impact on differences in household income?
a. differences in productivity.
b. differences in asset ownership.
c. differences in opportunities.
d. differences in location.

(9.10) 15. About what percentage of the U.S. population is classified as being "poor" *after* transfer payments are accounted for?
a. 6%.
b. 12%.
c. 18%.
d. 24%.

True/False *(Circle T or F.)*

(9.2) 16. Workers resent the introduction of new capital equipment because it results in lower wages. T or F

(9.3) 17. Minimum wage laws can increase employers' incentives to replace workers with machines. T or F

(9.5) 18. Sticky wages can result from union demands or minimum wage laws. T or F

(9.7) 19. The huge amounts of money paid to movie stars are a form of rent. T or F

(9.10) 20. Children are the poorest segment of American society today. T or F

9 Labor and Income Distribution / 135

Microeconomics Crossword Puzzle
(Chapters 5–9)

Across

5. Earnings from asset ownership.
6. Consumer _____, influenced by advertising, determines what is produced.
7. The smallest share of income receipts in the United States.
12. Purchasing goods because they are expensively chic is this "effect."
14. American companies were pioneers in this development in the 1970s.
15. The use of computer-controlled equipment to enhance production.
17. Holding companies established in the nineteenth-century to develop the then-feudal Japanese economy.
18. A movement to turn those natural monopolies that are not obviously "natural" over to the private sector.
20. A(n) _____ is opposed to employee-involvement programs.

Down

1. OPEC is an example.
2. In coming years, the shortage of this in Japan will likely cause their industries to become more capital-intensive.
3. These production costs do not change with the change in the quantity of goods or services.
4. They enable two or more people to pool their capital and/or talents to make a business successful.
8. These types of goods enrich our entire culture, not just individuals.
9. Enables consumers to obtain a greater utility from their income.
10. If demand for an item is this, the quantity demanded will decrease a great deal with a small increase in its price.
11. To protect the consumer, this government organization requires proper seat belts and secure gas tanks on automobiles.
13. Law that stated employers cannot "interfere with, restrain, or coerce employees."
16. The monetary value of a property less the amount of outstanding mortgages.
19. This organization tries to keep track of U.S. immigrants, legal or otherwise.

Chapter 10
Money

I. Chapter Outline

Although all of us are interested in money, most of us do not understand just exactly what money is, what it does, or where it comes from. Money is a very curious commodity. Coins, bills, and checks have little value in and of themselves. What can you do with a rectangular piece of paper or a small metal disc? The only value money has is that people are willing to accept it in exchange for the things that they really want—goods and services.

Introductory Article: That Curious Commodity

As long as you can carry it, people will accept it, and other people cannot easily reproduce (forge) it, anything can function as "money." Although everything from cows to tobacco has been used as money, most countries today use paper money. The use of paper money was introduced in the 1700s. Prior to 1913, private banks in the United States were allowed to issue their own paper money. With the formation of the Federal Reserve System in that year, the United States for the first time had a standardized type of paper money.

Economic Analysis

This chapter explores what money is and where it comes from by examining the following questions:

1. What Is Money?

   Important Concepts: Currency, Demand deposits, Near money, Money supply, M1, M2, M3, L

   Case Application: Dealing the Cards

2. What Does Money Do?

   Important Concepts: Medium of exchange, Unit of measurement, Store of value

   Case Application: P.O.W. Money

3. How Is Money Created?

   Important Concepts: Promissory notes, Government bonds

   Case Application: How to Create Money

4. How Is the Supply of Money Controlled?

   Important Concepts: The Federal Reserve System, Required reserves, Excess reserves, Discounting, Money multiplier, Open market operations

   Case Application: Cheap Money

Perspective: The Big Bank Controversy

II. Summary of Economic Analysis

1. In the United States, money consists primarily of **currency** in circulation (one-third of all money) and **demand deposits** in banks (two-thirds of all money).
2. Currency is produced by the federal government and is distributed through the economy by the banking system to satisfy the needs of businesses and households.
3. Demand deposits are checking accounts in banks and other financial institutions. Changes in the money supply result primarily from changes in the amount of demand deposits.
4. The usual measure of the money supply is **M1**, the total of coins and currency in circulation, demand deposits, and travelers' checks.
5. **Near money** consists of financial assets that are less **liquid** than money. These include **savings deposits, certificates of deposit,** and **shares in money market funds.**
6. In addition to M1, other measures of the money supply, such as **M2, M3,** and **L**, can be defined by adding different kinds of near monies to M1.
7. Money serves three basic functions: it serves as a **medium of exchange**, a **unit of measurement**, and a **store of value**.
8. Money is created and the money supply increases when individuals, businesses, and governments borrow money. The money supply decreases (or fails to increase) when loans are repaid and/or no new loans are being made.
9. Banks must hold a required percentage of their deposits as **required reserves.** Any deposits in excess of the required reserves are **excess reserves**. Excess reserves represent the amount of funds that banks have to lend.
10. The money supply in the United States is controlled by our central bank, called the **Federal Reserve System**, or simply the **"Fed."** The Fed controls the money supply by controlling the excess reserves available to banks.
11. The tools that the Fed uses to control the money supply include changing the level of required reserves, changing the **discount rate**, and **open market operations.**
12. When the ratio of required reserves to total deposits increases, banks will have less excess reserves to loan and the money supply will be unable to increase. When the ratio decreases, banks will have more money to loan and the money supply will increase.
13. The discount rate is the interest rate that regular banks are charged when they borrow money from the Fed. Lower rates result in more money being borrowed by banks and re-lent to businesses and individuals. This increases the money supply.
14. Open market operations refer to the Fed buying and selling existing government bonds from banks and individuals. When the Fed buys bonds it takes bonds out of the economy and replaces them with new reserves that can be loaned. When the Fed sells bonds, it takes potentially loanable funds out of the economy and replaces them with nonloanable bonds.
15. The price of money is the **interest rate**. The quoted interest rate, the one that people and businesses earn and pay, is called the **nominal interest rate** because it includes an inflation premium. The interest rate that is adjusted for inflation is called the **real interest rate.**

138 / Working With The Study of Economics, 4/E

III. Review of the Learning Objectives (Answers begin on p. 301.)

What Is Money?

MONEY

Currency
Currency is that part of the money supply that consists of coins and bills. Currency constitutes about one-fourth of the money supply. The amount of currency in circulation depends on the demands by individuals and businesses for holding their financial assets in the form of currency.

Demand Deposits
Demand deposits are liabilities of depository institutions that are payable on demand, such as checking accounts. Deposits payable on demand constitute nearly three-fourths of the money supply.

M1
The most commonly used measurement of the money supply includes currency, travelers' checks, demand deposits, and other checkable deposits such as negotiable order of withdrawal (NOW) accounts.

NEAR MONEY
Near money is a type of financial asset which can, more or less, easily be turned into money. This includes savings deposits, certificates of deposit (CDs), and shares in money market mutual funds.

(See page vi in the foreword "To the Student" for how to make the best use of this schematic outline.)

10.1. Discuss the history of money. *(Write in answers below.)*

A. Other than coins or currency, what are three things that have served as money in different societies?

1. _sea shell_
2. _cows_
3. _cigarettes_

B. Paper money was first introduced in the _17_ century by _goldsmith_ [what profession?].

C.
  1. Which early American leader wanted a strong national bank?
     Alexander Hamilton

  2. Which early American leader did not want a strong national bank?
     Thomas Jefferson

D. During the 1800s in the United States, what institutions were allowed to issue paper money?

10 Money / 139

E. In 1913, what U.S. institution was granted the sole right to issue paper money? *Any privately owned bank that was chartered by state or federal government.*

The Federal Reserve System (banks)

10.2. Define the M1 money supply and describe its components.

A. List the components of the M1 money supply.
1. *Currency (including coins)*
2. *checkable deposits*
3. *traveler's checks*
4. *ATS accounts*

B. The largest component of the M1 money supply is *checkable deposits*.

C. Why do U.S. dollar bills have value? *because people are willing to accept them as payment for goods or services*

D. Currency held by *banks* and/or the *government* is NOT considered part of the money supply.

10.3. Explain how near money differs from money and discuss how near money relates to the broader money definitions of M2, M3, and L.

A. Assets that can be converted from near money to money more easily than other assets are more *liquid*.

B. Rank the following from most liquid (1) to least liquid (5).
1. *5* A house.
2. *2* A savings account.
3. *4* An automobile.
4. *1* A checking account.
5. *3* 100 shares of AT&T.

C. What are three financial assets included in "L" but not in M1?
1. *commercial paper*
2. *saving bonds*
3. *short term government bonds*

D. Indicate which measure(s) of the money supply (M1, M2, M3, L) include each of the following.
1. *M1 M2 M3 L* Travelers' checks.
2. *M2 M3 L* ___ Your passbook savings account.
3. *M1 M2 M3 L* A checking account.

4. _L_ ___ ___ ___ Short-term government bonds.
5. _M3_ _L_ ___ ___ Large certificates of deposit (CDs).
6. _M1_ _M2_ _M3_ _L_ Coins and currency.
7. _M2_ _M3_ _L_ ___ Money market funds.

Case Application: What Isn't Money?

It is getting more difficult all the time to tell what money is—although this may not seem to be a problem to you. If you have $500, you can keep it in currency under your mattress, deposit it in a NOW account in a savings and loan association, or put it in a money market fund. It's all money to you. But it is not all money to the nation's monetary authorities. Currency and checkable accounts in depository institutions are considered money, but not money market funds.

The first money market fund was started in 1972. By 1988 the money market funds had grown to $338 billion. Most of the money was taken out of banks, especially savings and loan associations. Money market fund shareholders earned as high as 16% or 17% on their savings in the early 1980s, as compared to the maximum 5.5% which the government allowed the S&Ls to pay on checkable deposits. Checks can be written on the money market funds, although there is usually a minimum amount per check of $300 to $500. One drawback to the money market funds is that, unlike deposits in banks and S&Ls, the customer's money is not insured by the federal government. However, the assets of money market funds are invested in government and other blue-chip securities with short maturity periods of one month or up to one year. The risk can be minimized by investing in a money market fund holding only federal government securities.

Because people treat their money market fund accounts as disposable money, it can be arbitrary and misleading not to include those funds as part of the money supply.

The money supply situation became even more cloudy when the Depository Institutions Act of 1982 permitted banks to establish money market funds of their own. Under one new plan, a specified amount of a customer's deposits is kept in a checking account which pays the government-regulated interest rate. Amounts deposited over and above that minimum are automatically "swept" into a money market account paying the market interest rate. This type of account has blurred significantly the line between what is part of the money supply and what is near money.

It is not only increasingly difficult to tell what money is, it is even hard to tell what a bank is. Other financial institutions such as brokerage firms and insurance companies are taking on banking functions. For their part, the banks are moving into new areas of business. Financial institutions once limited to specified activities are now expanding into "supermarkets" of financial services. Deregulation of the industry is creating new opportunities and types of competition, but this change is accompanied by flux and uncertainty in the management of the nation's money supply.

Economic Reasoning *(Write your responses on a separate sheet. Answers begin on p. 302.)*

1. The expansion of money market funds represented an increase in what type of money?
2. Why are money market funds more like money than are certificates of deposit?
3. Is the deregulation of financial institutions a good idea? Why or why not?

What Does Money Do?

MEDIUM OF EXCHANGE	UNIT OF MEASUREMENT	STORE OF VALUE
Money is used in the role of an intermediary in the exchange of goods and services, in place of direct barter, because it simplifies making transactions.	The money unit serves as a common denominator in which the value of other things can be measured.	Money serves as a liquid form in which wealth can be held.
Attributes of a good medium of exchange: * Universally recognized * Adequate but limited supply * Not easily reproduced * Easily portable * Durable	**Attribute of a good unit of measurement:** * Should itself be stable in value	**Attribute of a good store of value:** * Should be liquid – readily convertible without loss of value

(See page vi in the foreword "To the Student" for how to make the best use of this schematic outline.)

10.4. List the three functions of money and explain the characteristics money must have in order to be functional.

A. List the three **functions** of money.

1. _medium of exchange_
2. _unit of measurement_
3. _store of value_

B. Using the numbering in the above list, indicate which function is being described in each of the following:

1. _3_ You hide your money under your mattress.
2. _2_ You estimate how much you should charge to do a job based on what you can buy with your earnings.
3. _1_ You pay $1.95 for a burger.
4. _1_ You pay tuition.
5. _2_ World oil prices are quoted in dollars.
6. _2_ Prices influence how much a producer will produce.

C. Why are credit cards not considered "money"? What necessary characteristic(s) do they lack?

Credit cards do not serve as a "store of value" or a unit of measurement. Also they are not money, they are I.O.U.'s / borrowing money.

D. List the five characteristics that money must have in order to be a good medium of exchange.

1. _universally recognized_

2. _not easily reproduced_
3. _portable_
4. _durable_
5. _adequate but limited supply_

E. Using the numbering from the above list, indicate which characteristic would be **missing** if each of the following were to be used as money (there may be more than one):

1. _5_ Flawless diamonds.
2. _4_ Dead fish.
3. _3+4_ Cows.
4. _5_ Pebbles.
5. _2_ Notebook paper.
6. _1_ Your IOUs.

Case Application: Primitive Money

Debate over the nature of primitive money has recently surfaced in anthropological circles. Are the foodstuffs, cattle, brass rods, bits of porcelain, and cowrie shells used in various primitive cultures really money? The Tiv in Nigeria, for example, have three separate classes of transactions. Foodstuffs are used to exchange within one class; cattle and brass rods are used in the second. Before slaves were freed, their price was quoted in cows and brass rods. The third class is limited to marriage arrangements and involves the "payment" of cattle. Services and labor, on the other hand, are acts of generosity, and to offer payments for them would be insulting.

Some anthropologists argue that the shells, cattle, and brass rods have a particular social value and a limited purpose. These goods do not serve as a medium of exchange except in special instances; often in the case of bride-price. Only special people may use the cattle or shells. These items act more as the concrete sign of a contract than as a medium of exchange. A person's concept of money is closely related to the society in which he or she lives. It can be misleading to assume that what we call money always has the same functions in different cultures.

One anthropological view maintains that the shell money of the Russell Island inhabitants was used in basically the same way as, say, U.S. money. Perhaps the most telling point against this stand is that there is little or no conversion of denominations of one class of shells into another class. Some classes of shells are obviously special-purpose money.

Economic Reasoning (Write your responses on a separate sheet. Answers begin on p. 302.)

1. When the price of slaves was quoted in cows and brass rods in Nigeria, which function of money were they performing?
2. Why should the lack of conversion of denominations of one class of shells into another class among the Russell Islanders indicate the shells do not serve the same function as money does in the United States?
3. Are there ways in which money in our society performs social functions as well as economic functions? For example?

How Is Money Created?

CURRENCY	PRIVATE BORROWING	GOVERNMENT BORROWING
The government prints paper money and mints coins in the amounts required by the public. The currency is disbursed to businesses and households through the banking system.	Borrowing from a bank results in increasing the money supply by increasing the amount of demand deposits. Repayment of a loan decreases the money supply.	When a local, a state, or the federal government sells bonds or Treasury bills acquired by banks, new demand deposits are created that increase the money supply just as in the case of private borrowing.

(See page vi in the foreword "To the Student" for how to make the best use of this schematic outline.)

10.5. Discuss how currency is affected by public demand and explain money creation.

A. Which of the following would result in an increase (I) in the demand for currency, and which would result in a decrease (D) in the demand for currency?

1. _I_ An increase in the use of automatic tellers (bank "cash machines") in shopping malls.
2. _D_ A very large increase in the interest rate paid on certificates of deposit.
3. _D_ A decrease in incomes.
4. _I_ The approach of the holidays.
5. _I_ Individuals trying to avoid paying income taxes.
6. _D_ A decrease in illegal activity.

B. When an individual, a business, or the government borrows money from a bank, the loan is usually in the form of which component of the money supply?
a checking account

C.
1. Have you ever received a student loan, a car loan, or any kind of loan from a bank? _no_
2. If so, how much of the loan did you actually see in "cold, hard cash"? _usually none_

D. When the money supply is increased (when money is created), it is usually done by increasing which component of the money supply?
checking accounts

E.
1. When someone gets a bank loan, does the amount of money that the borrower has change? How?
Yes, they usually have an increased balance in their checking accounts

2. When someone gets a bank loan, does anybody else **outside the banking system** have less money?

   no

3. What happens to the amount of money in an economy if someone gets a bank loan?

   It increases

Case Application: How the Government Creates Money

If the government needs money, it doesn't just crank up the printing presses and print currency. Instead, it prints bonds or Treasury bills and sells these government securities to the public, financial institutions, or other businesses. The money received from the sales of securities is deposited in the U.S. Treasury's bank accounts.

The Treasury writes checks drawing on the money from sales of securities to pay for government programs, public projects, or employees' salaries. The recipients of these checks, of course, deposit them in their own banks. The banks send them to the Federal Reserve banks in their districts. The checks are cleared by the Fed, reducing the Treasury's deposit balance and increasing the commercial bank's reserve account by like amount. Thus, the money becomes new reserves for the banking system, and these new reserves can result in a multiple expansion of the money supply.

The sale of government securities is most expansionary when they are acquired by the Fed or by other banks. When this happens, the funds used to purchase the securities are new money created by the credit expansion of the banking system. On the other hand, when the securities are sold to the public or to businesses other than banks, they may be paid for from existing demand deposits and thus would not represent an increase in the money supply.

Economic Reasoning *(Write your responses on a separate sheet. Answers begin on p. 302.)*

1. If the U.S. Treasury prints a $10,000 bond and you borrow $10,000 from your bank to purchase the bond, by how much is the money supply increased? Who is directly responsible for the expansion of the money supply, you or the government?
2. If the government paid its bills by printing currency rather than by selling government securities, would this increase the money supply more, less, or the same amount? Why?
3. The only government securities issued in the smaller denominations everyone can afford are savings bonds, which pay lower interest rates than other types of government securities. Is this fair? Why or why not?

How Is the Supply of Money Controlled?

THE FEDERAL RESERVE SYSTEM (FED)

The Fed is the central bank of the United States, a government institution which serves as a "banker's bank," provides for the monetary needs of the federal government, and controls the money supply. Control of the money supply is the Fed's most important function, which it accomplishes by the following means:

Reserve Requirements	Discounting	Open Market Operations
The Federal Reserve specifies the amount of reserves that banks must have on deposit with the Fed as a % of their deposit liabilities. The magnitude of the required reserve ratio determines the money multiplier. Thus by changing the banks' reserve requirement ratio, the Fed can permit a larger or smaller money supply.	The Fed can reduce the amount of bank lending by raising the discount rate that it charges the banks on funds they borrow from the Fed to supplement their reserves. Or the Fed can encourage bank lending and increase the money supply by reducing the discount rate that it charges the banks.	The Fed can draw funds out of bank reserves by selling government securities on the open market, thus reducing the amount of money the banks can create. Or it can encourage bank lending by buying bonds and Treasury bills on the open market, thus adding to bank reserves.

(See page vi in the foreword "To the Student" for how to make the best use of this schematic outline.)

10.6. Describe the Federal Reserve System.

A. The central bank of the United States is called the
   Federal Reserve System.

B.
   1. How many branches of the Federal Reserve are there in the United States?
      _12_
   2. Which branch of the Federal Reserve serves the area where you live?
      _____

C. What are the three functions of the "Fed"?
   1. _acts as a bankers bank_
   2. _serves the monetary needs of the federal government_
   3. _controls the money supply_

D. Some economists believe that the Fed has more economic power than any other institution in the United States. Which of the above functions do you think gives the Fed so much power?
   control of the money supply

146 / *Working With The Study of Economics, 4/E*

E.
1. How many members are there on the Board of Governors of the Federal Reserve? __7__
2. For how many years does each member of the board serve? __14__
3. Compare the terms of office for members of the Board of Governors and members of the House of Representatives, the Senate, or even the president of the United States. What advantage is there in these relative terms of office?

   pg. 303

10.7. Explain how the Federal Reserve System controls the money supply.

A. What are the three tools that the Fed can use to change the money supply?
1. changing the discount rate
2. changing the required reserve ratio
3. open market operations

B. Other than deposits by customers, what are two places from which banks can get money in order to increase reserves?
1. from the Fed through discounting
2. from other banks in the Fed Funds market

C. Indicate whether each of the following will result in an increase (I) or a decrease (D) in the money supply:
1. __I__ The Fed buys bonds from banks.
2. __D__ The Fed sells bonds to banks.
3. __D__ The discount rate is increased.
4. __D__ I buy bonds from the Fed and pay for them with a check.
5. __I__ The required reserve ratio is decreased.

D. Use the bank "balance sheet" to answer the questions that follow.

Bank Assets		Bank Liabilities	
Total Reserves	$100,000	Demand Deposits	$100,000
Loans			
Government Bonds	_____		_____
Total	$100,000		$100,000

1. If the required reserve ratio is 10%, how much must the bank put into required reserves?

   $10,000

2. How much will be left in excess reserves?

   $90,000

3. How much can the bank lend?

    $90,000

4. The money multiplier will be equal to

    10 (1 ÷ 0.1).

5. The money supply can increase by how much?

    $900,000 (10 × $90,000)

6. If the bank buys $20,000 in government bonds, how much will it have available to loan to individuals and businesses?

    $70,000

7. After the bank buys the government bonds, how much can the money supply increase?

    $700,000 (10 × $70,000)

E. Use the same balance sheet from Part A to answer the following questions, but now assume that the reserve ratio is equal to 20%.

1. How much must the bank put into required reserves?

    $20,000

2. How much will be left in excess reserves?

    $80,000

3. What is the money multiplier?

    5 (1 ÷ 0.2)

4. The money supply can be increased by how much?

    $400,000 (5 × $80,000)

5. If the bank buys $40,000 in government bonds, how much will it have available to loan to individuals and businesses?

    $40,000

6. After the bank buys the government bonds, how much can the money supply increase?

    $200,000 (5 × $40,000)

F. The interest rate (the price of money) is **inversely** related to the price of government bonds; that is, when bond prices increase the interest rate decreases, and vice versa.

1. If the Fed increases the amount of bonds it buys, what happens to the demand for bonds?

    increases

2. What happens to the money supply?

    increases

3. What happens to the price of bonds?

    increases

4. What happens to the interest rate?

    decreases

G.

1. If the Fed increases the amount of bonds that it sells to banks, what happens to the supply of bonds?

   increases

2. What happens to the money supply?

   decrease

3. What happens to the price of bonds?

   decreases

4. What happens to the interest rate?

   increases

H. The supply of money is usually considered to be **interest inelastic**. This means that the quantity supplied does not change as the price of money (the interest rate) changes.

   1. In the space provided, draw the supply curve for money (S_1) and a "typical" downward-sloping demand curve for money (D_1). Label the equilibrium interest rate R_1.

   2. Show what happens to the interest rate if the demand for money increases (D_2) while the supply of money does not change. Label the new interest rate R_2.

   3. On the same graph, show what happens if the supply of money increases (S_2). Label the new interest rate R_3.

   4. What might be one drawback of increasing the money supply in order to keep interest rates low?

      it might cause inflation

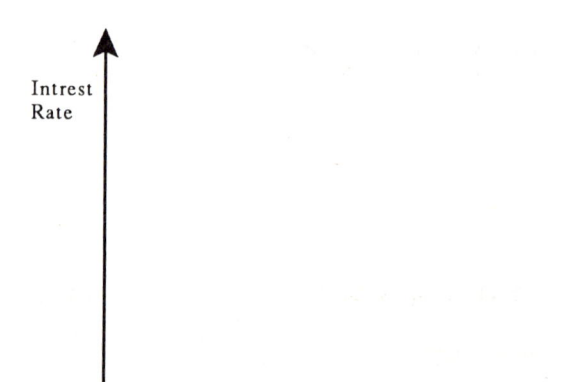

pg. 303

Case Application: Who's in Charge Around Here?

Who is in charge of the nation's banks? The Federal Reserve? The Comptroller of the Currency? The Federal Deposit Insurance Corporation? At present, authority over the 4,000-plus national banks is divided among all three.

This confusion of authority has led to proposals to delineate the spheres of control among the different agencies. A White House task force was designated to draft a plan to overhaul bank regulation. In essence, the plan would have stripped the Fed and the FDIC of their bank regulatory functions and set up a new federal banking agency under the Comptroller of the Currency. The FDIC would have confined its activities to insuring bank deposits, and the Fed's role would have been to serve as a central bank for its members and control the money supply.

The plan was torpedoed by Federal Reserve Board chairman Paul Volcker. He contended that, without its regulatory powers, "It would indeed be dangerous to look to the Federal Reserve to pick up the pieces in a financial crisis."

Economic Reasoning *(Write your responses on a separate sheet. Answers begin on p. 303.)*

1. The task force recommendation would reduce the authority of the Fed. What legislation expanded its authority in 1980?
2. What regulatory powers does the Fed need in order to implement monetary policy?
3. Should jurisdiction over the different areas of banking system control be assigned to specific agencies, or should the present system of divided authority be retained? Why?

IV. Practice Test *(Answers begin on p. 303.)*

Multiple Choice *(Circle the correct answer.)*

(10.1) 1. Paper money was first introduced by which of the following types of workers?
    a. bankers.
    b. spice and silk traders.
    c. goldsmiths.
    d. soldiers (Crusaders).

(10.1) 2. Which of the following was the subject of a debate between Thomas Jefferson and Alexander Hamilton?
    a. the use of paper money.
    b. the use of "fractional reserve" banking.
    c. the creation of a national bank.
    d. whether the states or the federal government should mint coins.

(10.2) 3. Which of the following is NOT a part of M1?
    a. currency.
    b. travelers' checks.
    c. checking accounts.
    d. savings accounts.

(10.2) 4. Which of the following is the "technical" term used to describe checking accounts?
    a. certificate accounts.
    b. demand deposits.
    c. time deposits.
    d. negotiated orders of withdrawal (NOW accounts).

(10.3) 5. Near money is _____ than money.
    a. more valuable
    b. scarcer

c. less liquid
d. less risky

(10.3) 6. Which of the following measures of the money supply includes the greatest number of different financial assets?
   a. M1.
   b. M2.
   c. M3.
   d. L.

(10.4) 7. To be "functional," money must be all of the following EXCEPT:
   a. durable.
   b. easy to reproduce.
   c. universally acceptable.
   d. portable.

(10.4) 8. Which of the following would NOT function well as money?
   a. bird scalps.
   b. cigarettes.
   c. dead fish.
   d. metal disks.

(10.5) 9. Which of the following determines the amount of currency that the Fed provides to the economy?
   a. the level of the interest rate.
   b. the level of cash transactions.
   c. the need to increase or decrease the money supply.
   d. the level of bonds in the economy.

(10.5) 10. The supply of money in an economy is usually controlled by controlling:
   a. the amount of money that is borrowed.
   b. the amount of money deposited in savings accounts.
   c. the amount of currency printed.
   d. the demand for money.

(10.6) 11. Which of the following is responsible for controlling the supply of money in the United States?
   a. Congress.
   b. the president.
   c. the Federal Reserve Bank.
   d. the Department of the Treasury.

(10.6) 12. Which of the following deal DIRECTLY with the "Fed"?
   a. individuals.
   b. businesses.
   c. banks.
   d. all of the above.

(10.7) 13. Which of the following would lead to an INCREASE in the money supply?
   a. The Fed sells government bonds.
   b. The discount rate is lowered.
   c. The required reserve ratio is increased.
   d. all of the above.

(10.7) 14. The money supply is most commonly changed by:
   a. changing the rate at which bills are printed.
   b. changing the discount rate.
   c. changing the required reserve ratio.
   d. changing the amount of government bonds bought and sold by the Fed.

(10.8) 15. Which of the following is a TRUE statement?
   a. When the Fed buys bonds, the money supply decreases and interest rates increase.

b. When the Fed buys bonds, the money supply decreases and interest rates decrease.
c.) When the Fed buys bonds, the money supply increases and interest rates decrease.
d. When the Fed buys bonds, the money supply increases and interest rates increase.

True/False *(Circle T or F.)*

(10.1) 16. Metal coins were first used in China. T or (F)

(10.2) 17. The largest measure of the money supply (L) is also the most commonly used measure of the money supply. T or (F)

(10.5) 18. The main determinant of changes in the money supply is the amount of money deposited in savings accounts. T or (F)

(10.6) 19. The United States did not establish a successful central bank until 1913. (T) or F

(10.7) 20. Increasing the required reserve ratio results in a decrease in the money supply. (T) or F

Chapter 11

Economic Instability

I. Chapter Outline

The standards by which an economy is evaluated are how well it deals with the problems of unemployment and inflation. Prior to the 1970s economists believed that the U.S. economy could suffer from one or the other, but not both at the same time. In the 1970s we found out that this unfortunately was not the case: the U.S. economy experienced both inflation and high unemployment at the same time.

Introductory Article: Fallout From the S&L Meltdown

A slowdown in one part of an economy can have negative effects on other parts of the economy. When the real estate boom in the southwest United States slowed down in the 1980s, real estate developers were unable to repay their loans to savings and loan associations. As a consequence, the S&Ls did not have enough reserves to cover their obligations to depositors. In the past, strict regulations that governed S&L lending practices would not have allowed such a situation to occur, but the spirit of deregulation that characterized the 1980s resulted in very lax supervision of S&L activity. Although a government-backed insurance fund existed in order to cover such S&L losses, the fund was soon depleted, and the federal government, through its taxpayers, will have to make up an estimated $500 billion of losses.

Economic Analysis

This chapter explores the phenomena of unemployment and inflation by examining the following questions:

1. What Causes Unemployment?

    Important Concepts: Frictional unemployment, Structural unemployment, Cyclical unemployment, Aggregate demand, Hidden unemployment

    Case Application: "Go West, Young Man, Go West"

2. What Causes Inflation?

    Important Concepts: Consumer price index, Demand-pull inflation, Cost-push inflation, Monetary inflation

    Important Model: The quantity equation

    Case Application: The High Cost of Loving

3. Is There a Trade-off Between Unemployment and Inflation?

    Important Concepts: The Phillips curve, Stagflation

    Important Model: Aggregate demand and supply

    Case Application: The Roller Coaster Ride

4. What Are the Consequences of Unemployment and Inflation?

Important Concepts: Income effects of unemployment, Real output effects of unemployment, Social effects of unemployment, Income effects of inflation, Real output effects of inflation

Case Application: Inflation—How High Is Up?

Perspective: Black Thursday and the Great Crash

II. Summary of Economic Analysis

1. The three reasons that people may be involuntarily out of work are **frictional unemployment**, **structural unemployment**, or **cyclical unemployment**.
2. Frictional unemployment results from job changes. It is not unexpected in a healthy economy, and it usually will be of short duration.
3. Structural unemployment results when skills become obsolete or there are geographic shifts in job locations.
4. Cyclical unemployment results from the inadequate **aggregate demand** for an economy's goods and services. It occurs when the economy is in a recession or a depression.
5. The reported number of unemployed persons includes only those who are unemployed and actively looking for work. This does *not* include **hidden unemployment**: those who are not counted because they are **discouraged** and have stopped looking, and those who work part-time when they desire full-time work (are **underemployed**).
6. **Inflation** is a continual rise in the general level of all prices in an economy.
7. The level of inflation is measured by price indices such as the **consumer price index**. These indices are computed by comparing the prices of goods in the same **market basket** at different points in time.
8. **Demand-pull** inflation is caused by the level of aggregate demand in product markets exceeding the productive capacity of the economy.
9. **Cost-push** inflation is caused by a rise in the prices of productive inputs (land, labor, and capital) in factor markets.
10. **Monetary inflation** occurs when the money supply increases faster than an economy's output of goods and services. The direct relationship between the money supply and the price level is shown by the **quantity equation**.
11. The **Phillips curve** shows the *inverse* relationship between the level of unemployment and the level of inflation.
12. The trade-off between unemployment and inflation shown by the Phillips curve is not constant over time. **Stagflation** occurs when the Phillips curve shifts so that *both* unemployment and inflation increase at the same time.
13. The **consequences of unemployment** include reduced household incomes, lower real output in the economy, and increased social and health problems.
14. Inflation reduces the **real income** of those whose incomes do not rise as fast as the price level. The effects of inflation on real output are unclear, but the longer the inflation lasts, the greater the negative effects on output.

III. Review of the Learning Objectives *(Answers begin on p. 303.)*

What Causes Unemployment?

FRICTIONAL UNEMPLOYMENT	STRUCTURAL UNEMPLOYMENT	CYCLICAL UNEMPLOYMENT
In a market economy there will always be people in between jobs. Those who are out of work for a short period of time while changing jobs constitute frictional unemployment in the economy. From the end of World War II to the 1970s, 3-4% frictional unemployment was considered normal.	When changes in market supply or demand conditions affect major industries or regions it can result in what is called structural unemployment. **Causes of structural unemployment:** * Decline in demand for a product * Increased foreign competition * Automation of production * Increased raw material costs * Lack of labor mobility between occupations or between regions	When aggregate demand in the economy is not sufficient to provide jobs for all those who are seeking work, cyclical unemployment results. When the economy is operating at production capacity there is full employment aggregate demand.

Hidden Unemployment
In addition to those officially counted as unemployed, there are others who have become discouraged about the possibility of finding a job and have given up looking. Consequently, they are not counted as unemployed, constituting hidden unemployment. There are other workers who are involuntarily working only part-time. They are not counted among the unemployed, even though they cannot find full-time jobs and are underemployed.

(See page vi in the foreword "To the Student" for how to make the best use of this schematic outline.)

(See page vi in the foreword "To the Student" for how to make the best use of this schematic outline.)

11.1. Describe the three major causes of unemployment. *(Write in answers below.)*

A. Indicate whether each of the following represents frictional (F), structural (S), or cyclical (C) unemployment.

1. _S_ Unemployed blacksmiths.
2. _C_ Assembly-line workers laid off during a recession.
3. _F_ A new graduate looking for her first job.
4. _S_ A Pittsburgh steelworker who loses his job when the steel mill moves to Alabama.
5. _S_ An unemployed oil worker in Houston during 1986.
6. _C_ A textile worker who loses her job when aggregate demand in the economy declines.
7. _S_ A textile worker who loses her job when the textile mill shuts down because of foreign competition.

B.
1. Which type of unemployment is a sign of a healthy economy?
   frictional

2. Which of type of unemployment is expected to last the shortest amount of time?
   frictional

3. Which type of unemployment is considered the most serious problem for the economy as a whole?
   cyclical

4. What type of unemployment exists when the economy is at **full employment**?
   frictional

C. Indicate which type of unemployment, frictional (F), structural (S), or cyclical (C) could be reduced by each of the following:

1. _F_ Publishing lists of all available jobs in an area.
2. _C_ Increasing the demand for goods and services in an entire economy.
3. _S_ Retraining programs.
4. _S_ Policies that increase the mobility of workers between different regions of the country.
5. _F_ Job placement services at high schools and colleges.

11.2. Explain why some unemployment is hidden.

A. To be classified as unemployed, a person must be unemployed **and** _actively seeking employment_.

B. Indicate whether each of the following would be officially counted (C) or not counted (N) as being unemployed (those not counted represent **hidden** unemployment).

1. _N_ A person works at a part-time job at night while looking for a full-time job during the day.
2. _N_ A person with a Ph.D. in economics works as a cab driver.
3. _C_ A person loses her job as a mechanic and is looking for a new job.
4. _N_ A person who has been unemployed for 6 months stops looking for work.
5. _N_ A new mother decides to leave her job in order to stay at home with her child.
6. _N_ A person is in prison because he lost his job as a bank robber when he got caught.
7. _N_ A person who works on an assembly line has her hours reduced from 40 to 25 hours per week because of a decline in aggregate demand.

C. The official unemployment rate is calculated by dividing the number of unemployed persons actively looking for work by the total labor force.

1. If the amount of hidden unemployment increases, what happens to the official unemployment rate?
   nothing

2. Every June the number of students looking for work causes the size of the labor force to increase. What effect will this have on the unemployment rate if none of the students finds a job?

It will increase

3. Does the existence of hidden unemployment mean that the official unemployment rate understates or overstates the actual unemployment rate in the economy?

understates

4. Does the existence of people "working" full-time in illegal activities mean that the official unemployment rate understates or overstates the actual unemployment rate in the economy?

overstates

Case Application: Where the Jobs Went

The unemployment level remained stubbornly high through the 1980s, despite the second longest economic expansion since World War II. With 6.5 million people out of work in 1989, more than 5% of the labor force, what happened to all of the jobs? Who was out of work and why? Would the jobs return or were they lost forever?

The answers to these questions were extremely important to the people out of work and to the future of the economy. Most of the jobs lost were blue-collar jobs. For unskilled workers the unemployment rate was 10% and for semi-skilled workers almost 9%. For white-collar workers, on the other hand, the unemployment rate was only 4% and for managerial and professional occupations only 2%.

Much of the blue-collar unemployment resulted from the decline of older manufacturing industries such as steel, rubber, textiles, and automobiles. Those heavy industries, once the foundation of the nation's prosperity, were being replaced by high-technology industries. Even if some of them, the automobile industry for example, recouped their markets, they needed to automate in order to be competitive with Japanese and other foreign producers. Many of the jobs were thus gone forever. It was estimated that at least 100,000 jobs would be permanently eliminated in the automobile industry, and a million jobs in manufacturing overall.

The high unemployment levels were also associated with an exceptionally large increase in the size of the labor force in the preceding decade. The members of the "baby boom" generation swelled the ranks of labor, and an increasing percentage of women were entering the job market, so the capacity of the economy to create new jobs was strained beyond the limit. In order to absorb the new entrants into the work force, the growth of output would have had to have been much higher than it was.

Economic Reasoning *(Write your responses on a separate sheet. Answers begin on p. 303.)*

1. The more than 100,000 jobs that were permanently lost in the automobile industry represented what type of unemployment?
2. About one in every four women workers who were displaced from jobs that they had held for three years or more gave up looking for a new job. Were they counted as unemployed? What type of unemployment did they represent?
3. What would you recommend to a 40-year-old steelworker, with a wife and four children to support, who lost his job when the steel mill shut down in Donora, Pennsylvania?

What Causes Inflation?

Measuring inflation		
The most commonly used measure of average prices in the economy as a whole is the consumer price index (CPI).		
DEMAND-PULL	**COST-PUSH**	**MONETARY**
When the demand for goods and services exceeds the production capacity of the economy, the excess demand spills over into demand-pull inflation. Inflation is compounded when prices are rising due to shortages as goods and resources are bought and held off the market by those who are speculating on a rise in the price.	Inflation can arise from changes in the costs of production of goods and services. An increase in prices of raw materials, labor, or capital results in cost-push inflation. Cost-push inflation may reinforce demand-pull inflation through labor contracts containing cost of living adjustment (COLA) clauses.	The monetarists maintain that inflation is caused by excessive growth of the money supply. **Quantity Equation** According to the quantity equation, the money supply times the velocity at which it changes hands equals the number of transactions times the average level of prices. $$M \times V = T \times P$$

(See page vi in the foreword "To the Student" for how to make the best use of this schematic outline.)

(See page vi in the foreword "To the Student" for how to make the best use of this schematic outline.)

11.3. State the meaning of inflation and the CPI.

A. Define inflation.

Inflation is the continual increase in the general level of prices

B.
  1. The most common measure of inflation is the *consumer price index*.
  2. This index is computed by comparing the price of the same *market basket* of goods in two different time periods.

C. The following represent the cost of the same market basket of goods purchased in successive years. If 1985 is the **base year**, use the data to construct a price index. (Use the following formula to compute the index.)

Price Index = $\dfrac{\text{(Cost in year of interest)}}{\text{(Cost in base year)}} \times 100$

Year	Cost of Market Basket	Price Index
1985	$200.00	100
1986	$220.00	110
1987	$230.00	115
1988	$250.00	125
1989	$260.00	130

D. The inflation rate between two years is calculated as the percentage change in the price index for those years. What are the inflation rates for the indices you computed in the previous question? (Use the following formula.)

$$\% \text{ Change} = \frac{(\text{Index in one year}) - (\text{Index in previous year})}{\text{Index in previous year}}$$

1985 to 1986 inflation rate equals __10%__.

1986 to 1987 inflation rate equals __4.5%__.

1987 to 1988 inflation rate equals __8.7%__.

1988 to 1989 inflation rate equals __4.0%__.

E. In terms of the circular flow model of the economy presented in chapter 3, demand-pull inflation arises in the __product__ market, and cost-push inflation arises in the __factor__ market.

11.4. Describe three causes of inflation and explain the usage of the quantity equation.

A. Identify the probable causes of inflation in each of the following instances:

1. The Fed buys increasing amounts of bonds.
   __monetary__

2. Even though real income and output do not change, everybody goes out and charges their credit cards up to their limits.
   __demand-pull__

3. The price of oil increases as a result of political unrest in the Middle East.
   __cost-push__

4. People see that prices are increasing and they stock up on goods.
   __demand-pull__

5. A large proportion of the economy receives cost-of-living adjustments.
   __cost-push__

B. Define each of the four components of the quantity equation:
   1. M. __the money supply__
   2. V. __the velocity of money__
   3. P. __the average price level__
   4. T. __the number of transactions__

C.
   1. What does M × V represent?
      __the number of dollars spent__

   2. What does P × T represent?

the value of all goods & services bought

D. Use the quantity equation to answer each of the following:

1. What happens to the price level if output does not change when the money supply decreases?

   price increase

2. What happens to the value of total purchases if increases in the money supply are offset by equal decreases in the velocity of money?

   It stays the same

3. If prices and the supply of money cannot change, what must happen if the number of transactions in an economy are increasing?

   The velocity of money must increase

Case Application: Talk About Inflation...

The United States experienced unprecedented levels of inflation—unprecedented since price controls were lifted at the end of World War II—in the late 1970s and the beginning of the 1980s. Prices rose at a rate of 13.3% in 1979 and 12.4% in 1980. This rate of inflation was very disturbing to the public and to policymakers in Washington, but compared to inflation rates in some other countries the U.S. inflation was quite tame.

How about an inflation of 3,400% in one year? That was the amount of inflation Bolivia experienced in 1985, with rates at times during the year even much higher. Argentina's inflation reached 672% and Israel's 374%. A tankful of gasoline costs in Israel an amount of shekels that would have purchased the car five years earlier.

Those extreme inflation rates were consequences of large government budget deficits and increases in the money supply. When a government is spending more than it collects in tax revenues, the extra money spent by the government is chasing the same resources as the money in the taxpayers' pockets. Hence, the prices of resources and finished products are bid up. When the government finances its deficit spending by putting more money into circulation, it compounds the inflation.

Economic Reasoning *(Write your responses on a separate sheet. Answers begin on p. 304.)*

1. If dinner in a Bolivian restaurant cost 10 Bolivian dollars at the end of 1984, what would a restaurant patron have to pay for the same meal at the end of 1985?
2. What types of inflation are described in this application?
3. Why do you think inflation was so much greater in those countries than in the United States?

Is There a Trade-off Between Unemployment and Inflation?

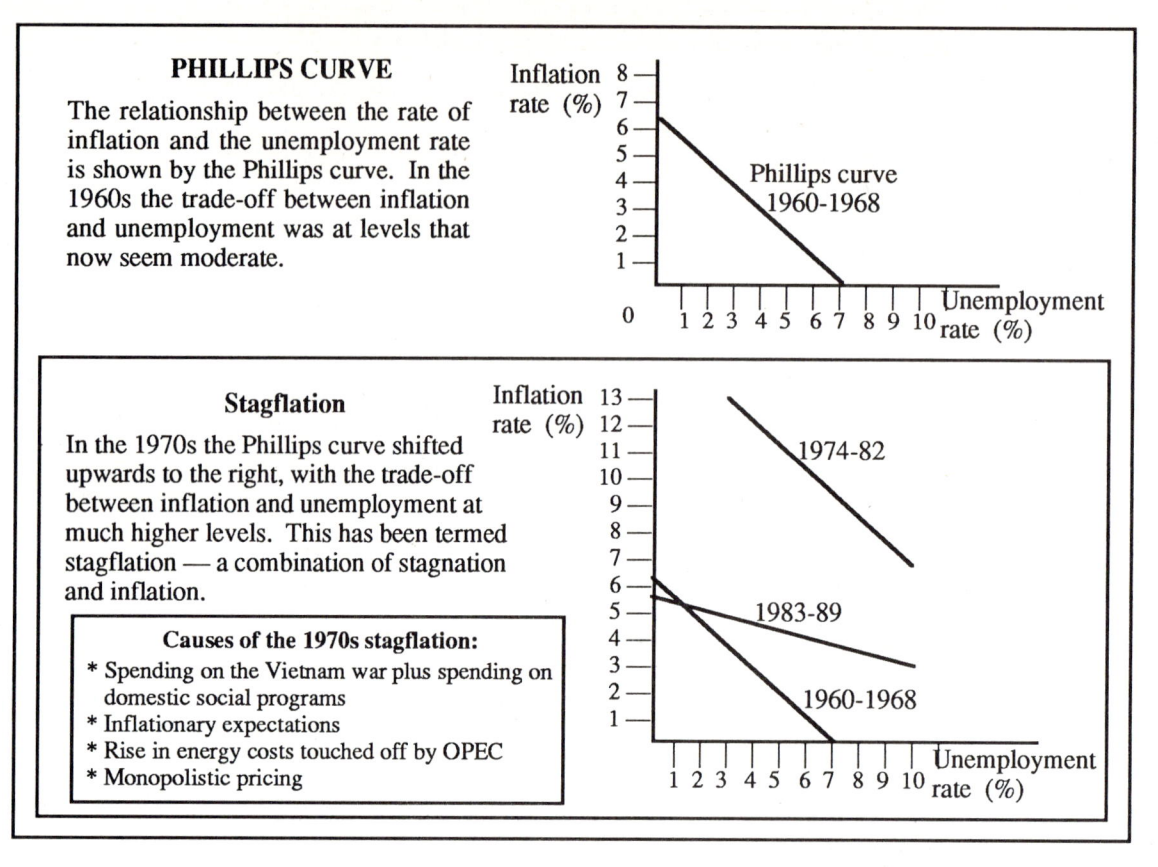

PHILLIPS CURVE

The relationship between the rate of inflation and the unemployment rate is shown by the Phillips curve. In the 1960s the trade-off between inflation and unemployment was at levels that now seem moderate.

Stagflation

In the 1970s the Phillips curve shifted upwards to the right, with the trade-off between inflation and unemployment at much higher levels. This has been termed stagflation — a combination of stagnation and inflation.

Causes of the 1970s stagflation:
* Spending on the Vietnam war plus spending on domestic social programs
* Inflationary expectations
* Rise in energy costs touched off by OPEC
* Monopolistic pricing

(See page vi in the foreword "To the Student" for how to make the best use of this schematic outline.)

(See page vi in the foreword "To the Student" for how to make the best use of this schematic outline.)

11.5. Explain the relationship between unemployment and inflation and use the Phillips curve to show this relationship.

A. According to the Phillips curve, inflation and unemployment are _inversely_ related.

B. Use the data provided below to construct a Phillips curve for the economy (be sure to label both axes).

Year	Unemployment	Inflation
1986	10%	1%
1987	8%	3%
1988	6%	6%
1989	4%	9%
1990	2%	12%

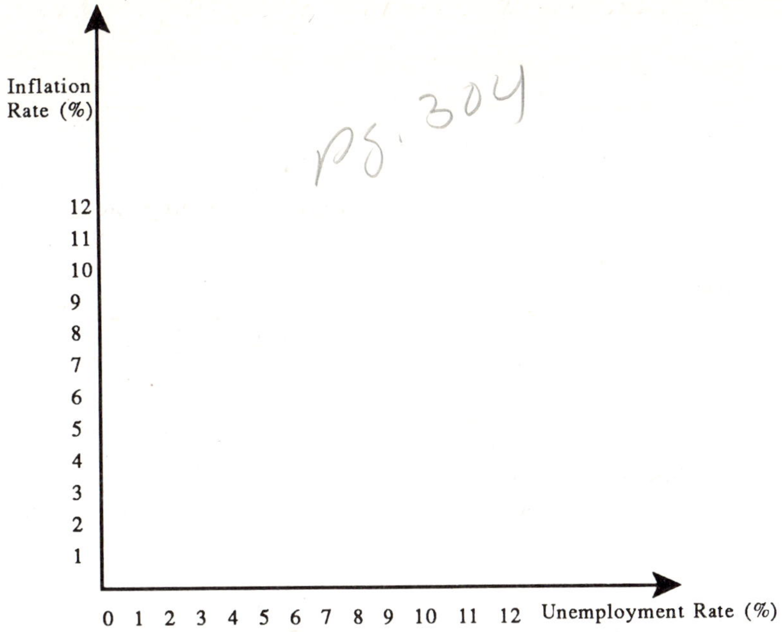

C. Use the space provided below to construct an aggregate supply and aggregate demand graph that reflects the economy described above (question B) in 1986 and 1990. (Be sure to label both axes and both AD curves.)

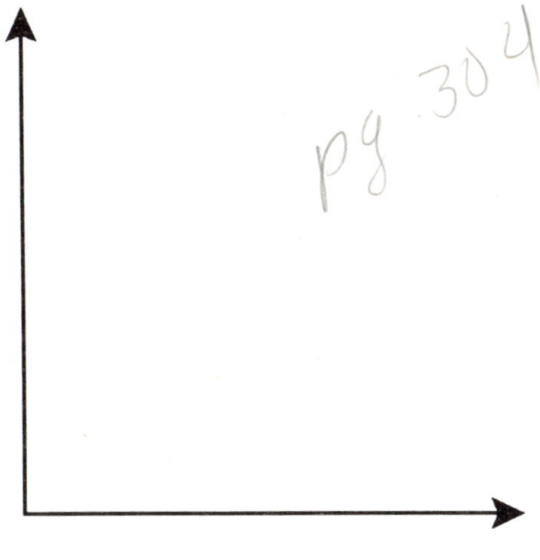

D. What **type** of inflation is described in the AS/AD graph that you constructed in question C?

demand-pull

E.

1. According to the Phillips curve, what is an opportunity cost of reducing inflation?

   higher unemployment

2. According to the Phillips curve, what is an opportunity cost of reducing unemployment?

   high inflation

11.6. Define stagflation and relate the price level to output and employment levels by use of the aggregate supply and aggregate demand curves.

A. When stagflation occurs, unemployment and inflation are ___directly___ related.

B. Use the space provided below to construct an AS/AD graph with the initial intersection in the stable price range of the AS curve. Then draw a new AD curve (AD$_2$) that indicates an increase in both output and prices.

C. Use the space provided below to construct an AS/AD graph with the initial intersection in the stable price range of the AS curve. Then draw a new AS curve (AS$_2$) that indicates an increase in prices and a **decrease** in output.

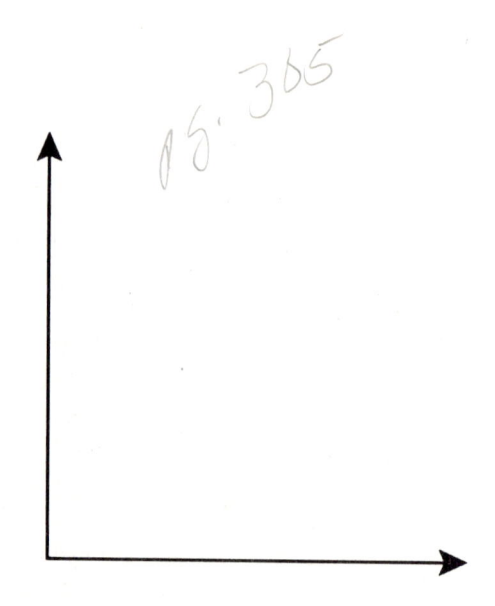

D. Which of the above graphs (question B or C) depicts the presence of stagflation? Explain _question C, both prices & unemployement are higher_

E. Use the aggregate supply and aggregate demand curves drawn below to answer the following questions about the quantity equation:

1. If aggregate demand shifts from AD_1 to AD_2, what happens to P and T?
   P: _same_ T: _increases_

2. If aggregate demand shifts from AD_2 to AD_3, what happens to P and T?
   P: _increase_ T: _increase_

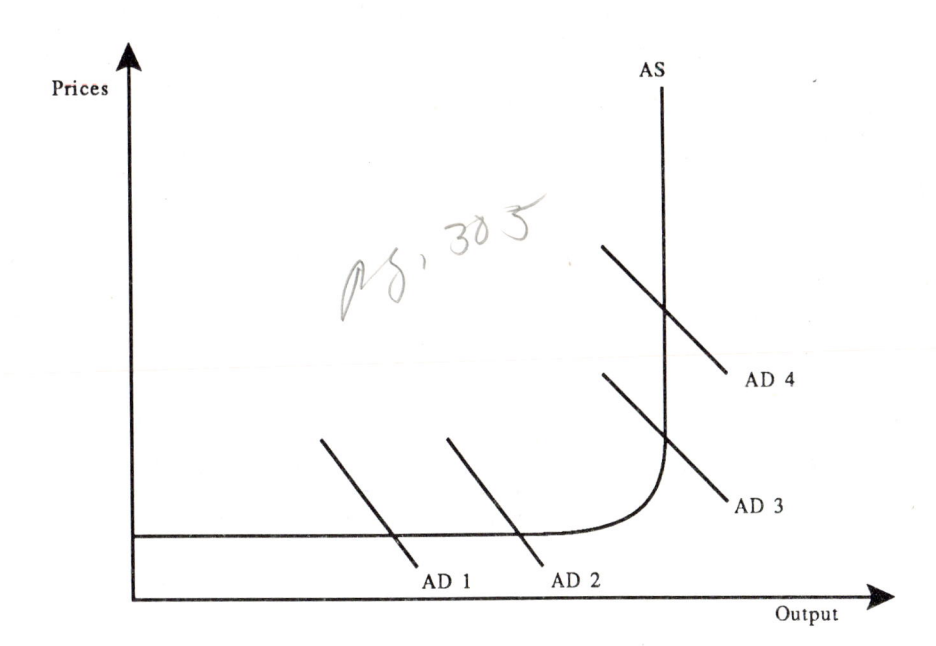

3. If aggregate demand shifts from AD_3 to AD_4, what happens to P and T?
   P: _increase_ T: _stays the same_

Case Application: Phillips Curve International

Traditionally, the countries of Western Europe have been willing to trade off more inflation for less unemployment than has the United States. The 4% unemployment rate, considered normal full employment in the United States, was excessive in the eyes of the Europeans. Unemployment rates that high would cause European governments to fall. Between 1960 and 1975, the unemployment rate in West Germany was never more than 1.6%, in Sweden not over 2%, and in France less than 3%. In Italy it never reached 4%, and in the United Kingdom it did so in only one year. There was an abhorrence of unemployment in Western Europe. On the other hand, those countries generally had higher inflation rates than did the United States.

The worldwide stagflation of the late 1970s and early 1980s dealt the European economies a severe blow from which they have not recovered. In 1989, when the unemployment rate in the United States was 5.3%, over 10% of the French labor force was unemployed, and in Italy 7.8%. The unemployment rates in Britain, West Germany, and other European countries were also higher than in the United States. Meanwhile, the inflation rates in some European countries, Britain and Italy for example, were also higher than in the United States. The upward shift in the Phillips curve in Western Europe was even greater than in this country.

Differences in the positions of the Phillips curve reflect such things as variations in industry structure, the age and skill composition of the labor force, institutional factors including labor union practices and the tax structures, and government economic policies. The economies of the European countries were hit even harder by the energy crunch than the U.S. economy was, because they are more dependent on foreign energy supplies.

Economic Reasoning *(Write your responses on a separate sheet. Answers begin on p. 305.)*

1. Prior to 1975, were the European countries operating more to the lower right or to the upper left on their Phillips curves, compared to the United States?
2. How did the rise in energy costs in the 1970s contribute to the upward shift in the Phillips curve in Western Europe?
3. In which direction on the Phillips curve do you think it is better for a country to be located, the lower right or the upper left? Why?

What Are the Consequences of Unemployment and Inflation?

UNEMPLOYMENT

Income effects
* Loss of income and fringe benefits (medical insurance) by unemployed
* Loss of income to others because of reduced purchasing power
* Reduced tax income and increased outlays for governments

Real output effects
* Each 1% of unemployment results in a reduction of $100 billion in output
* Lower real investment means less growth and reduced future output

Social effects
* Health problems (e.g., depression)
* Increased suicides
* Families break up
* Increased child abuse
* Increased crime

INFLATION

Income effects
* Reduced purchasing power of the $
* Reduced real income for fixed income receivers
* Reduced real wealth of savings
* Benefits those whose incomes rise faster than the inflation rate
* Benefits owners of real assets (e.g., precious metals, real estate)
* Benefits debtors

Real output effects
* Inflation initially stimulates output
* Near full employment, there arise bottlenecks in supplies
* Costs begin rising faster than prices
* Interest rates accelerate, discouraging new investment

(See page vi in the foreword "To the Student" for how to make the best use of this schematic outline.)

(See page vi in the foreword "To the Student" for how to make the best use of this schematic outline.)

11.7. Explain the consequences of unemployment and inflation.

A. List three undesirable consequences of unemployment.

1. _real output decreases_
2. _real incomes decrease_
3. _negative social effects_

B. Use the above list to indicate which consequence is represented in each of the following.

1. _3_ Suicides increase.
2. _1_ The economy produces fewer cars.
3. _2_ Living standards decrease.
4. _2_ Government tax receipts decrease.
5. _3_ Child abuse increases.

C. Indicate which of the following would benefit (B) and which would lose (L) as a result of unanticipated inflation.

1. _B_ Borrowers.
2. _L_ People on fixed incomes.

3. _L_ People who put their money under their mattresses.
4. _L_ People who put their money in savings accounts at fixed interest rates.
5. _L_ Lenders.
6. _B_ Members of strong labor unions.
7. _B_ Collectors of rare coins.
8. _B_ Homeowners.
9. _B_ The U.S. government.

D.
1. Describe a situation in which a business would benefit from inflation.

   A business will benefit if the price of its product is increasing faster than the prices of its inputs.

2. Describe a situation in which a business would be harmed by inflation.

   A business will suffer if the price of its inputs increase faster than the price of its output.

Case Application: Disinflation Losers

Lowering the rate of inflation has been a major economic goal, and inflation has been accused of robbing everybody's pocketbook. But as inflation came down, it appeared there were some losers from "disinflation" as well.

The people visibly hurt by the end of the high inflation rates included those who had purchased houses when real estate prices were rising at 5%–20% a year. Some purchased those houses at mortgage interest rates of 15% or more with the expectation that the continued rise in the value of real estate would enable them to refinance their loans in the future. The sudden end to those rising housing prices, even price declines in many areas, resulted in many foreclosures because owners could not meet the high mortgage payments and could not refinance. In a sense all homeowners suffered from the end of the inflation in housing prices. The rise in real estate prices, which was higher than the inflation of prices in general, had greatly increased the value of their homes as a financial asset. It made homeowners wealthier, although they might not be able to take immediate advantage of it. The end of inflation terminated their "windfall" gains in the value of their houses.

Others who suffered from the end of inflation were those who invested in gold, precious gems, or other commodities. Disinflation meant an end to the rising prices of those inflation hedges. As a result, there was a decline in the demand for them, and their value fell. The price of gold fell by over 50% in a two-year period. The price of diamonds nose-dived. Those who tried to protect themselves from inflation by investing in those commodities were savaged by the disinflation.

Government finances also suffered from the end of inflation. Inflation had accelerated government tax receipts and reduced the real cost of government debt. The disinflation and recession put a severe squeeze on government budgets. As a result, many government services had to be sharply curtailed.

Economic Reasoning *(Write your responses on a separate sheet. Answers begin on p. 305.)*

1. Whose wealth and income were negatively affected by an end to inflation?
2. How would a decline in the price of gold and other commodities be likely to affect the output of those commodities? Why?
3. Is disinflation as bad as inflation? Why or why not?

IV. Practice Test (Answers begin on p. 306.)

Multiple Choice (Circle the correct answer.)

(11.1) 1. Unemployment that results from a decrease in aggregate demand is called _____ unemployment.
- a. inflationary
- **b. cyclical**
- c. frictional
- d. structural

(11.1) 2. The type of unemployment that can be reduced by increasing training and retraining programs is _____ unemployment.
- a. inflationary
- b. cyclical
- c. frictional
- **d. structural**

(11.1) 3. For the economy as a whole, which type of unemployment represents the greatest problem?
- **a. cyclical.**
- b. frictional.
- c. structural.
- d. all of the above.

(11.2) 4. Which of the following is an example of "hidden" unemployment?
- a. A worker is laid off because of decreased demand for his product.
- b. A worker loses her job when she is replaced by a machine.
- **c. A worker works at a part-time job while desiring a full-time job.**
- d. A worker quits a job in order to find a better job.

(11.2) 5. "Underemployment" exists when a worker:
- a. is temporarily laid off from his or her job.
- b. works in illegal activities.
- c. works in the home (a housewife or househusband).
- **d. is overqualified for his or her job.**

(11.3) 6. Price indices are constructed by comparing the prices of:
- a. different market baskets at the same point in time.
- b. different market baskets at different points in time.
- c. the same market basket at the same points in time.
- **d. the same market basket at different points in time.**

(11.3) 7. Which of the following would NOT result in an increase in the rate of inflation?
- a. Oil prices increase because of political unrest in the Middle East.
- **b. The economy is suffering from excess productive capacity.**
- c. The Fed increases the money supply too quickly.
- d. Workers receive increased COLAs.

(11.3) 8. If prices double from the base year to the current year, the price index in the current year is equal to:
- a. 0.20.
- b. 50.00.
- c. 100.00.
- **d. 200.00.**

(11.4) 9. In the quantity equation, $(P \times T)$ represents which of the following?
- a. the total amount of money in an economy.
- b. the total number of times a dollar is spent.

        c. the total amount of money spent on goods and services.
        d. the total amount of inflation and unemployment in an economy.

(11.4) 10. Which of the following is the quantity equation?
        a. $M \times V = P \times T$.
        b. $P \times V = P \times T$.
        c. $C \times P = I$.
        d. $M \times T = P \times V$.

(11.4) 11. If the level of transactions and the velocity of money are fixed (constant), an increase in the supply of money will result in which of the following?
        a. an increase in output.
        b. a decrease in employment.
        c. an increase in prices.
        d. a decrease in inflation.

(11.5) 12. The Phillips curve shows the relationship between which of the following?
        a. inflation and the price level.
        b. inflation and unemployment.
        c. employment and unemployment.
        d. inflation and total output.

(11.5) 13. Which of the following is a TRUE statement?
        a. The Phillips curve does not shift over time.
        b. The Phillips curve shifted to show greater levels of both inflation and unemployment in the 1970s.
        c. The Phillips curve shifts when the level of unemployment changes.
        d. The Phillips curve shifts when the inflation rate changes.

(11.6) 14. Stagflation may occur as the result of which of the following?
        a. a rightward shift of the aggregate demand curve.
        b. a leftward shift of the aggregate demand curve.
        c. an upward shift of the aggregate supply curve.
        d. a downward shift of the aggregate supply curve.

(11.7) 15. Unemployment affects everyone because:
        a. it reduces the demand for goods and services.
        b. lost production is lost forever.
        c. the unemployed usually require tax-financed government assistance.
        d. all of the above.

True/False *(Circle T or F.)*

(11.1) 16. Frictional unemployment is not unusual in a healthy economy. T or F

(11.2) 17. A worker who has stopped looking for work is counted as being unemployed. T or F

(11.4) 18. Excess aggregate demand is more likely to lead to inflation in the long run than it is in the short run. T or F

(11.5) 19. The Phillips curve shows a direct relationship between inflation and unemployment. T or F

(11.7) 20. Because it is the biggest debtor in the world, the U.S. government will be a net loser if inflation occurs. T or F

Chapter 12

The Economy's Output

I. Chapter Outline

There are two different ways of measuring the total output of the economy. Although it is calculated differently, you will get the same total amount whether you add up the total amount of money spent or whether you add up the total amount of money earned. There are also two different explanations of what determines how much an economy produces: the demand-side and the supply-side points of view. Unlike the two different ways of measuring output, however, these two points of view come to distinctly different conclusions.

Introductory Article: Forecasting or Fortunetelling?

Despite the intricate complexity of modern statistical economic forecasting models, they are often no more reliable than the oracles at Delphi in ancient Greece at predicting the future. Problems which confront forecasters include unreliable data to put into their models and the unpredictable nature of the world and the events which shape it. Nonetheless, there is a strong demand by business and government for information which can be used to shape future plans. As an anonymous economist once pointed out, "Forecasting is difficult, especially about the future."

Economic Analysis

This chapter examines how the levels of total output and employment are determined in a market economy by addressing the following questions:

1. How Much Does the Economy Produce?

    Important Concepts: Expenditure categories, Income categories, Current and constant dollar GNP

    Case Application: Harry's Sub Shop

2. What Determines Domestic Output From the Demand-Side Point of View?

    Important Concepts: Consumption, Investment, Government and foreign demand, Equilibrium Output

    Important Model: Keynesian economic model

    Case Application: The Inventory Paradox

3. What Determines Domestic Output From the Supply-Side Point of View?

    Important Concepts: Supply-side economics, Say's Law, Incentives, Crowding out

    Case Application: Spending Like There Is No Tomorrow

Perspective: The Keynesian Revolution
    Biography—John Maynard Keynes

II. Summary of Economic Analysis

1. The **Gross National Product (GNP)** of an economy is the value of all the goods and services it produces in a given time period (usually one year).
2. An economy's GNP can be computed either by adding together all the **expenditures** on goods and services or by adding together all the **income** earned by producing these goods. Either method of measuring will result in the same value for GNP.
3. The expenditure method computes GNP by adding together the four types of expenditures that occur in a market economy: **personal consumption (C), private domestic investment (I), government spending (G),** and **net exports (X − M)**. Therefore, $GNP = C + I + G + (X - M)$.
4. The sum of all incomes earned as wages, rents, profits, and interest is equal to **National Income**. National Income plus **capital consumption allowances, indirect business taxes,** and other business transfers equals GNP.
5. In order to avoid **double-counting**, only the **value added** by each firm at each stage of the production is included when computing the size of the GNP.
6. **Current dollar GNP** is the value of GNP in current dollars, with no adjustment for inflation. **Constant dollar GNP** is the inflation-adjusted value of GNP.
7. The **demand-side** (Keynesian) view of the economy is that the size of the GNP depends on aggregate demand: the total amount of consumption, investment, government, and export demand.
8. Savings (S) and taxes (T) are **leakages** out of an economy's flow of income. Investment and government spending are **injections** into the flow of income.
9. **Equilibrium output** in the **Keynesian model** of an economy occurs whenever the level of leakages out of the economic flow are just offset by the injections into it: $(I + G) = (S + T)$.
10. Keynesian economics is based on the premise that the supply of goods and services in an economy will increase in response to increased demand. In contrast, early **supply-side** economic views were based on **Say's Law of Markets**, which states that "supply creates its own demand."
11. Modern supply-side economics emphasizes the importance of profit **incentives** in motivating an economy to increase its output. According to this view, big government and high tax rates discourage productive work and investment and consequently limit economic growth.
12. According to the supply-side point of view, a very real danger of increased government borrowing is that it **crowds out** private investment.

III. Review of the Learning Objectives *(Answers begin on p. 306.)*

How Much Does the Economy Produce?

GROSS NATIONAL PRODUCT
The measure of the total amount of goods and services produced in the economy is the Gross National Product (GNP). There are two methods of measuring GNP:

Expenditure categories	Income categories

C — personal consumption expenditures
I — gross private domestic investment
  (buildings, equipment, inventories)
G — government spending
X-M — net exports
  (exports minus imports)
 	
$\boxed{GNP = C + I + G + (X-M)}$
	National Income (NI)
	  Wages and salaries
	  Proprietor's income
	  Corporate profits
	  Interest
	  Rent
	+ Capital Consumption Allowances
	+ Indirect Taxes
	= GNP

Value added
To avoid double-counting in adding up the total amount of goods and services produced, only the value added at each stage of production is counted, excluding the cost of intermediate goods.

Current and constant dollar GNP
In order to measure real changes in GNP, eliminating the effect on figures of inflation, the current dollar values are adjusted by a price index to give the values in the constant dollar value of an earlier base year.

(See page vi in the foreword "To the Student" for how to make the best use of this schematic outline.)

12.1. Define the GNP and explain the two ways of measuring it and why they give the same result. *(Write in answers below.)*

A.

1. The *expenditure* approach to calculating GNP adds up all the money that people _____*spend*_____.

2. The *income* approach to calculating GNP adds up all the money that people _____*earn*_____.

B. In terms of the circular flow diagram:

1. the expenditure approach to calculating GNP adds up all the transactions in the ___*product*___ market.

2. the income approach to calculating GNP adds up all the transactions in the ___*factor*___ market.

C. The following table shows the prices received by producers at each stage of the production of a loaf of bread. Calculate the *value added* at each stage of

172 / Working With The Study of Economics, 4/E

production and indicate how much the production of a loaf of bread adds to GNP.

Producer	Price Received	Value Added
Wheat farmer sells to miller	$0.30	.30
Miller sells to baker	0.45	.15
Baker sells to wholesaler	0.65	.20
Wholesaler sells to retailer	0.85	.20
Retailer sells to customer	0.95	.10
	ADDITION TO GNP =	.95

D. GNP is a measure of the total amount of goods and services *produced in an economy in the current year*. With this in mind, indicate whether the dollar value of each of the following should be included (I) or not included (N) in this year's GNP.

1. __I__ Harry buys a meal at a restaurant.
2. __N__ Harry buys 100 shares of AT&T from a stockbroker.
3. __N__ Harry buys a 1984 Ford station wagon.
4. __I__ Harry buys a new pair of jeans.
5. __I__ Harry sells 1,000 bushels of wheat to the Chinese.
6. __I__ Harry sells 1,000 bushels of wheat to an American baker.
7. __I__ Harry mows his neighbor's lawn for $10.00.
8. __I__ Harry pays his housekeeper $100 per week.
9. __N__ Harry's wife cleans their house but is not paid for doing the job.

12.2. Explain the four types of expenditures that make up the total demand for goods and services.

A. Indicate whether each of the following expenditures is a part of consumption (C), government spending (G), investment (I), or exports (X):

1. __G__ The government buys a Stealth bomber.
2. __X__ A pair of Levi's jeans is sold in Rome.
3. __X__ French tourists buy New York City souvenirs.
4. __I__ A family buys a new house.
5. __C__ A family buys a Thanksgiving turkey.
6. __I__ A toy company increases its inventory.
7. __I__ An electric company buys a new generator.
8. __C__ A family pays its electric bill.

B. The same good could be classified as consumption, a government purchase, investment, or an export, depending on who the buyer is. Give an example of how each of the following goods could be classified as C, I, G, or X.

1. A pickup truck.
   C: It becomes a second family vehicle
   I: A landscaping company buys the truck
   G: Your town buys the truck & uses it for hauling leaves
   X: The truck is shipped to Russia

2. A television.
   - C: _You buy it & watch it_
   - I: _Your local news station buys it & uses it as a monitor_
   - G: _Your local school buys it & uses it in class_
   - X: _The TV is sold to China_

C. Which component of total expenditures:
   1. is the largest? _C_
   2. is the most stable over time? _C_
   3. depends the most on interest rates? _I_
   4. increases when we buy more French wine? _X_
   5. includes inventories? _I_
   6. depends on disposable income? _C_
   7. is directly related to savings levels? _I_
   8. is inversely related to savings levels? _C_

12.3. Define National Income and explain how it differs from GNP.

A. To determine GNP using the income approach, what two things must be added to National Income?
   1. _indirect business taxes_
   2. _capital consumption allowances_

B. What are two taxes that businesses pay directly to the government without the money ever becoming a part of someone's income? (Hint: they are state and/or local taxes)
   1. _sales taxes_
   2. _property taxes_

C. **Gross** national product measures total additions to output, not net additions. **Net** national product takes into account any existing goods that wear out while producing this year's new goods and services. What is the economic term for the difference between gross and net national product?

depreciation or capital consumption allowances

12.4. Define constant dollar GNP and show how it relates to current dollar GNP.

A.
   1. If an analyst wishes to compare changes in an economy's output over a number of years, she must first adjust the level of GNP to reflect changes in the _price level_ in each of the years.
   2. This implies that the analysts should compare the values of _constant dollar_ GNP rather than _current dollar_ GNP.

B. If **P** represents the average price level and **Q** represents the total amount of goods and services produced in an economy, then:
   1. constant dollar GNP equals _Q_.

2. current dollar GNP equals __P × Q__.

C. To convert current dollar GNP to constant dollar GNP, one must divide current dollar GNP (P × Q) by the appropriate price index (P) and then multiply by 100 (because the price index starts from a base of 100—see chapter 11). If constant dollar GNP is defined as Q, then:

$$\frac{(P \times Q)}{P} \times 100 = Q, \text{ or } \frac{\text{Current \$ GNP}}{\text{Price Index}} \times 100 = \text{Constant \$ GNP}$$

Use the above formula to calculate the level of constant dollar GNP from the given levels of current dollar GNP and the price index.

Year	Current Dollar GNP	Price Index	Constant Dollar GNP
1990	$2,000,000	100	2,000,000
1991	2,310,000	105	2,200,000
1992	2,640,000	110	2,400,000
1993	3,055,000	130	2,350,000
1994	3,500,000	140	2,500,000

D. In the previous question, the economy was in a recession in which year?

__1993__

E. If the price index increases each year, then which will be bigger, current or constant dollar GNP? Explain.

__Current dollar GNP will be greater because the prices of everything will be greater__

Case Application: Helen's Gift City, Inc.

Late in 1989, a gift store located in a shopping mall in a well-to-do suburban area of northern New Jersey was on the verge of bankruptcy. Internal management and external coordination problems with corporation headquarters in California appeared to be behind the trouble.

Helen Bidwell had always dreamed of owning her own business. At the end of December 1989, she bought the store. She reorganized, incorporated, and named it "Helen's Gift City, Inc."

Mrs. Bidwell has a good business mind, and she seemed to know where the "market" was for the gift industry. She immediately acquired a selection of merchandise in all materials and colors, from all geographic and national origins. Boutique specialities, costume jewelry, decorative hardware, flatware, figurines, sculpture, purse accessories, and woodenware were only a few of the items she carried. Because her line of giftware was so comprehensive in its appeal, she turned the store into a lucrative enterprise. By the year's end, Helen, who had some elementary accounting, drew up the income statement on the following page:

Helen's Gift City, Inc.
Account's Income Statement For the Year 1990

Sales		$200,000
Cost of gifts sold		
Merchandise	$90,000	
Wages and Salaries	60,000	
Rent	15,000	
Depreciation	10,000	
Excise Tax	14,000	
		−189,000
Gross Profit		11,000
Allowance for Corporation		
Income Tax	2,000	−2,000
Net Profit		$ 9,000

Based on the income statement of Helen's Gift City, Inc., Mrs. Bidwell's husband, who happens to be an economist, drew up the following national income accounts for the same year.

National Income Accounting
(for Helen's Gift City, Inc. 1990)

Sales	$200,000	
Purchases from all		
Intermediate firms		
(wholesale)	−90,000	
Value-added GNP		$110,000
Wages and Salaries	60,000	
Rent	15,000	
Capital-consumption allowance	10,000	
Business taxes	14,000	
Corporation income taxes	2,000	
Profit	9,000	
Income and other contributions		$110,000

Economic Reasoning *(Write your responses on a separate sheet. Answers begin on p. 306.)*

1. What was the contribution of Helen's Gift City to total output?
2. How much did the firm add to National Income? What accounts for the difference between its contribution to GNP and its contribution to NI?
3. Which provides the most useful information about Helen's Gift City, Inc., the business accounting statement or the national income accounting statement? Why?

What Determines Domestic Output from the Demand-Side Point of View?

KEYNESIAN ECONOMICS

One of the two principal interpretations of what determines total output is the demand-side analysis based on the writings of British economist John Maynard Keynes in the 1930s. The Keynesian model assumes four demand sectors, of which we consider at this point only the three domestic sectors.

Consumption
Consumption demand (C) is the largest flow of purchasing power into the economy. The size of C is determined for the most part by the amount of people's disposable income that they choose to allocate to consumption.

Investment
Investment demand (I) consists of the spending by businesses for equipment, factories, office buildings, and inventories. The investment also includes new residences. The corresponding allocation of income is savings (S) which flows to money markets.

Government
Government demand (G) is the purchases of goods and services by federal, state, and local governments. The corresponding outflow consists of the taxes (T) paid by households and businesses.

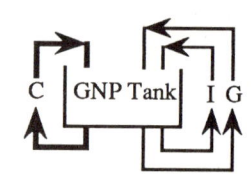

Equilibrium output

Total output is at the domestic equilibrium level, with no tendency to increase or decrease, when the aggregate demand from the three domestic demand sectors is just equal to the amounts allocated from income to the three sectors. The economy thus will not be rising or falling when C + I + G = C + S + T. Since the allocation of income to consumption expenditures is identical to consumption demand (C = C), the condition for equilibrium GNP can be stated as:

$$I + G = S + T$$

(See page vi in the foreword "To the Student" for how to make the best use of this schematic outline.)

12.5. Explain the Keynesian economic model and show under what conditions the output of the economy is at equilibrium.

A. According to the Keynesian economic model, the level of output in an economy depends upon the level of ___*aggregate demand*___.

B. The three leakages (excluding the foreign sector) from the GNP tank reenter the tank as additions to demand. Indicate each of the leakages and its corresponding addition.

   1. Leakage: *consumption*   Addition: *consumption*
   2. Leakage: *taxes*   Addition: *government spending*
   3. Leakage: *savings*   Addition: *investment*

C. Using the leakage/addition list constructed in the previous question, indicate what (if anything) will cause the leakage to be greater than the addition.

   1. *nothing; consumption will always equal consumption*

2. _If the government doesn't spend all its tax receipts_
3. _If available savings are not borrowed_

D. Indicate what happens to the level of output (GNP) in each of the following instances:
   1. Leakages exceed additions. _GNP falls_
   2. Additions exceed leakages. _GNP rises_
   3. Additions equal leakages. _GNP remains the same_

E.
   1. Most people think that saving some of their money is a wise thing to do. According to the Keynesian economic model, what is a negative aspect of saving?

      It reduces aggregate demand

   2. What is a positive aspect of saving?

      It results in lower interest rates and greater investment demand

F. Using the Keynesian point of view, indicate which of the following will result in GNP growth (G) and which will result in GNP decline (D).
   1. _D_ An increase in taxes.
   2. _G_ An increase in business investment.
   3. _G_ An increase in consumer spending.
   4. _D_ An increase in leakages.
   5. _G_ An increase in government spending.
   6. _G_ An increase in net exports.
   7. _D_ An increase in net imports.

G.
   1. When the government spends more than it receives in taxes, the result is a _budget deficit_.
   2. This will have what impact on GNP?

      It will cause it to increase

H.
   1. When the government spends less than it receives in taxes, the result is a _budget surplus_.
   2. This will have what impact on GNP?

      It will cause it to decrease

I. According to the Keynesian economic model, what do excess inventories represent?

   reduced aggregate demand

J.
1. According to the Keynesian model, can overproduction (the same as underconsumption) ever occur in an economy?

   yes

2. Describe overproduction in terms of the relationship between leakages and additions.

   leakages exceed additions

3. What will be the GNP consequences of overproduction?

   GNP will decline

Case Application: Changes in Demand

Most demand that makes up GNP is consumption demand, 66% in 1989. But changes in GNP are not attributable to changes in consumption. Consumption spending does not fluctuate a great deal; it does so mainly as a result of changes in GNP and income. Consumption expenditures generally follow income changes rather than initiating them.

The variability in the different demand sectors is showing in the following table:

Growth in Major Components of Real Gross National Product
1985–1989, percentage change

Component	1985	1986	1987	1988	1989
Real gross national product	3.4	2.7	3.7	4.4	2.9
Personal consumption expenditures	4.7	3.9	2.8	3.4	2.7
Business fixed investment	6.7	−3.3	3.9	8.4	3.5
Residential fixed investment	2.0	12.2	−0.5	−0.4	−2.7
Government purchases of goods and services	7.9	4.2	2.7	0.4	2.6
Federal	12.1	2.5	1.6	−3.2	2.5
State and local	4.7	5.5	3.4	5.1	2.7
Net exports	−24.2	−24.4	10.8	35.3	24.8
Exports	−1.2	8.4	13.5	17.6	10.8
Imports	3.4	11.8	7.5	6.8	6.4

Source: Department of Commerce, Bureau of Economic Analysis.

The most stable components of aggregate demand are consumption and government spending. Investment and net foreign demand are much more variable.

Economic Reasoning *(Write your responses on a separate sheet. Answers begin on p. 306.)*

1. In 1989, which GNP component was the weakest?
2. What was the effect of federal government expenditures on GNP in 1989?
3. In the national income accounts, consumption spending appears more stable than income. Is your spending more stable than your income? Why or why not?

What Determines Domestic Output from the Supply-Side Point of View?

SUPPLY-SIDE ECONOMICS
The main alternative explanation of what determines the total output of the economy is supply-side economics, which was the foundation of "Reaganomics."

Say's Law
The roots of supply-side economics go back to the ideas of J. B. Say. According to Say's Law of Markets, "supply creates its own demand" so that production creates enough income to purchase what is produced and there will not be overproduction and unemployment.

Incentives	Government deficits
Modern supply-side economics emphasizes the importance of incentives in determining output. Increasing the returns to producers by reducing taxes and other costs provides an incentive for them to produce more, thereby creating jobs and income to purchase what is produced. Reducing taxes also is assumed to result in larger savings, which makes more funds available for investment.	Supply-side economics emphasizes the negative effects of government deficits on the availability and cost of capital to investors in the private sector, with government borrowing crowding out private investment borrowing in the money market.

(See page vi in the foreword "To the Student" for how to make the best use of this schematic outline.)

12.6. Describe the meaning of Say's Law.

A. According to Say's Law, the level of aggregate demand in an economy will depend upon _aggregate supply or the level of income earned_.

B.

1. Prior to the Keynesian revolution, economists believed that if overproduction existed (if there were too many goods on the market), the problem would be corrected by _flexible wages & prices_.

2. Keynes argued that this would *not* occur because _there are powerful institutional forces that resist falling wages & prices_.

C. If Say's Law had been correct, what would have happened to end the Great Depression of the 1930s?
Wages & Prices would have fallen

D. In the space on the following page, draw demand (D_1) and supply (S_1) curves for the labor market. Draw a new demand curve (D_2) that represents a decrease in demand. Indicate the levels of employment and wages that J. B. Say believed would occur (Q_s and W_s), and the levels of employment and wages that J. M. Keynes believed would occur (Q_k and W_k).

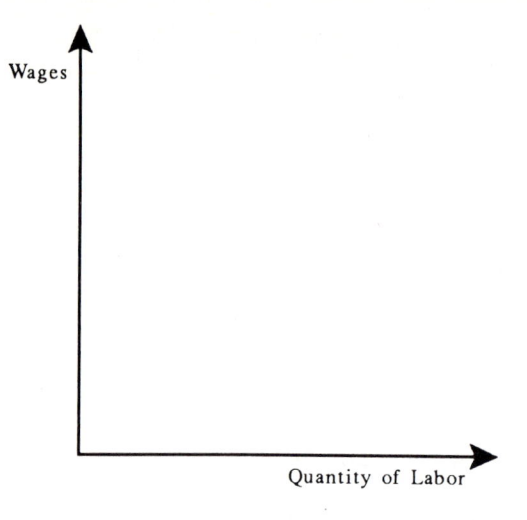

(Graph with axes: Wages (y-axis) and Quantity of Labor (x-axis), no curves drawn)

12.7. Explain how supply-side economics differs from demand-side economics.

A.

1. According to supply-side economists, the key to increasing output is increasing the _incentives to produce_.

2. Accordingly, supply-side economists believe that the best government policy for expanding output would be _to lower taxes_.

B. According to supply-side economists, lower tax rates will result in more output because they will increase

1. _savings_.
2. _investment_.
3. _labor supplies_.

C.

1. According to the Keynesian (demand-side) point of view, increased government deficits result in _increased_ aggregate demand and _increased_ levels of output.

2. According to the supply-side point of view, increased government deficits result in higher _interest rates_ that _decrease_ private investment and result in _decreased_ levels of GNP.

D. Indicate which of the following statements would be favored by demand-side (Keynesian) economists (D) and which would be favored by supply-side economists (S).

1. _D_ Government spending helps keep GNP high.
2. _S_ Transfer payments to the poor harm the economy.

3. __S__ High tax rates reduce output because they reduce incentives to produce.
4. __S__ Government borrowing crowds out private investment.
5. __D__ The most important benefit of lower taxes is increased disposable income and spending.
6. __S__ The most important benefit of lower taxes is increased savings and investment.
7. __S__ Private sector activity is more important than government activity in ensuring economic growth.

Case Application: Is War Good for the Economy?

The conventional viewpoint in the past was that war is good for the economy. The reasoning for such a view was found in the observation that the production of armaments and the supplying of troops with food, clothing, transportation, and other goods and services stimulated an increase in output and raised incomes.

The view of war as a cure for recession was bolstered by the experience at the beginning of World War II, as the United States supplied the Allies with armaments and civilian materials when hostilities began in Europe. Even before America entered the war, the increased production brought the country out of the depression of the 1930s and caused a rapid expansion to full employment.

On the other hand, when the United States became involved in war in the Persian Gulf in January 1991 there was concern that the war would make the recession that began in the previous quarter even worse. What was the cause of this change in the conventional wisdom about the effects of war on the economy?

In part, the changed opinion about the effects of war was peculiar to that particular war. It was anticipated that the war would reduce the supply of petroleum on world markets, raising the prices of gasoline, fuel oil, and energy as a whole. If that happened, production costs would rise throughout the economy, and consumers would have less money with which to buy goods and services.

Other causes of the changed expectations about the effect of war on the economy were more general. One change in the economy since World War II has been the decline in the relative importance of manufacturing in total output. A boost to the output of military hardware would have a smaller effect on overall economic activity than it did when manufacturing was the principal production sector.

But even more important in the changed thinking was the anticipated effect of the costs of the war and how they would impact the investment sector of the economy. With government spending increased by billions of dollars to wage war, it was feared that the rising government deficit would siphon off funds from the financial markets, leaving a shortage of funds for investment.

Economic Reasoning *(Write your responses on a separate sheet. Answers begin on p. 307.)*

1. Was the earlier conventional view of the effect of war on the economy based on demand-side or supply-side economics?
2. Was the expected impact of war on the economy at the beginning of the Persian Gulf war based on demand-side or supply-side economics? What were those anticipated effects?
3. Should the U.S. government take into account the expected effects of war on the economy when it decides whether to go to war? Why or why not?

IV. Practice Test (Answers begin on p. 307.)

Multiple Choice (Circle the correct answer.)

(12.1) 1. GNP measures:
   a. the total level of investment in an economy.
   b. the total output produced by an economy.
   c. the total disposable income in an economy.
   d. the total level of private sector output in an economy.

(12.1) 2. The largest component of GNP is:
   a. personal consumption spending.
   b. business investment.
   c. government spending.
   d. net exports.

(12.1) 3. Why will the income and expenditure approaches to measuring GNP result in the same total?
   a. All leakages eventually reenter the economy as additions to aggregate demand.
   b. Total aggregate demand is always equal to the sum of its four components (C, I, G, and X).
   c. Aggregate demand is by definition always equal to aggregate supply.
   d. Every dollar spent in an economy becomes someone's income.

(12.2) 4. Which of the following is NOT included as a part of investment spending when computing GNP?
   a. A family buys a new house.
   b. The government builds a new dam.
   c. A business increases its inventory stocks.
   d. An electric company builds a new generator.

(12.2) 5. Which of the following is NOT one of the four expenditure categories used when calculating GNP?
   a. investment.
   b. consumption.
   c. savings.
   d. net exports.

(12.3) 6. National Income:
   a. is equal to GNP.
   b. plus indirect taxes is equal to GNP.
   c. plus capital consumption allowances is equal to GNP.
   d. plus indirect taxes plus capital consumption allowances is equal to GNP.

(12.3) 7. National Income includes which of the following?
   a. taxes.
   b. investment.
   c. profits.
   d. imports.

(12.4) 8. Which of the following will always be true during periods of inflation?
   a. The expenditure approach to measuring GNP will result in larger values than the income approach.
   b. Consumption spending will become the most volatile part of aggregate demand.
   c. Current dollar GNP will be greater than constant dollar GNP.
   d. GNP will decline.

(12.5) 9. According to the Keynesian economic model, the equilibrium level of output occurs when:

    a. G + T = I + S.
    b. G + I = S + T. ✓
    c. G + T = C + S.
    d. G + I = C + S.

(12.5) 10. According to the Keynesian economic model, the most important factor in determining an economy's output is:
    a. the level of taxes.
    b. the level of aggregate demand. ✓
    c. the level of investment.
    d. the level of government spending.

(12.5) 11. According to the Keynesian economic model, which of the following will promote economic growth?
    a. Household savings increase.
    b. Investment exceeds savings. ✓
    c. Taxes exceed savings.
    d. Government spending decreases.

(12.6) 12. What is Say's Law?
    a. the idea that all earned income will be spent. ✓
    b. the law that restricted government spending and led to the Great Depression.
    c. an idea that served as the basis for the Keynesian revolution.
    d. the belief that lower taxes lead to greater output.

(12.6) 13. Prior to the Keynesian revolution in economic thought, economists believed that which of the following would protect an economy from prolonged recessions?
    a. flexible wages and prices. ✓
    b. the existence of government demand for goods and services.
    c. the growth of GNP.
    d. the existence of "crowding out."

(12.7) 14. Supply-side economists argue that which of the following is the key to economic growth?
    a. increased aggregate demand.
    b. incentives to produce. ✓
    c. a strong government sector.
    d. all of the above.

(12.7) 15. An example of "crowding out" occurs when:
    a. government tax revenues exceed government spending.
    b. government taxes reduce the incentive to produce.
    c. government borrowing results in less private investment. ✓
    d. government borrowing exceeds government tax revenues.

True/False *(Circle T or F.)*

(12.2) 16. Personal consumption expenditures are the most unstable part of aggregate demand. T or **F**

(12.3) 17. National Income is the total amount of income earned in an economy. **T** or F

(12.5) 18. According to the Keynesian economic model, GNP increases when "leakages" exceed "additions." T or **F**

(12.6) 19. Prior to the Keynesian revolution in economic thinking, economists believed that recessions could never last very long. **T** or F

(12.7) 20. Supply-side economists usually advocate a large government sector to ensure economic growth. T or **F**

Chapter 13
Public Finance

I. Chapter Outline

There are many goods and services that the market system cannot provide for the members of an economy. The market cannot provide national defense or public safety. The market cannot provide food, clothing, shelter, and medical care for those too poor to afford these basic necessities. When the members of a society collectively decide to provide goods and services, they do so through the institution we refer to as the "government" or the "public sector" of the economy. However, governments, whether local, state, or federal, are constrained by scarcity, just as individuals are. After determining where we, as a society, want our money spent, governments must collect money from us to pay for the programs by levying taxes.

Introductory Article: Lessons in Lip Reading

Despite repeated promises by politicians to reduce or eliminate the federal budget deficit, it continues to grow. Although it is easy to say that we should reduce government spending, a close examination of government programs shows that there are few places where spending can be reduced without imposing hardships on many. Reducing the deficit requires either less spending on the programs that Americans want and expect or increased taxes. Either of these will result in so much financial pain for some groups that we seem unable or unwilling to do either. Although the 1985 Gramm-Rudman bill requires automatic spending cuts to reduce the deficit, Congress has repeatedly found ways to avoid the bill's requirements, and the deficit continues to increase.

Economic Analysis

This chapter examines the issue of government (public) finance by addressing the following questions:

1. On What Do Governments Spend Money?

   Important Concepts: Transfer payments, Grants-in-aid, Entitlements, Federal expenditures, State and local expenditures
   Case Application: Privatization

2. Where Do Governments Get the Money to Spend?

   Important Concepts: Income taxes, Payroll taxes, Excise taxes, Sales taxes, Property taxes, Fiscal federalism
   Case Application: Social Insecurity

3. Who Pays for Government Spending?

   Important Concepts: Horizontal equity, Vertical equity, Benefits principle, Tax efficiency, Tax incidence, Proportional taxes, Progressive taxes, Regressive taxes
   Case Application: Whose Goose Is Getting Plucked?

Perspective: The Growth of Big Government

II. Summary of Economic Analysis

1. About one-third of the Gross National Product in the United States passes through federal, state, or local governments. However, after adjusting this amount for funds that are simply **transfer payments** from some individuals to others, governments purchase about one-fifth of all the goods and services produced.
2. The growth in federal government during the past two years has been in the areas of national defense (the largest single federal expenditure) and transfer payments.
3. Transfer programs make up over two-thirds of the federal government budget. Most transfer payments are **entitlements**, meaning that recipients are legally entitled to their benefits. Entitlement programs include **Social Security, Medicaid, Medicare,** veterans' benefits, and unemployment assistance.
4. The third largest single expenditure for the federal government is **interest on existing federal debt.**
5. The largest expenditure made by state and local governments is education spending.
6. Unlike the federal government, state and local governments must keep their budgets balanced and can pay for new programs only by raising taxes. A **taxpayer revolt** against increased taxes has put state and local governments under increasing financial pressure.
7. The largest source of revenue for the federal government is the **individual income tax.** Although they represent the second largest source of federal revenue, funds raised through the **payroll tax** are used only to finance the Social Security system.
8. State governments receive most of their revenue through the **sales tax** and local governments rely most heavily on the **property tax.**
9. Through the institutional arrangement known as **fiscal federalism,** state and local governments receive a significant share of their funds from the federal government in the form of grants.
10. A fair tax system requires **horizontal equity,** meaning that financially equal households pay the same amount of taxes. **Vertical equity** refers to the idea that those with greater financial means should pay more taxes.
11. The **benefits principle** of taxation refers to the idea that those who benefit from a government service should pay for it.
12. An **efficient tax** is one that does not result in a lower level of economic output or alter the economic behavior of citizens.
13. The **incidence of a tax** refers to who ultimately pays the tax.
14. If a person's tax payments *as a percentage of income* increase as income increases, the tax is **progressive.** If taxes decrease as a percentage of income as income increases, the tax is **regressive.** If the proportion of income taken in taxes is constant across all income levels, the tax is **proportional.**

III. Review of the Learning Objectives *(Answers begin on p. 307.)*

On What Do Governments Spend Money?

Size of government spending
— About 34% of all spending in the economy is channeled through governments.
— But governments account for only about 20% of purchases. The difference is transfer payments.

FEDERAL SPENDING	**STATE AND LOCAL EXPENDITURES**

— National defense is the largest item in the federal budget (26.2%)
— Other direct expenditures (4.6%)
— The balance of federal expenditures are transfer payments for
  * Social Security (20.4%)
  * interest on the national debt (14.6%)
  * Medicare and other health programs (12%)
  * grants-in-aid to state and local governments (10.9%)
	— Education absorbs the largest part of state and local budgets (29.7%)
	— Other large expenditures include
	  * income maintenance (18.3%)
	  * transportation (7.7%)
	  * police and corrections (7.3%)
	— Interest costs on state and local government debt amount to only 5.4% of their budgets

(See page vi in the foreword "To the Student" for how to make the best use of this schematic outline.)

13.1. Describe the size of government debt and deficits. *(Write in answers below.)*

A.

1. The size of the federal government budget *deficit* is calculated by subtracting _expenditures_ from _tax revenue_.

2. The size of the **actual** deficit in 1990 was about _$220 billion_.

3. The government *debt* is calculated by _adding together all past deficits_, and it is now equal to about _$3 trillion_.

B.

1. The Gramm-Rudman bill calls for _automatic spending reductions_ if the federal budget deficit is not reduced enough to meet certain targets.

2. What impact has Gramm-Rudman had on the size of the federal budget deficit? _not too much — the deficit has actually grown since the bill_

C. What are three ways that the government has avoided making the spending cuts required by the Gramm-Rudman bill?

1. _moving expenditures to prior years_
2. _treating Social Sec. Taxes as income instead of loans_
3. _making overly optimistic revenue forecasts_

D. What are two reasons why it is so difficult to get rid of federal government deficits?
   1. _It is politically difficult to reduce consvty benefit programs_
   2. _It is politically difficult to raise taxes_
E. Why is the federal budget deficit so much larger than state and local budget deficits?
   most states have constitutional restrictions that prohibit deficit financing
F. When calculating the size of the federal government's budget deficit, Social Security payroll tax receipts are counted as _income_ when they more accurately should be counted as _borrowed funds_.

13.2. Discuss the relative size of government economic activity.

A.
   1. Including transfer payments, governments account for what percent of all economic activity in the United States? _about 33%_
   2. Excluding transfer payments, governments account for what percent of all economic activity in the United States? _about 20%_
B. Most of the growth in federal spending over the past two decades has occurred in which two types of spending?
   1. _defense_
   2. _transfer payments_
C. The level of total spending is greatest at the _federal_ level, but public employment is greatest at the _state & local_ level of government.
D. How have the numbers of government employees changed during the past two decades at
   1. the federal level? _roughly constant_
   2. the state and local level? _nearly doubled_

13.3. List the most important types of federal government spending.

A. The three largest **specific** federal government expenditures are:
   1. _defense_
   2. _Social Security_
   3. _interest payments_.
B.
   1. Does the federal government have a bigger impact on the allocation of resources or on the allocation of incomes?
      allocation of income

2. How do you know? _transfer payments are a bigger part of the budget than direct payments_

C. Indicate which of the following expenditures **can** be reduced by Congress (C) and which **cannot** be reduced because they are entitlements or for some other reason (CN).

1. _CN_ Veterans' benefits.
2. _CN_ Social Security payments.
3. _CN_ Medicaid payments.
4. _C_ Defense expenditures.
5. _C_ Space exploration.
6. _CN_ Interest payments.
7. _C_ Environmental programs.
8. _C_ Education programs.

D. Which of the above programs (in part C) represent:

1. Collective goods? _4, 5_
2. Correcting for external economies? _7, 8_
3. Income redistribution? _1, 2, 3_

E. Excluding defense expenditures, **direct** expenditures made by the federal government account for _50_ percent of the federal budget.

F. What are three federal expenditures that you personally benefit from?

1. _defense_
2. _education_
3. _water projects_

13.4. List the most important types of state and local government spending.

A. The largest state and local government expenditure is for _education_.

B. State and local governments are allowed to borrow only in order to _finance capital projects_.

C. What two areas of spending have increased the most for state and local governments during the past decade?

1. _prisons_
2. _health care_

D. Indicate which of the following are financed **primarily** by the federal government (F) and which by state and local governments (SL).

1. _SL_ Education.
2. _SL_ Police and fire protection.

3. _SL_ Highways.
4. _SL_ Prisons.
5. _F_ Defense.
6. _F_ Income maintenance programs.
7. _F_ Space exploration.
8. _F_ Environmental cleanup.

E. Indicate three expenditure programs where your state or local government is undergoing some financial pressure.

1. _transportation_
2. _education_
3. _public safety_

Case Application: Renovating America

Between 1948 and 1951 the United States spent nearly $12 billion helping to rebuild the Western European countries after the devastation inflicted by World War II. But the cost of that reconstruction pales in comparison to the cost of rebuilding our own country's public facilities after decades of neglect. It is estimated that the cost of repairing our deteriorating highways, bridges, and dams, bringing our water and sewage systems to an adequate level, and renovating our decrepit public transportation equipment will amount to as much as $3 trillion.

The country's infrastructure of public facilities is deteriorating so rapidly due to lack of maintenance that failure to carry out a massive renovation program will result in increasing breakdowns, suspensions, and dangerous hazards in public services. According to a 1982 study done under the auspices of the Council of State Planning Agencies, published under the title *America in Ruins,* "the deteriorated condition of basic facilities that underpin the economy will prove a critical bottleneck to national economic renewal during this decade unless we can find new ways to finance public works."

Approximately one-fifth of our bridges are considered so hazardous they have either been closed or are restricted to only light traffic. Cities are being sued for injuries sustained when cars hit enormous potholes. Half of our cities are prevented from expanding because of inadequate water-treatment systems.

It is estimated that $33 billion will have to be spent on repairing the interstate highway system. It will cost many times that for repairs and maintenance of state highway systems and country roads. The Department of Transportation estimates that another $47 billion is needed for the nearly one-half of the nation's bridges, which are obsolete or unsound. The Army Corps of Engineers has determined that approximately one-third of all dams in highly populated areas are unsafe.

Economic Reasoning *(Write your responses on a separate sheet. Answers begin on p. 307.)*

1. Federal spending on renewal of the nation's public facilities would increase the size of which of the pie slices in Figure 3 on page 362 of the textbook?
2. What state and local government spending in Figure 4 on page 363 of the textbook will be affected by the need to renovate the infrastructure?
3. What priority would you give to renewing America's infrastucture in relation to other types of government spending? Why?

Where Do Governments Get the Money to Spend?

FEDERAL REVENUES	STATE AND LOCAL REVENUES
— The largest federal revenue source is personal income taxes (45%) — The second largest is payroll taxes and pension contributions (36.3%) — Corporate income taxes (10.5%) — Excise taxes (3.4%)	— Sales taxes (17.1%) — Property taxes (14.4%) — Federal transfers (13.7%) — Income taxes (12.6%) **Fiscal federalism** The system by which the federal government collects revenues which it transfers to lower government levels to finance their activities.

(See page vi in the foreword "To the Student" for how to make the best use of this schematic outline.)

13.5. Identify the principal sources of revenue for the federal, state, and local governments respectively.

A. Indicate which of the following revenue sources are used **primarily** by federal (F), state (S), or local (L) governments.

1. _F_ The personal income tax.
2. _S_ The sales tax.
3. _F+S_ Excise taxes.
4. _S+L_ Grants-in-aid.
5. _F_ The corporate income tax.
6. _L_ The property tax.
7. _F_ Payroll taxes.

B. What is an advantage of the federal government collecting taxes and giving grants to states and localities instead of state and local governments raising their own tax revenues? (HINT: think about the incidence of taxes and vertical equity.)

The federal tax system is more progressive than state & local tax systems. (more vertical equity) Pg. 308

C. Indicate which taxes might be paid in each of the following situations (there may be more than one).

1. A person gets a paycheck.

   income & payroll taxes
   ~~sales tax & excise tax~~

2. A person spends some of his or her paycheck.

sales tax & excise tax

3. A person saves some of his or her money in a savings account or buys corporate stocks that pay dividends.

income taxes on earned interest & dividends & corporate income taxes

4. A person saves some of his or her money and buys a house.

property taxes

D. The property tax in the United States is levied on both the value of land and the value of buildings on that land. Henry George was an American writer who argued that the property tax should be imposed on land only. Keeping in mind that people respond to incentives, how would removing the tax on the value of buildings and taxing only land affect

1. the supply of land?

No would not change, it can't.

2. the supply (size and number) of buildings?

Taxes are a cost of production that must be paid, & removing the tax on buildings would make them less expensive to build.

Case Application: Should the United States Have a Value-Added Tax?

It has been proposed by Al Ullman, former chairman of the House Ways and Means Committee, and by others as well, that the United States follow the lead of European countries and adopt a value-added tax (VAT) to levy government revenues. He suggests the VAT be substituted for part of the existing income taxes or for the payroll taxes.

A value-added tax is a type of federal sales tax, but unlike the present sales taxes, it is levied upon each producer at each stage of production according to the increase in the value of the product at that stage. The sum of the value-added taxes on the different production stages is passed on to the final purchaser of the product. In the shoe industry, for example, a leather tannery would pay a VAT as a percentage of the difference between the cost of the hides it purchased and the value of the finished leather that it sold to a shoemaker. The shoe manufacturer, in turn, would pay a VAT on the difference between the cost of the leather for the shoes and the value of the shoes sold to the wholesaler. The wholesaler and retailer would pay VATs on the markups they added to the cost of the shoes, and the final selling price for the shoes would include the total VAT paid by all of the firms involved in producing and distributing the shoes.

One of the advantages claimed for the VAT is that it does not reduce efficiency, investment, or work incentives in the way income taxes, payroll taxes, and corporate profit taxes are assumed to do. It would presumably encourage saving and investment while discouraging unnecessary consumption. Other advantages are that it is easily collected and difficult to evade. It is also suggested that it would put American producers on a more equitable competitive footing with foreign producers because imports would be subject to the VAT while exporting firms would get a rebate of the VAT on items exported. That is the system used by European countries, and it helps promote their exports and protect their domestic producers.

The introduction of a value-added tax in the United States might raise the prices of goods and services by 10% to 20%, depending on how much government revenue was needed to make up for a reduction in other taxes. A consumption tax such as VAT is inherently regressive because the lower a person's income, the higher a percentage of their income is spent on goods and services. Ullman proposes that this regressive aspect of VAT should be eliminated by exempting necessities such as food, housing, and medical care from the tax.

Economic Reasoning *(Write your responses on a separate sheet. Answers begin on p. 308.)*

1. If a value-added tax were imposed in the United States as a substitute for the existing Social Security taxes, approximately what percentage of federal government revenues would have to be collected by the VAT?
2. What is the basis for the supposition that income taxes, payroll taxes, and corporate profit taxes reduce efficiency, investment, and work incentives?
3. Is a value-added tax for the United States a good idea or not? If it were used as a substitute for existing taxes, which taxes should be reduced? Why?

Who Pays for Government Spending?

EQUITY	EFFICIENCY
Horizontal equity — People who are equally able to pay bearing the same tax burden. **Vertical equity** — Those with higher incomes paying a larger % of their income in taxes. **Benefits principle** — Taxes levied on the users of government services in proportion to the amount of use.	Taxes should be levied in such a way as to minimize their interference with the allocation of resources and their discouragement of production. **Sin taxes** — An exception to the above rule in the case of goods (tobacco, alcohol) that public policy wishes to discourage.

INCIDENCE
Taxes are often shifted by those on whom they are levied to others. The incidence of the tax is on those who ultimately pay it. Income taxes cannot be shifted, but excise and property taxes are. Corporate profits taxes and payroll taxes are likely shifted to consumers in the form of higher prices and to workers in the form of lower wages.

Progressive taxes	Regressive taxes	Proportional taxes
— a higher % of tax is levied on larger incomes.	— lower income earners pay a larger % of their income in taxes than higher earners.	— the same % of income is paid in taxes at different income levels.

(See page vi in the foreword "To the Student" for how to make the best use of this schematic outline.)

13.6. Explain the criteria for equity in taxation.

A.

1. The idea that people with equal incomes should pay equal taxes is referred to as *horizontal equity*.

2. The idea that taxes should be **directly** related to income is referred to as ___vertical equity___.

B. President George Bush has long supported a decrease in the *capital gains tax* so that capital gains are taxed at a lower rate than earned income. (Capital gains are the profits from the sale of assets.) Capital gains are primarily earned by people in the highest income categories. How would a reduction in the capital gains tax influence

1. horizontal equity?

_____
_____
_____

2. vertical equity?

_____
_____
_____
_____

C.
1. According to the benefits principle of taxation, who pays the tax that finances a specific government service?

___whoever uses that service___

2. Give one example of how the benefits principle is used in the United States.

___gas taxes are used to finance highway construction & maintenance___

D. What are two types of government goods or services that cannot feasibly be financed according to the benefits principle of taxation?

1. ___collective goods___
2. ___redistribution of income to the poor___

E. Which of the following taxes are based on the benefits going to the taxpayer (B), and which are based on equity (ability to pay) grounds (E)?

1. _E_ The personal income tax.
2. _B_ Highway gas taxes.
3. _B or E_ The Social Security payroll tax.
4. _E_ The general sales tax.
5. _E_ Luxury taxes.
6. _E_ Property taxes.
7. _B_ Entertainment taxes on concert or movie tickets.

13.7. Describe how "bad" taxes decrease economic efficiency.

A.
1. What are "sin taxes"?

___taxes on things considered sins - drinking & smoking___

2. Explain how sin taxes could be justified because of "external" costs.

smokers & drinkers effect their own health & the health of others through second-hand smoke & accidents

B. Indicate one way that each of the following tax policies may change behavior and cause a reallocation of resources.

1. Higher income taxes. *people may work less*
2. A new tax on buildings. *fewer new buildings*
3. Higher taxes on dividends. *fewer people investing in corporate stocks*
4. Lower taxes on capital gains. *more people buying & selling financial assets*
5. Taxes on yellow pencils. *people will switch to blue pencils*
6. Reduced tax deductions for charitable contributions.

people will give less to charity

13.8. Define what is meant by the incidence of a tax.

A. If the demand for a product is very **inelastic**, then people will continue to buy the product regardless of price increases. If the demand is **elastic**, people will switch to substitutes if the price of a product increases. Explain how the elasticity of demand can therefore influence the incidence of an excise tax.

If the demand is inelastic, the incidence will fall on the buyer

elastic - seller

B. Which of the following taxes is regressive, which is proportional, and which is progressive?

A		B		C	
Income	Tax	Income	Tax	Income	Tax
$10,000	$2,000	$20,000	$2,000	$10,000	$2,000
20,000	3,000	24,000	3,000	15,000	3,000
40,000	4,000	28,000	4,000	20,000	4,000

1. Tax A is *regressive*.
2. Tax B is *progressive*.
3. Tax C is *proportional*.

C. If after-tax incomes are less equally distributed than before-tax incomes, then the overall tax system must be

regressive.

D. Which of the following are regressive (R), progressive (P), and proportional (Pr) taxes?

1. *P* The federal income tax.

2. _R_ Sales taxes.
3. _R_ Payroll taxes.
4. _R_ Excise taxes.
5. _P/r_ The U.S. tax system as a whole.
6. _R_ Gasoline taxes.
7. _R_ The lottery.

Case Application: A Look at the Flat-Rate Tax

The 1986 tax reform bill was a semi-flat tax bill. In place of the progressive tax rate schedule it instituted a two-rate structure of 15% and 28%, depending on the level of income and whether the tax return was single or joint. The 1990 tax bill added a third step of 31% on higher incomes.

The advantage claimed for the flat-rate tax is that it should greatly simplify the tax system, making it easier and cheaper for people to calculate their taxes and for the government to administer the system. Since it eliminates a multiplicity of income exemptions from taxes, it should remove the existing inducements to invest in tax shelters and devise other ways of avoiding taxes. It is alleged that this increases the efficient allocation of our financial resources, reduces the time and expense allocated to tax accountants and lawyers, and otherwise provides incentives for productive efforts in place of tax-avoidance efforts.

As it turned out, although the reformed tax bill did eliminate most tax shelters, it was at least as complicated to calculate and administer taxes as before. In actuality, it increased the business of tax-preparation firms.

The main objection to the flat-rate income tax is that it makes the tax system more inequitable. Federal taxes other than the income tax, as well as state and local taxes, are largely regressive. They take a higher percentage of the incomes of low-income earners than of high-income earners. Only income taxes counterbalance the regressivity of the rest of the tax system with their progressive structure. The new tax structure does set the basic personal exemption higher in order to relieve the lowest income earners from paying income taxes.

Economic Reasoning *(Write your responses on a separate sheet. Answers begin on p. 308.)*

1. What is the effect of a flat-rate income tax on the vertical equity of our tax system?
2. How might a flat-rate tax increase the efficiency of the tax system?
3. Are you in favor of a pure flat-rate tax, the modified flat-rate tax bills passed in 1986 and 1990, or the previous progressive income tax system? Why?

IV. Practice Test *(Answers begin on p. 309.)*

Multiple Choice *(Circle the correct answer.)*

(13.1) 1. During the 1980s:
  a. "Reaganomics" eliminated the national debt.
  b. annual budget deficits increased and the national debt doubled.
  c. the size of annual budget deficits decreased, and the national debt was reduced.
  d. both annual budget deficits and the size of the national debt remained constant.

(13.1) 2. Which of the following is one of the ways that Congress has managed to avoid the budget-cutting provisions included in the Gramm-Rudman bill?
  a. Congress and the president make very optimistic budget forecasts.
  b. Expenditures are moved backwards to prior fiscal years.

c. Some expenditures are not included in the "official" budget, such as the S&L bailout.
d. Social Security tax collections are counted as income instead of as loans to the Treasury.
e. all of the above.

(13.2) 3. Excluding income transfers, governments in the United States spend _____ percent of GNP.
a. 10
b. 20
c. 33
d. 40
e. 50

(13.2) 4. Which of the following is a TRUE statement?
a. State and local government employment increased faster than federal government employment during the past 20 years.
b. Federal government employment has grown faster than overall employment during the past 20 years.
c. Both federal and state and local employment have grown at the same rate as overall employment during the past 20 years.
d. Government employment at all levels decreased during the past 20 years.

(13.3) 5. The three largest expenses of the federal government are:
a. defense, space exploration, and education.
b. defense, education, and Social Security.
c. defense, Social Security, and interest payments.
d. defense, foreign aid, Social Security.

(13.3) 6. Which of the following is NOT an entitlement program?
a. veterans' benefits.
b. Social Security.
c. grants-in-aid.
d. Medicaid.

(13.4) 7. The largest state and local government expenditure is spending for:
a. income transfers and income maintenance.
b. public safety (including police, prisons, and courts).
c. transportation (including roads and mass transit).
d. education.

(13.4) 8. State and local government budget deficits:
a. are collectively almost as large as the federal budget deficit.
b. are small or nonexistent because state and local governments are more responsible than the federal government.
c. do not usually exist because most state constitutions forbid state and local deficit spending.
d. have increased at about the same rate as the federal budget deficit.

(13.5) 9. The largest source of federal tax revenue is the:
a. sales tax.
b. individual income tax.
c. corporate income tax.
d. Social Security payroll tax.

(13.5) 10. The largest source of local tax revenue is the:
a. property tax.
b. income tax.
c. sales tax.
d. excise tax.

(13.6) 11. Which of the following helps achieve "vertical equity"?
a. the use of state lotteries instead of taxes.

b. reducing the federal deficit by increasing everybody's taxes equally.
c. the use of more sales taxes and less property taxes.
d. the use of a progressive income tax.

(13.6) 12. Which of the following functions of government could NOT be financed by depending on the benefits principle of taxation?
a. building roads.
b. providing fire protection.
c. providing a court (justice) system.
d. providing services for the poor.

(13.7) 13. A tax is "efficient" if:
a. it is easy to collect.
b. it cannot be shifted from the taxpayer to someone else.
c. it is fair.
d. it does not change people's economic behavior.

(13.8) 14. The "incidence" of a tax refers to which of the following?
a. who ultimately pays the tax.
b. the fairness (equity) of a tax.
c. the effect of the tax on economic behavior and the allocation of resources.
d. the size of the tax relative to the taxpayer's income.

(13.9) 15. Which of the following is a tax that cannot be passed on to others?
a. the property tax.
b. the sales tax.
c. the corporate income tax.
d. the individual income tax.

True/False *(Circle T or F.)*

(13.1) 16. As a result of the Gramm-Rudman Bill, federal budget deficits declined during the 1980s. T or F

(13.4) 17. State and local governments are usually forbidden from borrowing for any purpose. T or F

(13.5) 18. Property taxes are the primary source of local government revenues. T or F

(13.6) 19. Overall, the United States tax structure became more progressive during the 1980s. T or F

(13.8) 20. The incidence of the Social Security payroll tax falls on both workers and employers. T or F

Chapter 14

Policies for Economic Stability and Growth

I. Chapter Outline

Economic growth, full employment, and stable prices are generally accepted by most economists as desirable economic goals. There is substantial disagreement, however, on the best ways to achieve these goals. Some economists believe that government intervention causes more problems than it cures and advocate a minimum of such intervention. Among those that believe that government intervention is necessary to achieve the above goals, there is disagreement as to whether the best policies are those that are based on changing government spending and taxation levels (fiscal policy) versus those that are based on changing the money supply (monetary policy). Finally, there are significant disagreements between those that advocate policies that influence demand (Keynesian economics) and those that advocate policies that influence the supply side of the economy (supply-side economics).

Introductory Article: The Legacy of Reaganomics

After a severe recession in 1982, the economic policies of the Reagan administration (1981 to 1988) were associated with steady economic growth, low unemployment, and stable prices. The period between 1982 and 1990 represented the longest peacetime economic expansion in American history. Many economists are concerned, however, that this excellent economic performance came at a price that will be paid for by future generations. Record budget deficits resulted in a doubling of the national debt during the 1980s, and the United States went from being the world's largest international lender to being the world's largest international borrower. Savings and investment decreased, income inequality increased, the nation's infrastructure began to crumble, and the banking system ended the 1980s teetering on the brink of disaster. Only time will tell if the true legacy of Reaganomics will be the boom of the 1980s or paying for that boom in 1990s.

Economic Analysis

This chapter examines the ways that the federal government can influence the nation's economy by addressing the following questions:

1. What Can the Government Do About Unemployment and Inflation?

    Important Concepts: Fiscal policy, Cyclically balanced budgets, Functional finance, Monetary policy

    Case Application: Who's at the Wheel?

2. How Does Fiscal Policy Help Stabilize the Economy?

    Important Concepts: Discretionary fiscal policy, The multiplier, Automatic stabilizers

    Important Models: Keynesian and supply-side economic models

    Case Application: Investment Incentives or Tax Loopholes?

3. How Can Monetary Policy Help Stabilize the Economy?

>   Important Concepts: Open market operations, Reserve requirements, Discounting, Velocity of money, The monetary rule
>
>   Important Model: The quantity theory
>
>   Case Application: Target Practice at the Fed
>
> 4. How Can Economic Growth Be Increased?
>
>   Important Concepts: Investment/GNP ratio, Capital/output ratio, Labor-force participation rate, Human capital
>
>   Case Application: Investing in the Future

Perspective: Monetarism—Does Money Matter?

>   Biography—Milton Friedman

II. Summary of Economic Analysis

1. Economic **stabilization** refers to policies that promote growth, employment, and price stability in an economy.
2. The two principal policy tools used to stabilize the economy are **fiscal policy** and **monetary policy**.
3. Fiscal policy is the use of federal government spending, taxing, and **debt management** to influence economic growth and price stability.
4. The way that the government manages its budget can have significant impacts on the economy. Three different budget philosophies are the **annually balanced budget**, the **cyclically balanced budget**, and **functional finance**.
5. **Discretionary fiscal policy** refers to intentional changes in tax or spending policies specifically designed to influence economic activity in a certain way.
6. **Keynesian economic theory** argues that discretionary fiscal policy should consist of government spending making up for inadequate or excessive aggregate demand. **Supply-side economic theory** argues that fiscal policy should be directed at stimulating savings and private investment.
7. The impact of any fiscal policy is magnified through the **multiplier** effect because increases in spending create income for individuals and/or businesses, and this income is in turn spent and becomes income for others.
8. **Automatic stabilizers** are built into the economy to help keep demand up during recessions and decrease demand during expansions. These automatically shield the economy from dramatic fluctuations in economic activity without requiring any action by the government.
9. **Monetary policy** consists of adjusting the money supply and interest rates in order to influence economic activity. Monetary policy is implemented by the Federal Reserve System.
10. Monetary policy can be used either to control interest rates or to control the supply of money. The level of interest rates affects the economy by influencing investment. The impact of the supply of money on the economy can be evaluated by means of the **quantity equation**.
11. A problem with using monetary policy to control interest rates is that the timing of the Fed's actions becomes very important. A problem with using monetary policy to control the money supply is that the definition of the money supply and the velocity of money are constantly changing.
12. Increased **economic growth** is essential to increased standards of living.
13. To a large extent, economic growth depends on the quantity of capital in an economy. This is measured by the **investment/GNP ratio**. The quality of this capital, as measured by the **capital/output ratio**, also influences the level of economic growth.

14. The **labor-force participation rate** measures the quantity of labor that is working with an economy's capital. **Human capital** investment improves the quality of that labor.

III. Review of the Learning Objectives (Answers begin on p. 309.)

What Can the Government Do About Unemployment and Inflation?

FISCAL POLICY

One arm of government stabilization policies is fiscal policy — the use of federal spending, taxing, and debt management to influence general economic activity.

BUDGET PHILOSOPHIES

Annually balanced budget

An objective of balancing the federal budget each year rules out any discretionary fiscal policy by the government to counteract economic instability in the private sector.

Cyclically balanced budget

Balancing the federal budget over the course of the businesses cycle, with surpluses in boom years covering deficits during recessions, would make active government fiscal policy possible.

Functional finance

Pursuing fiscal stabilization policies without regard to budget balance is functional finance.

MONETARY POLICY

Monetary stabilization policies are under the control of the Federal Reserve System. The Fed implements monetary policy through its powers to manage the money supply by changing the reserves of depository institutions — reducing them to tighten the money supply in order to combat inflation or expanding them to loosen the money supply in order to encourage business expansion in a recession.

(See page vi in the foreword "To the Student" for how to make the best use of this schematic outline.)

14.1. Discuss economic policies in the 1980s and their consequences. *(Write in answers below.)*

A. List three positive consequences of economic policies in the 1980s.

1. *economic growth*
2. *low unemployment*
3. *low inflation*

B. List three negative consequences of economic policies in the 1980s.

1. *record budget deficits*
2. *growing inequality of income*
3. *international trade deficits*

C. President Reagan claimed that the federal budget could be balanced by **reducing taxes**.
   1. This was an exercise in _supply_-_side_ economic policy.
   2. The tax cuts were designed so that people would _save_ their extra disposable income, resulting in increased _investment_.
   3. However, the policy failed to work because people _spent_ their extra disposable income.

D. Suppose that you applied for every credit card you could get and charged each card up to its maximum amount. How would this be similar to U.S. economic policy in the 1980s, and what consequences would it have for the future?
   Like the U.S., if you borrowed a lot you could have a good time living beyond your means. pg. 309

14.2. Identify the government's two major instruments of stabilization policy.

A. Recall that aggregate demand is equal to C + I + G + (X–M).
   1. How could fiscal policy increase C?
      by decreasing personal taxes
   2. How could fiscal policy increase I?
      by decreasing business taxes
   3. How could monetary policy increase I?
      by reducing interest rates

B. Match the stabilization policies below with the following uncontrollable event that could cause the policy to be **ineffective**.
   1. Supply-side tax cuts are made in order to stimulate investment. _d_
   2. Demand-side (Keynesian) tax cuts are made in order to stimulate aggregate demand. _c_
   3. The Fed lowers the discount rate in order to increase economic activity. _a_
   4. The Fed increases the discount rate in order to decrease economic activity. ___

      a. Businesses decide not to borrow because their expectations about the future are gloomy.
      b. The velocity of money increases.
      c. People save their extra disposable income.
      d. People spend their extra disposable income.

C. Suppose the United States economy is at the peak of a business cycle and fiscal policy is to be used to slow the economy down. How can an unexpected war in the Middle East frustrate the intent of fiscal policy?

Increased military expeditures would require an increase in government expeditures

D. How can "rational expectations" counteract a Fed policy of increasing the money supply to lower interest rates and stimulate investment?

Expecting higher inflation, lenders would raise the nominal interest rate

E. How can "rational expectations" counteract a government fiscal policy of cutting taxes and running a budget deficit in order to stimulate aggregate demand? (HINT: What effect will current deficits have on future taxes, and how will future taxes be paid?)

People might save their extra disposable income in order to pay future taxes, thus demand would not increase.

F. What are the effects of the following policies on GNP (Up or Down)? Indicate whether the policy is a fiscal policy (F) or a monetary policy (M).

	F/M	Up/Down	
1.	F	down	Taxes increase.
2.	M	up	The discount rate falls.
3.	M	up	The Fed buys bonds.
4.	F	up	Government spending increases (Keynesian theory).
5.	F	down	Government spending increases (Supply-side theory).

14.3. Differentiate between annually balanced budgets, cyclically balanced budgets, and functional finance.

A. Independent of fiscal policies, the federal budget usually runs deficits during recessions and surpluses during expansions.

1. Suppose the economy is in a recession. How could requiring an annually balanced budget make the recession worse?

   pg. 309

2. Suppose the economy is at the peak of a business cycle. What problem could be caused by requiring an annually balanced budget?

   pg. 309

B. If the budget is to be cyclically balanced, then it will run a ___surplus___ during ___expansions___ and a ___deficit___ during ___recessions___.

C. Even though there have been a number of expansions during the past 30 years, the federal government has not had a surplus since 1969. Even if Congress believes in cyclically balanced budgets, why is it politically so much easier to have a deficit than it is to have a surplus?

Surpluses require either less spending on things that constituents want, higher taxes, or both. These are unpopular w/ voters.

D. Indicate whether each of the following is most descriptive of an annually balanced budget (A), a cyclically balanced budget (C), or functional finance (F).

1. ___C___
The government should run a deficit during recessions.

2. ___F___
Permanent budget deficits are acceptable.

3. ___A___
Government spending would need to be cut during recessions.

4. ___A___
This would cause higher highs and lower lows in the business cycle.

5. ___C___
Current deficits should be balanced by future surpluses.

Case Application: The Balanced Budget Amendment

A proposed amendment to the U.S. Constitution would require an annually balanced budget. Proponents of such an amendment maintain Congress has been unwilling to curb the large federal deficits that have fueled inflation, increased the national debt, and caused higher interest rates. They claim a constitutional amendment is necessary to prevent the government from running deficits except in times of emergency.

The text of one proposed balanced budget amendment is as follows:

SECTION 1. Prior to each fiscal year, the Congress shall adopt a statement of receipts and outlays for that year in which total outlays are no greater than total receipts. The Congress may amend such statement provided revised outlays are no greater than revised receipts. Whenever three-fifths of the whole number of both houses shall deem it necessary, Congress in such statement may provide for a specific excess of outlays over receipts by a vote directed solely to that subject. The Congress and the president shall, pursuant to legislation or through exercise of their powers under the first and second articles, ensure that actual outlays do not exceed the outlays set forth in such statement.

SECTION 2. Total receipts for any fiscal year set forth in the statement adopted pursuant to this article shall not increase by a rate greater than the rate of increase in national income in the year or years ending not less than six months nor more than 12 months before such fiscal year, unless a majority of the whole number of both Houses of Congress shall have passed a bill directed solely to approving specific additional receipts and such bill has become law.

SECTION 3. The Congress may waive the provisions of this article for any fiscal year in which a declaration of war is in effect.

SECTION 4. Total receipts shall include all receipts of the United States except those derived from borrowing and total outlays shall include all outlays of the United States except those for repayment of debt principal.

SECTION 5. The Congress shall enforce and implement this article by appropriate legislation.

SECTION 6. This article shall take effect for the second fiscal year beginning after its ratification.

Economic Reasoning *(Write your responses on a separate sheet. Answers begin on p. 309.)*

1. Could Congress circumvent the requirement for a balanced budget? How?
2. What would be the consequences for implementing fiscal policy if the balanced budget amendment were to pass?
3. Are you in favor of or opposed to the balanced budget amendment? Why?

How Does Fiscal Policy Help Stabilize the Economy?

DISCRETIONARY FISCAL POLICY

Keynesian	Supply-side
Keynesians focus on the use of fiscal policy to compensate for inadequate or excessive demand in the private sector by increasing government spending and decreasing taxes in a recession or by reducing government spending and increasing taxes in a period of inflation.	Supply-side fiscal policy would reduce both taxes and government spending in a recession. The decreases in taxes would be directed toward savers rather than consumers.

Multiplier
The impact on the economy of a change in taxes or government spending is increased by the multiplier effect:

$$\text{Multiplier} = \frac{1}{\text{savings rate} + \text{tax rate}}$$

AUTOMATIC STABILIZERS
Besides discretionary fiscal policy, there are various automatic stabilizers in government spending and taxing, such as transfer payments and progressive tax rates, that counteract recession and inflation.

(See page vi in the foreword "To the Student" for how to make the best use of this schematic outline.)

14.4. Explain how discretionary fiscal policy works from the Keynesian and supply-side viewpoints.

A. Indicate which of the following are Keynesian (K) and which are supply-side (S) views of the way that different policies affect the economy.

1. __S__ Tax cuts to upper-income groups will increase saving and investment.
2. __K__ Tax cuts to lower-income groups will stimulate aggregate demand.
3. __S__ Budget deficits "crowd out" private investment.
4. __K__ Budget deficits stimulate the economy.
5. __S__ If the government used fewer resources, more resources would be free to increase private spending.
6. __S__ Government policies should be directed toward increasing the economy's productive capacity.

7. _K_ Government spending is sometimes necessary in order to get the economy out of a recession.

B. Which of the two types of policy prescriptions, Keynesian or supply-side, takes a longer-run view of economic policy? How do you know?

Supply side takes longer because it takes more time to increase the supply of productive resources than it does to increase spending

C.
1. _Keynesian_ economic policy is directed at increasing economic activity by "filling up the GNP tank."
2. _Supply-side_ economic policy is directed at increasing the size of the GNP tank.

14.5. Describe the multiplier effect.

A. For each of the following savings and tax rates, indicate the size of the **multiplier** and how much income will increase from an initial expenditure of $100 (include the original $100 in your calculations of how much income will increase).

	Savings Rate	Tax Rate	The Multiplier Equals	Total Income Will Increase
1.	0.10	0.00	10	$1000
2.	0.10	0.10	5	$500
3.	0.20	0.10	3	$300
4.	0.40	0.10	2	$200
5.	0.50	0.50	1	$100

B. What would the multiplier be equal to if savings rates and tax rates together approached zero?

It would approach infinity

C.
1. Is there an inverse, direct, or constant relationship between the savings rate and increases in income?

inverse

2. The "consumption rate" is equal to (1 – the savings rate): as the savings rate increases the consumption rate decreases, and vice versa. With this in mind, can you think of a good economic justification for encouraging people to spend rather than save?

Spending increases aggregate demand and increased consumption rates increase the size of the multiplier

3. The savings rate and tax rate in the United States both decreased during the 1980s. From a Keynesian point of view, what impact would this have on income in the United States?

It would cause it to increase

D. Suppose the government determined that incomes needed to be increased by $1 billion in order to bring the economy out of a recession. How much would the government need to spend in direct spending (G) in each of the following situations?
1. The multiplier equals 5. *$200,000,000*
2. Tax plus savings rates equal 0.25. *$250,000,000*
3. Tax plus savings rates equal 0.10. *$100,000,000*

14.6. Define and give examples of automatic stabilizers.

A. Automatic stabilizers cannot reverse a trend in economic activity, but they can *"cushion" downturns & upturns*.

B.
1. During downturns in the economy, automatic stabilizers *increase aggregate demand*.
2. During upturns in the economy, automatic stabilizers *decrease aggregate demand*.

C. Which of the components of aggregate demand is most influenced by automatic stabilizers? *consumption*

D. Indicate (with a check) which of the following are automatic stabilizers.
1. ✓ Unemployment compensation.
2. ✓ Progressive income taxes.
3. ___ Defense spending.
4. ✓ Aid to Families with Dependent Children.
5. ___ Property taxes.

Case Application: What Happens to Tax-Cut Dollars?

A principal point of contention between Keynesian and supply-side proponents concerns the proper function of tax reductions. According to the Keynesians, tax-cut money should be used by consumers to purchase goods and services—thereby stimulating output, employment, and incomes. Supply-siders, on the other hand, believe tax-cut dollars should go into savings, which would be available for real investment—thereby reducing costs, increasing output, creating jobs, and increasing incomes.

Tax legislation in the 1980s was oriented toward tax reductions for business and high-income taxpayers who have a larger propensity to save. Fully 35% of the total tax-cut dollars went to the 5.6% of income earners making over $50,000 a year. Increases in Social Security taxes and tax bracket creep resulting from inflation ate up all of the tax-cut dollars of those earning less than $50,000 a year.

The supply-side strategy requires an increase in the savings rate. However, research has shown the savings rate to be quite constant over time. Furthermore, although the average savings rate is greater for high-income earners than for low-income earners, the marginal propensity to save is about the same for both groups. Those earning over $50,000 a year are no more likely to save their tax-cut dollars than those earning under $50,000.

Another assumption of the supply-side tax cuts was that increasing the after-tax rate of return on savings would cause an increase in the savings rate. Studies do not support this assumption. Some people are induced to save more when the after-tax rate of return is increased. However, people whose objective is a specific level of future income from their assets can achieve that objective with a lower savings rate when the after-tax rate of return on savings is increased. These two groups cancel each other out, leaving the overall rate of savings unaffected by changes in the after-tax rate of return.

Economic Reasoning *(Write your responses on a separate sheet. Answers begin on p. 310.)*

1. What discretionary fiscal policy measure is discussed in this application?
2. Does the multiplier effect work on tax-cut dollars as well as on government expenditure dollars? How?
3. Was the tax legislation passed in the 1980s wise and effective fiscal policy? Why or why not?

How Can Monetary Policy Help Stabilize the Economy?

MONETARY POLICY TOOLS		
Open Market Operations Fed offers to buy or sell government securities on the open market. Buying increases bank reserves and encourages expansion of money supply, while selling decreases reserves and reduces money supply.	**Discount rate changes** Fed reduces discount rate on loans to banks in order to encourage an increase in reserves and expand money supply, raises discount rate to discourage bank borrowing of reserves and to reduce money supply.	**Required reserve ratio** Fed reduces the % of the banks' liabilities that they must have on deposit in their reserves in Federal Reserve Bank to permit increase in money supply, increases % to reduce money supply.
CONTROLLING INTEREST RATES The target of Fed monetary policy prior to Oct. 1979 was the control of interest rates. Bringing about a decline in interest rates stimulated economic activity, while raising interest rates was deflationary.		**CONTROL OF THE MONEY SUPPLY** In 1979 the target of monetary policy was changed to control of the money supply. The Fed sets a target for growth of the money supply sufficient to finance expansion of the economy, but restrictive enough to prevent inflation.

(See page vi in the foreword "To the Student" for how to make the best use of this schematic outline.)

14.7. Explain how monetary policy is implemented.

A. Indicate what effect (increase or decrease) each of the following will have on the supply of money (MS), interest rates (r), investment (I), and aggregate demand (AD).

1. The Fed lowers the discount rate.
   MS *up* r *down* I *up* AD *up*
2. The Fed buys bonds in the open market.
   MS *up* r *down* I *up* AD *up*
3. The Fed increases reserve requirements.
   MS *down* r *up* I *down* AD *down*

B.

1. Prior to 1979, the aim of the monetary policy carried out by the Fed was to

control interest rates.

2. The Fed was criticized because it sometimes made mistakes in the _timing_ of its policies.

C.
1. Since 1979, the Fed's monetary policy has concentrated on controlling the _supply of money_.
2. One problem with this policy is that the _velocity of money_ is not constant.
3. A second problem is that financial deregulation has resulted in new types of accounts that function both as _demand_ deposits (money) and _saving_ accounts (near money).

D. The demand for money increases when the aggregate demand for goods and services increases.

1. Using the graph below, graphically show what happens if the Fed **decreases** the supply of money in order to reduce inflation while the government uses fiscal policy to **increase** economic activity.

2. What impact would the Fed's policy have on government plans to increase economic activity?
   a. Interest rates would _rise_.
   b. Investment would _fall_.
   c. Aggregate demand would _fall_.

3. Would the Fed's actions help or hinder the government's fiscal policy efforts?
   hinder.

pg. 310

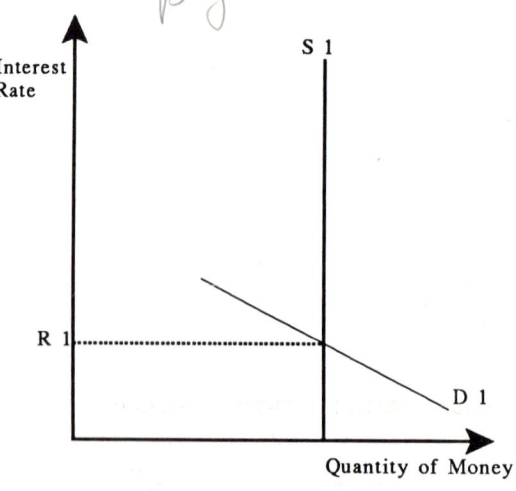

[Graph: Interest Rate vs Quantity of Money, showing S 1 (vertical supply line), D 1 (downward sloping demand), intersecting at R 1]

E. When the government undertakes expansionary fiscal policy to stimulate the economy, it usually increases the demand for money.

1. Using the graph below, graphically show what happens if the Fed **increases** the supply of money while the government is conducting expansionary fiscal policy.

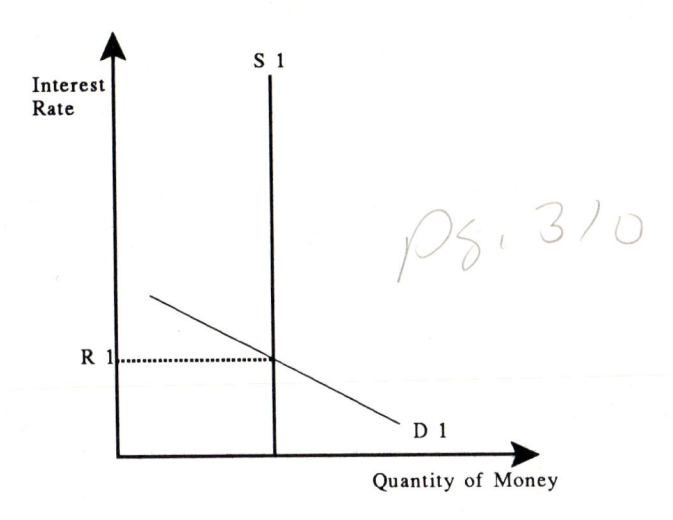

[Graph: Interest Rate vs Quantity of Money, showing vertical supply curve S 1, downward-sloping demand D 1, intersecting at R 1. Handwritten note: "pg. 310"]

2. What would be the effect on interest rates if the Fed **did not** increase the money supply?

   they would increase

3. What would be the effect on interest rates if the Fed **did** increase the money supply?

   they would be lower

4. What would be a **negative** consequence of keeping interest rates low in this situation?

   It might be inflationary

F. According to monetarists, the quantity theory of money (M × V = P × T) shows that increasing the money supply at the same rate of growth as increases in transactions (output) will result in stable prices.

   1. What assumption is necessary for this argument to be correct?

      a constant velocity of money

   2. Is this assumption consistent with reality? *no*

Case Application: The Interest Rate Yo-Yo

In 1981 more than 2,000 construction firms went out of business. They went broke because housing construction fell to the lowest level in years, with hundreds of thousands of construction workers out of a job. The National Association of Realtors lost 70,000 members between 1978 and 1981. Other industries also had high mortality rates. In two and a half years some 2,600 automobile dealerships closed their doors. There was a 41% jump in business failures in 1981 as small businesses and farmers suffered foreclosures.

This havoc in the business world was not caused by a major depression but rather by sky-high interest rates—rates as high as 23% for construction loans alone. Potential housing buyers were unable or unwilling to take out mortgage loans at interest rates of

16% or 17%. Consequently, many construction firms were forced into bankruptcy by the banks that underwrote their construction loans.

New car dealers were in the same sort of bind, often paying $142 a month in interest costs on every $10,000 automobile they had in inventory. With new car sales moving so slowly, the interest costs simply became more than many dealers could handle.

It was previously unheard-of for established businesses with excellent credit ratings to pay a prime rate over 20%, as they did for a short time in 1981. Home builders, farmers, and other small businesses frequently had to pay a premium of 2 or 3 percentage points above the prime interest rate. The super-high interest rates were a part of the government strategy for bringing down the inflation rate. It was a strategy that exacted a high price from thousands of small business owners.

With escalating government debt in the early 1990s, the question is being asked whether we may repeat the sky-high interest rate experience of a decade earlier.

Economic Reasoning *(Write your responses on a separate sheet. Answers begin on p. 310.)*

1. One reason interest rates were so high in 1981 was because of Federal Reserve open market operations. How would open market operations result in raising the interest rates paid by businesses?
2. As a result of the 1979 change in Federal Reserve Board strategy from controlling interest rates to controlling the money supply, interest rates have fluctuated widely. What are the consequences of wide fluctuations in interest rates?
3. Do you think the objective of controlling the money supply justifies the wide swings in interest rates? Why or why not?

How Can Economic Growth Be Increased?

IMPORTANCE OF ECONOMIC GROWTH
Our standard of living is largely determined by the rate of growth, and a higher growth rate makes it easier to solve many economic problems.

Increasing capital investment	Increasing capital efficiency	Increasing labor-force participation rate	Increasing investment in human capital
Economic growth can be increased by raising the proportion of the nation's output that we put into the formation of capital.	Increasing the quality of capital investment by the substitution of more technologically advanced equipment and also production methods is a major source of economic growth.	Economic growth is increased when a larger % of the population is active in the nation's labor force. Increased participation by women in the labor force in the last two decades has contributed in a quite significant way to U.S. economic growth.	The quality of the labor force is a determinant of the rate of economic growth. Investment in education and also in more occupational and on-the-job training increases the growth rate.
Investment/GNP ratio The fraction of each year's GNP that is allocated to creating investment goods.	**Capital/output ratio** The ratio of the cost of new investment goods to the value of annual output produced by those goods.		

(See page vi in the foreword "To the Student" for how to make the best use of this schematic outline.)

14.8. Explain the investment/GNP ratio and the capital/output ratio and describe their importance.

A.

1. What is the primary opportunity cost of increasing the investment/GNP ratio? _current consumption_

2. What is the primary benefit of increasing the investment/GNP ratio? _A higher standard of living in the future_

B. Increased productivity is indicated by a(n) _decrease_ in the capital/output ratio.

C. Are the investment/GNP and capital/output ratios measures of the quality or quantity of capital in an economy?

1. Investment/GNP ratio _quantity_
2. Capital/output ratio _quality_

D. Indicate which of the following will result in an improved investment/GNP ratio (I) and which will result in an improved capital/output ratio (C).

1. _C_ Improved technology.
2. _I_ Lower interest rates.
3. _C_ Better human capital.
4. _C_ The use of process innovations.
5. _I_ A longer-term profit perspective.
6. _I_ A smaller federal budget deficit.
7. _C_ Computer-assisted manufacturing techniques.
8. _C_ Just-in-time manufacturing techniques.

E. List three types of **public** investment that can lead to improved economic growth.

1. _highway improvements_
2. _water projects_
3. _human capital investment (education)_

14.9. Describe the effects on economic growth of the labor-force participation rate and investment in human capital.

A. Do the labor-force participation rate and human capital investment reflect increased labor quantity or quality?

1. Participation rate _quantity_
2. Human capital _quality_

B. What are three reasons for the increased labor-force participation rate in the United States?

1. _"baby boomers" entering the labor force_
2. _more women working outside the home_

212 / *Working With The Study of Economics, 4/E*

    3. *more workers working longer years (retiring later)*

C. What are two ways that people can invest in their human capital?

    1. *formal education*

    2. *on-the-job training*

D. Similar to investing in physical capital, a person investing in human capital must compare the costs of the investment to the expected benefits.

    1. What is a person's biggest cost of investing in human capital?

    foregone wages while in school or lower wages during on-the-job training

    2. Why would you expect an **inverse** relationship between a person's age and that person's investment in human capital?

    the older someone is, the fewer remaining work years available to get the returns

E. Rank the following in the order of time that it takes for each to occur (1 is the quickest, 4 the slowest).

    1. _1_ Increases in the labor-force participation rate.

    2. _2_ Increases in the investment/GNP ratio.

    3. _4_ Increases in productivity stemming from human capital investment.

    4. _3_ Increases in the capital/output ratio.

Case Application: How to Grow

A growing economy is one that spends today to increase tomorrow's production. Money and effort are poured into education and research, as well as into new and better machines. However, disagreements arise over the relative effectiveness of money and time invested in different areas. The table below shows the relationship between changes in spending for research and development (R&D) and changes in Gross National Product.

**Average Annual Percentage Changes in
Research and Development Outlays and Gross National Product**
Constant Dollars, 1961–1988

Percent Change

	1961–65	1966–70	1971–75	1976–80	1981–88
R&D Outlay	6.5	1.2	−0.2	4.1	4.4
GNP	4.7	3.2	2.6	3.7	3.0

    The figures on average annual changes in research and development outlays and Gross National Product show a correlation between the two for each period. Lower rates of increase in research and development spending are associated with lower rates of increase in Gross National Product.

    This relationship does not necessarily show that changes in research and development spending cause changes in Gross National Product, however. The benefits of research and development outlays may not show up in the growth of GNP for a period of time, perhaps years after the research and development takes place. The relationship may very well be the other way around: changes in the rate of growth of GNP may cause changes in the rate of growth of research and development outlays.

    Another contributor to growth in GNP is education. The following chart shows the median years of education completed by those aged 25 and over.

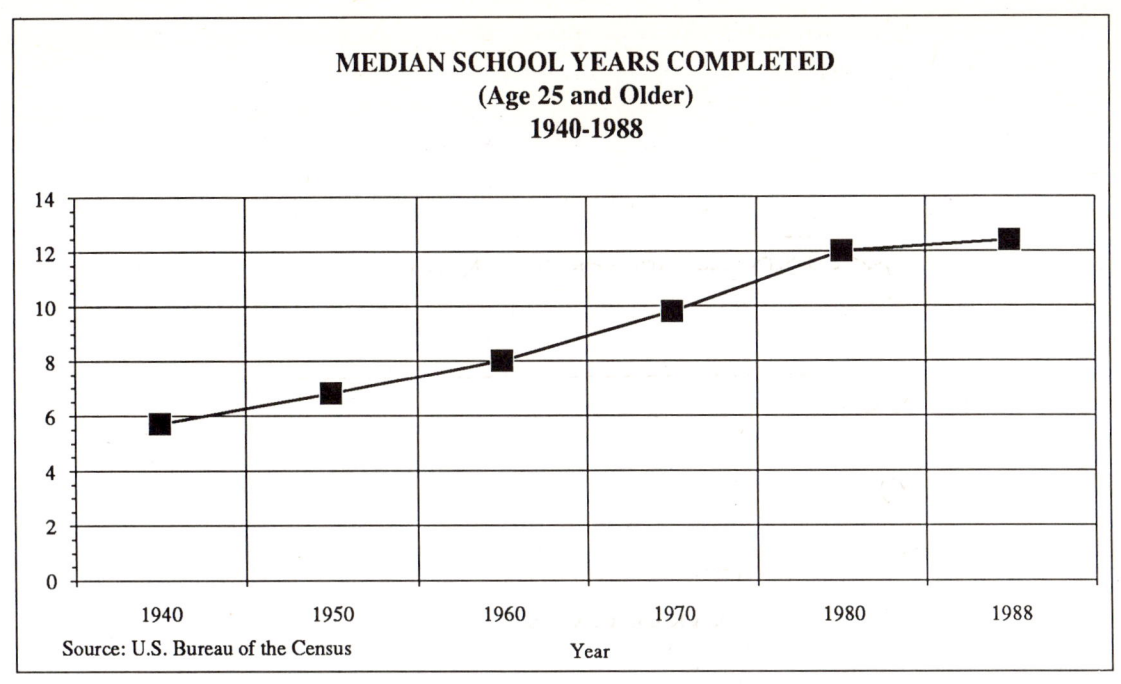

MEDIAN SCHOOL YEARS COMPLETED
(Age 25 and Older)
1940-1988

Source: U.S. Bureau of the Census

There was a steep increase in the median number of school years completed up to 1980. That increase slowed significantly in the decade of the 1980s. It rose only from 12 to 12.4 years of school completed. Considering the increasingly technical nature of production and the necessity for a more skilled and trained work force, the economic growth rate is jeopardized.

Economic Reasoning *(Write your responses on a separate sheet. Answers begin on p. 311.)*

1. What are the factors discussed in this application that affect economic growth?
2. Why should the rate of growth of R&D increase when GNP is growing faster and decrease when GNP growth slows?
3. Judging from the relationships shown in the data in this application, what measures do you think should be taken to increase the rate of growth in GNP?

IV. Practice Test *(Answers begin on p. 311.)*

Multiple Choice *(Circle the correct answer.)*

(14.1) 1. Which of the following was NOT a legacy of Reaganomics?
    a. lower inflation in the 1980s.
    b. sustained economic growth in the 1980s.
    c. smaller budget deficits in the 1980s.
    d. lower unemployment in the 1980s.

(14.1) 2. One policy of the Reagan administration was to balance the federal budget by:
    a. increasing taxes and cutting spending.
    b. lowering taxes and stimulating capital investment.
    c. increasing taxes and stimulating economic growth.
    d. lowering taxes and increasing consumer spending.

(14.2) 3. Fiscal policy includes all of the following EXCEPT:
    a. controlling interest rates.
    b. controlling the size of government spending.
    c. automatic stabilizers.
    d. tax changes.

(14.2) 4. Monetary policy is controlled by:
   a. Congress.
   b. the Federal Reserve System.
   c. the Department of the Treasury.
   d. all of the above.

(14.3) 5. Which of the following problems might result from an annually balanced budget?
   a. an increased money supply and inflation.
   b. decreased aggregate demand that could make an existing recession worse.
   c. Congress using fiscal policy to obtain political, rather than economic, objectives.
   d. higher interest rates and less investment.

(14.3) 6. The goal of **functional finance** is to:
   a. keep the federal budget in balance.
   b. keep the economy growing.
   c. prevent inflation.
   d. all of the above.

(14.4) 7. According to Keynesian economic policy, the objective of tax cuts is to:
   a. increase government spending.
   b. stimulate saving and investment.
   c. increase the money supply.
   d. increase consumer spending.

(14.4) 8. According to supply-side economic policy, the objective of tax cuts is to:
   a. increase government spending.
   b. stimulate saving and investment.
   c. increase the money supply.
   d. increase consumer spending.

(14.5) 9. The size of the **multiplier** depends on:
   a. the velocity of money.
   b. tax and savings rates.
   c. the level of government spending.
   d. the size of the budget deficit.

(14.5) 10. The multiplier shows how much a change in _____ affects the level of _____.
   a. taxes; government spending
   b. spending; income
   c. saving; investment
   d. interest rates; investment

(14.6) 11. Which of the following is considered to be an **automatic stabilizer**?
   a. investment in public infrastructure.
   b. unemployment compensation.
   c. health care.
   d. defense spending.

(14.7) 12. If the money supply increases at the same rate as output, prices will remain stable as long as:
   a. the federal budget is balanced.
   b. taxes do not change.
   c. the capital/output ratio remains constant.
   d. the velocity of money is constant.

(14.7) 13. A monetary policy by "rule" would involve which of the following?
   a. adjusting the money supply to keep interest rates constant.
   b. Congressional review of the Fed's monetary policies.
   c. adjusting monetary policy so that it does not conflict with fiscal policy.
   d. increasing the money supply at the same rate that GNP increases.

(14.8) 14. Increasing the investment/GNP ratio will result in:
- a. an improved standard of living in the future.
- b. higher interest rates.
- c. increased consumption spending at the present time.
- d. improvements in the quality of capital.

(14.9) 15. The labor-force participation rate in the United States:
- a. is a measure of the quality of U.S. labor.
- b. decreased steadily in the 1970s because of high income taxes.
- c. is among the highest in the world.
- d. is directly related to investment in human capital.

True/False *(Circle T or F.)*

(14.1) 16. Total federal spending as a percentage of GNP declined during the Reagan administration. T or F

(14.3) 17. Requiring an annually balanced budget would make it very difficult to implement fiscal policy. T or F

(14.4) 18. As predicted, the supply-side tax cuts of 1981 resulted in increased saving and investment. T or F

(14.5) 19. The formula used to calculate the multiplier implies that income will increase the most when people have low savings rates. T or F

(14.7) 20. Fiscal policy involves adjusting taxes, government spending, and interest rates. T or F

Macroeconomics Crossword Puzzle

(Chapters 10–14)

Across

1. Both the money supply and total income are affected by this process.
5. This type of federal aid to state and local governments can be used for any purpose.
8. The largest revenue source for the federal government.
9. This type of inflation comes from supply-side economics.
11. British economist who developed the demand-side analysis of how the economy works.
13. A period of generally rising prices in the economy as a whole.
14. The most commonly used measure of changes in the general price level of an economy.
16. The paper money that the U.S. federal government printed in order to help finance the Civil War.
18. Social Security is this type of payment.
20. This type of tax is one of the largest sources of state and local government revenues.

Down

2. When measuring the economy, this should equal the value of output.
3. The price of money.
4. _____ increases the money supply.
6. The economic policies followed by the United States in the 1980s.
7. _____ income determines the amount of consumer spending.
10. The central bank of the United States (slang).
12. The functional _____ economic philosophy sees noninflationary full employment as the most important economic goal.
15. It provides instruction to workers in small firms to train them in computer-aided manufacturing.
17. This clause, built into labor union contracts, automatically raises wages when the CPI reaches a specified point.
19. The total sum of all incomes earned in production for an economy.

Chapter 15

International Trade

I. Chapter Outline

Specialization and trade between different countries, like specialization and trade between individuals, lead to gains for both trading partners. By doing what each does best and engaging in trade, the total amount of goods and services available to each trading partners increases. Some specific individuals and businesses, however, may suffer losses when consumers buy less-expensive or better-quality imported products instead of domestically produced goods and services. As a consequence, these parties would prefer to limit trade by imposing tariffs, quotas, and other trade restrictions.

Introductory Article: New Kid on the Bloc

By removing barriers to free trade among its members, the European Economic Community will form one integrated economy in place of the 12 separate economies that existed prior to 1992. In many ways, EC92 will be very similar to the United States: the 12 independent countries will function economically like the 50 states. While this should lead to increased economic activity and growth within the European Community, many onlookers fear that it may lead to increased trade restrictions and less trade with countries outside Europe.

Economic Analysis

This chapter examines the pluses and minuses of international trade by addressing the following questions:

1. Why Do We Trade with Other Countries?

   Important Concepts: Imports, Exports, Absolute advantage, Comparative advantage, Specialization, Increasing costs, Limited specialization

   Case Application: Barter Is Back

2. Who Benefits and Who Is Hurt by Foreign Trade?

   Important Concepts: Consumer, producer, and worker benefits, Import-competing goods, Mobility of capital and labor

   Case Application: Steel Industry Does an About Face

3. How Do We Restrict Foreign Trade?

   Important Concepts: Tariffs, Bilateral trade negotiations, Multilateral trade negotiations, Most-favored nations, GATT, Quotas, Non-tariff barriers, Export embargoes

   Case Application: Protection Japanese Style

4. Should Foreign Trade Be Restricted?

   Important Concepts: Protectionism, Infant industry argument, Terms of trade, Neomercantilists, Trade adjustment assistance

   Case Application: Bastiat's Petition

   Perspective: Smoot-Hawley Revisited

II. Summary of Economic Analysis

1. International trade can be based on either **absolute** or **comparative advantage**.
2. When a country has either type of advantage, it can gain by **specializing** in the production of one good and trading it for other goods.
3. Specialization is **limited** because of **increasing costs**.
4. Because it results in a greater selection and/or lower prices, **consumers benefit** from foreign trade.
5. Many **producers benefit** from foreign trade because it gives them access to raw materials that can be found only in other countries, and it provides them with larger markets for their output.
6. When domestic output is exported, **workers benefit** from foreign trade because our exports provide jobs for domestic workers.
7. Producers and workers in **import-competing industries** can suffer if consumers purchase available imported goods instead of domestically produced goods.
8. If import-competing firms decline at the same time that exporting industries are growing, capital and labor should move from the former to the latter. Unfortunately, labor and capital are not always **mobile** between different types of production, and, as a consequence, they may suffer unemployment. **Trade adjustment assistance** is given by governments to firms and workers injured by foreign competition.
9. Taxing imported goods by placing a **tariff** on them raises their prices and improves the competitive position of domestic firms.
10. Domestic firms can also be protected from import competition by imposing **quotas** that limit the quantity of certain goods that can be imported.
11. **Non-tariff barriers** to trade include licensing, testing, labeling, and other bothersome details that make it difficult for consumers to import foreign products.
12. **Export embargoes** prohibit the sale of certain goods to other countries in order either to protect domestic technology or to impose economic hardships on unfriendly countries.
13. In order to increase trade, countries often reduce tariffs and quotas through **bilateral trade negotiations** with another country. To reduce confusion and multiple tariff structures, **most-favored nation clauses** extend such reductions to all nations that reciprocate.
14. Beginning in 1947, the United States and other countries began to negotiate trade agreements simultaneously through **multilateral trade negotiations**.
15. Among their arguments against free trade, **protectionists** claim that American workers need help in competing with cheap foreign labor, that imports reduce domestic aggregate demand and reduce GNP, and that **infant industries** need protection from import competition while they develop.
16. The amounts of a country's imports and exports can be influenced by the **terms of trade**—the relative prices of imports and exports.
17. The **mercantilists** were seventeenth-century economists who believed that a country's wealth came from its stocks of gold and that gold should not be exported. **Neomercantilists** are modern economists who believe that a country's comparative advantage lies in its technology and that a country should avoid exporting this technology.

III. Review of the Learning Objectives (Answers begin on p. 311.)

Why Do We Trade With Other Countries?

ABSOLUTE ADVANTAGE
When a country has the resources that enable it to produce one good more cheaply than a second country and the second country has the resources to produce a another good more cheaply than the first country, each country will benefit from producing the good in which it has an absolute advantage and trading part of its production for the good in which it has a disadvantage.

COMPARATIVE ADVANTAGE
When one country has an absolute advantage over a second country in the production of two goods but has a greater advantage in the production of one of the two goods than the other, it will benefit both countries for each to produce the good in which it has a comparative advantage and trade with the other country for the good in which it has a comparative disadvantage.

SPECIALIZATION
Nations tend to specialize their production in accordance with their available resources. Those countries with an abundance of capital relative to labor specialize in high-technology industries, while countries that lack large capital resources specialize in labor-intensive industries.

Increasing costs
For most products, specialization is not complete. Because the amounts of resources that are suited to the production of a particular good are limited, as more of the good is produced there are increasing production costs that prevent the country from producing all of the good that it consumes. The difference is imported.

(See page vi in the foreword "To the Student" for how to make the best use of this schematic outline.)

15.1. Explain the difference between absolute and comparative advantage. *(Write in answers below.)*

A. Suppose Mexico can produce 3 units of textiles and 6 units of oil with 1 unit of labor. Also suppose that Nigeria can produce 1 unit of textiles and 4 units of oil with one unit of labor.

1. Mexico has a(n) __absolute__ advantage in the production of both goods.

2. One unit of textiles costs Mexico __2__ units of oil.

3. One unit of textiles costs Nigeria __4__ units of oil.

4. Which country is the low-cost producer of textiles?
   __Mexico__

5. One unit of oil costs Mexico __½__ units of textiles.

6. One unit of oil costs Nigeria __¼__ units of textiles.

7. Which country is the low-cost producer of oil?
   __Nigeria__

8. Which country has a comparative advantage in the production of oil?
   Nigeria

9. Which country has a comparative advantage in the production of textiles?
   Mexico

10. Who should trade what for what?
    Mexico should trade textiles for Nigerian oil

15.2. Explain why specialization is sometimes complete but normally is limited.

A. Under what conditions will complete specialization characterize the trade between two countries?
   Only when each country produces a good that is not produced in the other

B.
   1. What does a straight-line (uncurved) production possibility frontier imply about the cost of one good relative to the other as production increases?
      A straight line PPF implies that costs are constant

   2. In actuality, PPFs are curved because costs
      increase as the output of a specific good increases.

   3. This is due to the fact that resources are not
      perfectly adaptable (mobile) to all uses.

   4. When the PPF is curved, it indicates that the last unit of any good produced is extremely
      expensive.

   5. Because of this, specialization will be
      limited.

15.3. Compare the types of goods exported by the United States with the types of goods imported.

A. Indicate whether each of the following is best characterized as a United States import (I) or export (E):
   1. *I* Petroleum.
   2. *I* Autos and auto parts.
   3. *E* Food and animal products.

4. _I_ Textiles and clothing.
5. _E_ Chemicals.
6. _E_ Aircraft and parts.

B. Where do people and businesses in other countries get the dollars necessary to buy goods and services from American producers?

from American purchases (imports) of their products

C. The United States tends to specialize in the export of goods that are _capital_ (technology) intensive while importing goods that are _labor_-intensive.

Case Application: U.S. Farmers Selling Overseas

The United States is a major source of food and other agricultural products for the rest of the world. We export a large percentage of the crops grown in this country. In 1988 we exported an estimated 40.7% of the acreage of crops harvested in this country. This was higher than the previous record of 40.5% of U.S. crops exported in 1983.

However, the increase in the fraction of our output exported abroad was due only in part to an increase in the quantity of exports. It was also the result of a decline in the total acreage of crops harvested in 1988. The quantity of our exports was actually somewhat less than in 1983 but the highest amount since then.

The United States is by far the world's leading exporter of agricultural products. The following table shows the percentage of world exports accounted for by the United States for various major crops. The data is for 1987, the last year for which complete world statistics are available.

United States Share of World Agricultural Exports
Selected Crops, 1987

Commodity	United States as % of World Exports
Wheat	41.5
Corn	78.2
Soybeans	72.5
Rice	18.5
Tobacco (unmanufactured)	14.2
Vegetable oils	8.3
Cotton	28.4

The United States produces 11% of the wheat grown in the world, but it supplies over 41% of total world wheat exports. This is down somewhat from the nearly one-half (48.2%) that it supplied in 1981. It is still dominant in world soybean production and exports but not to the extent that it once was, as a result of increased planting of soybeans in Brazil.

Although the United States produces only 1.3% of the world rice output, it accounts for 18.5% of world rice exports. Some Asiatic countries, for whom rice is the main dietary staple, import rice grown in the United States more cheaply than they can grow it themselves.

In 1988, Asiatic countries received 45% of the agricultural exports of the United States. Almost half of that amount was purchased by Japan alone. Western Europe was the destination of 21% of our exports, down from 35% in 1970. The largest consumer of American farm products in Europe was the Netherlands, which purchased nearly twice as much as any other European country. Latin American countries took over 13% of our exports, half again as much as their share in 1970.

Economic Reasoning (Write your responses on a separate sheet. Answers begin on p. 311.)

1. Judging from the data on U.S. exports as a percentage of world exports, in what agricultural crop did the United States apparently have the largest efficiency advantage over the rest of the world?

2. Since the United States accounts for such a large percentage of world corn exports, it obviously has an advantage in corn production. Why, then, does it not completely specialize in corn production?
3. Because exporting so much of our agricultural output tends to raise domestic food prices, some people say we should limit food exports in order to hold down the cost of living at home. What is your opinion about this proposal?

Who Benefits and Who Is Hurt by Foreign Trade?

BENEFITS

Consumer benefits

Consumers benefit from foreign trade by being able to consume some products that would not be available without trade. More importantly, consumers benefit by being able to purchase many products at lower costs than if there were no foreign trade both because of the lower prices of imported goods and because competition from imports holds down the prices of domestic goods.

Producer and worker benefits

Domestic industries that use imported inputs benefit. More importantly, export industries, their workers, and their suppliers benefit from the sales to markets abroad.

LOSSES

Import-competing firms' and workers' losses

Competition from imports can be costly to the domestic firms and their workers in lost sales and lower prices. These costs are similar to the costs of competition from new domestic producers or from new substitute products.

Mobility of capital and labor
The costs of free trade to import-competing firms and workers can be minimized by mobility of capital and labor to alternative employments.

Domestic consumers of export industries

The export of part of the output of an industry tends to raise the price of the good to domestic consumers.

(See page vi in the foreword "To the Student" for how to make the best use of this schematic outline.)

15.4. Describe the effects of foreign trade on economies.

A. The following tables show the production possibilities for oil and textiles produced in Mexico and Nigeria, assuming that these are the only two goods produced by both countries and that no trade takes place.

MEXICO

	A	B	C	D	E
Oil	0	2	4	6	8
Textiles	4	3	2	1	0

NIGERIA

	A	B	C	D	E
Oil	0	1	2	3	4
Textiles	16	12	8	4	0

1. What is the opportunity cost of a unit of oil in Mexico?

½ unit of textiles

2. What is the opportunity cost of a unit of textiles in Mexico?

   2 units of oil

3. What is the opportunity cost of a unit of oil in Nigeria?

   1/4 unit of oil

4. What is the opportunity cost of a unit of textiles in Nigeria?

   4 units of oil

5. In the spaces provided below, draw the production possibility frontiers for each country.

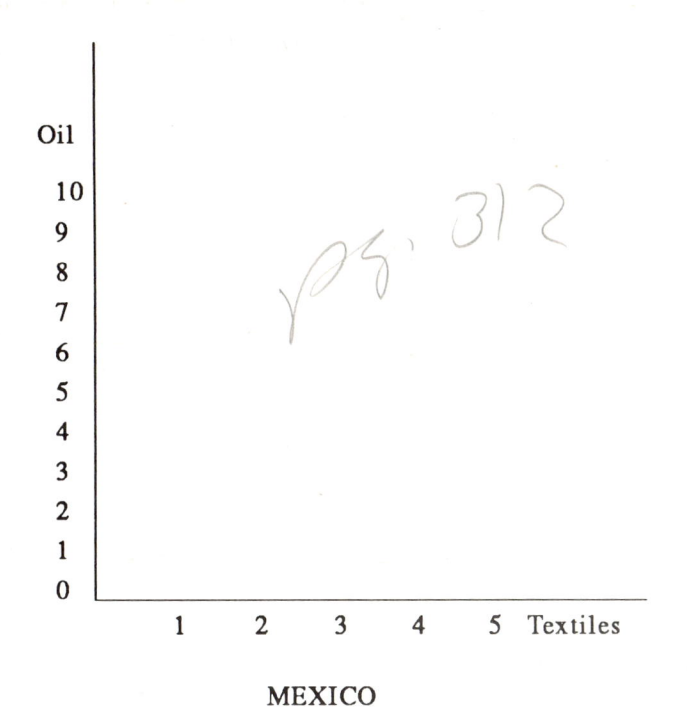

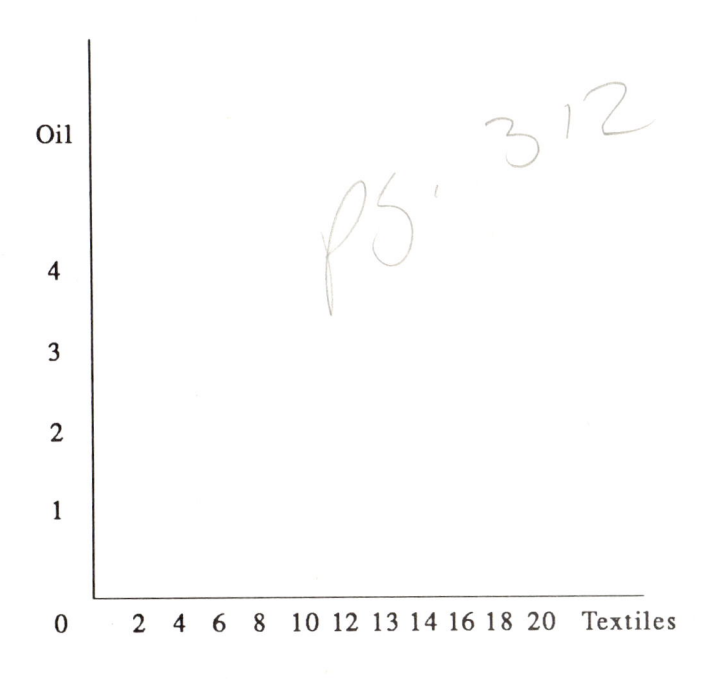

pg. 312

MEXICO

pg. 312

NIGERIA

6. Suppose that Nigeria produces only textiles (16 units) and Mexico produces only oil (8 units) and that they trade oil for textiles at terms of trade equal to 2 units of textiles for 1 unit of oil. If Mexico gives up 3 units of oil in exchange for 6 units of textiles from Nigeria, then:

   a) Mexico will now have __5__ units of oil and __6__ units of textiles.

   b) Nigeria will now have __3__ units of oil and __10__ units of textiles.

   c) Compare these two combinations of oil and textiles to production possibility C on the above production possibility frontiers for both countries. (Plot the new points as point **X**.) How do they compare? _Both have more of each good — they are better off after specialization & trade_

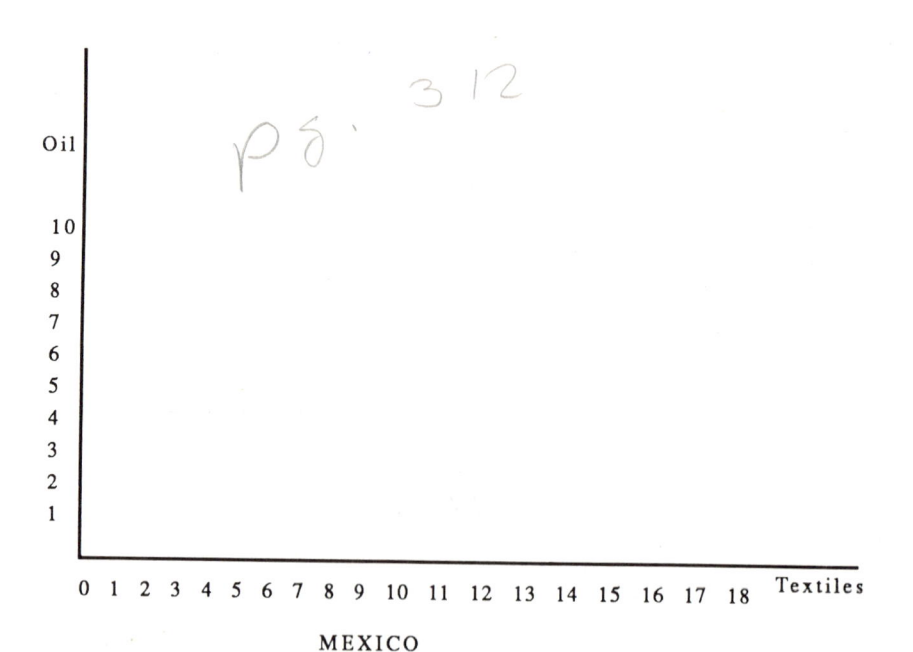

7. With trade, one production possibility for Mexico is to produce 8 units of oil and trade it all for 16 units of textiles. Plot this point (0 oil, 16 textiles) in the space provided below and draw the new PPF for Mexico by connecting this to the point where Mexico produces 8 oil and 0 textile units. Draw in the previous PPF that represented no trade.

pg. 312

Oil

10
9
8
7
6
5
4
3
2
1

0 1 2 3 4 5 6 7 8 9 10 11 12 13 14 15 16 17 18   Textiles

MEXICO

8. With trade, one production possibility for Nigeria is to produce 16 units of textiles and trade it all for 8 units of textiles. Plot this point (0 textiles, 8 oil) in the space provided below and draw the new PPF for Nigeria by connecting this to the point where Nigeria produces 16 textile and 0 oil units.

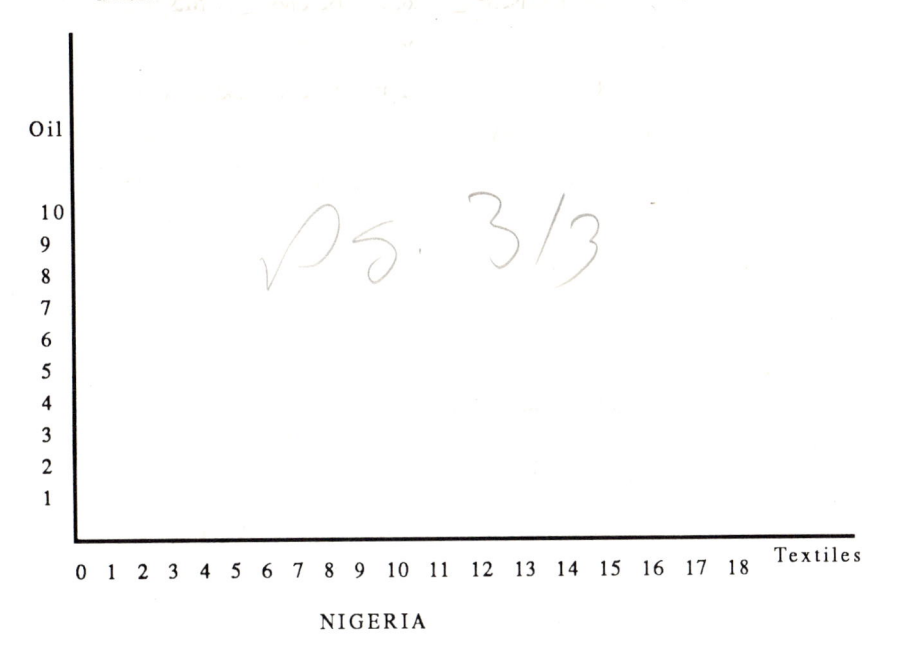

Oil

```
10
 9
 8
 7
 6
 5
 4
 3
 2
 1
   0  1  2  3  4  5  6  7  8  9  10 11 12 13 14 15 16 17 18   Textiles
```

NIGERIA

9. What conclusions can you draw from your analysis in parts 7 and 8?

Trade moves the PPF to the right for both countries, allowing them to attain previously unattainable combinations of both goods.

15.5. Specify who benefits and who loses as a result of foreign trade.

A. What are three imported goods that you buy and/or use?

1. Clothes
2. Cars
3. Radio

B. For each of the three goods listed above, indicate the best possible **domestic** substitute available to you.

1. _____
2. _____
3. _____

C. For each of the three goods listed in part A, indicate a firm or worker in America who loses as a result of your buying an imported product.

1. _____
2. _____
3. _____

D. The discussion of foreign trade in the textbook implies that free trade is beneficial to economies in general. More specifically, the arguments assume that the purpose of trade is to benefit which group in every economy?

Consumers

E. Indicate one American group that is helped and one group that is hurt by foreign trade in each of the following instances:

1. The Japanese produce high-quality, low-cost autos.
   Helped _American consumers_
   Hurt _American auto workers_

2. American farmers agree to sell wheat to the Soviet Union.
   Helped _American farmers_
   Hurt _American bread consumers_

3. The American government imposes new tariffs on imported shoes.
   Helped _American shoe producers_
   Hurt _American shoe buyers_

4. War in the Middle East results in reduced oil imports.
   Helped _American energy companies_
   Hurt _American consumers_

F. What **type** of unemployment (frictional, structural, or cyclical) results when imports increase and labor is not mobile enough to move to new jobs in exporting industries?

structural

G. What are at least three industries in the United States that have suffered because of increased imports during the past 20 years?

1. _autos_
2. _steel_
3. _textiles_

Case Application: The Top U.S. Exporters

According to Table 1 on page 427 of the textbook, the country's leading exporting firm is Boeing. It sells $11 billion in aircraft and parts overseas. That is over half of its total sales. General Motors, on the other hand, second in exports at $10.2 billion, is the world's largest manufacturing firm; and its overseas sales amount to only a small part, 8%, of its total sales. Because over nine-tenths of its market is domestic, its main interest is in protecting that segment.

Although Boeing, as the largest exporter, depends to a very great extent on the export market, there are also other businesses to whom exports are important because they constitute a large share of their business. In the previous case application, for example, it was brought out that U.S. farmers depend on export markets for over 40% of their sales.

Other major companies with a high dependence on the export markets are Caterpillar, a manufacturer of farm equipment (29.6% of sales), and electronics producers Motorola (24.1%), Unisys (23.8%), and Hewlett-Packard (22.1%).

Economic Reasoning *(Write your responses on a separate sheet. Answers begin on p. 313.)*

1. Among the top 10 exporters shown in Table 1 on page 427 in the text, what industry accounted for the largest amount of export sales? Did that industry also lead in total export sales of all U.S. industries as shown on the same page? If not, what industry did?
2. Are there other industries that do not export much or any of their production but still benefit from international trade? If so, what types of industries are they and how do they benefit?
3. What do you think is the explanation for the success of the leading exporters?

How Do We Restrict Foreign Trade?

TARIFFS	QUOTAS
Taxes on imports are not imposed primarily for revenue but rather to shelter domestic firms from foreign competition. They may be based either on value or on quantity.	Restrictions imposed on the quantity of a good that may be imported may be set in terms of physical quantity or value and may be by country or in total.

Bilateral trade negotiations reduce the trade restrictions between two countries. Most-favored nation clauses in trade agreements extend trade concessions to other countries.	NON-TARIFF BARRIERS Protectionist measures in addition to tariffs and quotas include label of origin requirements, additional tests and inspections, and intentionally slow customs clearance.
Multilateral trade negotiations reduce the trade restrictions among many nations simultaneously. The General Agreement on Tariffs and Trade (GATT) provides for non-discrimination between nations.	EXPORT EMBARGOES Exports may be restricted, rather than imports, to keep new technologies out of the hands of other countries or for political reasons or to hold down domestic prices.

(See page vi in the foreword "To the Student" for how to make the best use of this schematic outline.)

15.6. Compare the different types of restrictions imposed on foreign trade.

A. A tariff on an imported good is similar to any increase in the cost of production. In the following space, draw a demand and supply curve that shows the **domestic** market for a product before and after the imposition of a tariff. Indicate the pre- and post-tariff equilibrium prices and quantities.

228 / *Working With The Study of Economics, 4/E*

Price

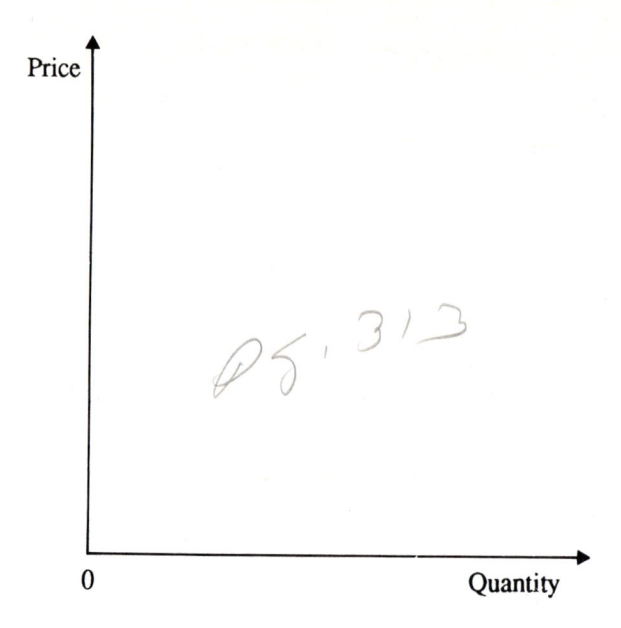

0   Quantity

pg. 313

B. Quotas are effective at reducing trade only if the quota is less than the equilibrium quantity in the domestic market. In the space below, draw a demand and supply curve that shows the **domestic** market for a good before a quota is imposed. Then show what happens to the supply curve if a quota lower than the equilibrium quantity is imposed. Indicate the quota limit by Q_q and the new domestic price by P_q.

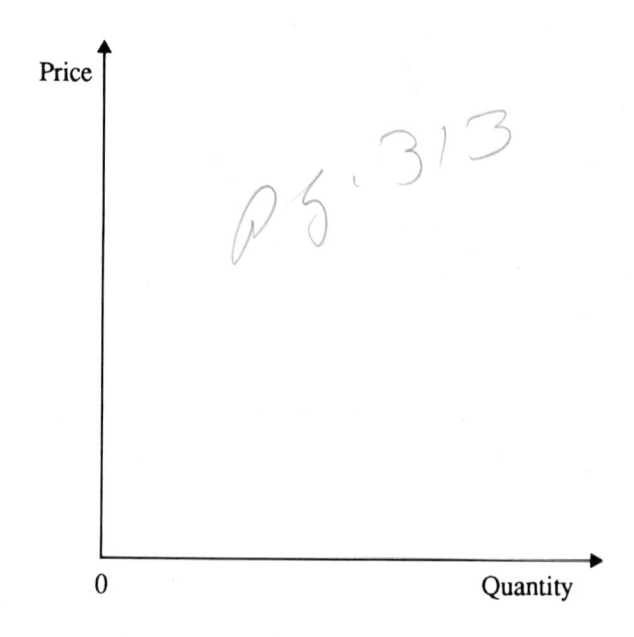

Price

0   Quantity

pg. 313

C. Suppose the demand for an imported product increases. In which case—quotas or tariffs—will the price increase be the greatest? Why?

pg. 314

_____

_____

_____

D. What are three reasons that the United States may place an export embargo on exports to a particular country?

1. _politics_
2. _to protect technological advantage_
3. _national security_

E. Be creative and make up three non-tariff barriers that the United States could use to limit the import of Peruvian anchovies.

1. _____
2. _____
3. _____

15.7. Discuss the different vehicles for trade negotiations and define "most-favored nation" treatment.

A. GATT is an example of what type of trade negotiations?
multilateral

B.
1. What bill did Congress pass in 1930 in order to raise tariffs?
Smoot-Hawley
2. What was the effect of this bill?
It reduced international trade

C.
1. What is a major problem that can arise from numerous bilateral trade agreements between one country and several others?
confusion resulting from different tariff rates w/ different countries on the same product
2. What type of trade "clause" is designed to reduce or eliminate this problem?
most favored nation clauses
3. What do these clauses do?
they give the favored nation all tariff reductions that are negotiated w/ any other country

Case Application: Made-in-America Japanese Cars

The United Auto Workers union pushed hard for a new type of trade restriction—new, at least, for this country. It is called a "local content" law. The local content law would require that foreign automobile producers selling more than 500,000 cars in the United States each year do most of the manufacturing of those cars in this country, as much as 90%. The local content requirement would be less for foreign producers selling under 500,000 cars a year, and those selling less than 100,000 cars a year would be exempt.

Such a requirement would affect not only the large Japanese automobile firms such as Toyota, Nissan, and Honda but might also affect American automobile companies that are moving toward the production of "world cars," in which many of the components are produced abroad. For that reason, American automobile firms have not been enthusiastic about a local content law. Furthermore, they are concerned that other countries might pass similar laws, thus restricting their ability to sell American cars in countries which do not presently have an automobile industry.

Mexico utilized a local content law to help develop its domestic automobile industry. Before passage of the law, American automobile producers had manufactured the automobile parts in the United States and shipped them to Mexico to be assembled for sale in the Mexican market. During the 1960s, Mexico required the companies to produce an increasing percentage of the parts in Mexico. This forced the firms to set up training programs for Mexican workers to teach them the skills necessary for automobile production. In this way, Mexico not only founded an automobile industry, but also developed its human capital.

Economic Reasoning *(Write your responses on a separate sheet. Answers begin on p. 314.)*

1. Is a local content law more like a tariff, a quota, or a non-tariff barrier?
2. What would be the effect of a U.S. local content law on comparative advantage?
3. What might be a useful trade policy for a developing country like Mexico might not be appropriate for an industrialized country such as the United States. Do you think that a local content law would have the same results in the two countries? Why or why not?

Should Foreign Trade Be Restricted?

TRADITIONAL PROTECTIONIST ARGUMENTS

Cheap foreign labor	Increase aggregate demand	Infant industry
The argument for protecting American workers against competition from cheap foreign labor ignores the fact that workers' real income is primarily determined by their productivity, and productivity that is low means low wages but high real costs.	Restricting imports increases demand in the industries that compete with imports, but it reduces demand and reduces employment in export industries because of retaliation.	If there is a new industry which has the potential to be efficient and competitive, it may be justified to protect the industry from foreign competition while it matures. This is the only one of the traditional protectionist arguments that generally has recognized validity among economists.

TERMS OF TRADE ARGUMENT

Imposing trade protection to lower the average price of imports relative to exports can obtain more imports per unit of exports, but is subject to retaliation.

NEOMERCANTILIST ARGUMENT

Like the mercantilists of Queen Elizabeth's time, today's neomercantilists want to restrict trade in order to maintain the advantages of technological superiority.

BALANCE-OF-PAYMENTS ARGUMENT

Restricting imports to eliminate a basic deficit in the balance of payments would subject a nation to retaliation by the countries affected.

(See page vi in the foreword "To the Student" for how to make the best use of this schematic outline.)

15.8. Evaluate the arguments in favor of trade restrictions.

A.

1. How do the levels of exports and imports effect aggregate demand in an economy?

    Exports _increase_
    Imports _decrease_

2. How do they effect domestic employment?

    Exports _increase_
    Imports _decrease_

B.

1. American workers earn higher wages than many foreign workers because they are more productive. This means that American firms can hire American workers and still be quite profitable. What is the main reason that American workers are so productive?

    They have more & better capital to work with

2. Explain why American workers, especially production workers, would accept the **neomercantilist** argument.

C. The American steel and auto industries have consistently argued for protection from foreign competition. Can they use the **infant industry** argument to support their case? Explain.

Case Application: Politics and Trade

Controls over trade are often used by governments or interest groups to reach political goals. In the name of national security and defense, many companies in the United States are not permitted to trade with certain countries. In 1982, in reaction to the imposition of martial law in Poland, President Reagan placed an export embargo on equipment and technology for the Soviet Union's gas pipeline to Western Europe. The restriction applied not only to American firms but also to European companies making equipment under license from U.S. patent holders. Some of the European firms, which already had contracts with the Russians for delivery of the equipment, ignored the embargo, straining the relationships between the United States and some of its allies. This use of trade sanctions to enforce diplomatic policy was widely criticized and did not succeed in its objective.

The effect of government policies on trade is sometimes indirect. Farm subsidies in the United States or shipbuilding subsidies in Britain can affect the competitive prices of grain, ships, or shipping in the world market. American shipowners are concerned about the low rates charged by the Soviet merchant marine because the Soviets do not have to make a profit on shipping and the government underwrites any losses.

In developing countries, import tariffs are often an easy and effective way for the government to raise revenue. At the same time, arguments for protection of infant industries for an appropriate period of time could be well justified. Thus, tariffs can also be used selectively to encourage some industries and to discourage others. A multinational corporation may find, as in Venezuela, that only a certain percentage of its invested capital can leave the country where it has built a plant.

In developed countries, even though there is no justification for the infant industry argument, people from special interest groups still use it along with other arguments—typically national security and the saving of jobs at home. Foreign competition can cause structural dislocations in developed countries and increased costs in terms of unemployment and bankruptcies. One solution is to use a temporary tariff on the imports and to use the proceeds to move the affected workers and businesses into other, less-threatened sectors of the economy. However, the high visibility of the public funds given to the affected workers raises political questions. Legislators will find it easier to set quotas or even raise tariffs than to pay out funds for adjustment assistance. In short, politics gains, free trade loses.

Economic Reasoning *(Write your responses on a separate sheet. Answers begin on p. 314.)*

1. How did the U.S. embargo on equipment for the Soviet gas pipeline resemble the neomercantilist position?
2. Why is the infant industry argument more justified for developing countries than for developed countries? What problem may result from restricting imports to foster infant industries in any country?
3. Do you believe in the use of trade sanctions as an instrument of foreign policy? Why or why not?

IV. Practice Test *(Answers begin on p. 314.)*

Multiple Choice *(Circle the correct answer.)*

(15.1) 1. Which of the following is a TRUE statement?
   a. Trade can be beneficial only if one trading partner has an absolute advantage.
   b. Trade can be beneficial only if one trading partner has a comparative advantage.
   c. Trade can be beneficial only if each trading partner has a comparative advantage in producing its export product.
   d. Trade can be beneficial if either a comparative or an absolute advantage exists.

(15.1) 2. A country that has a comparative advantage in producing good X:
   a. will make economic profits by selling X.
   b. will be the low-cost producer of good X.
   c. will be the high-price seller of good X.
   d. will import good X.

(15.1) 3. The United States tends to have a comparative advantage in the production of:
   a. labor-intensive goods.
   b. capital-intensive goods.
   c. energy-intensive goods.
   d. land-intensive goods.

(15.2) 4. Which of the following tends to limit specialization in the production and export of a specific good?
   a. decreasing capital/labor ratios as output expands.
   b. increasing costs due to resources that are not perfectly mobile between different industries.
   c. increasing labor-force participation rates that lead to declining productivity.
   d. increasing tariffs and quotas as output and exports increase.

(15.2) 5. Complete specialization can exist only when:
   a. there are no barriers to free trade.
   b. both trading countries have an absolute advantage in producing the good that they export.
   c. a particular good is produced only in one of the two countries that are engaging in trade.
   d. both trading partners have most-favored nation status.

(15.3) 6. The largest category of goods exported by American firms is:
   a. machinery.
   b. autos.
   c. food and animal products.
   d. chemicals.

(15.3) 7. The largest category of goods imported by Americans is:
   a. machinery.
   b. autos.
   c. petroleum.
   d. textiles and clothing.

(15.4) 8. Increased levels of U.S. imports will result in:
   a. leakages from the U.S. GNP tank.
   b. increased unemployment in the United States.
   c. reduced aggregate demand in the United States.
   d. all of the above.

(15.4) 9. Increased amounts of foreign trade can have which of the following impacts on a country's production possibility frontier?
   a. it can make the curve flatter.
   b. it can make the curve less flat (more bowed).
   c. it can cause the curve to move to the left.
   d. it can cause the curve to move to the right.

(15.5) 10. Which of the following would be a potential loser from increased exports of American wheat to the Soviet Union?
   a. American farmers.
   b. Soviet bread consumers.
   c. American bread consumers.
   d. Soviet bakers.

(15.5) 11. Which of the following would gain from increased imports of Japanese cars?
   a. American auto manufacturers.
   b. American auto workers.
   c. American gasoline producers.
   d. American car buyers.

(15.6) 12. Why would the prices of American cars increase if a tariff is imposed on Japanese cars?
   a. The price of a complement would increase.
   b. The price of a complement would decrease.
   c. The price of a substitute would increase.
   d. The price of a substitute would decrease.

(15.6) 13. The effect of a quota on an imported good is to:
   a. make the domestic demand curve for the good perfectly inelastic.
   b. make the domestic demand curve for the good perfectly elastic.
   c. make the domestic supply curve for the good perfectly inelastic.
   d. make the domestic supply curve for the good perfectly elastic.

(15.7) 14. GATT is an example of:
   a. most-favored nation treatment.
   b. multilateral trade negotiations.
   c. a non-tariff barrier to trade.
   d. a quota system.

(15.8) 15. Neomercantilists oppose:
   a. the use of tariffs and quotas.
   b. trade adjustment assistance.
   c. the exporting of technology.
   d. complete specialization.

True/False *(Circle T or F.)*

(15.2) 16. Complete specialization can exist only when an absolute advantage is present. T or **F**

(15.3) 17. Machinery is both the biggest U.S. import and the biggest U.S. export. **T** or F

(15.5) 18. Workers in import-competing industries are harmed by foreign trade. **T** or F

(15.6) 19. U.S. firms have difficulty selling goods in Japan because of high Japanese tariffs on imported goods. T or **F**

(15.7) 20. GATT (the General Agreement on Tariffs and Trade) was initiated in 1986. T or **F**

Chapter 16

International Finance and the National Economy

I. Chapter Outline

Even if all trade barriers between countries were removed, other difficulties for trade would remain. For example, different countries use different currencies, and one currency must be exchanged for another in order to make purchases in a different country. Since a country pays for its imports through its exports, it is also necessary to determine a method of payment when imports exceed exports.

Introductory Article: Alice in the Wonderland of International Finance.

Is a weak dollar good or bad for an economy? It depends on whom you ask, or, to put it another way, it depends on whose goose is getting plucked. Importers (such as consumers and raw material importers) dislike a weak dollar because it means imported goods will be more expensive. On the other hand, exporters and workers in exporting industries like a weak dollar because it means that their exported goods will be less expensive to foreigners, and import-competing goods will become more expensive in this country.

Economic Analysis

This chapter examines how countries pay for their imports and how this affects the domestic economy, by analyzing the following questions:

1. How Do We Pay for Imports?

    Important Concepts: Foreign-exchange market, Correspondent banks, Exchange rates, IMF, Depreciation, Appreciation, Devaluation, Revaluation

    Case Application: The Hunt for the Elusive Ecu

2. What Happens When Exports and Imports Do Not Balance?

    Important Concepts: Balance of payments, Current account, Balance of trade, Capital account, Basic deficit, Residual accounts

    Case Application: The World's Biggest Debtor

3. What Is the Relationship Between International Finance and the National Economy?

    Important Concepts: Economic equilibrium

    Case Application: Selling America

Perspective: Bring Back Gold?

II. Summary of Economic Analysis

1. Instead of using barter to conduct international transactions, businesses exchange their different currencies in **foreign-exchange markets**. After buying a trading partner's currency, an entrepreneur can then use the currency to buy goods in that country.

2. Foreign-exchange transactions for business purposes are usually done through **correspondent banks** in major financial centers.
3. When **exchange rates** are fixed, the price of one currency does not change with changes in its demand or supply in the foreign-exchange markets. Shortages of a currency are met by reserves from each country's central bank or by borrowing from the **International Monetary Fund (IMF)**.
4. If shortages of one country's currency persist under a system of fixed rates, the country will **revalue**, or raise, the price of its currency. Persistent surpluses of a country's currency are met by a **devaluation**, or decrease in the price of its currency.
5. International financial markets today use a system of **freely fluctuating exchange rates** in which the price of one country's currency changes constantly depending on its demand and supply.
6. If people in the United States (or any other country) want to import increased amounts of goods from another country, the demand for that country's currency will increase and it will **appreciate**, or become more expensive. This, in turn, makes that country's goods more expensive and reduces the amount of goods that the United States imports.
7. If a country is importing more than it exports, it will be supplying the exchange markets with more of its currency while other countries have little demand for this currency. When the supply of a country's currency exceeds the demand for it, the currency will **depreciate**, or become less expensive. This, in turn, will make this country's goods less expensive and its exports will increase.
8. The accounting record of a country's imports and exports is shown in its **balance of payments**. Exchanges of goods and services are reported in the **current account**.
9. The difference between the volume of goods and services exported and imported is called a country's **balance of trade**. If exports exceed imports, the balance is **favorable**, otherwise it is **unfavorable**.
10. In addition to the current account of goods and services, a country's balance of payments includes its **long-term** and **short-term capital accounts**. The long-term account compares the annual imports and exports of capital (investment), and the short-term account compares the international transfers of liquid funds such as bank deposits.
11. When total imports exceed total exports, the difference between the two is called a country's **basic deficit**.
12. One way in which a country can deal with a basic deficit is simply to pay for its imports with its currency. This amounts to the exporting country giving the importing country credit, and the currency it holds serves as an IOU that can be redeemed for the importing country's goods in the future.
13. Another way that a country with a basic deficit can pay for its imports is by using gold or some other internationally accepted form of payment. Transfers such as these are called **residual accounts**.
14. Still another way for a country with a basic deficit to pay for its imports is to ask the IMF to loan it the currency it needs to pay the exporters to whom it is in debt.
15. If a basic deficit persists, a country's currency will be worth less and less to its trading partners, while their currency will be increasingly more valued. As a result, the currency of a country with a basic deficit will depreciate relative to its trading partners' currencies. Eventually, this will reduce the first country's imports, increase its exports, and eliminate its basic deficit.
16. A country's spending on imported goods results in money flowing out of its GNP tank, while the spending by others on its exports results in money flowing into its tank.
17. When imports exceed exports, there is a net flow out of a country's GNP tank, and aggregate demand, GNP, and employment will all fall.
18. When imports exceed exports, there will also be an excess supply of a nation's currency in the hands of foreign businesses. This currency will either stay in the

238 / Working With The Study of Economics, 4/E

bank for later use, or it will be used to buy assets in the country that has the basic deficit. In effect, a country with a basic deficit (such as the United States) trades its assets for imported goods and services.

19. **National economic equilibrium** occurs when leakages from the GNP tank—Savings (S) plus Taxes (T) plus Imports (M)—are equal to injections into the tank—Investment (I) plus Government Spending (G) plus Exports (X).

20. During the 1980s in the United States, (S+T) was less than (I+G), so M needed to exceed X in order to bring the economy into equilibrium. A large part of these imports was in the form of liquid assets borrowed to finance our federal budget deficit.

III. Review of the Learning Objectives *(Answers begin on p. 314.)*

How Do We Pay for Imports?

FOREIGN-EXCHANGE MARKET

The conversion of one currency into another takes place in the foreign-exchange market, which is not a place but a set of banks and other institutions in the United States and other countries that deal in foreign currencies.

EXCHANGE RATES

SYSTEM	CHANGES IN RATES
Freely fluctuating exchange rates — Exchange rates are allowed to float in response to demand and supply in the foreign-exchange market.	**Depreciation** — The market exchange value of a currency falls due to a change in its market demand or in its supply.
	Appreciation — The currency's value rises due to a change in its market demand or supply.
Fixed exchange rates — Governments stipulate the rate at which their currencies will exchange for other currencies and support that rate.	**Devaluation** — The government lowers the exchange value of its currency.
	Revaluation — The government raises the exchange value of its currency.

(See page vi in the foreword "To the Student" for how to make the best use of this schematic outline.)

16.1. Explain how payments are made for imports. *(Write in answers below.)*

A. The price of an imported good has two parts. First, an importer must purchase some of the other country's currency in the _foreign-exchange_ market, and then it must purchase the good it wants to import.

B.

1. If 1 dollar buys 5 francs, one franc buys _.20_ dollars.

    1/5 20 cents

2. If 1 dollar buys 4 francs, one franc buys __.25__ dollars. *¼ or 25 cents*
3. If 1 dollar buys 10 francs, one franc buys __.10__ dollars. *⅒ or 10 cents*

C. Assume that a U.S. importer of perfume can buy 5 French francs for one dollar.
  1. How many francs can the American importer buy for a dollar? __1.5 francs__
  2. If a bottle of perfume costs 100 francs, how much does it cost in dollars? __$20__
  3. If the perfume increases in price to 120 francs, how much does it cost the American importer? __$24__
  4. If the price of the perfume is still 100 francs but the American importer now gets only 4 francs for a dollar, how much does the perfume cost the importer in dollars? __$25__

D. Assume that a French importer of blue jeans must pay 5 francs for 1 dollar.
  1. How many dollars can the French importer buy for 1 franc? __.20__
  2. If a pair of blue jeans costs 15 dollars, how much does it cost in francs? __75 f__
  3. If the price of the blue jeans increases to 18 dollars, how much do they cost in francs? __90 f__
  4. If the price of the jeans is 15 dollars, but the French importer needs only 4 francs to buy 1 dollar, then the price of the jeans in francs is __60 f__.

E.
  1. If francs become cheaper for Americans, dollars become __more expensive__ to the French.
  2. As a result, the price of French imports becomes __less expensive__ to Americans, and
  3. the price of American imports becomes __more expensive__ to the French.

F.
  1. If francs become more expensive for Americans, dollars become __less expensive__ to the French.
  2. As a result, the price of French imports becomes __more expensive__ to Americans, and
  3. the price of American imports becomes __less expensive__ to the French.

16.2. Distinguish between fixed and freely fluctuating exchange rates and explain how the rate of exchange is determined under each system.

A. When Americans demand pounds, they buy them with dollars, increasing the world's supply of dollars. When the British demand dollars, they buy them with pounds, increasing the world's supply of pounds. According to this:
  1. The demand for pounds is the same as the __supply of dollars__, and
  2. the demand for dollars is the same as the __supply of pounds__.

B. Assume that under a system of fixed exchange rates, 1 dollar is set to equal 1/2 a British pound (1 pound = $2). Now suppose that because of increased demand

240 / *Working With The Study of Economics, 4/E*

for British woolens, there is an increased demand for British pounds. The demand curve for pounds shifts from D_1 to D_2, while the supply curve for pounds remains unchanged. This will result in an increase in the supply of dollars from S_1 to S_2, while the demand for dollars remains unchanged. In the space provided below, draw the demand and supply curves for both pounds and dollars.

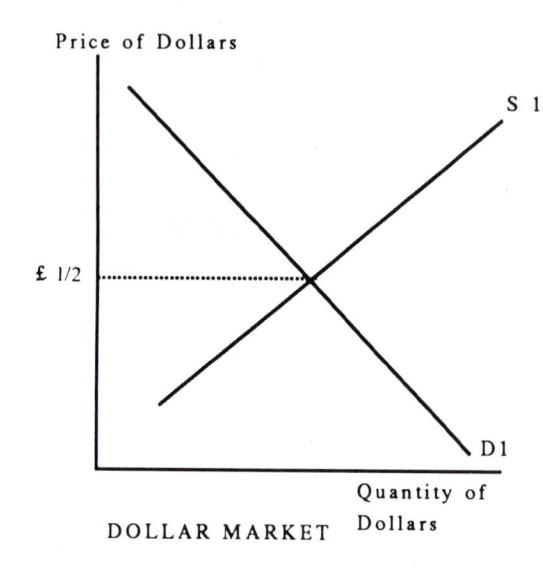

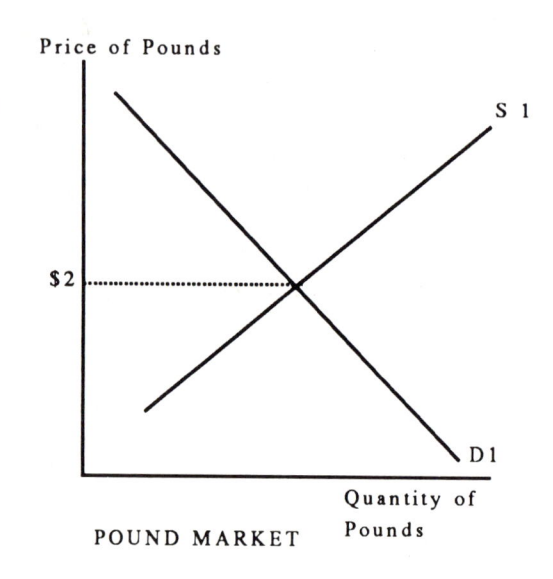

[Two supply-and-demand graphs: the DOLLAR MARKET showing Price of Dollars vs Quantity of Dollars, with equilibrium at £ 1/2, curves S1 and D1; and the POUND MARKET showing Price of Pounds vs Quantity of Pounds, with equilibrium at $2, curves S1 and D1.]

pg. 315

C.

1. In the above exercise, the graphs show that with a fixed exchange rate there would be a ___shortage___ of pounds. Show this on the graph.

2. How could this be eliminated if exchange rates are fixed?
   ___The British pg. 315___

D.
1. In part B above, the graphs show that with a fixed exchange rate there would be a ___surplus___ of dollars. Show this on the graph.
2. How could this be eliminated if exchange rates are fixed?

   _____pg. 315_____

E. The demand and supply for dollars in terms of pounds and the demand and supply for pounds in terms of dollars are shown below. Initially, the foreign-exchange markets are in equilibrium with 1/2 pound = 1 dollar and 1 pound = 2 dollars.

   Now suppose that an increase in the demand for American jeans increases the demand for dollars and *exchange rates are allowed to fluctuate*. Show what happens in the markets for pounds and dollars and indicate possible new prices for each currency. (HINT: when analyzing the pound market, remember the relationship between the demand for one currency and the supply of the other from part A, above.)

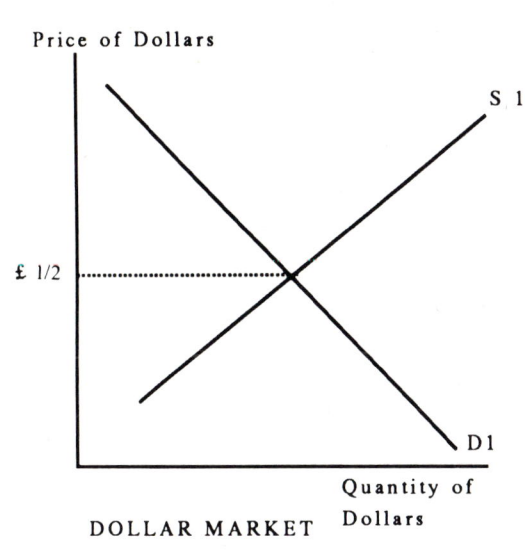

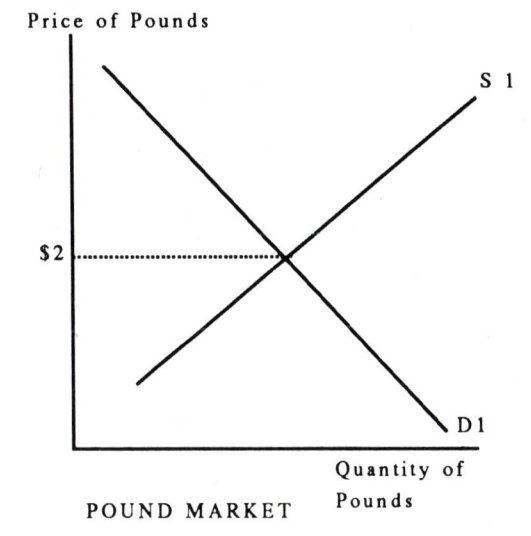

Price of Dollars — S 1, D 1, £ 1/2
DOLLAR MARKET — Quantity of Dollars

Price of Pounds — S 1, D 1, $2
POUND MARKET — Quantity of Pounds

pg. 315

16.3. Differentiate between currency depreciation, currency appreciation, devaluation, and revaluation.

A. If trade between Britain and the United States resulted in a surplus of dollars and a shortage of pounds under a system of **fixed** exchange rates, equilibrium in the foreign-exchange markets would require that
   1. the pound be _revalued_ and
   2. the dollar be _devalued_.

B. If trade between Britain and the United States resulted in a surplus of dollars and a shortage of pounds under a system of **fluctuating** exchange rates, equilibrium in the foreign-exchange markets will occur when
   1. the pound _appreciates_ and
   2. the dollar _depreciates_.

C.
   1. If exchange rates are fixed, a country can make its goods cheaper to other countries by _devaluing_ its currency.
   2. This will lead to increased _exports_ and
   3. increased levels of _employment & GNP_
   4. What would be a negative aspect of this type of policy?
      Citizens of the country would be able to buy fewer imported goods

D. Is there any way for a country to influence the value of its currency under a system of freely fluctuating exchange rates? Explain.
   Yes. A country can cause the value of its currency to appreciate by buying its own currency Pg. 316

E. Indicate whether each of the following will cause the U.S. dollar to appreciate (A) or depreciate (D).
   1. _D_ Inflation increases in the United States, making U.S. goods more costly in other countries.
   2. _A_ Interest rates are higher in the United States than in other countries.
   3. _A_ There is an increase in the demand for U.S. exports.
   4. _D_ The United States continually runs trade deficits with its trading partners.
   5. _A_ The threat of war causes people in other countries to put their assets in the United States because it is safe.

Case Application: The End of the World Credit Binge

The Mexican peso crisis in August 1982 signaled the end of a decade-long orgy of borrowing by developing countries that totaled some $360 billion. This credit consisted of private loans extended by U.S. and Western European banks to governments and private companies in Asian, African, Latin American, and Central European countries. A lot of the money, however, consisted of petrodollars, the earnings of the oil-exporting countries, which were recycled through Western banks to the borrowing nations.

Mexico was the biggest borrower, its foreign debt quadrupling between 1975 and 1982. Much of the borrowed money went to Pemex, the Mexican national oil company, for investment in new oil, gas, and petrochemical production facilities. As a result of its heavy international borrowing, Mexico was scheduled to make payment of $43 billion in interest and repayment on its foreign debts in 1982. This was nearly one-fifth of its national product and amounted to three times its estimated oil export earnings for the year. With world petroleum prices sagging due to the oil glut, Mexico did not have sufficient foreign exchange to satisfy its debt service obligations. As a result, in August the peso was devalued by nearly one-half to 70 pesos to the dollar. In September the private Mexican banks were nationalized and taken over by the government, and an interim loan was negotiated from the U.S. government to cover Mexico's foreign obligations until it could renegotiate its debt with the foreign banks. There was worldwide concern that a default by Mexico on the foreign loans could cause the banks which had extended it vast amounts of credit, based on its rapid growth rate and anticipated oil export earnings, to collapse.

A key to keeping Mexico from having to default on its foreign obligations was the participation by the International Monetary Fund in the financial rescue mission. Although the IMF would provide only $4.5 billion of the $15 billion to $20 billion needed, Mexico's agreement to the tough austerity measures imposed on it by the IMF was essential to obtain agreement from the private foreign banks to renegotiate their loans. These austerity measures included a reduction of Mexican deficit spending on government development projects and a lowering of the inflation rate.

Mexico was not the only country in trouble because of excessive foreign borrowing. Argentina, Bolivia, Brazil, Chile, Costa Rica, Peru, Poland, Romania, Venezuela, Yugoslavia, and a number of small African countries were also in danger of bankruptcy. If Mexico, Brazil, or some of the others were to default on their foreign obligations, the whole international financial structure could collapse as it did in the 1930s.

Economic Reasoning *(Write your responses on a separate sheet. Answers begin on p. 316.)*

1. Was Mexico employing a freely fluctuating exchange rate or a fixed exchange rate system? How can you tell?
2. How can petrodollars be recycled through Western banks to borrowing countries like Mexico?
3. The Mexican government resented the terms imposed by the IMF as a condition for extending it additional credit because Mexico felt that the demands infringed on its sovereignty. Do you think the IMF is justified in telling governments how to manage their internal affairs? Why or why not?

What Happens When Exports and Imports Do Not Balance?

BALANCE OF PAYMENTS

The annual accounting record of all transactions between a country's residents and residents of the rest of the world is the country's balance of payments.

MERCHANDISE AND SERVICES TRADE	CAPITAL FLOWS
Current account — The current account records imports and exports of goods and services. **Balance of trade** — The difference between merchandise exports and imports.	**Long-term capital account** — The long-term capital account records the flow of public and private investment into and out of a country. **Short-term capital account** — The short-term capital account records the flow of liquid funds such as bank deposits between countries.

Basic deficit
If the claims against a country from its merchandise and service trade, long-term capital, and other spontaneous transactions exceed the claims by the country on the rest of the world, the difference is the country's basic deficit.

Residual accounts
The residual accounts record balancing short-term capital and gold movements to cover a basic deficit.

(See page vi in the foreword "To the Student" for how to make the best use of this schematic outline.)

16.4. Define balance of payments and list the different accounts in the balance of payments.

A. Indicate whether each of the following would be classified as an export (E) or an import (I) and whether it would be counted in the current (C), short-term capital (ST), or long-term capital account (LT).

	Export or Import	Type of Account	
1.	I	C	An American tourist visits Spain.
2.	I	LT	An American firm builds a factory in France.
3.	E	ST	An American in Maine earns interest on a money market fund in Germany.
4.	E	LT	A Japanese company buys a U.S. building.
5.	E	C	A British citizen buys a pair of Levi's.
6.	E	ST	A Finnish citizen buys a 90-day U.S. government Treasury bill.
7.	I	C	A Californian eats imported sushi.

16.5. Distinguish between a favorable and an unfavorable balance of trade.

A.
1. A favorable balance of trade occurs when _exports_ exceed _imports_.
2. This is favorable to _exporters + export workers_ because it results in increased sales.
3. It is not necessarily favorable to _consumers_ because it reflects reduced choice.
4. A favorable balance of trade will eventually cause a country's currency to _appreciate_.

B.
1. An unfavorable balance of trade occurs when _imports_ exceed _exports_.
2. This is unfavorable to _exporters + export workers_ because it results in decreased sales.
3. It is not necessarily unfavorable to _consumers_ because it reflects increased choice.
4. An unfavorable balance of trade will eventually cause a country's currency to _depreciate_.

C. Assuming freely fluctuating exchange rates, if country X has a favorable balance of trade, then:
1. the world's demand for X's currency will be _increasing_.
2. the value of X's currency will _increase_.
3. the prices of imported goods in X will _decrease_.
4. the volume of X's imports will _increase_.
5. the prices of X's exports to others will _increase_.
6. the volume of X's exports will _decrease_.
7. as a result of #4 and #6, X's **trade deficit** will _disappear_.

D. Assuming freely fluctuating exchange rates, if country Y has an unfavorable balance of trade, then:
1. the world's demand for Y's currency will be _decreasing_.

2. the value of Y's currency will _decrease_.

3. the prices of imported goods in Y will _increase_.

4. the volume of Y's imports will _decrease_.

5. the prices of Y's exports to others will _decrease_.

6. the volume of Y's exports will _increase_.

7. as a result of #4 and #6, Y's **trade surplus** will _disappear_.

E. Summarize the effects of a system of freely fluctuating exchange rates on nations' trade surpluses and trade deficits.

_pg. 316_

16.6. Explain basic deficit and the role of the residual accounts in the balance of payments.

A. What are three ways that a country can offset a **basic deficit**?

1. _outflows of gold or similar internationally accepted assets_
2. _borrowing funds from the IMF_
3. _it can sell its assets to other countries_

or it can allow its currency to depreciate

B. Are basic deficits more or less likely to persist if exchange rates are freely fluctuating? Explain.

_pg. 316_

C.
1. A country never really runs a total trade deficit because every transaction on one side of the balance of payments is offset by a payment on the other. Existing trade deficits are brought into balance by _residual accounts_.

2. These accounts are payments in the form of _gold_ or _similar assets_.

Case Application: U.S. International Trade Position Takes a Nosedive

The last decade has seen dramatic changes in the United States' position in world trade. Judging by the behavior of its current account balance, the changes have been extraordinary.

Up until the 1970s the current account was close to being in balance. The values of U.S. exports and imports of goods and services were nearly equal, with a small but fairly consistent export surplus. (See chart below.) During the decade of the 1970s the behavior of the current account balance became much more erratic. The surpluses and deficits became much larger, but over the course of the decade they tended to cancel out.

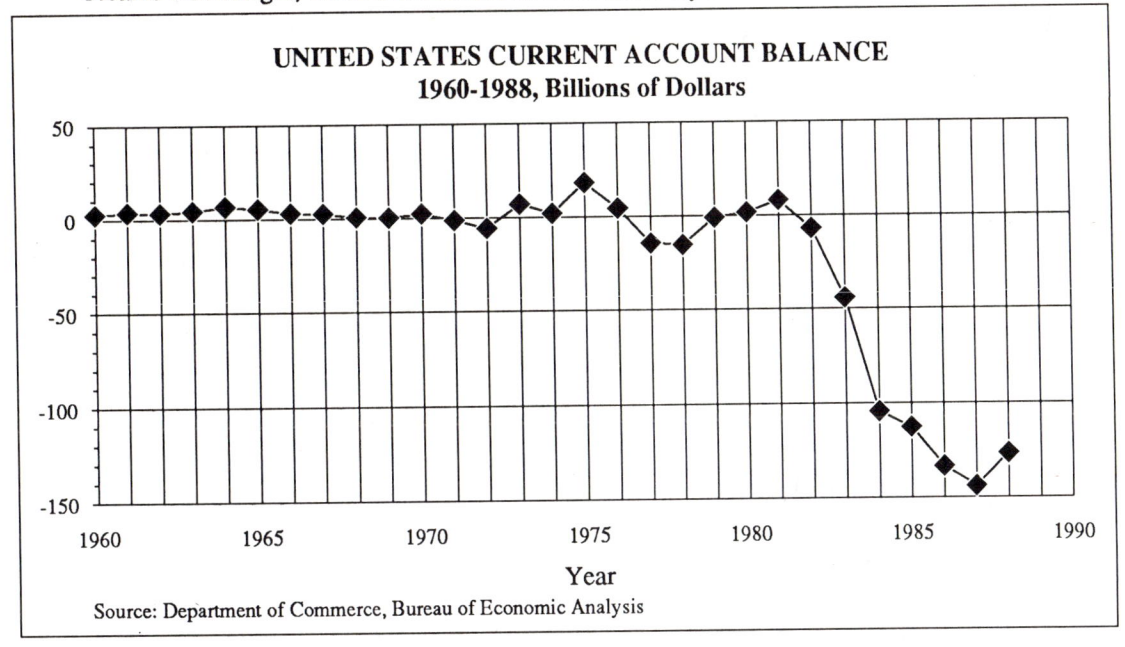

UNITED STATES CURRENT ACCOUNT BALANCE
1960-1988, Billions of Dollars

Source: Department of Commerce, Bureau of Economic Analysis

Not so in the 1980s. Beginning in 1982 the current account balance took an unprecedented nosedive. It plunged to a low of –$144 billion in 1987. It recovered somewhat to –$127 billion in 1988, but the prospects for any significant improvement remained in doubt for some time to come.

Economic Reasoning (Write your responses on a separate sheet. Answers begin on p. 316.)

1. What types of balance of payments transactions are NOT included in the data shown in the chart?
2. What would you expect to happen to the exchange rate for the dollar as a result of the changes shown in the chart? Why?
3. What do you think are the reasons for the drastic plunge of the U.S. current account balance in the 1980s?

What Is the Relationship Between International Finance and the National Economy?

FOREIGN SECTOR

The foreign sector of the economy consists of the country's external trade. Adding net foreign demand (X − M) to the domestic demand sectors (C + I + G) gives the aggregate demand for the nation's output of goods and services.

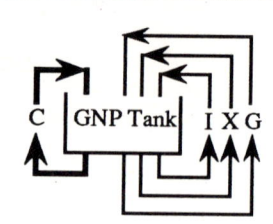

NATIONAL ECONOMIC EQUILIBRIUM

In the past decade the domestic sectors of the economy have been out of equilibrium because investment and government spending exceeded savings and taxes. The GNP has been in equilibrium as a result of the deficit in the foreign sector. The payments for the U. S. import surplus were invested by foreigners in the private sector and in government securities.

$I > S$
$G > T$
$X < M$
$I + G + X = S + T + M$

(See page vi in the foreword "To the Student" for how to make the best use of this schematic outline.)

16.7. Explain national economic equilibrium and illustrate with a schematic GNP tank diagram.

A. National economic equilibrium occurs when __A__ + __I__ + __X__ = __T__ + __S__ + __M__.

B.
 1. __I__, __S__, and __M__ are leakages out of the GNP tank.
 2. Changes in each of these are __inversly__ related to growth in GNP.

C.
 1. __G__, __I__, and __X__ are injections into the GNP tank.
 2. Changes in each of these are __directly__ related to growth in GNP.

16 International Finance and the National Economy / 249

D. Label each of the flows in the GNP tank diagram below:

(2C's, G, I, M, S, T, X)

[Diagram: GNP TANK with HOUSEHOLDS on left; top inflows labeled C, G, X, I; bottom outflows labeled C, T, M, S; connected to FINANCIAL MARKET (labeled E.3), FOREIGN SECTOR, and GOVERNMENT BUDGETS (labeled E.6)]

E. Assume that the above GNP tank diagram represents the U.S. economy during the 1980s.

1. In relation to the GNP tank, was more flowing into or out of the financial markets?

   More was flowing out of the financial markets

2. Where did the "extra" funds in the financial sector go to or come from?

   They came from foreign lenders

3. Depict your answer to #2, above, on the GNP tank diagram by drawing an arrow and labeling it **E.3**.

4. In relation to the GNP tank, was more flowing into or out of the government budgets?

   More was flowing out of the government

5. Where did the "extra" funds in the government budgets go to or come from?

   They came from foreign lenders

6. Depict your answer to #5, above, on the GNP tank diagram by drawing an arrow and labeling it **E.6**.

F.

1. Suppose a country saves more than it invests and raises more in taxes than its government spends. Draw a GNP tank diagram in the space provided that shows this situation and indicate with a "+" those sectors which have inputs greater than outputs. Assume that there are no barriers to flows between financial markets, the foreign sector, and government budgets.

pg. 317

2. According to the diagram that you drew, which sector(s) must be net lenders and which sector(s) must be net borrowers?
   Lender(s) _government & financial markets_
   Borrower(s) _foreign sector_

3. According to the diagram that you drew, what *must* be the relationship between this country's exports and imports?
   It must be exporting more than it imports

4. What is an example of a country that fits the description of the country described in this problem?
   Japan

16.8. Show how an import surplus allows the economy to consume more than it produces.

A. America's trade deficit has received a great deal of negative publicity. However, there has been one positive aspect of the deficit. What is it? (HINT: think of *short-term* consequences.)
   _pg. 318_

B. If the United States consistently imported more than it exported throughout the 1980s, then it must have supplied the rest of the world with lots of dollars that were not used to buy American exports. Where do you think these dollars have gone?
   _pg. 318_

C. What (if any) will be the price of consuming more than we produce in the United States, and who will pay this price?

pg. 318

16.9. Describe the role of foreign investment in compensating for insufficient domestic savings and taxes.

A. Assume that the U.S. economy is in equilibrium with $S + T + M = I + G + X$. What would be the consequences if foreign investment in the United States suddenly declined?

1. What would have to happen in the government sector?

    It would find it difficult to borrow & would need to cut back on spending or raise taxes.

2. What would be the consequences for GNP?

    It would decrease as G decreased (or T increased) or aggregate demand decreased

3. What would have to happen in the financial markets?

    The same as in the government sector — investment would fall

4. What would be the consequences for GNP?

    The same — GNP would decrease as I decreased

5. What would be the consequences of all of the above for consumer spending?

    There would be money available for consumers to spend

B.
1. Does foreign investment to build factories or buy real estate in the United States represent exports or imports?

    exports

2. Do the profits generated from foreign investments in the United States represent exports or imports?

    imports

Case Application: A Penny Saved Is a Rare Occurrence

The United States is a big spender. The national savings rate—gross national savings as a percentage of Gross National Product—is the lowest of any major country.

This inclination to spend rather than save affects both the private and government sectors. As individuals, as businesses, and as a nation we have accumulated record levels of debt. In the private sector this has led to a massive number of bankruptcies. But the United States cannot take a Chapter 11 escape from its obligations. It must meet them in full.

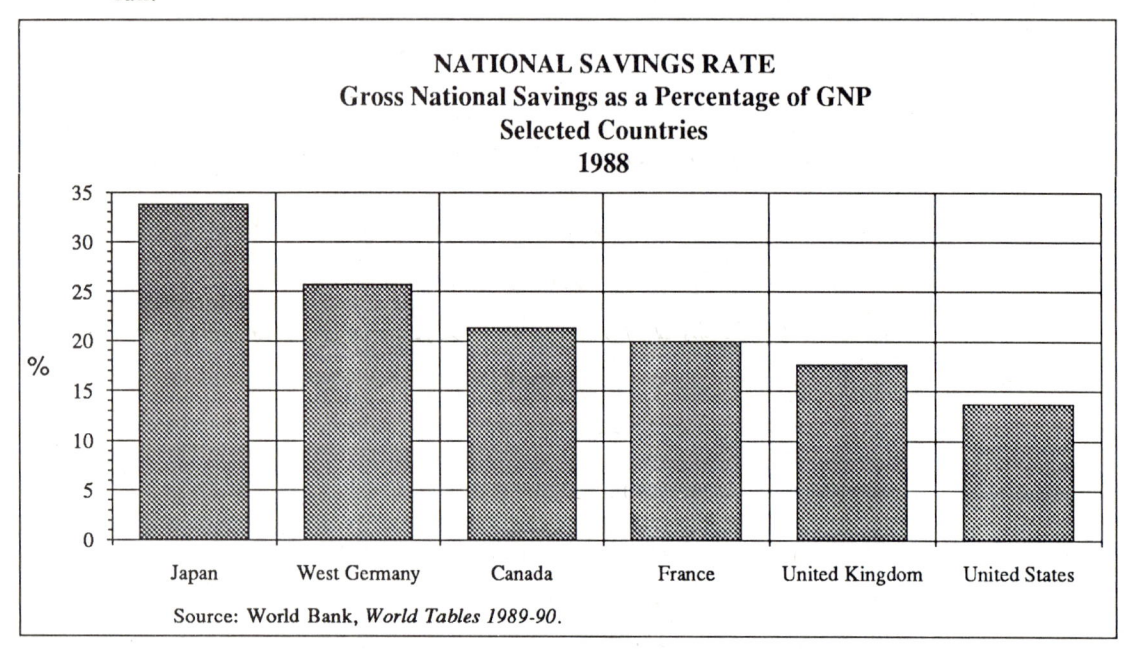

NATIONAL SAVINGS RATE
Gross National Savings as a Percentage of GNP
Selected Countries
1988

Country	%
Japan	~34
West Germany	~26
Canada	~21
France	~20
United Kingdom	~17
United States	~13

Source: World Bank, *World Tables 1989-90*.

The Japanese have the highest rate of savings. As a nation, they consume less than two-thirds of their output. The next most thrifty are the Germans, who save more than one-fourth of their output. It is hardly a coincidence that the two countries with the highest national savings rate are the two countries with the strongest, most competitive economies internationally.

Economic Reasoning *(Write your responses on a separate sheet. Answers begin on p. 318.)*

1. Referring to Figure 3 on page 459 in the text, if the U.S. savings (S) flow were greater, which of the other flows would be less?
2. What effect does the low national savings rate in the United States have on the country's international financial position?
3. Should any measures be taken to increase the national savings rate in the United States? If measures were to be taken, what should they be?

IV. Practice Test *(Answers begin on p. 318.)*

Multiple Choice *(Circle the correct answer.)*

(16.1) 1. Ultimately, a country pays for its imports with:
    a. its own currency.
    b. its exports.
    c. its investments in other countries.
    d. credit.

(16.1) 2. Which of the following is traded in foreign-exchange markets?
- a. claims on foreign assets.
- b. short-term capital assets.
- c. physical quantities of goods and services.
- d. currencies from different countries.

(16.2) 3. Under a system of freely fluctuating exchange rates, the price of a country's currency is determined by:
- a. the International Monetary Fund.
- b. each country's central bank.
- c. multilateral currency negotiations.
- d. the relative demand for and supply of that currency.

(16.2) 4. Under a system of fixed exchange rates, a shortage of country A's currency in world markets will be eliminated by:
- a. an increase in the price of country A's currency.
- b. increased supplies provided at the set price by country A's central bank.
- c. the substitution of another country's currency for country A's currency in exchange markets.
- d. a devaluation of country A's currency.

(16.3) 5. Under a system of freely floating exchange rates, an increase in the demand for Japan's products will result in:
- a. an appreciation of Japan's currency.
- b. a depreciation of Japan's currency.
- c. a revaluation of Japan's currency.
- d. a devaluation of Japan's currency.

(16.3) 6. Under a system of fixed exchange rates, a country can increase the amount of goods that it **imports** through _____ of its currency.
- a. an appreciation
- b. a depreciation
- c. a revaluation
- d. a devaluation

(16.4) 7. Records of merchandise imports and exports are contained in a country's:
- a. trade account.
- b. current account.
- c. capital account.
- d. residual account.

(16.5) 8. Who is helped when country A has a favorable balance of trade?
- a. consumers in country A.
- b. a resident of country A who buys a lot from country A's exporting industries.
- c. workers in export industries in country A.
- d. import-competing firms in country A's trading partners.
- e. Everyone in country A benefits from a favorable balance of trade.

(16.5) 9. Who benefits from an unfavorable balance of trade in country A?
- a. consumers in country A.
- b. workers in country A's export industries.
- c. consumers in country A's trading partners.
- d. workers in country A's import-competing industries.
- e. Nobody in country A gains from an unfavorable balance of trade.

(16.6) 10. A country that has a basic deficit will have:
- a. a positive residual account balance.
- b. a positive trade balance.
- c. an inflow of gold or similar assets.
- d. an appreciating currency.

(16.6) 11. Which of the following can be used to offset a basic deficit in the United States?
   a. an outflow of gold from the United States.
   b. foreign countries holding more idle dollars.
   c. outflows of short-term capital assets from the United States.
   d. loans from the IMF.
   e. all of the above. *[e circled]*

(16.7) 12. National economic equilibrium requires that:
   a. I + X + T = S + M + G.
   b. X + M + T = S + G + I.
   c. S + M + T = G + X + I. *[c circled]*
   d. S + G + X = T + M + I.

(16.7) 13. To restore economic equilibrium in the United States during the 1980s, increased imports were necessary:
   a. to offset increased exports.
   b. because savings and taxes were less than government spending and investment. *[b circled]*
   c. because the dollar was depreciating.
   d. so that the residual account could be used to offset the basic deficit in the United States.

(16.8) 14. The price of import surpluses in the 1980s will be:
   a. an appreciation of the dollar.
   b. the necessity of producing more than we consume in the future. *[b circled]*
   c. an increased residual account in the future.
   d. less trade in the future.

(16.9) 15. The biggest threat to the United States of foreign investment in the United States is:
   a. the political power that it gives to foreign interests.
   b. the increase in imports that such investment represents.
   c. the increase in exports that such investment represents.
   d. the possibility that this investment will be withdrawn. *[d circled]*

True/False *(Circle T or F.)*

(16.2) 16. Under a system of fixed exchange rates, a surplus of a nation's currency can be eliminated by devaluing the currency. **T** or F

(16.3) 17. An increase in inflation in France will result in the appreciation of the French franc. T or **F**

(16.4) 18. A country's balance of payments will always balance when **all** short- and long-term transactions are taken into account. **T** or F

(16.5) 19. A favorable balance of trade in Italy results in benefits for Italian consumers. T or **F**

(16.8) 20. An import surplus is necessary for a country to consume more than it produces. **T** or F

Chapter 17

Alternative Economic Systems

I. Chapter Outline

Every society must devise a way to answer the basic economic questions of what to produce, how to produce, and for whom to produce. Different societies, however, have developed alternative economic systems that answer these questions in quite different ways. A comparison of the different types of systems, from market economies to command economies, reveals that they have had varying degrees of success in achieving economic and socioeconomic goals. The crumbling of the command economies in the Soviet Union and Eastern Europe indicates that the world is moving (sometimes violently) toward increased reliance on the use of market economies to allocate scarce resources.

Introductory Article: Revolution from Above

After the Russian Revolution of 1917, a number of countries abandoned market-oriented economies and replaced them with planned economic systems. Now, for the first time in history, the planned economies are undergoing a transition in the other direction. The introduction of *perestroika* in the Soviet Union during the 1980s was meant to reform its planned economy and make the consumer sectors of the economy more responsive to market forces. Revolutions of any kind represent dramatic changes, and such changes do not take place easily or overnight. A society that has done things one way for generations cannot easily or rapidly adapt to a new social order. Although the economic changes taking place in the Soviet Union may lead to an improved economy in the long run, the short-run transition from a command to a market economy is proving to be painful.

Economic Analysis

This chapter compares alternative economic systems by analyzing the following questions:

1. What Are the Alternatives to Capitalism?

    Important Concepts: Capitalism, State socialism, Communism, Market socialism, The welfare state

    Case Application: The Yugoslavian Way

2. How Do Alternative Economic Systems Resolve the Basic Economic Questions?

    Important Concepts: Gosplan, Control figures, Priority sectors, Gosbank

    Case Application: Little Lions?

3. How Does the Performance of Alternative Economic Systems Compare?

    Important Concepts: Static efficiency, Dynamic efficiency, Correcting distortions, *Perestroika, Glasnost*

    Case Application: Exploiting the Environment

Perspective: Marx on Capitalism

II. Summary of Economic Analysis

1. Although commonly referred to as **communism**, the economies of the Soviet Union and its Eastern European neighbors were, until the 1990s, actually examples of **state socialism**. Under this system, the government owns all productive resources (the means of production) and makes all economic decisions.
2. **Market socialism** is somewhere in between state socialism and free enterprise. The government owns most of the means of production, but the market system is used extensively to allocate goods and services in product markets.
3. A **welfare state** exists when the government controls the transportation, communications, and energy industries while the remainder of the economy is generally market-oriented. Welfare states typically use very progressive income tax structures to achieve relatively equal income distributions.
4. **Gosplan** was the central planning agency in the Soviet Union that was responsible for making all production decisions. Gosplan would develop broad **control figures** for most industries, and different ministries would then use the figures to generate specific targets for specific plants.
5. After receiving its production targets, each Soviet plant would estimate its needed resources and would forward its requests up the chain of command to Gosplan.
6. New capital investment and national defense were **priority sectors** emphasized by Gosplan, and taxes were used to discourage consumption.
7. All financial transactions necessitated by Gosplan were handled by **Gosbank**, the government bank.
8. Unlike the system of state socialism typified by Gosplan, market socialist economies generally abandon rigid central control. Government activity, however, is still much greater than it is in market economies.
9. Under a system of state socialism, central authorities dictate **how** goods are produced because they dictate the type and amount of investment in each sector of the economy. Technological change and innovation in the way goods are produced are slow to develop because there are few incentives for individual plants to produce efficiently.
10. Although most workers in state socialist economies receive lower wages than their Western counterparts, they have fewer expenses because food, housing, and medical care are heavily subsidized by the government.
11. The main determinant of the distribution of income in a welfare state is the highly progressive tax system.
12. The goals of all economic systems are generally the same: efficiency, growth, full employment, and price stability.
13. In terms of **static efficiency**, the record of the Soviet Union indicates that state socialism has been unsuccessful in using its resources efficiently.
14. By making investment in physical and human capital priority sectors, the Soviet economy was able to generate high rates of growth (**dynamic efficiency**) through the 1970s.
15. State socialist economies have much more stable prices than market economies, but these inflexible prices often result in surpluses and shortages that cannot be removed by price fluctuations. Long lines and large savings balances are signs of pent-up inflation waiting to break loose.
16. State socialist economies have low unemployment rates because workers cannot be fired or laid off, but this inflexibility prevents workers from moving to jobs where they are most highly valued.
17. With respect to **socioeconomic goals**, state socialism is superior at providing job security while market economies are superior at providing economic freedom. Sadly, neither system has been very successful in promoting environmental protection.

III. Review of the Learning Objectives *(Answers begin on p. 318.)*

What Are the Alternatives to Capitalism?

STATE SOCIALISM (communism, authoritarian socialism)	MARKET SOCIALISM (regulated market economy)	WELFARE STATE (democratic socialism)
Production Means of production owned by the government. Allocation and pricing decisions are made by a central planning authority. **Income distribution** Supposed to be relatively equal, but the government and ruling party officials enjoy a much higher real income. **Government** Self-perpetuating government by the ruling party. It provides extensive public services and income security.	**Production** Means of production, with some exceptions, are owned by the government. Major allocation decisions made by authorities, but production methods and mix of consumer goods determined in the marketplace. **Income distribution** Income incentives provided by market, but real income largely determined by the government's policies. There are some labor union effects. **Government** Customarily authoritarian, but recently some with democratic elections. Extensive public services and income security.	**Production** Means of production largely in private hands, except for some basic industries. The pricing and allocation decisions along with the production methods are mainly determined in the marketplace. **Income distribution** Money incomes determined by market forces, but after-tax incomes egalitarian as a result of highly progressive taxes, income transfers, and social services. Strong labor unions. **Government** Democratically elected. It may employ indicative planning. Extensive public services and income security.

(See page vi in the foreword "To the Student" for how to make the best use of this schematic outline.)

17.1. Explain the distinctions between capitalism, state socialism, market socialism, and the welfare state. *(Write in answers below.)*

A. Indicate which economic system or systems correspond to the characteristics below: **C** for capitalism, **MS** for market socialism, **SS** for state socialism, and **WS** for the welfare state. (More than one economic system may apply in each case.)

1. _MS, SS_ Government ownership of most basic industries.
2. _SS_ Central planning for all production.
3. _MS, SS_ Wages determined by the government.
4. _C, WS_ Private ownership of most of the means of production.
5. _C, WS_ Prices determined by market forces.
6. _MS, SS_ The means of production owned primarily by the government.
7. _WS_ High marginal tax rates and income redistribution.
8. _WS_ Strong labor unions playing important roles.
9. _MS_ Income determined in factor markets.
10. _WS_ Government traditionally democratically elected.

B. Use the same abbreviations as in Part A to list the four types of economic systems in the appropriate order:

1. _SS_ Most government control of the economy.
2. _MS_ Second most government control.
3. _WS_ Third most government control.
4. _C_ Least government control.

C. Use the same abbreviations as in Part A to indicate which type of system best describes the **current** economic system used in the following countries:

1. _MS_ The Soviet Union.
2. _MS_ Hungary.
3. _SS_ China.
4. _C_ Canada.
5. _C_ The United States.
6. _C_ Japan.
7. _WS_ Great Britain.
8. _SS_ Cuba.
9. _MS_ Yugoslavia.
10. _WS_ Sweden.

D. Use the same abbreviations as in Part A to indicate which of the types of economic systems each of the following is most associated with:

1. _SS_ Karl Marx.
2. _MS_ Oskar Lange.
3. _MS_ Mikhail Gorbachev.
4. _C_ Milton Friedman.
5. _MS_ Marshall Tito (the leader of Yugoslavia after 1948).
6. _SS_ Fidel Castro.
7. _C_ Boris Yeltsin.
8. _C_ Friedrich von Hayek.

Case Application: Down Argentina Way

At the time of World War II the Argentine economy was sixth largest in the world, with a GNP comparable to that of Canada. Today it is below thirtieth in the world—comparable to the GNP of Turkey—and headed lower. How did a country so rich in natural resources and with a skilled and literate labor force fall so far in less than five decades?

A quick answer is that it was brought down by a unique economic system that has been characterized as "socialism without planning." Under dictator General Juan Perón, who ruled the country from 1946 to 1954 and again from 1973 to 1974, industry and services were nationalized. (Some 30% of the country's productive capacity is still state-owned now.)

Perón subsidized government industries with funds from the private sector, particularly agriculture and the landowners. As a result, in the country once world-famous for its beef production, steaks have become unaffordable for much of the population. Productivity declined, services deteriorated, and inflation rose rapidly.

Nevertheless, Perón maintained his power base for a long time by transferring income from the propertied class to the working class. He was a populist dictator who catered to the powerful labor unions and associated his regime with the aspirations of the masses of poor and underprivileged. He provided a network of social services. (His populist image was reinforced by the popularity of his wife, Evita, among the masses of Argentina.) Although Perón passed away in 1974, the Justicialista party, the descendant of his Peronista party, governs the country.

Today the Argentine government is broke, spending $1 for every 40¢ in revenue that it takes in. It has the third largest foreign debt in Latin America, after Brazil and Mexico. In per capita terms, its foreign debt is the highest. The economy is in shambles, with hyperinflation that left prices over 30,000 times higher at the end of the 1980s than they were at the beginning of the decade.

According to an Argentine economist who is also a member of the national Congress, "We have been living in socialism without planning; capitalism without markets. We must reduce the size of the public sector of the economy." Public opinion surveys show that about 70% of the population is in favor of privatization. The still-powerful labor unions, however, may block any changes that threaten to reduce their power.

Economic Reasoning *(Write your responses on a separate sheet. Answers begin on p. 318.)*

1. What type of economic system is characterized by the powerful labor unions found in Argentina?
2. In what ways was the system adopted by Perón similar to state socialism, and in what ways was it different?
3. Was the popularity of Juan Perón among Argentines justified? Why or why not?

How Do Alternative Economic Systems Resolve the Basic Economic Questions?

WHAT TO PRODUCE
Five-year plans
The basic planning instrument in centrally controlled economies has been the five-year plan.

Gosplan	Gosbank
In the Soviet Union, Gosplan, which acts as the central planning agency, gathers information about the economy and leadership priorities (e.g., on the consumption-investment mix).	The state bank, Gosbank, handles all financial transactions among enterprises and through this monitors input use and production output.
Control figures	**Priority sectors**
Gosplan establishes control figures for about 2,000 major commodity groups which are sent to economic ministries that set production targets for each enterprise.	The priority sectors are given first preference in the allocation of the resources. The USSR priorities have been investment for growth and the military.

HOW TO PRODUCE
Production methods in a centrally planned system are for the most part dictated by the allocation of investment goods by the planning authority.

FOR WHOM TO PRODUCE
Income distribution in the USSR is based on wage incentives to allocate labor where it is needed. High officials receive large bonuses and non-wage benefits.

(See page vi in the foreword "To the Student" for how to make the best use of this schematic outline.)

17.2. Compare the way in which a system of state socialism answers the basic economic questions of what, how, and for whom to produce with the way a market system answers these questions.

A. Fill in the following blanks with the following terms: Gosplan, Gosbank, five-year plan(s), control figure(s), an economic ministry, priority sector(s). (Some terms will be used more than once.)

1. Prior to *perestroika,* broad production goals in the U.S.S.R. were established by _five-year plans_.

2. These included the designation of _priority sectors_ that were considered to be the most important parts of the economy.

3. Based on all this, _Gosplan_ made production allocations by industry.

4. These production decisions were then put into the form of _control figures_ for about 2,000 commodity groups.

5. These were further narrowed down into targets for specific enterprises by _economic ministries_.

6. The specific industries would then estimate their resource needs and make a request to their _economic ministries_.

7. These requests would then be sent back up the line to _Gosplan_.

8. All necessary financial transactions were controlled by _Gosbank_.

B. Fill in the following blanks with the following terms: financial markets, market prices, factor markets, profits, entrepreneurs. (One term will be used more than once.)

1. In a market system, the basic production goals are set by _entrepreneurs_ as they try to determine what people want to buy.

2. Decisionmakers get their information about what to produce from the _market prices_ of their goods.

3. The necessary resources to produce this output are obtained in _factor markets_.

4. If these scarce resources are more highly valued elsewhere, this information will be transmitted to the decisionmaker through _market prices_.

5. Goods will be produced only if they generate _profits_ for the firm.

6. If the firm needs additional capital, it will obtain it in the _financial markets_.

C.
1. In a state socialist economy, _planners_ determine what gets produced.
2. What gets produced in a state socialist economy is therefore what is considered best for _society_.
3. In a market economy, _consumer demand_ determines what gets produced.
4. What gets produced in a market economy is therefore what is considered best for _the consumer_.

D.
1. What determines where workers work in a state socialist economy? Workers are given incentives to work in jobs where their skills are most highly valued by _planners_.
2. In a market economy, workers have incentives to work where their skills are most highly valued by _employers_.

Case Application: Food Production in the Soviet Union

The structure of Soviet agriculture is divided into three sectors, the most important of which is collective farming. There are nearly 36,000 collective farms producing about 45% of all Soviet agricultural output. Each collective farm is organized like a cooperative, and each member uses machinery and equipment that is jointly owned. A large part of the collective output—80%—must be sold to the state at an unfavorable price. The incomes of workers on collective farms are lower than those of other workers.

The second sector of Soviet agriculture is state farming. The almost 12,700 state farms (*sovkhozy*) produce about 31% of total agricultural output. All the state farms are directly controlled and administered through the planning system. Each farmer works on the state farm as a hired laborer and earns a wage.

The third component of Soviet agriculture is the private plot sector. Each farmer in a collective or state farm can own and work up to one acre of private land. Although it occupies only 3% of the arable land, this sector produces about one-quarter of the food supply.

About 34% of the Soviet population is engaged in agricultural production, whereas the comparable figure in the United States is only 2%. The Soviets, however, are unable to feed their own population, while the United States has often had the headache of surpluses. The agricultural drag in the Soviet Union is attributed to many factors, such as the natural conditions of climate and soil and the limited investment in capital and chemical fertilizer. The most important factors, however, are the failure of the bureaucratic planning hierarchy, the lack of an incentive system, and the lack of research facilities and organization.

As a result of these problems, the Soviet Union has become increasingly dependent on food imports. Recently it has been importing at least one-fourth of its grain consumption. One cause of the grain shortage is the high percentage of grain production used for seed for the next year's harvest. In the Soviet Union, 16% of the crop goes for seed to plant, compared to only 2% in the United States. One reason for this is the greater U.S. reliance on corn, a more productive seed grain than wheat.

An important element of the Gorbachev reforms was a proposal to privatize agriculture by allowing farmers to lease the land for as long as 50 years and work it as their own, selling their produce for whatever they could get. Subsequently, however, to placate conservatives in the government and in the population, Gorbachev decided to hold a referendum on the privatization of farmland before going ahead with the plan.

Economic Reasoning *(Write your responses on a separate sheet. Answers begin on p. 318.)*

1. Was agriculture one of the priority sectors in Soviet economic planning?
2. What difficulties and deficiencies are there in the resolution of the "how to produce" food question in the Soviet Union?
3. If you were a member of the Council of Ministers of the Soviet Union, would you vote to privatize agriculture? If you were a farmer? If you were a consumer on a low budget? Give your reasons in each case.

How Does the Performance of Alternative Economic Systems Compare?

EFFICIENCY	PRICE STABILITY	FULL EMPLOYMENT	GROWTH
Static efficiency The static efficiency is measured at a given point in time. Levels of productivity of both the labor and capital in the USSR are low. **Dynamic efficiency** Dynamic efficiency is the performance of an economy over a period of time.	Theoretically, USSR's government can keep prices almost perfectly stable because they are established by state agencies. But now that the Soviets are more concerned about the rational allocation of scarce resources, they are raising prices in response to shortages.	Officially, the USSR guarantees jobs for everyone and earlier had full employment. But under *perestroika* the rate unemployed has climbed.	Soviet annual growth in its real GNP from the 1920s to the 1960s was exceptional, unmatched by any other country either in aggregate or per capita terms. Since then, however, USSR growth has stagnated.

SOCIOECONOMIC GOALS

Environmental protection
Because of planning failure to include environmental costs, the USSR has severe pollution problems, the worst instance being the consequences of the Chernobyl nuclear power plant explosion.

Security
There was a high degree of job and basic needs security in the Soviet Union under central planning, but the *perestroika* transition period has led to unemployment and social distress.

Equality
Income is generally more evenly distributed than in the West, except for high officials.

Freedom
Economic freedom has been limited by the absence of private ownership and by the requirements of planning. The Soviets traded off economic freedom for stability and security.

(See page vi in the foreword "To the Student" for how to make the best use of this schematic outline.)

17.3. Evaluate the relative performance of state socialism and market economies in terms of each of the following: efficiency, price stability, unemployment, and growth.

A. State socialism in the Soviet Union was successful at generating _dynamic_ efficiency but was unsuccessful at generating _static_ efficiency.

B.
1. What essential aspect of market economies that eliminates shortages and surpluses is absent in state socialism?

   flexible prices

2. What essential aspect of market economies that causes workers and businesses to produce more efficiently is absent in state socialism?

   profit incentives

C.
1. What is an example of one industry where the Soviet Union and other state socialist economies have been more efficient than the United States?

   public transportation

2. Is this unique to state socialist economies?

   no. pg. 319

D. What are two indicators of suppressed inflation in the Soviet Union?
   1. *large savings balances*
   2. *long lines at stores*

E.
1. What is one advantage of the price controls used in state socialism?

   they help maintain stable prices

2. What is one disadvantage of the price controls used in state socialism?

   prices cannot contribute to economic efficiency by using to eliminate shortages

F. What are the two most important factors in explaining the high growth rates achieved by the Soviet Union through the 1960s?
   1. *high labor force participation rates*
   2. *investment in human capital*

G.
1. What is one advantage of the state socialist policy of forbidding enterprises from laying off workers?

   it helps achieve the goal of full employment

2. What is one disadvantage of the state socialist policy of forbidding enterprises from laying off workers?

   labor (workers) is not allocated to its most efficient use

264 / Working With The Study of Economics, 4/E

17.4. Compare the alternative economic systems in how well they achieve socioeconomic goals.

A. Indicate which of the following socioeconomic goals are best achieved with state socialism (SS) and which with market economies (M):

1. _SS_ Universal access to good health care.
2. _M_ Economic freedom.
3. _SS_ Old-age security.
4. _SS_ Job security.
5. _SS_ Equity.
6. _M_ Political freedom.
7. _M_ Environmental safety.
8. _SS_ Maternity benefits.

B. What is one essential thing absent in **both** market and state socialist economies that has resulted in the pollution of their air and water?

No owners of air & water with an incentive for property rights with which to protect them

C. List five examples of environmental damage in the Soviet Union.

1. _Lake Baikal has been polluted by paper mills_
2. _The Volga has been polluted w/ raw sewage_
3. _Radioactive fallout from the Chernobyl nuclear plant_
4. _Draining the Aral Sea_
5. _One cannot drink the tap water in Leningrad_

Case Application: Business Cycle Hits Eastern Europe

The Great Depression in the 1930s was worldwide—almost. The United States had a high 25% unemployment, and some of the European countries suffered even more. Meanwhile, the economy of the Soviet Union was booming along. Unemployment was virtually nonexistent, and real Gross National Product was growing at a healthy rate. The experience of the 1930s seemed to validate the communist doctrine that business cycles were a capitalistic "disease" from which communism was immune.

In order to avoid infection from this disease, the Soviet Union under Josef Stalin did very little business with Western countries. Except for receiving wartime supplies from the Allies during World War II, the Soviet Union was largely self-sufficient during Stalin's time. Today, however, the Soviet Union—and to an even greater extent, the countries of Eastern Europe—are heavily dependent on trade with the West.

The 1970s increase in petroleum prices and the world recession in the early 1980s created severe macroeconomic problems for the communist countries. Stagflation was even worse in the communist bloc than it was in the West. Output was stagnant in both groups of countries, but it was at a much lower level in the communist bloc. There were sharp increases in prices, especially for food. In 1982 the prices of meat and various other food items in Czechoslovakia, Romania, and Hungary increased from 20% to 35% and in Poland as much as 400% for some items.

During the 1970s Eastern European countries such as Poland and Czechoslovakia borrowed heavily from European and American banks in order to acquire Western imports. With the economic slump in the 1980s and the decline in their export earnings, and with the Soviet Union cutting off its subsidized petroleum, these countries were unable to meet their foreign debt obligations. They needed financial assistance from the West and renegotiation of their loans in order to avoid defaulting. In order to meet their obligations and satisfy their creditors, they had to restrict imports severely and impose a program of "belt-tightening" on their populations.

Then in the 1990s, with their rejection of communism and turn toward a market system, they faced the twin horrors of capitalism—inflation and unemployment. Especially in the transition period from controlled to market economies, they found that greater economic instability is the price that market systems pay for efficiency.

Economic Reasoning *(Write your responses on a separate sheet. Answers begin on p. 319.)*

1. In the 1930s the Soviet Union achieved macroeconomic goals better than Western countries did. Which two primary economic goals did it succeed at better than the West?
2. Some Western experts allege that an economic slump is worse for command economies than for market economies because their static efficiency is lower due to the rigidity of their systems. Why might an increase in petroleum prices create more problems for command economies than for market economies?
3. Do you think that Stalin was right in avoiding trade with the West for the economic well-being of the communist countries? Why or why not?

IV. Practice Test *(Answers begin on p. 319.)*

Multiple Choice *(Circle the correct answer.)*

(17.1) 1. The expression used to describe the Soviet Union's attempted move from state to market socialism is:
   a. glasnost.
   b. yeltsin.
   c. chernobyl.
   d. perestroika.

(17.1) 2. The type of economic system in which the government exerts the most control over the economy is:
   a. capitalism.
   b. the welfare state.
   c. market socialism.
   d. state socialism.

(17.1) 3. The Soviet Union is currently switching to which kind of economic system?
   a. capitalism.
   b. the welfare state.
   c. market socialism.
   d. state socialism.

(17.1) 4. China currently employs which kind of economic system?
   a. capitalism.
   b. the welfare state.
   c. market socialism.
   d. state socialism.

(17.1) 5. In which of the following types of economic systems do labor unions play the largest role?
   a. capitalism.
   b. the welfare state.
   c. market socialism.
   d. state socialism.

(17.2) 6. The basic attribute of market economies that promotes efficiency and that is missing in state socialism is:

a. the profit motive.
b. democratic governments.
c. employment security.
d. price stability.

(17.2) 7. Which of the following laid out the broad economic goals of the Soviet Union prior to the 1990s?
a. Gosplan.
b. the Economic Ministry.
c. the Priority Sector.
d. five-year plans.

(17.2) 8. What guides managers' decisions in state socialist economies?
a. attempting to maximizing profits.
b. attempting to allocate resources efficiently.
c. attempting to meet quotas.
d. attempting to conserve scarce resources.

(17.2) 9. Which of the following is the most accurate reflection of the Soviet economy prior to the 1990s?
a. Financial incentives were used only to increase the productivity of managers.
b. Financial incentives were used throughout the economy for both managers and workers.
c. Financial incentives were provided only in the agriculture industry.
d. Financial incentives were never used.

(17.3) 10. Market economies have their biggest advantage over state socialism in promoting which of the following goals?
a. static economic efficiency.
b. equity.
c. price stability.
d. full employment.

(17.3) 11. The Soviet Union was able to generate more economic growth than the United States through the 1960s by putting more emphasis on:
a. technologically improved capital.
b. increasing capital/output ratios.
c. investment in human capital.
d. the agricultural sector.

(17.3) 12. Correcting distortions is the expression used by the Soviet Union to describe:
a. damage to the environment.
b. deviations from five-year plans.
c. price increases.
d. laid-off workers.

(17.3) 13. The existence of long lines in the Soviet Union is evidence of:
a. shortages caused because prices are not allowed to rise.
b. unstable prices.
c. the poor quality of Soviet goods.
d. hidden unemployment.

(17.4) 14. Which of the following is the site of a major nuclear accident in the Soviet Union?
a. Chernobyl.
b. Lake Baikal.
c. Lake Ladoga.
d. the Aral Sea.
e. all of the above.

(17.5) 15. A cost of full employment in state socialist economies is:
a. price instability.

b. an inefficient allocation of labor resources.
c. slow economic growth.
d. poor quality output.

True/False *(Circle T or F.)*

(17.1) 16. Most Western European countries use economic systems best described as market socialism. T or F

(17.1) 17. The economy of Great Britain is best described as being a welfare state. T or F

(17.2) 18. Gosbank is the Soviet planning agency responsible for allocating resources to various sectors of the Soviet economy. T or F

(17.3) 19. The Soviet Union has consistently experienced slower rates of economic growth than the United States. T or F

(17.4) 20. Although neither system can be called successful at protecting the environment, state socialist countries seem to be doing a better job than countries with market economies. T or F

Chapter 18

World Economic Development

I. Chapter Outline

Two-thirds of the world's population lives in nonindustrialized countries with low living standards and numerous obstacles to economic development. Overpopulation, malnutrition, illiteracy, depleted natural resources, inappropriate public policies, and soaring debt all make it increasingly difficult for economies to pull themselves out of poverty. Adding even more to the problem, increased industrialization and economic growth will put increased pressures on the already threatened ecology of spaceship Earth.

Introductory Article: China's Great Leap Backward

Although it contains one-fifth of the world's population, China is one of the world's poorest countries in terms of income per person. Attempting to increase its people's incomes, China has applied different policy prescriptions to its economy. One prescription that worked was the "contract system" employed in the 1980s that allowed farmers and businesses to sell output in excess of government quotas in free markets. Partly as a result of this system, China's economy grew almost 10% per year from 1981 through 1988. Unfortunately for the Chinese, public corruption and the less equal distribution of income that accompanied the more open economy have led to a backlash against free markets and increased control by the central government.

Economic Analysis

This chapter examines the problems of less-developed countries by addressing the following questions:

1. How Do Standards of Living Compare?

    Important Concepts: LDCs, Headcount index of poverty, Poverty gap, Income distribution, Social indicators

    Case Application: A Tale of Two Countries

2. What Makes Countries Poor?

    Important Concepts: Vicious circle of poverty, Economic surplus, Overpopulation, Exploitation, Economic policies

    Case Application: The Example of India

3. What Are the Prospects for World Economic Development?

    Important Concepts: The population bomb, The debt bomb, The environmental bomb, The Brady Plan

    Case Application: South of the Border

Perspective: The Malthusian Dilemma

        Biography—Thomas Robert Malthus

II. Summary of Economic Analysis

1. Two-thirds of the world's population lives in **less-developed countries (LDCs)** where the standard of living is low and poverty is widespread.
2. Most LDCs are located in South Asia and sub-Saharan Africa.
3. The World Bank measures the existence and level of poverty through the use of the **headcount index** and the **poverty gap** index. The former measures the percentage of people below the poverty line and the latter indicates the gap between per capita incomes and the poverty line.
4. Examining the per capita income in a country can be misleading because per capita figures do not take into account the **distribution of income** in a country.
5. In addition to economic indicators, the World Bank compiles social indicators of economic development such as **life expectancy**, **infant mortality rates**, and **adult literacy**.
6. One reason for the lack of economic development in LDCs is the lack of an **economic surplus** that can be used to increase the quantity and quality of a country's capital. Another is the lack of investment in human capital to improve worker literacy.
7. **Overpopulation** contributes to a lack of economic development because increases in output need to be shared among an increasing number of people.
8. A history of **external exploitation** has hindered the development of LDCs because the industrialized nations of the world used them as sources of raw materials without adding to their industrial infrastructure.
9. Powerful families control much of the land and other means of production in LDCs, and they have used their position to **internally exploit** their poor countrymen in order to enrich themselves.
10. Inefficient public policies such as keeping food prices too low and barring the free trade of imported goods have contributed to the poverty in LDCs.
11. A ticking **population bomb** makes it difficult to increase economic growth because increased numbers of people require increased amounts of food, energy, and other resources that must be diverted from any economic surplus.
12. The increasing amount of money owed to foreign lenders has resulted in a **debt crisis** that limits growth because most foreign trade earnings must be used to pay interest instead of being used for new investment.
13. Increasing growth in LDCs will create an **environmental bomb** as increased industrialization will increase the demand for energy and put an increased strain on an already fragile ecology.

270 / Working With The Study of Economics, 4/E

III. Review of the Learning Objectives (Answers begin on p. 319.)

How Do Standards of Living Compare?

POVERTY
Most of the world's population lives in the less-developed countries (LDCs) of the Third World that have per capita incomes of only a few hundred dollars a year.

Poverty Line
The World Bank has established a poverty line range for the LDCs of $275 to $370 income per person per year.

Headcount Index	Poverty Gap
The percentage of a nation's population that falls below the poverty line.	The total amount that would be required to bring all of a nation's population above the poverty line.

Income distribution
A highly skewed income distribution in many LDCs makes the poverty problem more acute.

Social indicators
Various social indicators give a more complete picture of a nation's living standards.
* Growth in per capita GNP
* Adult illiteracy rate
* Life expectancy at birth
* Infant mortality rate

(See page vi in the foreword "To the Student" for how to make the best use of this schematic outline.)

18.1. Discuss the ways of comparing living standards among countries and explain how China compares with other less-developed countries. *(Write in answers below.)*

A. What are three **economic** indicators that can be used to compare living standards among countries?

1. _GNP_
2. _per capita GNP_
3. _growth of GNP_

B. What are three **social** indicators that can be used to compare living standards among countries?

1. _adult illiteracy_
2. _life expectancy_
3. _infant mortality_

C. China compares favorably with other low-income countries in which economic and/or social measures of living standards?

1. _GNP growth_
2. _literacy rate_

3. *life expectancy*
4. *infant mortality rates*

D. China compares unfavorably with other low-income countries in which economic and/or social measure of living standards?

1. *per capita GNP*

E. In addition to minimum standards for necessities, the World Bank establishes minimum standards for **amenities** based on different cultures. What are three amenities that are "necessary" for life in the United States that probably are not necessary in an LDC?

1. *a telephone*
2. *indoor plumbing*
3. *electricity*

18.2. Name the regions where poverty is most prevalent and list four low-income countries in those regions.

A. In which three regions of the world is poverty the most prevalent?

1. *South Asia*
2. *East Asia*
3. *sub-Saharan Africa*

B. List four countries in the region that you listed first in Part A (either low- or lower-middle-income countries).

1. *India*
2. *Bangladesh*
3. *Afganistan*
4. *Sri Lanka*

C. List four countries in the region that you listed second in Part A (either low- or lower-middle-income countries).

1. *Indonesia*
2. *China*
3. *Thailand*
4. *Laos*

D. List four countries in the region that you listed third in Part A (either low- or lower-middle-income countries).

1. *Nigeria*
2. *Kenya*
3. *Tanzania*
4. *Zambia*

Case Application: Report on Africa

Famine in Africa (see the first case application in this book on page 4) is only one of the problems plaguing the continent. According to a World Bank report, the African nations are not doing too well on the development front. The report, titled *Accelerated Development in Sub-Saharan Africa,* states that the development of the crucial agricultural sector is being badly mismanaged by African countries. Their policies are to keep food prices artificially low in order to provide cheap food for the growing urban populations. This has resulted in a decline in food output. There has been a fall in farm productivity in spite of $5 billion in foreign aid money for the development of African agriculture.

Some of the problems of agricultural production in Africa are due to drought, lack of irrigation, infestations, inadequate transportation facilities, and political disorders. In Ethiopia and the Sudan, even though the rains have come, the civil wars have prevented food distribution. Similarly, in Angola, Liberia, and Mozambique, civil wars have created hundreds of thousands of refugees, kept farmers from planting, and cut off the populations from food and water supplies.

But the greatest obstacles to improved productivity in Africa are government mismanagement and destructive politics. Even Kenya, which was long considered the showpiece of black African economic development, is facing an agricultural crisis. In Zimbabwe, the former British colony of Rhodesia, the best agricultural land is still in the hands of the white population, although the number of whites in the country has decreased from 280,000 before independence to less than 125,000 today.

The population growth rates in Africa are among the highest in the world, 3.8% a year in Kenya, 3.7% in Zambia, and 3.5% in Tanzania, for example. Because of the policy of maintaining low food prices and the consequent depression of incomes in the agricultural areas, the burgeoning populations gravitate toward the cities. There are not sufficient jobs for the growing urban populations and unemployment is rampant.

Economic Reasoning *(Write your responses on a separate sheet. Answers begin on p. 320.)*

1. In Table 1, on page 507 of the textbook, showing the basic indicators for different groups of economies, Nigeria is the only sub-Saharan country listed. How does its economic performance compare to the other four largest low-income countries?
2. Life expectancy in Nigeria is 19 years less than in China, and its infant mortality rate is more than three times higher. What conditions in Africa discussed in the case application might contribute to this?
3. What policies do you think African governments should adopt with respect to agriculture and food prices?

What Makes Countries Poor?

LACK OF CAPITAL, TECHNOLOGY, AND HUMAN CAPITAL
In order to break out of the vicious circle of poverty, a country needs an economic surplus over and above consumption needs to allocate to investment in real capital and human capital for intensive growth.

OVERPOPULATION
The standard of living depends on the amount of goods and services available relative to the numbers of people. A large and rapidly growing population absorbs all of the economic surplus, trapping the country in a vicious circle.

EXPLOITATION
The legacy of external exploitation in their colonial past may have retarded economic development for the LDCs. However, a greater obstacle to development may be the internal exploitation of one class by another, with ownership of land usually concentrated in the hands of a wealthy elite class that controls the government.

ECONOMIC POLICIES
Policies pursued by a number of LDCs have inhibited economic growth. These policies include the exploitation of agriculture by holding down agricultural prices to provide cheap food for residents of the cities and protectionist measures to favor import-substitution industries.

(See page vi in the foreword "To the Student" for how to make the best use of this schematic outline.)

18.3. Explain the problems that cause countries to be poor.

A. What is an economic surplus and why is it necessary for economic growth?

pg. 320

B. What are three factors leading to a lack of economic surplus in LDCs?

1. *overpopulation*
2. *low initial investment*
3. *little human capital*

C. Which three of the four factors that lead to economic growth (chapter 14) are missing in LDCs?

1. *increased investment GNP ratios*
2. *low capital/output ratios*
3. *investment in human capital*

274 / Working With The Study of Economics, 4/E

D. In which of the four alternative economic systems discussed in chapter 17 would you expect there to be the **least** amount of internal exploitation of workers? Why?

pg. 320

E.

1. What two groups benefit from the presence of barriers to imports in an LDC?

producers & labor unions

2. How is the overall economy of an LDC harmed by the presence of barriers to imports?

The people in the LDC must rely on high cost, low quality import substitutes

Case Application: Do You Like Company? How About 10 Billion?

The world population has doubled since 1950 to 5.3 billion people. In 40 years, at current rates of increase, it will double again. More than 90% of the increase will come in the poor countries of the world. Will those countries be able to feed, house, clothe, educate, and otherwise provide for the increased numbers of people and at the same time generate the real savings necessary to increase their production efficiency?

In earlier centuries, population increase and prosperity went hand in hand. But in modern times, particularly in the second half of this century, income has been low where there is faster population growth. One reason why there is no longer a correspondence between prosperity and population growth is the introduction of improved public health services such as vaccines, antibiotics, and medical treatment into even the poorest areas, dramatically reducing death rates from epidemics and other health problems.

There is a population/education vicious circle at work in the LDCs. Poverty results in low levels of education, and education is associated with lower birth rates. In Ecuador, for example, women who have never gone to school give birth to an average of eight children, while those with at least 7 years of education have an average of fewer than three children. Low literacy levels in LDCs result in high birth rates, which perpetuate the poverty that causes the low literacy.

In the 1980s the United States pulled funding from the International Planned Parenthood Federation and ended support for the United Nations Fund for Population Activities. In the first year of his administration, President Bush vetoed a bill to restore U.S. aid for population planning abroad.

Economic Reasoning (Write your responses on a separate sheet. Answers begin on p. 320.)

1. Does Table 1 in the text (p. 507) indicate that poverty is associated with illiteracy? What is the indication?
2. Are the population-education vicious circle and the vicious circle of poverty described in the text related? How are they different from each other?
3. Should the United States reinstate funding for international programs to reduce reproduction rates in the poor countries? Why or why not?

What Are the Prospects for World Economic Development?

THE POPULATION BOMB	THE DEBT BOMB	THE ENVIRONMENTAL BOMB
The high rate of population growth in the less-developed countries is a threat to their development prospects and to the ability of world agriculture to satisfy all the food needs of future populations. The large population pressures on food and other resources, on energy, and on the environment are potentially a bomb that could destroy living standards and create not only domestic but international conflicts.	Of immediate concern to the LDCs as well as to the creditor countries that lent them vast sums of money is the debt crisis triggered by the fall in oil prices and in the prices of other primary products that were counted on to provide the export income to service and repay the debts. Widespread defaults on the loans would create an international financial crisis, but the austerity imposed to avoid defaults has caused domestic unrest in the LDCs.	There are external costs of industrialization imposed on the environment in the LDCs that are very great. The costs are not internalized because of the shortage of funds to do that. Solving the problem of global warming promises to be hampered by the obstacles LDCs face in reducing their emissions.

UTOPIA OR APOCALYPSE

Inability to cope with the population bomb, the debt bomb, the environmental bomb, and the other problems of the LDCs could result in a super inflation, a worldwide depression, World War III, or wars of redistribution. Or the problems may be overcome with technological and organizational tools, guided by Adam Smith's "invisible hand."

(See page vi in the foreword "To the Student" for how to make the best use of this schematic outline.)

18.4. Explain the significance of the population growth rate in economic development.

A. Thomas Malthus was concerned that the world would suffer from food shortages because:

1. populations grow at a(n) _geometric rate_
2. while food supplies grow at a(n) _arithmetic rate_.

B. Suppose a population doubles each year while corn production increases by 1,000 ears per year. Use this information to fill in the following table:

Population	Ears of Corn	Ears per Person
100	1,000	10.00
200	2,000	10.00
400	3,000	7.50
800	4,000	5.00
1,600	5,000	3.12

C. What kind of mathematical relationship exists between a country's income and its population growth rate?

an inverse relationship

D. In addition to pressures on the available food supply, population growth in developing countries also puts pressure on:

1. _energy resources_
2. _the environment_

E. As sad as it may be, what two "natural" factors are currently limiting the population growth in the world's poorest countries?

1. _starvation_
2. _high infant mortality rates_

18.5. Describe the role of foreign indebtedness with respect to the LDCs.

A. Fill in the following blanks with the following: vicious circle of poverty, increased, decreased, interest, primary products, loans, economic surplus, economic reform.

1. Most of the world's underdeveloped debtor nations have economies that are based on the export of

   _____.

2. When inflation was high during the 1970s, the prices of these products

   _____.

3. This led foreign banks to think that these countries were good credit risks, and they increased their _____ to them.

4. When the prices of these products collapsed during the 1980s, the income earned by these countries

   _____.

5. This led to a situation where these countries could not afford to make their _____ payments.

6. If these countries attempt to make these payments, there will be even less resources available to build a(n)

   _____.

7. As a result, these countries will be caught in a

   _____.

8. One possible solution is the Brady Plan, which allows debtor countries to reduce their existing loans if they agree to

   _____.

B.

1. Inflation is not always so bad for everybody. Who gains from inflation—borrowers or lenders?

   _____

2. If inflation had increased in the 1980s, what would have happened to the price of primary products?

_____

3. How would this have affected the ability of poor debtor nations to pay their debts?

_____

_____

18.6. Discuss the relationship between economic development and environmental pollution.

A. What are three ways that the United States has attempted to reduce pollution?

1. *pollution control devices on cars*
2. *scrubbers on manufacturers smoke stacks*
3. *the construction of municipal sewage treatment plants*

B. What is one cost associated with each of the pollution control efforts listed in Part A?

1. *more expensive cars & lower mileage*
2. *having scrubbers instead of more products*
3. *having fewer local schools, roads, & clinics*

C.
1. Describe the relationship between the reduction of pollution and the output of goods and services.

It's an inverse relationship
pg. 321

2. Which countries of the world can best afford to reduce pollution?

the developed countries

D. What are two examples where richer countries might be better off in the long run by helping poorer countries improve their environments? (One was mentioned in chapter 17.)

1. *pg. 321*

2. *pg. 321*

Case Application: Growth Prospects for the LDCs

The World Bank has made projections of the growth rates of the less-developed countries for the period 1989–2000 compared to the projected growth rates for the industrial countries. The accompanying table shows past growth rates and the World Bank projections of growth in the real Gross Domestic Product (GDP) and the GDP per capita for the industrial countries and for the LDCs by geographic region.

Comparative Growth Rates
Real Gross Domestic Product by Country Group
Selected periods, 1965–2000

Group and region	Real GDP Growth Rates (%) Trend 1965-80	Recent 1980-89	Forecast 1989-2000	Real GDP Per Capita Growth (%) Trend 1965-80	Recent 1980-89	Forecast 1989-2000
Industrial	3.7	3.0	3.0	2.8	2.5	2.6
Less-developed	5.9	4.3	5.1	3.4	2.3	3.2
Sub-Saharan Africa	5.2	1.0	3.7	2.0	−2.2	0.5
East Asia	7.3	8.4	6.6	4.8	6.7	5.1
South Asia	3.6	5.5	5.1	1.2	3.2	3.2
Eastern Europe	5.3	1.4	1.9	4.5	0.8	1.5
Middle East, North Africa, & other Europe	6.3	2.9	4.3	3.9	0.8	2.1
Latin America & Caribbean	6.0	1.6	4.2	3.4	−0.6	2.3

Source: World Bank, *World Development Report 1990*.

The World Bank is optimistic about the growth prospects for the less-developed countries as a whole. The decade of the 1980s was a period of depressed economic growth, especially in per capita terms. Compared to the preceding 15 years, per capita GDP growth fell by one-third in the 1980s. The World Bank forecasts that in the 1990s the LDCs as a whole will nearly regain the growth rates of the earlier period.

However, there are wide differences in the projections for different areas. Sub-Saharan Africa is expected to return to a positive per capita growth rate in the 1990s after suffering declining living standards in the 1980s. The forecast growth is only one-half of 1%, but even this slight improvement is dependent on what happens to population growth.

Latin America and the Caribbean countries, which also experienced negative per capita growth in the 1980s, are projected to grow at nearly the same rate as the industrialized countries in this decade. This expectation hinges on the success of population programs and the Brady Plan. The nations of Asia, especially East Asia, are expected to perform much better than the industrial world.

The newly freed economies of Eastern Europe are a question mark. If they can successfully and quickly make the transition to market economies, they may do much better than projected by the end of the decade. If the transition is slow and beset with problems, they may do worse.

Economic Reasoning *(Write your responses on a separate sheet. Answers begin on p. 321.)*

1. Why is the per capita Gross Domestic Product in sub-Saharan Africa in the 1990s forecast to increase by only one-third of the size of the increase in Eastern European countries, despite the fact that the rise in real GDP will be nearly twice as great?
2. Why does the forecast for per capita growth in Latin America depend on the success of population programs and the Brady Plan? Explain.
3. Do you expect the gap in living standards between the industrial countries and the LDCs to get larger or diminish? Why?

IV. Practice Test (Answers begin on p. 321.)

Multiple Choice (Circle the correct answer.)

(18.1) 1. China is doing comparatively **worse** than many other LDCs in which of the following areas?
   a. growth in per capita GNP.
   b. population control.
   c. life expectancies.
   d. investment as a share of GNP.

(18.1) 2. According to the World Bank, China is classified as being:
   a. low-income.
   b. lower-middle-income.
   c. upper-middle-income.
   d. upper-income.

(18.1) 3. The headcount index of poverty does not accurately reflect the level of poverty in a country because it does not account for:
   a. the quality of life in that country.
   b. the long-term outlook for a country.
   c. the distribution of income in that country.
   d. the level of income in that country relative to similar countries.

(18.2) 4. Poverty is most prevalent in which of the following regions?
   a. Latin America and the Caribbean.
   b. South Asia.
   c. East Asia.
   d. sub-Saharan Africa.

(18.2) 5. Which of the following is NOT classified as being a low-income country by the World Bank?
   a. China.
   b. India.
   c. Tanzania.
   d. South Africa.

(18.2) 6. The largest concentrations of poverty occur in areas that are:
   a. sparsely populated rural areas.
   b. densely populated rural areas.
   c. small urban areas.
   d. densely populated urban areas.

(18.3) 7. An economic surplus is necessary in order for a developing country to improve its:
   a. labor-force participation rate.
   b. population growth rates.
   c. investment/GNP ratio.
   d. import/export ratio.

(18.3) 8. Increases in total GNP will not increase per capita GNP if:
   a. the capital/output ratio does not change.
   b. the investment/GNP ratio does not increase.
   c. the labor-force participation rate increases.
   d. the population grows faster than output.

(18.3) 9. The presence of a few large landowners taking advantage of the masses of people in a country is an example of:
   a. appropriation.
   b. exploitation.

c. reprobation.
d. colonization.

(18.4) 10. An example of a country that has dramatically reduced its population growth rate is:
a. India.
b. Kenya.
c. Mexico.
d. China.

(18.4) 11. The region of the world with the fastest growing population is:
a. South Asia.
b. East Asia.
c. sub-Saharan Africa.
d. Latin America and the Caribbean.

(18.4) 12. Rapid population growth has negative impacts on:
a. nutrition levels.
b. pollution levels.
c. energy use.
d. all of the above.

(18.5) 13. A major cause of the debt crisis among LDCs is:
a. too much investment in infrastructure.
b. the declining productivity of workers.
c. declining prices for raw materials.
d. the internal exploitation of workers.

(18.5) 14. Which of the following is required of LDCs that wish to have their debts reduced through the Brady Plan?
a. increasing their imports.
b. decreasing their exports.
c. nationalizing more industries.
d. reducing government spending.

(18.6) 15. Which of the following is a TRUE statement?
a. With proper planning, Mexico has been able to increase its economic growth while reducing pollution.
b. Increased economic growth has been accompanied by increased pollution in nearly all LDCs.
c. There is nothing that the developed nations of the world can do to reduce pollution in the LDCs.
d. As a general rule, the less developed a country is, the lower the pollution levels it has.

True/False *(Circle T or F.)*

(18.1) 16. China generally lags behind other LDCs in the basic social indicators of well-being. T or F

(18.2) 17. Most of the world's poverty is concentrated in sub-Saharan Africa. T or F

(18.3) 18. The exploitation that results in poverty can come from both inside and outside a poor country. T or F

(18.5) 19. The reduction in worldwide inflation during the 1980s increased the debt crisis in the LDCs. T or F

(18.6) 20. The world's underdeveloped countries may be poor in material goods, but they have much cleaner environments than the developed countries of the world. T or F

World Economics Crossword Puzzle

(Chapters 15–18)

Across

3. The lowering of the foreign-exchange rate of a currency by government regulation.
5. The supplementary index devised by the World Bank to determine how far per capita incomes would have to be raised to take a country out of poverty.
11. A belief that a country will retain a comparative advantage only as long as it retains a technological lead over other countries.
12. _____ efficiency is measured at a particular time.
14. This proposed to alleviate the indebtness of LDCs by supplying them with additional loans.
16. Unrestricted trade.
17. _____ efficiency is measured by estimating over a period of time.
18. It established five-year plans for production allocations.
19. From the late 1940s to the early 1970s, the exchange rate for major Western countries remained _____.

Down

1. This is of more concern to many LDCs than the overpopulation problem.
2. His answer to the critics of socialism would be for the central planning board to set the price of goods by trial and error.
4. The foreign-exchange market does this to currency.
6. This economic system uses high marginal tax rates on upper incomes to distribute per capita income more evenly than capitalism.
7. It handled all financial transactions among the enterprises in the Soviet Union.
8. Supplies foreign currency to a nation on a short-term loan basis.
9. The official unit of account for the European Economic Community.
10. It contains over 420 million people classified as poor.
13. Taxes on imports.
15. Worth $5 trillion plus, with 320 million people.

Answers to Chapter Questions

Chapter 1
What Is Economics?

Review of the Learning Objectives

1-1. A. scarcity. B. economic good. C. wants. D. 1, 4, 5, 7.

1-2. A. 1.land. 2.labor. 3.labor. 4.capital. 5.capital. 6.land. 7.capital. B. (answers will vary) classroom; instructor; desk; book; blackboard.

1-3. A. predict. B. testing hypotheses. C. observation; gathering data; make a hypothesis; accept the hypothesis.

Case Application: **Famine in Africa**

1. Forests (wood, woodlands), topsoil, rainfall. (Food is a product, not a resource.)
2. The famines are caused by drought and deforestation, which reduce the amount of moisture in the air and cause erosion of the topsoil.
3. The answer to this question is open-ended because there are different possible answers, depending on your personal value judgments. Forbidding Ethiopians to cut firewood would help save the forests and thereby lessen droughts and reduce erosion. On the other hand, the poor in Ethiopia do not have affordable alternatives for fuel to heat and cook.

What Are the Tools of Economics?

Review of the Learning Objectives

1-4. A. 1.history. 2.statistics. 3.institutions. B. 1.statistics. 2.institutions. 3.history. 4.institutions. 5.statistics. C. describe; analyze.

1-5. A. concepts; models. B. 1.C. 2.C. 3.M. 4.C. 5.M. 6.M. 7.M. C. 1.diagrams. 2.words. 3.mathematical equations.

Case Application: **Hot or Cold? Cost-Benefit Analysis**

1. A cost-benefit analysis is a type of economic model.
2. Statistics are one factual tool used in this analysis, such as the data on costs of improvements and savings on utility bills. History is also involved, such as the historical experience that utility bills rise at 10% a year. The institutional behavior of the firm is also involved, such as the policy that the company should provide good working conditions for its employees even if that resulted in reduced profitability.
3. Open answer. Many executives in businesses believe that their principal responsibility is to maximize the profits of the company, what they refer to as "the bottom line." If the company is a corporation, they feel they owe it to the stockholders to earn as high a profit rate as possible, so long as they abide by legal and ethical standards. Other officers of firms believe company policies must take into account the welfare of their employees, the community, or society at large. They believe companies have social responsibilities as well as profit responsibilities. In any event, executives should consider long-run profits rather than short-run profits. Spending money to improve the comfort and health of the company's employees may improve the long-run profitability of the company.

What Are the Uses of Graphs?

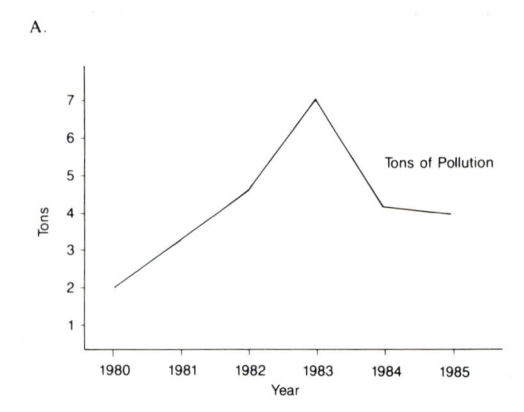

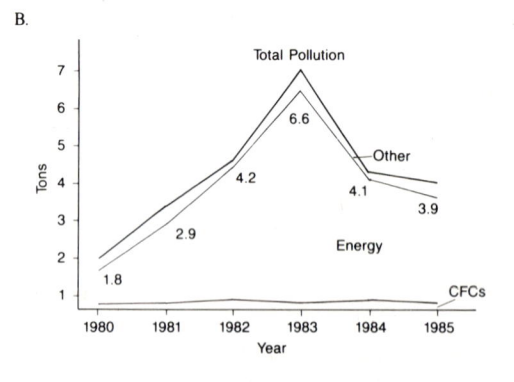

Review of the Learning Objectives

1-6.

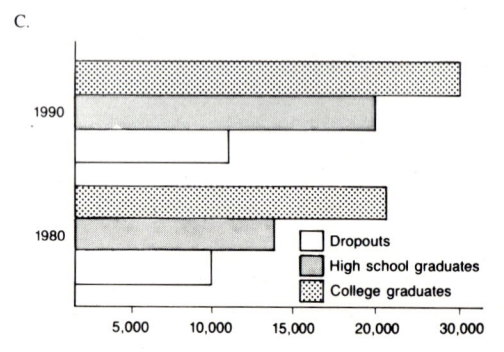

Answers to Chapter Questions / 283

D.

[Pie chart: 0-2 lbs. 10%, 2.1-4.0 lbs. 45%, 4.1-6.0 lbs. 20%, 6.1-8.0 lbs. 15%, 10%]

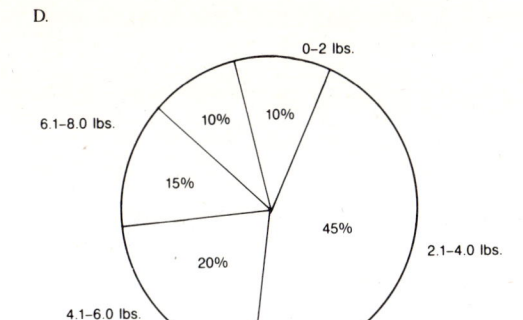

1-7. A. variables. B. inverse. C. direct. D. charts; diagrams.

1-8.

A. [Line graph: Pages vs. Hours, showing Carlos, Bob, Agnes]

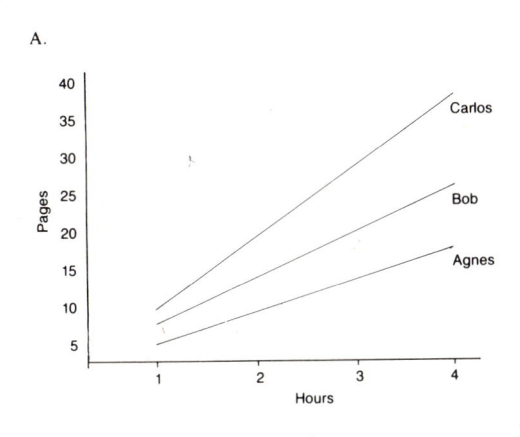

B. [Line graph: Buggies vs. Weeks, rising from 5 to 25 then flat]

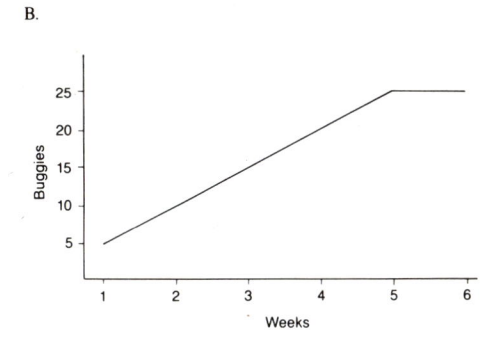

C. [Graph: Cannons vs. Olive Trees, with points (8C, 4T), (5C, 10T), (0C, 20T)]

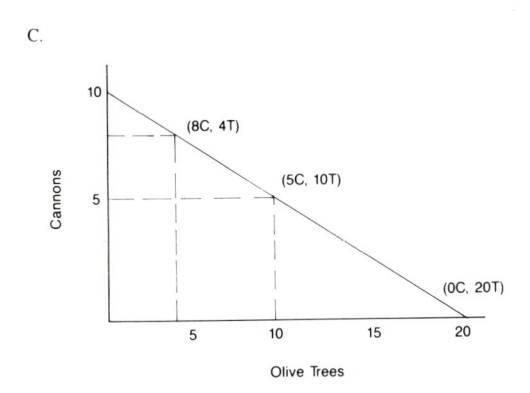

D. [Graph: Pecks of Peppers Remaining vs. Hours, showing 48 Pecks Remaining at 4 hours, line from 80 to 10]

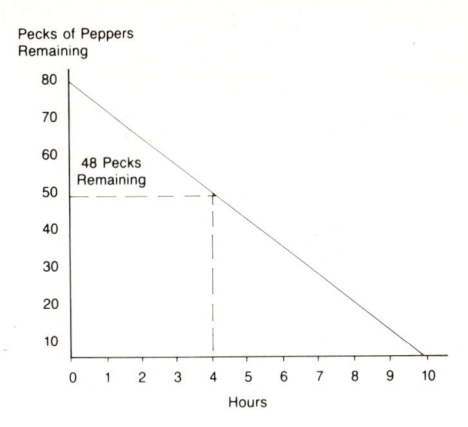

Case Application: **Air Quality in the United States**

1. The best charts to use would be a column chart or a bar chart because they are good for comparing the values of variables over time. An alternative would be a line graph of the time series variety with a separate labeled line for each gas. The vertical axis shows the quantity of gas emissions in millions of metric tons and the horizontal axis shows the years.

2. The relationship between the quantity of gaseous emissions and air quality is an inverse one. The vertical axis would normally show air quality (because it is the dependent variable) and the horizontal axis would show the quantity of gaseous emissions. The curve relating the two variables should slope downward to the right, indicating an inverse relationship.

3. Open answer. If you put more value on a clean environment and think the cost is worth it, the answer would be yes. If you think that the cost is too high and we cannot afford it or that there are more pressing needs for our funds and real resources, the answer would be no.

Answers to Practice Test

1.c. 2.b. 3.c. 4.b. 5.a. 6.d. 7.c. 8.a. 9.c. 10.d. 11.c. 12.d. 13.d. 14.b. 15.b. 16.T. 17.F. 18.F. 19.F. 20.T.

Chapter 2

How Do We Make Economic Choices?

Review of the Learning Objectives

2-1. A. scarcity. B. (answers will vary) better health care; better roads; a safer environment. C. (answers will vary) attending class instead of playing ball; watching TV instead of studying; sleeping instead of getting up. D. (answers will vary) 1. more help for the poor. 2. using the land for a park. 3. eating breakfast. 4. going to a concert.

2-2. A. Because of scarcity, everything has a cost. B. (answers will vary) Mr. Jones might think that the cost is the hospitals that could have been built; Ms.

Applegate might think that the cost is the teacher's aide she might have had. C. (answers will vary) 1.baking brownies. 2.going to a movie. 3.planting turnips. 4.the money you could earn on a job. 5.fishing. 6.buying something at the mall. D. any other scrumptious dessert **plus** the added calories!

2-3. A.

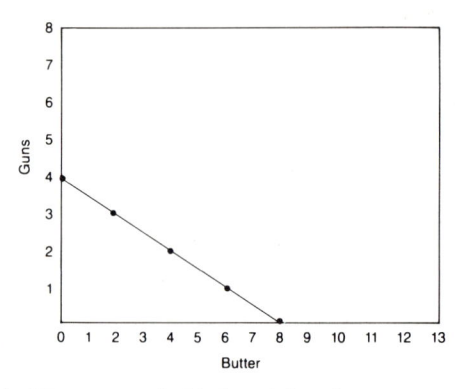

1. First, second, third, and fourth guns each cost 2 units of butter. 2.constant costs.

B.

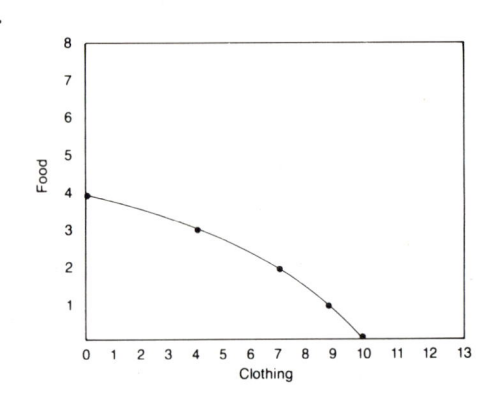

1. First—1 unit of clothes; Second—2 units; Third—3 units; Fourth—4 units. 2.increasing costs. C. Constant costs (part A) imply resources are perfect substitutes for one another. Increasing costs (part B) imply the more realistic situation where resources are not perfect substitutes. D. model.

Case Application: A Question of Oil

1. We need to determine the trade-offs between the uses of petroleum for gasoline, fuel oil, lubricants, raw material for synthetics, and so forth.
2. The opportunity cost of the gasoline produced with a gallon of petroleum is the amount of fuel oil that could have been produced with that gallon of petroleum, since gasoline and fuel oil are the two most important uses for petroleum. A diagram showing the opportunity costs of the uses of petroleum would have the amount of gasoline that could be produced on one axis and the amount of fuel oil that could be produced on the other axis. The curve showing the opportunity costs slopes downward to the right. The opportunity costs increase as more of the petroleum is used to produce one of the products because some components of crude oil are better suited for making gasoline and other components better suited for making fuel oil. Therefore, the curve showing the opportunity costs is not a straight line but curves toward the axes.
3. Open answer. The answer depends on how you relatively value environmental goals, such as perserving nature and wildlife, compared to the value of other uses for our natural resources, such as producing more gasoline.

What Are the Basic Economic Questions?

Review of the Learning Objectives
2-4. A. 1.what and who. 2.how. 3.how. 4.what. (note: ultimately, each of these may affect "who") B. what.

Case Application: **Is Coal the Heir to the Energy Throne?**
1. The decision between underground tunneling or surface strip mining illustrates the "how" decision—how to produce the coal.
2. The reallocation of our resources has resulted from petroleum prices that are higher than before and the increased costs of nuclear power and our heightened awareness of its dangers. These considerations have increased the attractiveness of coal as a substitute, and more resources are being devoted to coal production.
3. Open answer. Some people believe coal should be substituted for nuclear power in producing electricity, even if it results in an increase in air and water pollution, because nuclear power is dangerous due to the possibility of an accident and the problems of radioactive waste disposal. Others believe we should not use more coal to produce electricity if it increases air and water pollution because that results in damaging the environment, people's health, and the quality of life.

What Are Society's Economic Goals?

Review of the Learning Objectives
2-5. A. 1.efficiency. 2.price stability. 3.full employment. 4.growth. B. 1.growth. 2.price stability. 3.efficiency (or growth). 4.full employment (or growth).

2-6. A. 1.household incomes. 2.increased output. B. growth.

C.

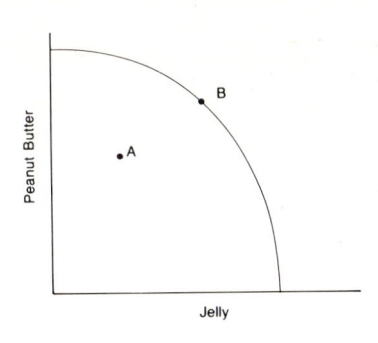

[Graph: Peanut Butter vs. Jelly PPF with points A (inside) and B (on curve)]

2-7. A. 1. & A.2.

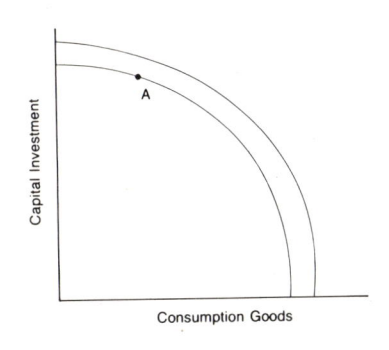

[Graph: Capital Investment vs. Consumption Goods with two PPF curves and point A]

B. (answers will vary) 1.a new auditorium. 2.a new water treatment plant. 3.new highways. 4.robots. 5.a new computer system.

2-8. A. 1.efficiency (or growth); safe environment. 2.efficiency (or growth); job security. 3.price stability; equity. 4.growth; equity.

Case Application: **A Plastic World**

1. The expansion of the plastics industry in recent years has definitely contributed to achieving the goal of economic growth. It most probably also has contributed to achieving the goal of full employment, despite the job losses in the older steel, wood, and fibers industries, because of the jobs created in the industry itself and the jobs created by industries using plastic.

2. An increasingly troublesome trade-off resulting from the growth of the plastics industry is the environmental pollution from the accumulating plastics garbage on land and in the oceans. Another trade-off is the loss of economic security by those workers who have been laid off in the more traditional materials industries because of the competition from plastics.

3. Open answer. On the environmental side, the answer is yes. If plastics garbage continues to accumulate in the environment, it will not only be aesthetically damaging and thus lower the quality of life, but it will be harmful to some animals, birds, and sea life. On the side of maximizing economic efficiency and minimizing costs, the answer is no. It is more costly to produce biodegradable plastics than standard plastics. It requires more resource inputs, and therefore we could not have as much consumption of other things as well as plastics.

Answers to Practice Test

1.a. 2.c. 3.d. 4.b. 5.d. 6.a. 7.d. 8.a. 9.c. 10.b. 11.a. 12.c. 13.d. 14.a. 15.b. 16.T. 17.F. 18.F. 19.T. 20.T.

Chapter 3

Why Are Economic Systems Needed?

Review of the Learning Objectives

3-1. A. comparative. B. absolute. C. comparative.

3-2. A. specialize; efficiency; lower. B. interdependent. C. (open answers) 1.pluck chickens. 2.make their own clothes. 3.repair their own roofs. D. boredom on the job.

Case Application: **From Farm to City**

1. People are more interdependent now than they were in 1790 because there is more specialization of production. In 1790 most families were rural and produced nearly everything they needed: food, clothing, shelter, tools, and so on. With industrialization and the movement to cities, families became dependent on others to supply their needs because they were now workers specialized in a particular type of production.

2. The growth of large metropolitan areas illustrates the principle of comparative advantage because they are efficient at providing services and many types of products. They have a comparative advantage in the types of production that benefit from population concentration, such as commerce, financial services, and communication. They are dependent on rural areas for those things, such as food, that are not as easily produced in densely populated areas.

3. Open answer. The answer to this question depends largely on people's value systems. If they think simpler life-styles, knowing one's neighbors, and self-sufficiency are the most important attributes, they might prefer a more rural society. If they believe

higher living standards, the availability of more goods and services, and economic growth are the most important characteristics, they might prefer urbanization of society.

What Are the Principal Types of Economic Systems?

Review of the Learning Objectives

3-3. A. 1.C. 2.T. 3.M. 4.C. 5.T. 6.M. B. (open answers) 1. provides water. 2. leases land to ranchers. 3. inspects beef. C. command (centrally directed) economy; mixed economy. D. I can't.

Case Application: **Digging a Subway in Calcutta**

1. The use of manual labor rather than machinery is characteristic of traditional economies. The Calcutta subway is being dug in the fashion and with the implements that are traditional in India. The fact that it is a government project makes it characteristic of a mixed economy.

2. Private enterprise uses the production methods that are least expensive for the output obtained. If manual labor is cheaper than using machinery for the work to be done, which may be the case in India, where labor is plentiful and capital scarce, private enterprise as well as government may use traditional rather than modern methods of production.

3. Open answer. The answer to this question depends on how we evaluate the goals of efficiency versus full employment. If we make efficiency the overriding concern, the subway should be built by the method that minimizes total cost. On the other hand, if we consider providing jobs for unemployed workers as important or more important than maximizing production efficiency, the subway should be built by manual labor, even if that raises the total cost of construction.

How Does a Market System Resolve the Three Basic Economic Questions?

Review of the Learning Objectives

3-4. A. profit. B. more; less. C. less; more. D. land, labor, and capital; wages, rent, and interest. E. finished goods; money payments.

3-5. A. 1.F. 2.P. 3.P. 4.F. 5.F. 6.P. 7.F. 8.P. B. 1. a restaurant; a household kitchen. 2. a law office; a student's room. 3. a construction company; fixing a house's leaky pipes.

3-6. A. and B.

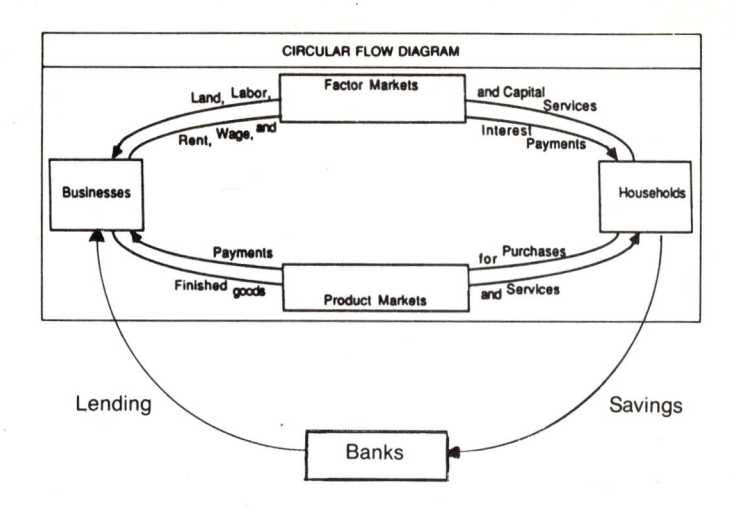

```
                    CIRCULAR FLOW DIAGRAM
              Land, Labor,   Factor Markets   and Capital
                 Rent, Wage, and            Services
                                         Interest Payments
         Businesses                                    Households
                      Payments                 for Purchases
                   Finished goods  Product Markets   and Services

              Lending                              Savings
                            Banks
```

C. earn; earn.

Case Application: **The Shale Age—Not Yet**

1. Shale oil would be sold in a factor market because it requires additional processing to refine it into finished petroleum products. Only when it is sold directly to a consumer in the form of gasoline, heating oil, motor oil, or other final products is it sold in a product market.

2. The oil companies will proceed with the development of shale oil when the profit incentives are adequate. Since they have petroleum reserves in wells that are cheaper to exploit at the present time than the shale oil, they are not willing to risk large investments in the projects. Furthermore, bringing shale oil to market would reduce the value of their existing reserves in wells. Further increases in oil prices or the development of shale oil by other companies or by the government would likely spur the oil companies to develop their lease holdings.

3. Open answer. One position is that energy is a critical need for the country, both for civilian and national defense purposes. If it is worthwhile for the government to finance space exploration, it is certainly worthwhile to do at least as much to solve our energy problems. The opposite position is that the government should keep out of the energy business because it would spend tax money wastefully and energy would cost more than if the development is left to private enterprise.

Answers to Practice Test

1.c. 2.b. 3.a. 4.b. 5.c. 6.d. 7.d. 8.c. 9.b. 10.c. 11.d. 12.d. 13.d. 14.b. 15.b. 16.F. 17.T. 18.F. 19.T. 20.F.

Chapter 4

What Forces Determine Prices in the Marketplace?

Review of the Learning Objectives

4-1. A. 1.increase; decrease. 2.decrease; increase. B. 1.I. 2.S. 3.S. 4.I. C. 1.price; quantity; inverse. 2.price; quantity; direct. D. There are fewer available substitutes for electricity, medicine, and salt. E.

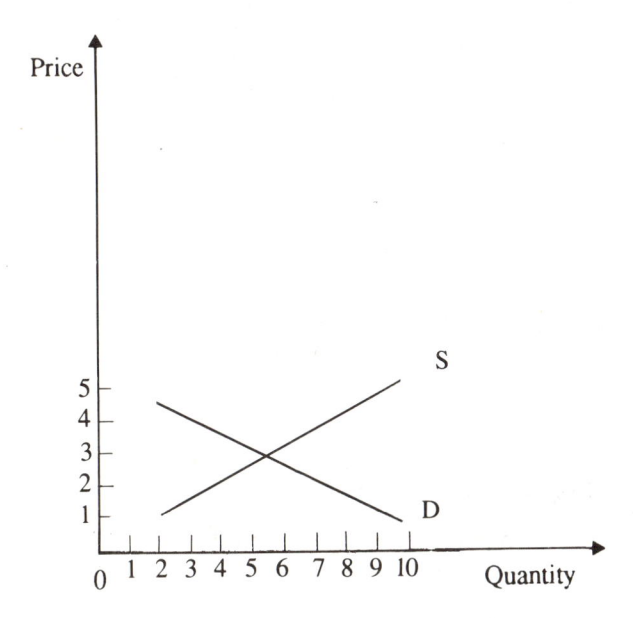

4-2. A. 1.shortage; 8 jars. 2.surplus; 8 jars. 3.$3. 4.

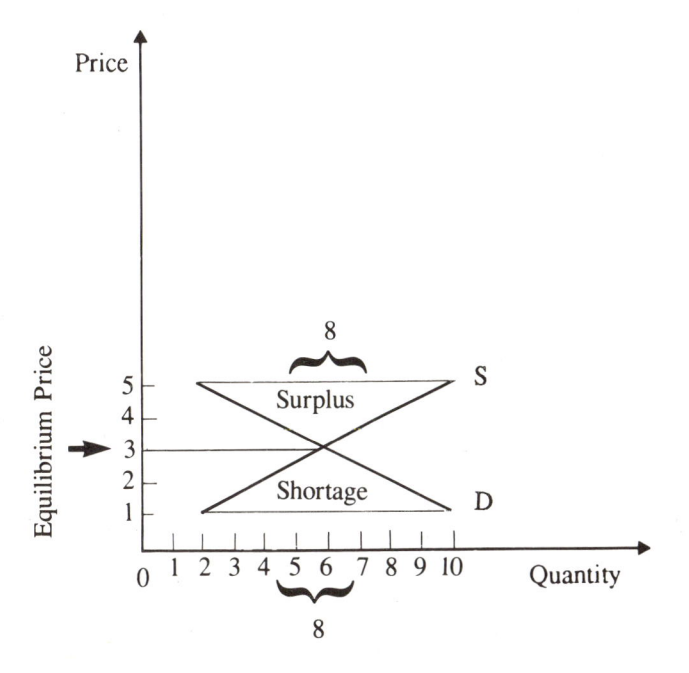

B. 1.surplus. 2.fall. 3.increase; decrease. 4.surplus; disappear. C. 1.shortage. 2.rise. 3.decrease; increase. 4.shortage; disappear. D. equilibrium; surpluses; shortages.

Case Application: **The Grain Drain**

1. The failure of the Soviet grain harvest resulted in increasing the demand schedule for American wheat. Increased foreign demand was added to the domestic demand. This shifted the demand curve outward to the right.

2. The increased Soviet demand for wheat initiated the rise in the price of American wheat, but the Soviets purchased wheat at a contracted price which was less than $3 per bushel. It was the American flour millers competing for the remaining supply that pushed the price of wheat above $3 per bushel.

3. Open answer. One view was that we should not have sold the wheat to the Soviets since it resulted in raising the price of a basic staple of the American diet and caused an increase in the cost of living. The opposite view, the one probably held by most economists, was that American farmers should be allowed to sell their wheat to the Soviets or anyone else willing to pay the price. If the Soviet wheat buyers outsmarted our negotiators and got the wheat at a bargain price, that's another question, and we should be more clever in the future. However, agricultural exports are very important to the farmer and to our economy in general and should not be restricted in order to hold down the prices of agricultural products at home.

What Determines Demand?

Review of the Learning Objectives

4-3. A. 1.tastes and preferences. 2.price of complements. 3.price of substitutes. 4.population. 5.income. B. 1.I. 2.D. 3.I. 4.D. 5.I.

Case Application: **Upscale Munching**

1. The determinants of demand responsible for the sales of gourmet snack products are the increase in the population size of that market, an increase in incomes, and changing tastes and preferences.

2. The cause of the change in the effective demand of the baby-boom generation is their entry into the labor force and advancement to higher-paying jobs. The increase in their incomes has allowed them to indulge their tastes for higher-quality snack foods.

3. Open answer. Some people might consider the super-premium ice creams overpriced, since regular ice cream that is much less expensive can be very tasty. Others believe that the super-premium is worth the extra cost not only because it tastes better but because it is made with less artificial additives and more natural ingredients. The factors that need to be considered are the tastes and preferences of the consumers, their incomes, and the price and availability of the substitute.

What Determines Supply?

Review of the Learning Objectives

4-4. A. 1.W. 2.W. 3.WN. 4.WN. 5.W. 6.W. B. production costs.

4-5. A. productive capacity. B. capital. C. 1.the dining room capacity. 2.the number of chairs. 3.classroom (number of desks). 4.factory size.

Case Application: Black Walnut Worth Gold

1. The rustling of black walnut trees adds to the short-run supply of black walnut veneer. It shifts the short-run supply curve outward to the right.

2. The long-run supply curve for black walnut trees depends upon the length of growing time for the trees to reach maturity. With fertilizing and special care the long run can be reduced from 60 to 80 years to 30 years.

3. Open answer. Perhaps laws such as the one in Missouri should be enacted to discourage rustling of black walnut trees grown by individuals or in our national parks. On the other hand, such laws may be difficult to enforce and they impose the burden of responsibility on log buyers, who claim that it is unfair.

Why Do Prices Change?

Review of the Learning Objectives

4-6. A. 1.income. 2.price of substitutes. 3.price of complements. 4.tastes and preferences. 5.size of the market population. B. 1.decrease; decrease. 2.increase; increase. 3.increase; increase. 4.decrease; decrease.

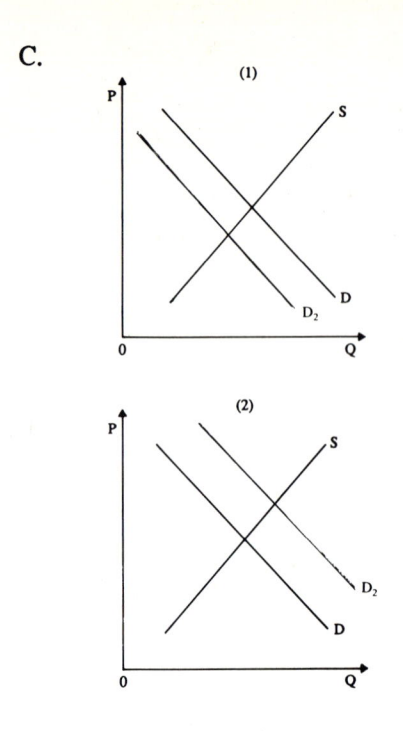

C.

D. 1.price decreases; quantity decreases. 2.price increases; quantity increases.

E.

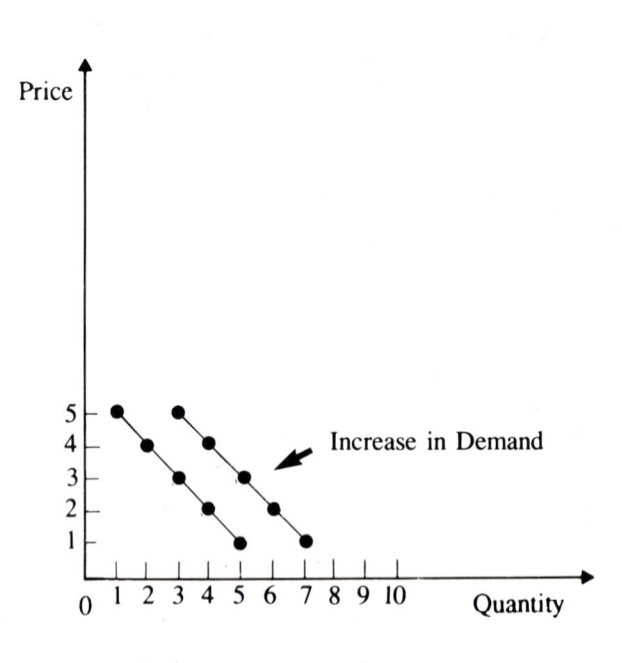

4-7. A. 1.increase; decrease. 2.decrease; increase. 3.decrease; increase. 4.increase; decrease. B. lower prices and more goods and services.

Answers to Chapter Questions / 289

C.

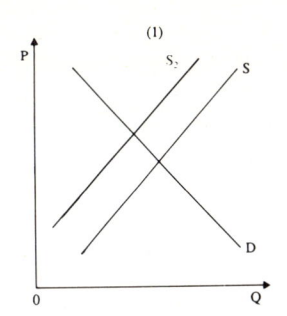

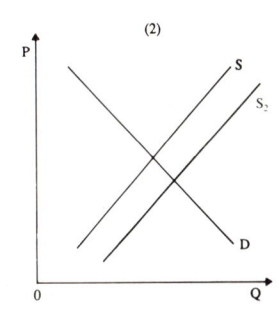

(1) [Supply and demand graph with S shifting to S₂ leftward]

(2) [Supply and demand graph with S shifting to S₂]

D. 1. price increases; quantity decreases. 2. price decreases; quantity increases.

4-8. A. 1. quantity supplied increases. 2. quantity supplied decreases. 3. quantity demanded increases. 4. quantity demanded decreases. B. 1. quantity supplied decreases. 2. quantity supplied increases. 3. quantity demanded decreases. 4. quantity demanded increases.

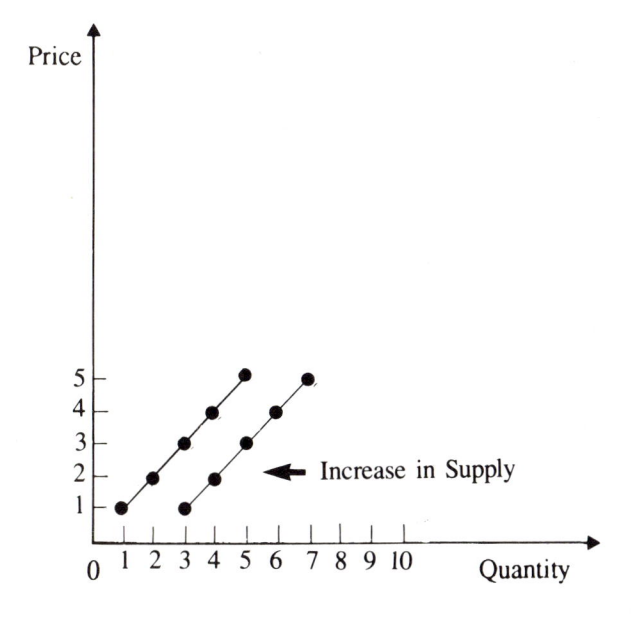

C. [Graph showing Price vs Quantity with parallel upward-sloping supply lines indicating "Increase in Supply"]

Case Application: Do Boycotts Work?

1. If consumers respond to a boycott by reducing the amount of the product they would normally buy at any given price, the demand curve shifts backward to the left.

2. A boycott results in lower prices in the short run because the shift in demand causes sellers to move down their supply schedule to a lower price. However, in a competitive industry such as the cattle industry the lower prices may cause a reduction in investment in the industry, which shifts the long-run supply curve backward to the left, resulting in higher prices in the long run.

3. Open answer. From the consumers' point of view, boycotts are fair when the price of something goes up much more rapidly than the consumers' incomes, and they cannot afford the higher prices. From the producers' point of view, boycotts are unfair because they may not be responsible for the higher prices that result from increased costs. To the producers, boycotts are a conspiracy that might force them out of business.

Answers to Practice Test

1.a. 2.c. 3.b. 4.d. 5.b. 6.a. 7.c. 8.d. 9.c. 10.a. 11.a. 12.a. 13.c. 14.c. 15.c. 16.T. 17.F. 18.F. 19.T. 20.T.

Crossword Puzzle for Chapters 1-4

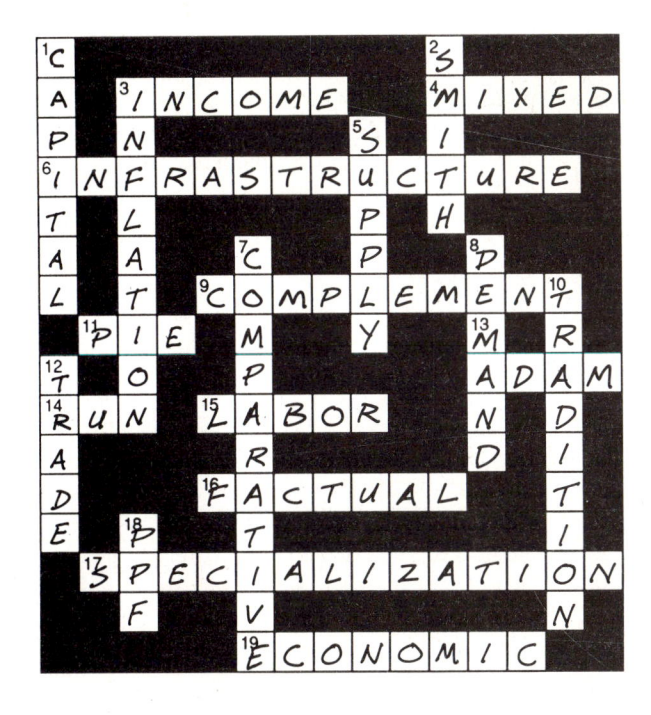

[Completed crossword puzzle with answers including: CAPITAL, INCOME, MIXED, INFRASTRUCTURE, SI, COMPLEMENT, PIE, ADAM, RUN, LABOR, FACTUAL, SPECIALIZATION, ECONOMIC]

Chapter 5

What Choices Do Consumers Make?

Review of the Learning Objectives

5-1. A. quantity demanded. B. inelastic; elastic. C. 1.availability of substitutes. 2.the price of the good relative to your budget. D. 1.I. 2.E. 3.E. 4.E. 5.I. 6.I.

5-2. A. There must be perfect substitutes. B. There are no substitutes. C. 1.PI. 2.PE. 3.PI. 4.PE. 5.RE. 6.RE. 7.RI. 8.RE.
D.

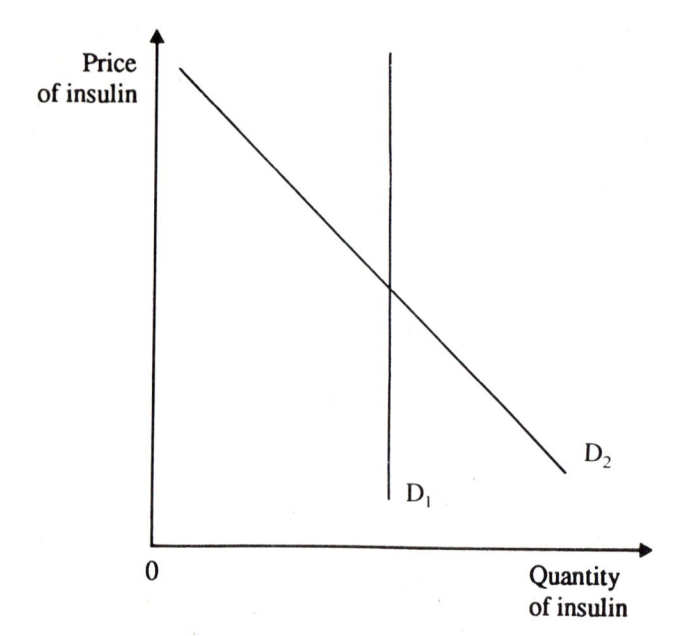

E.

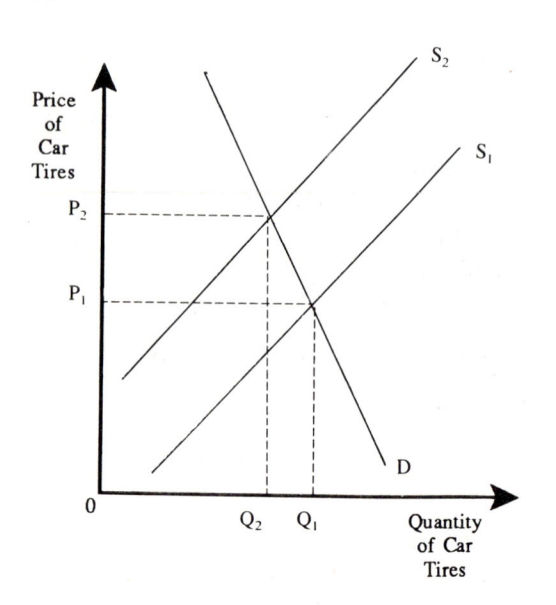

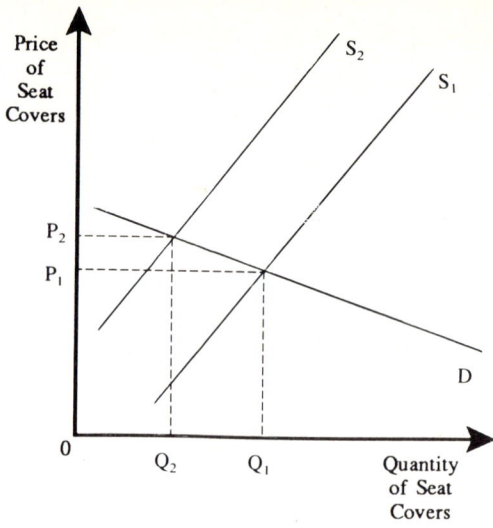

5-3. A. (1) 2.0. (2) 1.0. (3) 0.10. (4) 0.00. (5) infinite. B. Answers will vary for the example part of the question. 1.RE; broccoli. 2.UE; frozen vegetables. 3.RI; toothpaste. 4.PI; insulin. 5.PE; wheat.

5-4. A. It produces what consumers want. B. Good question. Producers would need to guess, or perhaps tradition or a central administration would answer the "what to produce" question. C. Supply reacts to demand.

5-5. A. 1.pay taxes. 2.spend. 3.save. B. APS = .15; APC = .85. C. 1.C. 2.C. 3.S. 4.C. D. They will be hurt because people will be spending and buying less. They will be helped because increased saving leads to more funds available to borrow for investment.

Case Application: **Going to the Movies**

1. The Gardners consider going to the movies a luxury. This is indicated by their unwillingness to pay the higher ticket prices and by Martin's statement that if the price of groceries continues to rise they will substitute groceries for movie attendance.

2. It appears the Gardners' demand for theater movies is relatively elastic because they are substituting bicycle rides, picnics, and rental tapes or television for going to the movies.

3. Open answer. The answer depends upon the individual's preference for attending movies in comparison to other forms of leisure-time spending. If people rank movies very high on their preference scale relative to other types of activities, $6 may not be too much to pay for a ticket. If, on the other hand, there are substitute activities that cost less and provide almost as much satisfaction, $6 may be too high a price for a movie ticket. Another criterion is the amount of the individual's income. Those with high incomes may not consider $6 tickets too high, while those with lower incomes do consider it too high.

How Do Consumers Make Choices?

Review of the Learning Objectives

5-6. A. shoes and only shoes. B. diminishes; less. C. 1.water (I would die without it). 2.diamonds (I value the **next** diamond more than the **next** glass of water). 3.I have so much water that the marginal utility of the next glass is very small. I have so few diamonds that the marginal utility of the next one is still very high.

5-7. A.1.

	MU	TU
First cone	4	4
Second cone	3	7
Third cone	2	9
Fourth cone	1	10
Fifth cone	−1	9

2.2. 3.negative marginal utility—a stomachache!

5-8. A. 1.3 of each. 2.74 utils. 3.Yes—marginal utilities are equal. 4.1 video game, 2 books, and 1 record.

Case Application: **Life-style and Consumer Choice**

1. Large cars do not necessarily have greater utility than compact cars. The utility of an automobile depends not only on its carrying capacity, but also on such things as fuel efficiency, ease of parking, and the reflection of personal taste and life-style. Those who do not need a car with a large carrying capacity may find that a compact car has greater utility for them.
2. Convenience does have diminishing marginal utility. This is apparent both from consumer behavior and from economic analysis of the trade-offs of convenience. Although convenience foods have greatly increased in popularity, they have not entirely displaced other types of foods—which would have been the case if they did not have diminishing marginal utility. The popularity of gourmet cooking schools and the demand for fresh produce and meats proves that convenience foods have diminishing marginal utility. The more time we save from the use of convenience foods, the less valuable is the saving of additional time by further increasing consumption of convenience foods.
3. Open answer. The answer depends on the circumstances of the individual household. Many people have cut back on the use of convenience foods because of tighter household budgets. In other cases, financial pressures have caused additional members of the household to enter the working force, resulting in an increased necessity to resort to convenience foods or to go out more for meals.

How Can Consumers Make Better Choices?

Review of the Learning Objectives

5-9. A.1–A.4 Answers will vary, but just about any food, medicine, or natural fabric would apply. B.1–B.4 Answers will vary. C. Answers will vary. D. 1.word of mouth. 2.consumer publications or consumer shows on public TV and public radio. 3.more reliable because they do not have a vested interest in selling a product like an advertiser does.

Case Application: **Do You Have Time for Your Possessions?**

1. The most common means by which consumers find out about the availability of new products is through advertising.
2. Purchasers could make better choices if they had information about the rate of failure and the frequency and cost of servicing the products that they buy.
3. Open answer. It would certainly help consumers to make better choices if they had that information. (For a few things, such information is already required—refrigerator manufacturers are required to post on a refrigerator the average yearly energy cost of operating it.) On the other hand, there is a cost involved in gathering, validating, and disseminating such information that would be passed on to consumers in a higher price for the product. Also, it would require government agencies to enforce the regulation—a cost to taxpayers.

Answers to Practice Test

1.a. 2.b. 3.a. 4.d. 5.a. 6.a. 7.b. 8.c. 9.d. 10.c. 11.b. 12.c. 13.d. 14.a. 15.d. 16.F. 17.T. 18.F. 19.T. 20.F.

Chapter 6

What Are the Forms and Economic Functions of Business Firms?

Review of the Learning Objectives

6-1. A. 1.PR. 2.C. 3.PR. 4.C. 5.PA. B. 1.C. 2.PR. 3.PA. 4.PR. 5.C. 6.C. C. 1.C. 2.PA. 3.PR. 4.C. 5.PA & PR. D. The managers may be more interested in **their own** well-being than in the stockholders' income. For example, big company cars, fancy desks, and "business" trips to Bermuda do not help the stockholders.

6-2. A. organize production; allocate resources. B. 1.(I) Consumers are environmentally conscious. (O) Production is geared toward the use of glass vs. plastic. (A) Manufacturers of glass benefit relative to manufacturers of plastic. (C) The bottling machine is new capital. 2.(I) People want oats. (O) Harvesting becomes capital-intensive and specialized. (A) The manufacturer of the harvester earns money. (C) The harvester is new capital.

Case Application: The Progressive Bike Shop

1. The Progressive Bike Shop was a limited partnership. Pat's parents invested in the business for a percentage return of the net earnings. This made them partners in the business.

2. The Progressive Bike Shop performed all four economic functions of a business. Pat and Jeff decided what goods and services would be offered in the economy by establishing a bicycle sales and service firm. Deciding to rent the storefront location in the inner city was an example of determining how goods and services would be provided. Deciding how the net receipts would be divided up affected the allocation of purchasing power by resolving the "for whom" question, which was also affected by providing their retail services to the campus community. Finally, the renovation of the store premises represented an increase in the economy's real capital investment.

3. Open answer. Locating the bike shop in a deteriorated neighborhood may have been a good idea from a business standpoint because of the low rent overhead, which reduced the costs of operation, and because the neighborhood population contained an age group of potential customers. From a socioeconomic standpoint, it was a good idea because it helped to revitalize a run-down area. On the other hand, it might not have been a good business decision if the store's marketing area did not have sufficient purchasing power to provide adequate sales revenues for the firm to succeed. If the business failed, it would have been bad for the neighborhood as well as for the owners.

What Determines a Firm's Profits?

Review of the Learning Objectives

6-3. A. Fixed costs exist only in the short run because in the long run the firm has time to alter any and all productive capacity. B. 1.F. 2.V. 3.V. 4.V. 5.F. 6.F. 7.F. C. depreciation; productive life; obsolete.

6-4. A. 1.zero. 2.variable. 3.fixed; variable. B. TC: 10, 22, 32, 40, 46, 50, 56, 66, 80, 100, 130. MC: 12, 10, 8, 6, 4, 6, 10, 14, 20, 30. AC: 22, 16, 13.3, 11.5, 10, 9.3, 9.4, 10, 11.1, 13. C. TR: 0, 10, 20, 30, 40, 50, 60, 70, 80, 90, 100. MR: 10, 10, 10, 10, 10, 10, 10, 10, 10, 10. D. Purely competitive. E. Profit: -10, -12, -12, -10, -6, 0, 4, 4, 0, -10, -30. F. 1.Total revenue will increase because the effect of increased price dominates the effect of decreased quantity. 2.Total revenue will decrease because the effect of increased price is dominated by the effect of decreased quantity.

6-5. A. 1.total revenue; total cost. 2.marginal revenue; marginal cost. 3.total revenue; total cost. B. 1. 5 and 8 units of output. 2.less than 5; greater than 8. 3.greater than 5; less than 8. 4. 7 units of output (note: it is actually somewhere between 6 and 7 units of output. Also note that MR = MC at a level of 2 units of output, but this is where profits are minimized!).

C.

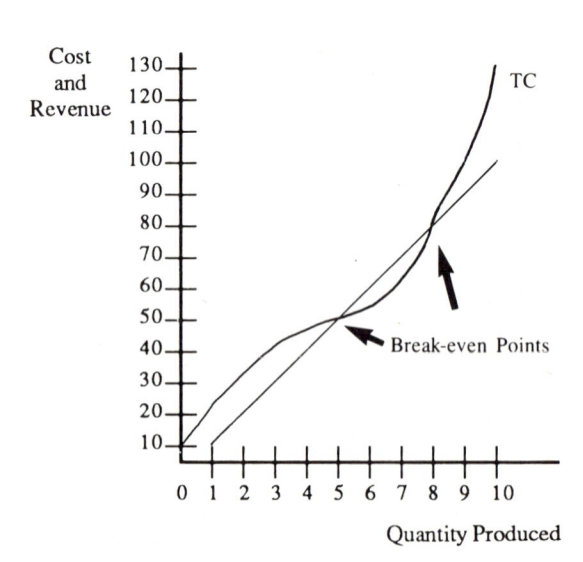

D. 1.

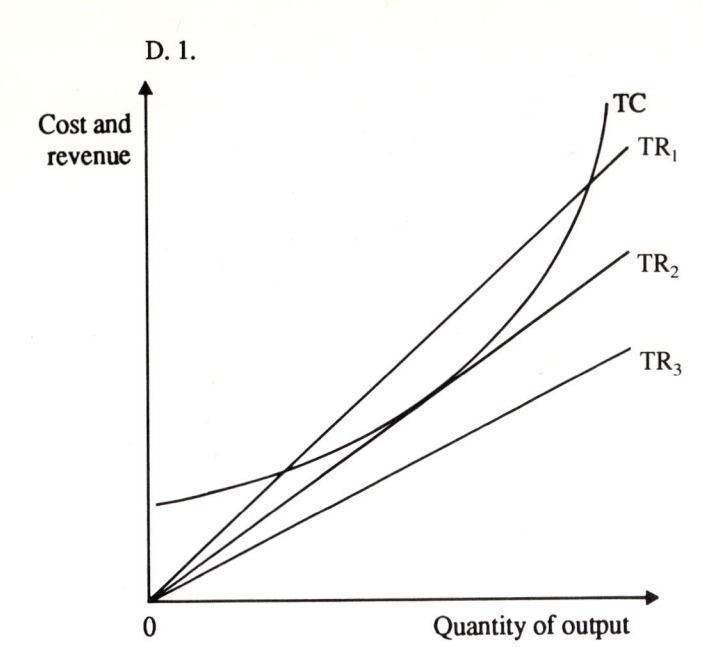

[Graph: Cost and revenue vs Quantity of output, showing TC, TR₁, TR₂, TR₃ curves]

2. lower prices.

6-6. A. 1.economic; normal return. 2.normal return. 3. lose money. B. TR₁ or TR₂. C. 1. $100,000 − $60,000 = $40,000 accounting profit. But her opportunity costs include $25,000 lost salary and $20,000 lost interest. Her net profit is a $5,000 loss! 2.She may stay in business for two reasons. First, she may expect business to improve—the first year is usually the toughest. Second, she may enjoy being her own boss enough to "subsidize" her business with her labor and capital.

Case Application: **The Fortunes of the Progressive Bike Shop**

1. The $26,400 cost of the merchandise was a variable cost because it was directly related to the volume of sales.
2. Economic costs not included in the $43,200 total costs were the compensation to Pat and Jeff for the labor time they put in the business and a normal return on the $6,000 of their capital investment in the business.
3. Open answer. Pat's parents put up over two-thirds of the capital invested in the business. They were entitled to a return on their investment. Such small businesses are risky investments and they stood a chance of losing their $14,000. Therefore, 20% of the net receipts might be a fair return. However, the way the net receipts were calculated they were greatly overstated. If Pat and Jeff had been paid a salary out of the receipts for the time they put into the business, the firm would not have shown a profit during its first year of operation. It might have been fairer if the return to Pat's parents' investment was calculated on the basis of net earnings after compensating Pat and Jeff for their time.

How Does Industry Market Structure Affect Price and Output Decisions?

Review of the Learning Objectives

6-7. A. Check 2, 3, 4, 5, and 6. B. Check 1, 2, 4, 6, and 7.

6-8. A. increase; fixed; decreasing. B. buy more land and plant corn. C. Because one factor of production must be fixed for diminishing returns to exist, they can exist only in the short run. D. Diminishing returns set in with the 6th unit of output.

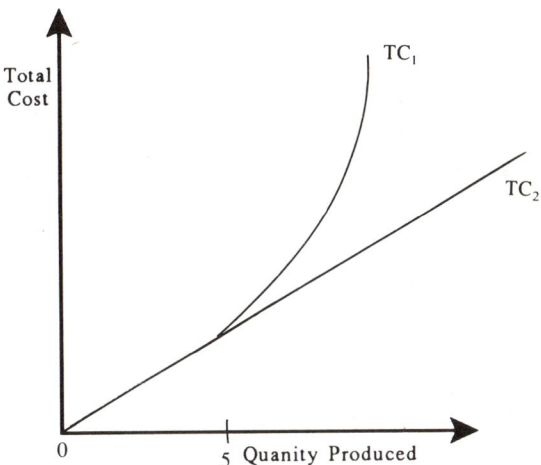

E.

[Graph: Total Cost vs Quantity Produced, showing TC₁ and TC₂ curves, with 5 marked on x-axis]

6-9. A. The correct order is: 7, 3, 5, 2, 1, 4, 6. B. 1.Prices and profits would have stayed high for existing firms. Consumers would not have gotten as much oat bran as they wanted. 2.Profits induced new firms to enter the industry and allocate their scarce resources to the production of oats—what consumers want. C. The correct order is: 6, 2, 1, 7, 5, 3, 4.

6-10. A. 1.PM. 2.DC. 3.SM. 4.SM. 5.PM. 6.PM. 7.DC. 8.DC. 9.SM. 10.PM. B. TR: 0, 100, 180, 240, 280, 300, 300, 280, 240, 180, 100. MR: 100, 80, 60, 40, 20, 0, -20, -40, -60, -80. C. 1. 6 or 7 units. 2.only 3 (the fourth would cost $41 but only earn $40). 3.differentiated competition, pure monopoly, shared monopoly. D. 1.DC, PM, SM. 2.DC, PM, SM. 3.DC, SM. 4.DC, PC. 5.ALL. 6.ALL. 7.DC, PC. 8.SM. 9.SM.

Case Application: **Wheat Farmers in Debt**

1. The fact that he had to accept the going market price for his output. He had no choice in determining the price, but had to take it or leave it.
2. This application illustrates that under purely competitive conditions economic profits tend toward zero because profitable crop conditions result in more wheat being planted, and the increased supply reduces the price. The price decline results in profits disappearing.
3. Open answer. Farmers are engaged in a business that provides a necessity of life but that is subject to varied unpredictable conditions over which they have no control. The unstable effects of weather, insects, and crop diseases are magnified by the unpredictability of prices in the competitive markets for farm products. The uncertainties of farming combined with its importance to our economy have been justifications for government farm price-support programs. These programs have been attacked for misallocating resources by encouraging the production of unneeded crops, for contributing to inflation by artificially raising food prices, for subsidizing mainly the large farmers, who are already wealthy and do not need government assistance, and for bureaucratic waste.

Answers to Practice Test

1.c. 2.c. 3.d. 4.b. 5.e. 6.c. 7.d. 8.c. 9.a. 10.c. 11.a. 12.b. 13.c. 14.c. 15.c. 16.F. 17.F. 18.T. 19.F. 20.F.

Chapter 7

What Determines Industry Performance?

Review of the Learning Objectives

7-1. A. (order of answers may vary) 1.productivity. 2.quality. 3.responsiveness to the market. 4.responsiveness to social concerns. B. 1.quality. 2.responsiveness to social concerns. 3.responsiveness to the market. 4.quality. 5.productivity. 6.quality. 7.quality. C. 1.responsiveness to the market. 2.quality.

7-2. A. How to produce. B. greater/smaller. C. (answers will vary) 1.more burgers served per employee. 2.more cases litigated per hour. 3.more electricity from a given amount of coal or oil.

7-3. A. (answers will vary) 1.radiation leaks. 2.too much fat. 3.blurry print. 4.too much "snow." B. (answers will vary) 1."At Ford, quality is job 1." 2.Maytag's lonely repairman. 3.Any American car company that compares its cars to Japanese cars. C. Winning the award will lead to more business and more profits.

7-4. A. (answers will vary) 1.discriminate in hiring practices. 2.use packaging made of CFCs. 3.dump their fry grease in a local stream. B. 1.boycotts by consumers. 2.fines levied by the government. C. 1.environmental protection. 2. equity.

Case Application: **Academic Theory Put Into Practice**

1. Productivity was increased by the consolidation of the sales staff so that they were not competing with each other for the same accounts. Responsiveness to the market was evidenced by the firm's concentration on producing a long-lasting bulb that reduced worker fatigue and errors. (Incidentally, this bulb would improve production efficiency at the businesses that purchased it.) You could even say that the firm was satisfying social objectives by providing such a bulb.
2. An employee stock ownership plan should provide the company's workers with more incentive to produce a quality product efficiently. The larger the sales and the more efficiently the company operates, the greater will be the company's profits and the higher the value of the employee's stock.
3. Open answer. As a teacher of business and law, Professor Lyons is doubtless up-to-date on management theory. On the other hand, it is often said that academics do not make good executives because managers frequently have to make decisions without undue delay on the basis of incomplete knowledge.

How Can Industry Performance Be Improved?

Review of the Learning Objectives

7-5. A. direct. B. decline. C. (answers will vary) 1.use of uniform product codes (bar codes). 2.use of computers. 3.use of robots. D. 1.short time horizon. 2.use of investment funds for speculation. 3.high interest rates. E. A lower current standard of living because of lower consumption spending, as evidenced by the high prices the Japanese must pay for food and housing.

7-6. A. 1.L. 2.L. 3.M. 4.L. B. inconsistent.

C. 1.

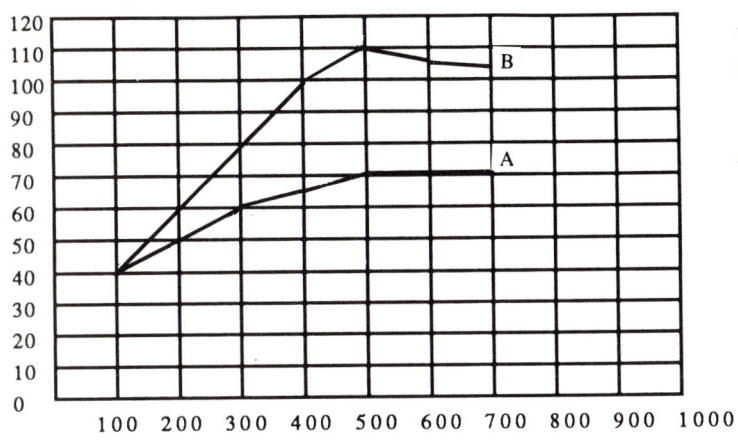

[Graph with x-axis 0-1000 and y-axis 0-120, showing curve A rising from 40 to about 70 and leveling off, and curve B rising from 40 to about 110 then slightly declining]

2. B learns faster. 3. A—after output reaches 300; B—after output reaches 400.

7-7. A. research and development. B. capital. C. 1.the military. 2.universities. D. No. First of all, it earns only a normal profit and has no funds left over for R&D. Second, since there is perfect information, a firm could not profit by innovation.

7-8. A. How to produce. B. 1.EC. 2.PI. 3.PI,EC. 4.PI. 5.HC. C. producing goods and services.

7-9. A. employee involvement. B. 1.SM. 2.SP. 3.SM. 4.PS. C. the United States, Japan. D. 1.unions. 2.middle management.

Case Application: The Factory of the Future Is Next

1. The routing of circuit boards directly to the final assembly area rather than to a warehouse and the shipment of finished computers directly out the door are examples of just-in-time manufacturing.

2. Next has invested heavily in automated equipment in order to maintain quality as well as reduce production costs. The fact that it produces a state-of-the-art computer in a state-of-the-art factory suggests that it is at the forefront of R&D. Its just-in-time production and the use of its workers to monitor production and look for problems rather than do the assembly themselves are examples of organization of production for better productivity.

3. Open answer. Next may or may not succeed, despite its advanced production methods, depending on the public acceptance of its computer, the software available for it, the state of the computer market overall, and a variety of other factors. In the computer industry, a latecomer to the industry faces a difficult barrier to overcome.

What Are the Effects of Industry Concentration on Performance?

Review of the Learning Objectives

7-10. A. high prices (profits). B. 1.H. 2.L. 3.H. 4.H. 5.L. 6.H. C. Monopoly, shared monopoly. D. 1. 40%. 2. 40%. 3. 12%. E. industry 3.

7-11. A. aggregate. B. 1.AM. 2.A. 3.AM. 4.A. 5.AM.

7-12. A. 1.mergers. 2.economies of scale. 3.predatory business practices. B. predatory business practices. C. 1.high prices. 2.inefficient resource allocation. 3.higher costs. 4.unnecessary product differentiation. D. (answers may vary) 1.breakfast cereal. 2.toothpaste 3.perfume.

Case Application: **Rent-A-Kidney Business: Dialysis for Profit?**

1. The home dialysis equipment industry is a shared monopoly. One firm sells almost 50% of all home equipment sold.

2. The hospital-based dialysis service industry does not have the same market structure as the home dialysis equipment industry. National Medical Care, the largest firm, has only 16% of the hospital-based business. Consequently, it can be concluded that the largest four firms have less than 50% of the industry sales.

3. Open answer. It could be argued that private firms provide dialysis service more economically than it would be provided directly by government agencies. Furthermore, it is not unusual for firms doing business under government programs to make high profits because such programs are frequently in new areas of technology and involve such business risks as on-and-off funding. Others would argue that government funding of programs provides excessive profits that would not exist in a purely free-enterprise market, and such humanitarian programs should not be tainted with large profits being siphoned off by private industry. Also, high profits from government-funded programs may result in a misallocation of resources.

Answers to Practice Test

1.c. 2.c. 3.b. 4.a. 5.b. 6.b. 7.d. 8.c. 9.a. 10.c. 11.c. 12.a. 13.d. 14.a. 15.c. 16.F. 17.T. 18.F. 19.T. 20.F.

Chapter 8

What Does the Government Do to Regulate Monopoly?

Review of the Learning Objectives

8-1. A. 1.ICA. 2.CKA. 3.CA. 4.CA. 5.SA. B. 1.monopolization. 2.collusion. C. There are too many firms for either effective collusion or attempted monopolization. D. No. It would be prohibited as a form of collusion under either the Sherman or Clayton Act.

8-2. A. In order to promote international competitiveness. B. The National Co-operative Research Act of 1984. C. There might be a duplication of effort. For example, three different firms may be independently working on the same brake problem. D. Collusion between the two firms such as a price-fixing or market-sharing scheme.

8-3. A. economies of scale. B. Average costs (and prices) would be higher for each of the smaller firms. C. (answers will vary) 1.local electric company. 2.local phone company. 3.local cable TV company. D. Fixed costs: high; Variable costs: low; Marginal costs: low.

8-4. A. government ownership and operation. B. Answers will vary. C. 1.finding accurate cost information. 2.determining a "fair" rate of return. D. 1.probably not. 2.probably so. E. a "normal profit."

8-5. A. 1.The demand is probably inelastic because of few substitutes. 2.You would probably raise the price. 3.Probably not. 4.Regulate their prices or pay the bill. B. 1.established companies. 2.labor unions. C. You should check 2 and 5.

8-6. A. competitive (either pure or differentiated competition). B. You should check 1, 3, and 4. C. Prices and profits fell.

Case Application: Water, Water, Everywhere, And Not a Drop (That's Fit) to Drink

1. The trend in government policies in recent years has been to decrease the role of government in the business sector.
2. The fact that there was only one company supplying water to Dedham and Westwood meant that, even though the citizens were extremely unhappy with the water they were getting, they had no choice but to buy it. Since a water utility is a natural monopoly, there was no competition to force an improvement in the service.
3. Open answer. Water is essential to life, and the purity of our water supplies is important to us. We look to government to protect the interests of the public, especially where natural monopolies are concerned. On the other side of the question is the argument that we cannot afford absolute purity of water or practically anything else. (Besides, there is no such thing as completely pure water unless it is distilled, and distilled water is not recommended for drinking on a regular basis because it lacks the minerals our bodies need.) The market is a better regulator of business than the government. If people are dissatisfied with the water from the tap, they can purchase bottled water.

Why Does the Government Produce Goods and Services?

Review of the Learning Objectives

8-7. A. 1.CG. 2.PS. 3.CG. 4.CG. 5.PS. 6.PS. 7.PS. 8.CG. B. (answers will vary) 1.local schools. 2.trash pick-up. 3.libraries. C. You could not exclude non-payers. D. Determining how much the citizens value the good (the city cannot use the price mechanism to "force" people to reveal how much they value a service).

8-8. A. 1.EC. 2.EC. 3.EE. 4.EE. 5.EE. 6.EC. 7.EC. 8.EC.

B. 1.

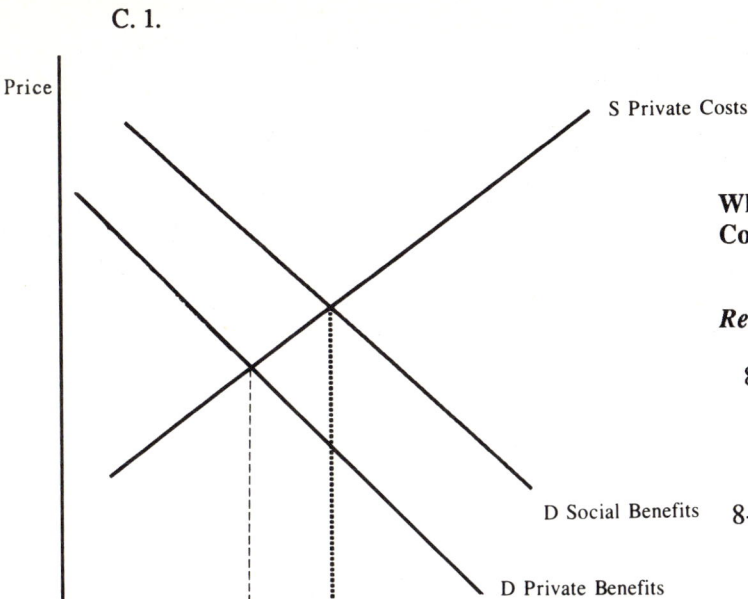

2. less.

C. 1.

[Graph: Price vs Quantity showing S Private Costs (upward sloping), D Social Benefits and D Private Benefits (downward sloping), with Qpo and Qso marked on quantity axis]

2. greater. D. Too many goods are produced when external costs are present, and too few are produced when external economies are present. E. 1. less pollution. 2. less congestion (or 3. less dependency on foreign energy sources.)

Case Application: Should the Government Be in the Railroad Business?

1. The government subsidy of Amtrak cannot be justified in terms of equity because it is not primarily lower-income people who take advantage of the government subsidies to rail passenger traffic.

2. There are external economies associated with rail passenger and freight traffic. Rail transportation is more energy-efficient and less polluting than highway or air transportation. Railroads reduce congestion on the highways, reduce the need for petroleum, reduce air pollution, and reduce the crowding of airports and flight paths. In addition, they help towns that are too small for an airport to compete for business and to remain viable places to live because of convenient transportation.

3. Open answer. The arguments for the government to dispose of Amtrak are: the government should not be in competition with other transportation suppliers; private business does a better job of resolving the allocation questions than government agencies; and the government can save the money it spends on subsidies to Amtrak. The arguments against disposing of Amtrak are: the reason the government took it over in the first place was because the private railroads were neither serving the public well nor making profits; the government has invested a great deal in upgrading Amtrak; ridership is increasing and the government subsidy diminishing; and railroads are an essential component of a nation's transportation system, with substantial external economies that many communities and individuals would sorely miss if the services were terminated.

What Is the Role of the Government in Protecting Consumers, Workers, and the Environment?

Review of the Learning Objectives

8-9. A. 1. SEC. 2. DOT. 3. CPSC. 4. OSHA. 5. FDA. 6. FTC. B. Most of us do not have the information to make informed decisions. C. agriculture. D. by paying wage premiums for dangerous work.

8-10. A. free. B. 1. command-and-control regulations. 2. eco-taxes. 3. the sale of emission allowances. C. 1. 100 tons for $750. 2. Have firm X clean up 100 tons for only $500. 3. Firm X would be willing to clean up 100 tons if firm Y made it worth its while, and firm Y would be willing to pay up to $500. D. 1. "third parties." 2. customers. E. 1. higher electric prices. 2. perhaps fewer jobs in the electric industry.

Case Application: Declaration of Air Pollution Emergency

1. The external costs associated with steel production in Allegheny County included air pollution, which resulted in many health problems, and decreased visibility, which interfered with traffic.

2. In order to internalize the external costs of its steel production operation, the U.S. Steel Corporation would have to install fabric filters for electric arcs, high-energy wet scrubbers for open-hearth and basic oxygen furnaces, and electrostatic precipitators for smokestacks. This would increase production costs, which would raise the price of steel and reduce the quantity of steel production. This can be shown on a demand-supply diagram by a shift of the supply curve to the left. The equilibrium price on the new supply curve is higher and the equilibrium quantity lower than on the previous supply curve.

3. Open answer. Those who believe reducing air pollution and the effects it has on health and safety are the most important considerations would favor forcing U.S. Steel to internalize its external costs. Those who believe unemployment is the most important consideration would not.

Answers to Practice Test

1. d. 2. d. 3. c. 4. b. 5. d. 6. c. 7. c. 8. c. 9. a. 10. b. 11. a. 12. d. 13. c. 14. b. 15. c. 16. T. 17. F. 18. F. 19. T. 20. T.

298 / *Working With The Study of Economics, 4/E*

Chapter 9

What Determines Wages in a Market Economy?

Review of the Learning Objectives

9-1. A. 1. supply. 2. decrease. 3. it prevents wages from falling.
4.

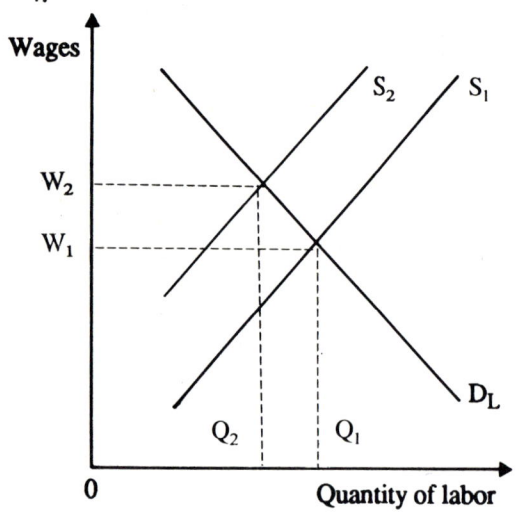

B. 1. D. 2. D. 3. I. 4. I.

C. 1-4.

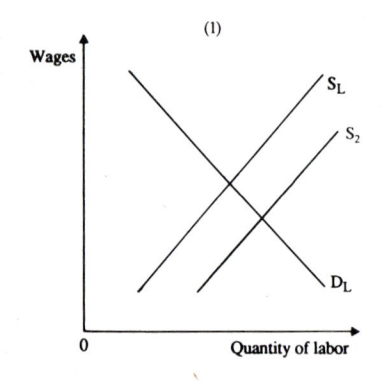

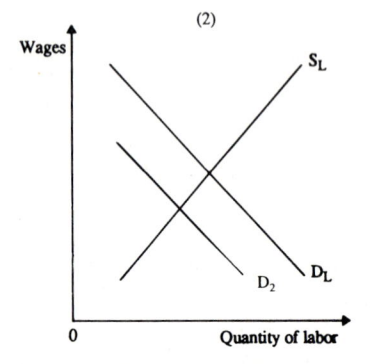

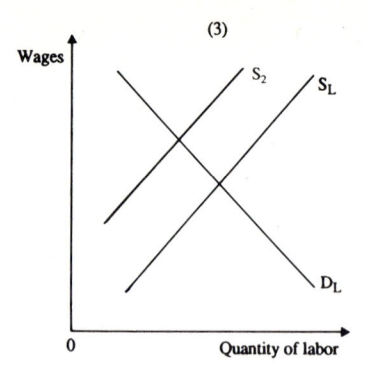

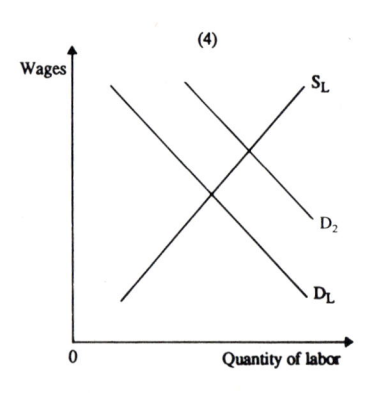

D. 1 & 2.

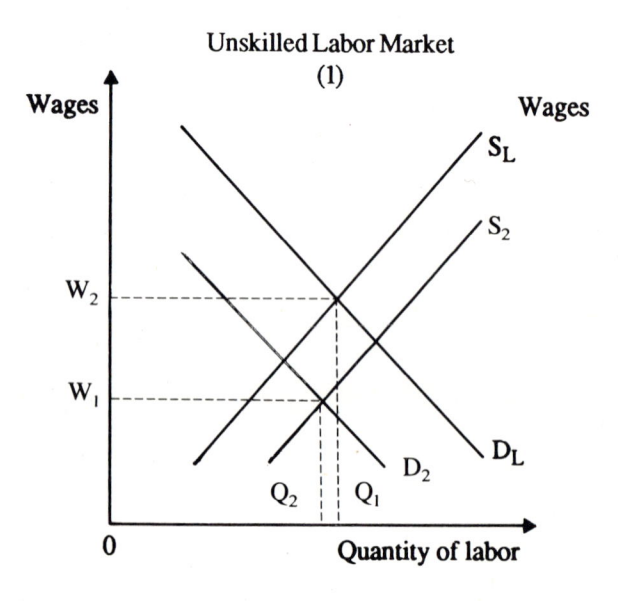

Unskilled Labor Market

Answers to Chapter Questions / 299

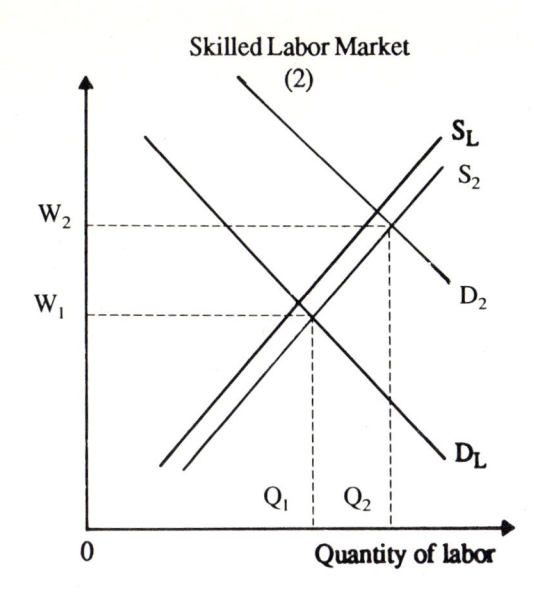

[Skilled Labor Market (2) graph: S_L and S_2 supply curves, D_L and D_2 demand curves, showing W_1, W_2 on wage axis and Q_1, Q_2 on quantity of labor axis]

E. (answers may vary) Dishwashers may earn only the minimum wage while computer technicians earn excellent salaries.

9-2. A. 1.will increase. 2.will increase. B. 1.will decrease. 2.will decrease. C. 1.I. 2.D. 3.I. 4.I. 5.I.

9-3. A.

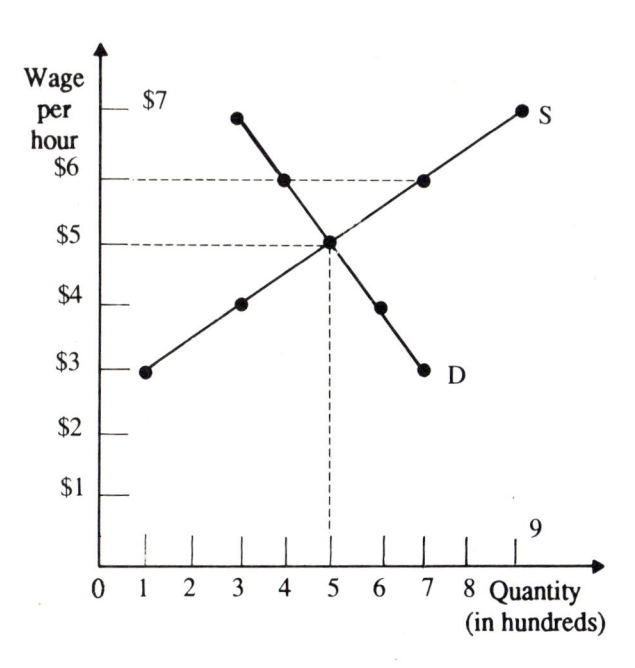

[Graph: Wage per hour ($1-$7) vs Quantity (in hundreds, 0-9), with supply curve S and demand curve D intersecting at $5, quantity 5; dashed line at $6 showing surplus]

B. $5 C. 1. **On graph above**

2. 200. 3. 100. 4.a surplus of 300 workers (unemployment). D. They have no effect.

9-4. A. 1.Wagner Act (National Labor Relations Act). 2.National Labor Relations Board. B. 1.S. 2.W. 3.W. 4.S. 5.S. 6.W. C. 1.strikes. 2.boycotts. D. 1.higher wages. 2.better working conditions.

9-5. A. 1. they do not adjust to decreases in the demand for labor. 2.No (nobody resists a raise!).

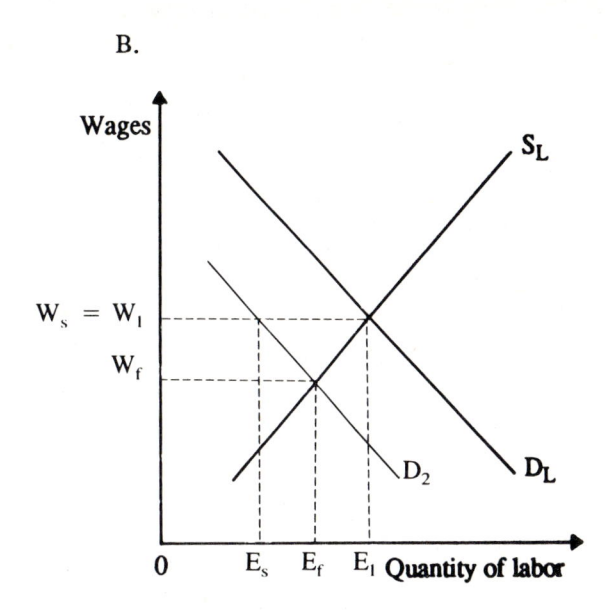

B.

[Graph: Wages vs Quantity of labor, supply curve S_L, demand curves D_L and D_2; showing W_s = W_1 and W_f on wage axis, E_s, E_f, E_1 on quantity axis]

C. 1.minimum wage laws. 2.unions. (or 3.workers simply resist wage cuts.) D. It depends. If I was one of those who kept their jobs, I would prefer sticky wages. On the other hand, if I was one of those who could keep only their jobs at a lower wage, I would prefer flexible wages.

Case Application: **Coal and Black Gold**

1. The loss of jobs in coal mines after 1941 can be explained in part by the substitution of petroleum for coal. Since the demand for coal miners is derived from the demand for coal, the substitution of petroleum for coal in many uses reduced the number of jobs available in coal mining.

2. The success of John L. Lewis in raising the wages of coal miners made labor in coal mining relatively more expensive than investment in capital equipment. This created a cost advantage for strip mines, which use more heavy equipment and less labor.

3. Open answer. Before John L. Lewis became president of the United Mine Workers, the wages, living standards, and working conditions of coal miners were very poor. Many died from black-lung disease, mine accidents, overwork, and poor nutrition and health care. Many generations grew up living under these conditions. Lewis believed it was better for the children of miners to be forced to seek jobs elsewhere than to continue in the mines under such circumstances. For those who remained in mining, the union succeeded in greatly improving their living

standards and working conditions. The opposition to Lewis's union activity maintained that miners were free to seek other work any time they chose to, and taking away their bread and butter by forcing many mines to close due to the high labor costs was not beneficial for the miners, mine owners, other businesses which depended on the mines, or coal users.

What Determines Other Incomes?

Review of the Learning Objectives

9-6. A. 1.wages and salaries. 2.profits. 3.interest. 4.rent. B. wages and salaries. C.rent. D. 1.f. 2.a. 3.c. 4.d. 5.e. 6.b.

9-7. A. Numbers 1, 3, 4, and 6 should be checked. B. 1.The supply curve is vertical. 2.Long run. In the short run the supply of many items is fixed and rent-like returns can be made. For example, the supply of fresh fruits and vegetables is vertical in the very short run.

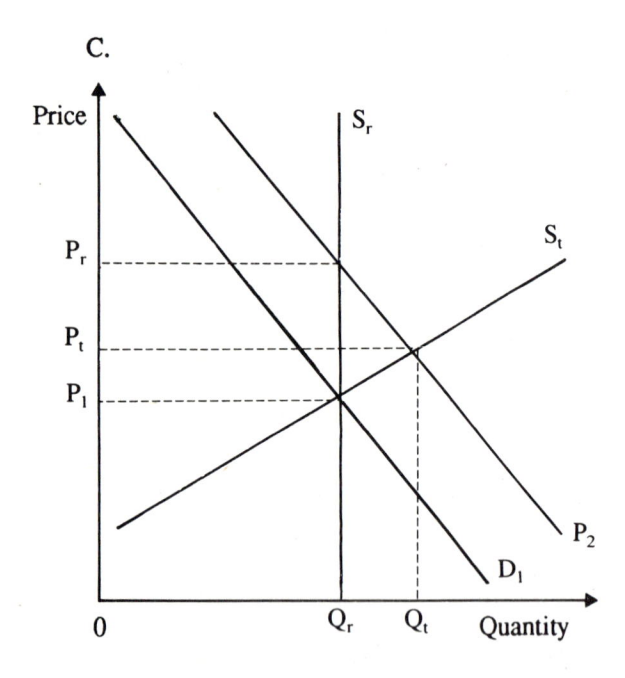

C.

D. The price of good R increased more because there was no offsetting increase in the quantity supplied to keep the price lower.

Case Application: **How Much Is a Nose Guard Worth?**

1. The supply of National Football League games is best represented by supply curve S_1 in Figure 8 on page 241 of the textbook. The number of games is perfectly inelastic, at least in the short run, and does not vary with the price for which tickets can be sold.

2. The salary earned by Jim Kelly is more like a rent payment than a wage payment because its level is determined entirely by demand and not at all by supply. Jim Kelly would be willing to work as a quarterback at only a fraction of the salary he receives if the demand for his services were lower. The high salary of gifted quarterbacks does not result in an increase in the number of such quarterbacks in the labor market, as would be the case with labor in general. The salary is therefore more like a rent on a resource in limited supply.

3. Open answer. It seems only fair for players who do their jobs equally well and contribute equally to the success of the team, whatever position they are playing, to receive the same wage. However, it is the market that determines prices, and in the entertainment business those who have the most popular appeal receive the largest incomes. In the theater and movies, for example, character actors frequently have more acting ability than the stars but are paid much less.

What Causes Unequal Distribution of Income?

Review of the Learning Objectives

9-8. A. The functional distribution shows where income comes from, the personal distribution shows who gets how much of it. B. 1.$400,000; $200,000; $100,000; $60,000; $40,000. 2. 50%; 25%; 12.5%; 7.5%; 5%.

3.

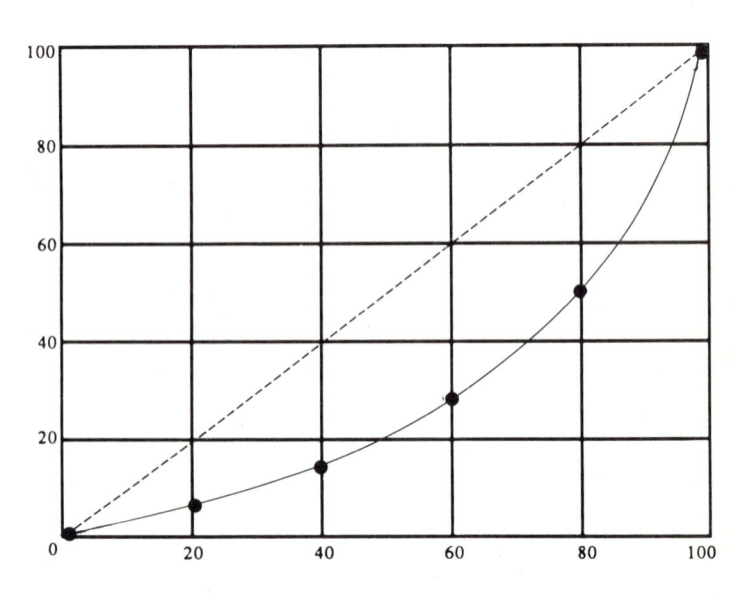

C. 1.D. 2.D. 3.D. 4.I. 5.I. D. 1.an equal distribution of income. 2.the less equal is the distribution of income.

9-9. A. (order of answers will vary) 1.ability. 2.opportunity. 3.asset ownership. B. 1.opportunity. 2.ability. 3.ability. 4.opportunity. 5.asset ownership. 6.asset ownership (or opportunity). C. by the sale of assets that they own and sell (capital gains). D. 1.women. 2.blacks. 3.Hispanics.

Case Application: **The New Poor**

1. The "old poor" were poverty-stricken because of such handicaps as lack of education, physical or mental disability, or exclusion from the work force. The "new poor" are poverty-stricken because of declining demand in a number of industries, putting many experienced workers out of a job.
2. The "new poor" will move out of poverty first when economic conditions improve because a rising number of job openings will be available to them, whereas the "old poor" are likely to still be excluded.
3. Open answer. Private welfare agencies should aid everyone in need of help regardless of the reason for their conditions. On the other hand, it could be argued that the "old poor" are more in need of assistance than the "new poor" because they have been in poverty longer, have fewer resources to fall back upon, and will continue to be in poverty after the "new poor" have found jobs.

What Is the Answer to Poverty?

Review of the Learning Objectives

9-10. A. food. B. 1.$12,000. 2.$20,000. 3.1/5. 4.1/5. 5.1/3. 6.The reported numbers understate the true number of people in poverty. C. 1.AFDC. 2.Medicaid. 3.Food Stamps. D. 1.Education and equal opportunities. 2.Transfer payments. E. A plan that gives households money when their own income is below a certain guaranteed level instead of taking taxes from the household. The main advantage is that such programs do not provide disincentives to work.

Case Application: **Increased Opportunities for the Handicapped**

1. The number of handicapped poor has been reduced since 1973 by the enactment of federal and state legislation prohibiting employer discrimination against the handicapped.
2. Affirmative action programs to employ the handicapped are needed because there is a prejudice against hiring them. They frequently can be valuable employees, but fears on the part of employers about possible consequences prevent their being considered for jobs in the absence of affirmative action programs.
3. Open answer. Yes, the government should subsidize firms that hire the handicapped because they can make a contribution to output, and income they earn reduces the need for government welfare payments and other assistance. No, the government should not subsidize firms to hire the handicapped because it could result in less efficiency in the production process, and the market should determine resource allocation without government intervention.

Answers to Practice Test

1.d. 2.b. 3.d. 4.c. 5.a. 6.b. 7.b. 8.c. 9.a. 10.c. 11.d. 12.a. 13.c. 14.b. 15.b. 16.F. 17.T. 18.T. 19.T. 20.T.

Crossword Puzzle for Chapters 5-9

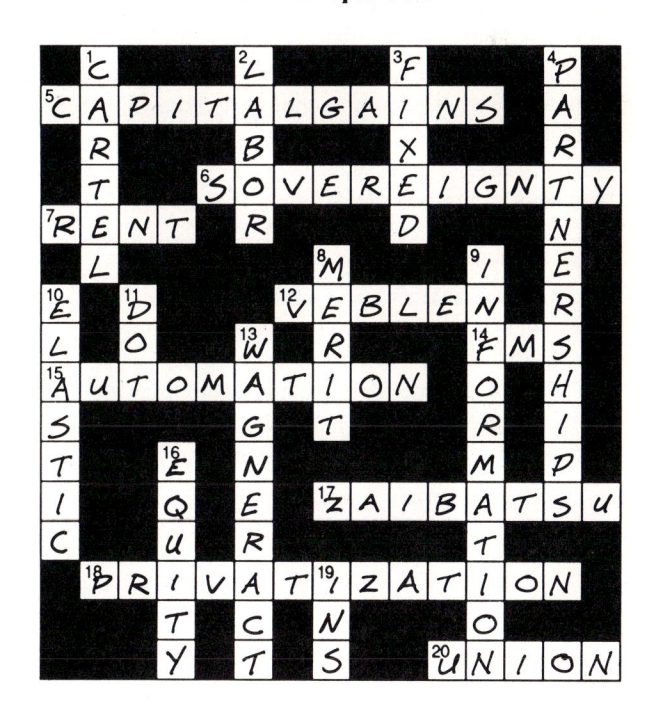

Chapter 10

What Is Money?

Review of the Learning Objectives

10-1. A. (answers will vary) 1.sea shells. 2.cows. 3.cigarettes. B. 17th; goldsmiths. C. 1.Alexander Hamilton. 2.Thomas Jefferson. D. Any privately owned bank that was chartered by a state or federal government. E. the Federal Reserve System (Bank).

10-2. A. 1.currency (including coins). 2.checkable deposits. 3.travelers' checks. 4.ATS accounts. B. checkable deposits. C. only because people are willing to accept them as payment for goods and services. D. banks; government.

10-3. A. liquid. B. ranking: 5, 2, 4, 1, 3. C. 1.commercial paper. 2.savings bonds. 3.short-term government bonds. D. 1.M1, M2, M3, L. 2.M2, M3, L. 3.M1, M2, M3, L. 4.L. 5.M3, L. 6.M1, M2, M3, L. 7.M2, M3, L.

Case Application: What Isn't Money?

1. The expansion of money market mutual funds represented an increase in near money.

2. Money market mutual funds are more like money than are certificates of deposit because they are more liquid. Investments in money market mutual funds can be withdrawn immediately with no penalty, usually simply by writing a check. Investments in certificates of deposit, on the other hand, cannot be withdrawn by check and cannot be withdrawn before maturity without a penalty being imposed.

3. Open answer. The advantages of deregulating financial institutions are: it increases competition in the financial services market and allows different types of financial institutions to compete on an equal basis. Disadvantages are: some financial institutions may not be able to survive (see the introductory article for chapter 11 in the text) and some types of loans, such as those for home mortgages, may be more difficult and costly to obtain because other types of lending are more profitable.

What Does Money Do?

Review of the Learning Objectives

10-4. A. 1.medium of exchange. 2.unit of measurement. 3.store of value. B. (using the numbering from A) 1.3. 2.2. 3.1. 4.1. 5.2. 6.2. C. Credit cards do not serve as a "store of value" or a unit of measurement. Also, credit cards are not money; they are a means of *borrowing* money. D. 1.universally recognized. 2.not easily reproduced. 3.portable. 4.durable. 5. adequate but limited supply. E. (using the numbering from D) 1.5. 2.4. 3.3, 4. 4.5. 5.2. 6.1.

Case Application: Primitive Money

1. When the price of slaves was quoted in cows and brass rods, those items were performing the function of a unit of account.

2. The lack of conversion of denominations of one class of shells into another class among the Russell Islanders indicates the shells do not serve the same function as money does in the United States because money must be convertible into different denominations (e.g., five $1 bills for a $5 bill) in order to serve as a universal means of exchange.

3. Open answer. Some possible ways in which it could be said that money performs social as well as economic functions in our society include lighting a cigar with a $100 bill to display affluence, leaving a very small tip for a rude waiter to show dissatisfaction, or leaving a quarter under the pillow of a child from the "tooth fairy."

How Is Money Created?

Review of the Learning Objectives

10-5. A. 1.I. 2.D. 3.D. 4.I. 5.I. 6.D. B. a checking account (demand deposit). C. 1.Answers will vary. 2.Usually none. D. checking accounts. E. 1.Yes, they usually have an increased balance in their checking accounts. 2.No. 3.It increases.

Case Application: How the Government Creates Money

1. If the U.S. Treasury prints a $10,000 bond and you borrow the $10,000 from your bank to purchase the bond, the money supply is increased by $10,000. You are directly responsible for the expansion of the money because it was your loan from the bank that increased the supply of money, not the printing of the bond by the Treasury.

2. If the government paid its bills by printing currency rather than by selling government securities, the result would be a greater increase in the money supply because some of the money paid for government securities represents a reduction in the privately held money stock.

3. Open answer. The lower interest rates paid on savings bonds can be called unfair to small investors because they do not have sufficient funds to purchase higher-denomination government securities. On the other hand, it could be argued that those who purchase U.S. savings bonds have the freedom to choose between those and other types of investments, and purchasing savings bonds may be considered patriotic.

Answers to Chapter Questions / 303

How Is the Supply of Money Controlled?

Review of the Learning Objectives

10-6. A. Federal Reserve System. B. 1.12. 2. Answers will vary. C. 1.acts as a banker's bank. 2.serves the monetary needs of the federal government. 3.controls the money supply. (4.the Fed also "clears" checks for individuals and businesses.) D. control of the money supply. E. 1.7. 2.14. 3.Because members of the Board of Governors have such long terms, they do not need to depend on the "kindness" of politicians in order to keep their jobs. This allows them to avoid political pressure.

10-7. A. 1.changing the discount rate. 2.changing the required reserve ratio. 3.open market operations. B. 1.from the Fed through discounting. 2.from other banks in the Federal Funds market. C. 1.I. 2.D. 3.D. 4.D. 5.I. D. 1.$10,000. 2.$90,000. 3.$90,000. 4.10 (1 ÷ 0.1). 5.$900,000 (10 × $90,000). 6.$70,000. 7.$700,000 (10 × $70,000). E. 1.$20,000. 2.$80,000. 3.5 (1 ÷ 0.2). 4.$400,000 (5 × $80,000). 5.$40,000 6.$200,000 (5 × $40,000). F. 1.increases. 2.increases. 3.increases. 4.decreases. G. 1.increases. 2.decreases. 3.decreases. 4.increases.

H. 1, 2, & 3.

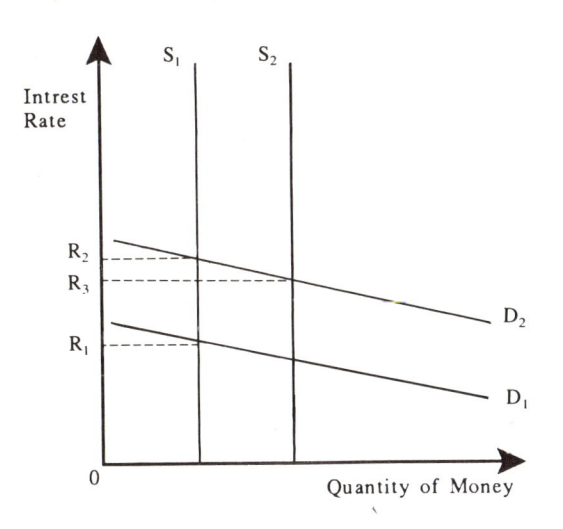

[Graph showing Interest Rate vs Quantity of Money with supply curves S₁ and S₂ (vertical), demand curves D₁ and D₂ (downward sloping), and interest rate levels R₁, R₂, R₃ marked]

4.It might cause inflation.

Case Application: Who's In Charge Around Here?

1. The Depository Institutions Deregulation and Monetary Control Act of 1980 (the Monetary Control Act) expanded the authority of the Fed by making nonmember banks and other depository institutions subject to the same Fed regulations as those banks that are members of the system and providing them with the Fed's services, for which they must pay a fee.

2. The principal regulatory power that the Fed needs in order to implement monetary policy is mandating the required reserve ratio, which the banks must maintain.

3. Open answer. The overlapping authority of the three bank regulatory agencies may result in duplication of activities and responsibilities. Especially in these times of widespread bank failures due to unsound lending practices, there should be clear regulatory responsibility by a single agency over a specific banking activity. On the other hand, the Federal Reserve has the primary responsibility for implementing a sound monetary policy and should have broad regulatory authority rather than being confined to a service and policy-making role.

Answers to Practice Test

1.c. 2.c. 3.d. 4.b. 5.c. 6.d. 7.b. 8.c. 9.b. 10.a. 11.c. 12.c. 13.b. 14.d. 15.c. 16.F. 17.F. 18.F. 19.T. 20.T.

Chapter 11

What Causes Unemployment?

Review of the Learning Objectives

11-1. A. 1.S. 2.C. 3.F. 4.S. 5.S. 6.C. 7.S. B. 1.frictional. 2.frictional. 3.cyclical. 4.frictional. C. 1.F. 2.C. 3.S. 4.S. 5.F.

11-2. A. actively seeking employment. B. 1.N. 2.N. 3.C. 4.N. 5.N. 6.N. 7.N. C. 1.nothing. 2.It will increase. 3.understates. 4.overstates.

Case Application: Where the Jobs Went

1. The more than 100,000 jobs permanently lost in the automobile industry represented structural unemployment. They were lost by an increase in automation of automobile production methods and by an increase in the share of the U.S. automobile market accounted for by foreign car imports.

2. Women who lost their jobs because of the recession and did not try to find new jobs were not counted as unemployed because only those actively seeking jobs are considered unemployed. The women who did not seek new jobs represented hidden unemployment.

3. Open answer. A 40-year-old steelworker with a family who lost his job would have difficult alternatives. One possibility would be to try to scrape by on unemployment compensation, as long as it lasted, and then on savings in hopes the steel mill would reopen. Another possibility would be to move his family to a state with a lower unemployment rate than Pennsylvania in hopes of finding other work for which he was qualified. A third possibility would be for him to attempt to obtain retraining for a different type of work in an expanding industry. All of these choices involve difficulties and dangers for the economic security of his family.

What Causes Inflation?

Review of the Learning Objectives

11-3. A. Inflation is a continual increase in the general level of prices. B. 1.consumer price index (CPI). 2.market basket. C. 1985: 100; 1986: 110; 1987: 115; 1988: 125; 1989: 130. D. 1985 to 1986 = 10%; 1986 to 1987 = 4.5%; 1987 to 1988 = 8.7%; 1988 to 1989 = 4.0%. E. product; factor.

Case Application: **Talk About Inflation...**

1. The restaurant dinner would have cost 340 Bolivian dollars at the end of 1985. This is calculated by multiplying 10 Bolivian dollars by 3,400%. (Note that 3,400% of a number is 34 times the number, since the decimal point is moved two places to the right when expressing a percentage.)

2. The types of inflation described in this application are demand-pull and monetary inflation.

3. Open answer. Likely reasons why the inflation rates are so much greater in those countries than in the United States are: they have smaller economies than the United States so that a monetary disturbance is not as easily absorbed as it is in the large U.S. economy; they have had more severe economic problems, such as the Arab-Israeli conflict and the Argentine war over the Falkland Islands and the subsequent overthrow of the military government; and probably the main difference is that they do not have a monetary control as effective as the Fed in the United States.

Is There a Trade-off Between Unemployment and Inflation?

Review of the Learning Objectives

11-4. A. 1.monetary. 2.demand-pull. 3.cost-push. 4.demand-pull. 5. cost-push. B. M = the money supply; V = the velocity of money; P = the average price level; T = the number of transactions. C. 1.M × V represents the number of dollars spent. 2.P × T represents the value of all goods and services bought. D. 1.Prices increase. 2.It stays the same. 3.The velocity of money must increase (each dollar must be spent more times).

11-5. A. inversely.

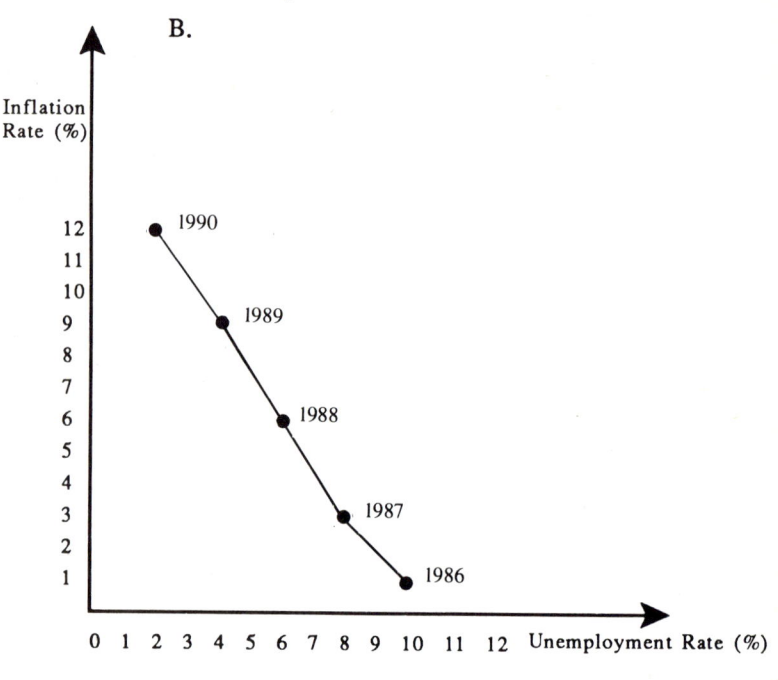

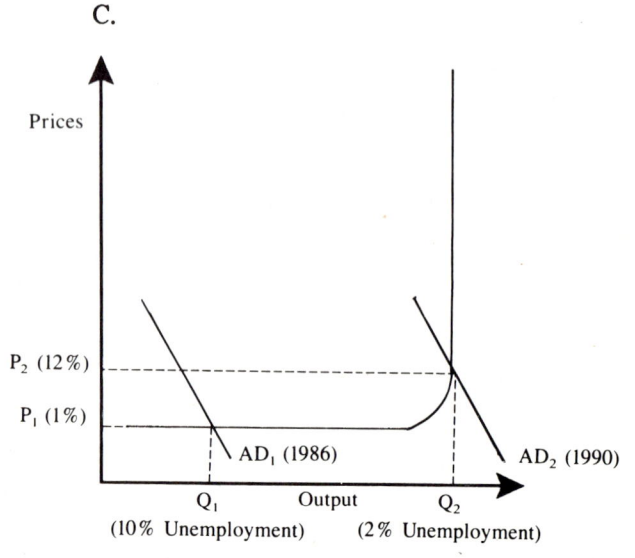

B.

C.

D. demand-pull. E. 1.higher unemployment. 2. higher inflation.

11-6. A. directly.

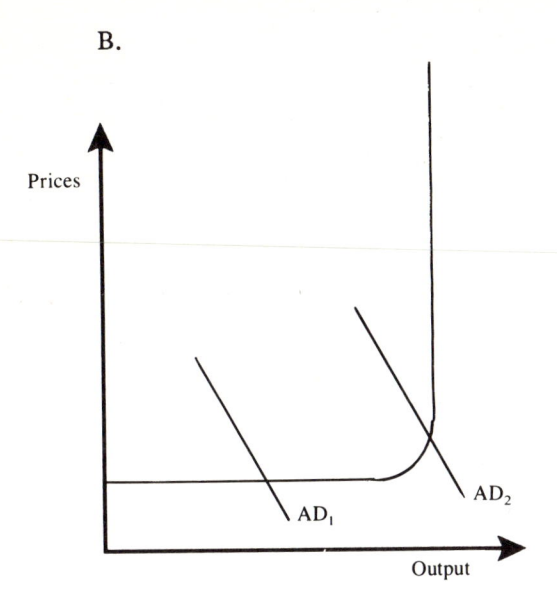

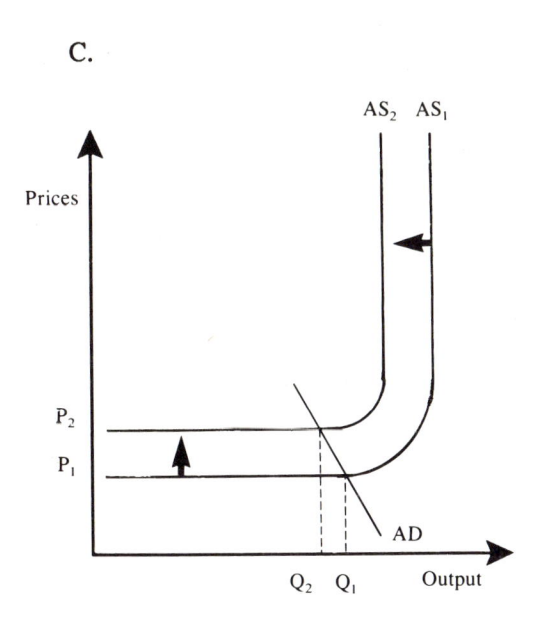

B.

[Graph: Prices vs Output, showing AD₁ and AD₂ curves with an L-shaped aggregate supply curve]

C.

[Graph: Prices vs Output, showing AS₁ shifting left to AS₂, with AD curve; P₁ rises to P₂, Q₁ falls to Q₂]

D. question C; both prices and unemployment are higher. E. 1.P stays the same, T increases. 2.Both increase. 3.P increases, T stays the same.

Case Application: Phillips Curve International

1. Prior to 1975, the European countries were operating more to the upper left on their Phillips curves, with higher inflation rates and lower unemployment rates compared to the United States.

2. The rise in energy costs in the 1970s made European production costs higher, which both raised the inflation rate and made their industries less competitive in the marketplace, thus slowing their economies and causing unemployment. The combination of higher prices and higher unemployment was represented by an upward shift in the Phillips curve.

3. Open answer. Answering this question is complicated and uncertain, depending on the assumptions and value judgments adopted. The upper-left portion of the Phillips curve imposes the costs of inflation such as a burden on those with fixed incomes and possible declines in the efficiency and growth of the economy. On the other hand, it minimizes the human, social, and output costs of unemployment. The lower-right location on the Phillips curve increases those unemployment costs while minimizing the costs of inflation.

What Are the Consequences of Unemployment and Inflation?

Review of the Learning Objectives

11-7. A. 1.Real output decreases. 2.Real incomes decrease. 3.negative social effects. B. (using the preceding numbering) 1.3. 2.1. 3.2. 4.2. 5.3. C. 1.B. 2.L. 3.L. 4.L. 5.L. 6.B. 7.B. 8.B. 9.B. D. 1.A business will benefit if the price of its product is increasing faster than the prices of its inputs. 2.A business will suffer if the price of its inputs increases faster than the price of its output.

Case Application: Disinflation Losers

1. The wealth and income of those who had purchased real assets such as houses, gold, precious gems, or commodities were negatively affected by an end to inflation. Debtors lose out when disinflation sets in, and the incomes of governments are also affected.

2. A decline in the price of gold and other commodities would be likely to affect the output of those commodities because of the law of supply. Unless the supply is perfectly inelastic, a price decline will result in reductions in their output.

3. Open answer. A severe disinflation could be worse than inflation. A collapse of prices such as that occurring in the early 1930s would cause many business failures and high unemployment. A

Answers to Practice Test

1.b. 2.d. 3.a. 4.c. 5.d. 6.d. 7.b. 8.d. 9.c. 10.a. 11.c. 12.b. 13.b. 14.c. 15.d. 16.T. 17.F. 18.F. 19.F. 20.F.

Chapter 12

How Much Does the Economy Produce?

Review of the Learning Objectives

12-1. A. 1.spend. 2.earn. B. 1.product. 2.factor (resource). C. The values added equal: .30; .15; .20; .20; and .10. The addition to GNP equals .95. D. 1.I. 2.N. 3.N. 4.I. 5.I. 6.I. 7.I. 8.I. 9.N.

12-2. A. 1.G. 2.X. 3.X. 4.I. 5.C. 6.I. 7.I. 8.C. B. (answers will vary) 1.C: It becomes a second family vehicle. I: A landscaping company buys the truck. G: Your town buys the truck and uses it for hauling leaves. X: The truck is shipped to Russia. 2.C: You buy it and watch it. I: Your local news station buys it and uses it as a monitor. G: Your local school district buys it and uses it in class. X: The television is sold to China. C. 1.C. 2.C. 3.I. 4.X. 5.I. 6.C. 7.I. 8.C.

12-3. A. 1.indirect business taxes. 2.capital consumption allowances (depreciation). B. 1.sales taxes. 2.property taxes. C. depreciation or capital consumption allowances.

12-4. A. 1.price level. 2.constant dollar; current dollar. B. 1.Q. 2.P × Q. C. 1990: $2,000,000; 1991: $2,200,000; 1992: $2,400,000; 1993: $2,350,000; 1994: $2,500,000. D. 1993. E. Current dollar GNP will be greater because the prices of everything (on average) will be greater.

Case Application: Helen's Gift City, Inc.

1. The contribution of Helen's Gift City to total output was $110,000. This was the value added by the firm to GNP; i.e., its sales revenue minus its purchases from other firms.

2. The firm added $86,000 to National Income. The difference between its contribution to GNP and its contribution to NI is accounted for by the firm's capital consumption allowance and business taxes.

3. Open answer. From the standpoint of the firm, the Account's Income Statement is the most useful organization of the information because it shows the total costs subtracted from sales to determine the firm's profit. The national income accounting statement is the most useful for determining the contributions of the firm to GNP.

What Determines Domestic Output From the Demand-Side Point of View?

Review of the Learning Objectives

12-5. A. aggregate demand. B. 1.leakage: consumption; addition: consumption. 2.leakage: taxes; addition: government spending. 3.leakage: savings; addition: investment. C. 1.nothing; consumption will always equal consumption. 2.if the government does not spend all its tax receipts. 3.if available savings are not borrowed. D. 1.GNP falls. 2.GNP rises. 3.GNP remains the same. E. 1.It reduces aggregate demand. 2.It results in lower interest rates and greater investment demand. F. 1.D. 2.G. 3.G. 4.D. 5.G. 6.G. 7.D. G. 1.budget deficit. 2.It will cause it to increase. H. 1.budget surplus. 2.It will cause it to decrease. I. reduced aggregate demand. J. 1.yes. 2.leakages exceed additions. 3.GNP will decline.

Case Application: Changes in Demand

1. In 1989 the weakest GNP component was residential fixed investment, which fell 2.7% below the already declining level of previous years.

2. The effect of government expenditures was to stimulate demand and raise GNP in 1989. The increased level of government spending from the year before helped to offset the decline in residential investment.

3. Open answer. Most people attempt to maintain their life-styles in spite of fluctuations in their incomes. Some, however, may be cautious and reduce their spending sharply if their incomes fall, in order to have a savings cushion in case their incomes fall further.

What Determines Domestic Output From the Supply-Side Point of View?

Review of the Learning Objectives

12-6. A. aggregate supply or the level of income earned. B. 1.flexible wages and prices. 2.there are powerful institutional forces that resist falling wages and prices. C. Wages and prices would have fallen.

D.

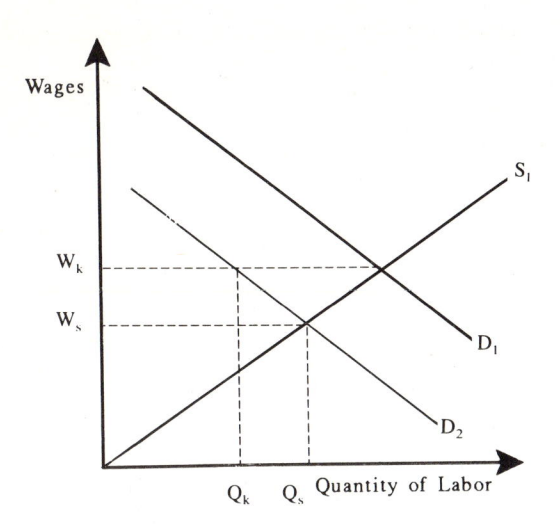

[Graph showing Wages on vertical axis and Quantity of Labor on horizontal axis. Supply curve S₁ slopes upward; demand curves D₁ and D₂ slope downward, with D₁ above D₂. Points W_k, W_s on vertical axis and Q_k, Q_s on horizontal axis.]

12-7. A. 1.incentives to produce. 2.to lower taxes. B. 1.savings. 2.investment. 3.labor supplies. C. 1.increased; increased. 2.interest rates; decrease; decreased. D. 1.D. 2.S. 3.S. 4.S. 5.D. 6.S. 7.S.

Case Application: **Is War Good for the Economy?**

1. The earlier conventional view of the effect of war on the economy was a demand-side view because it was based on the results of adding the demand for goods and services for the war effort to existing demand, thus increasing total demand.

2. The anticipated effects were supply-side effects such as the additional supply costs due to higher energy prices and the crowding-out effect on investment resulting from larger government spending to pay for the war.

3. Open answer. One response might be that effects of war on the economy should be disregarded because moral, political, and security considerations are more important in deciding whether to go to war. The opposite opinion might be based on the positions that the government should consider the welfare of its own citizens above all, that the costs of war—material, financial, and personal—are too high, and that in the long run a healthy economy is the best security.

Answers to Practice Test

1.b. 2.a. 3.d. 4.b. 5.c. 6.d. 7.c. 8.c. 9.b. 10.b. 11.b. 12.a. 13.a. 14.b. 15.c. 16.F. 17.T. 18.F. 19.T. 20.F.

Chapter 13

On What Do Governments Spend Money?

Review of the Learning Objectives

13-1. A. 1.expenditures, tax revenue. 2.$220 billion. 3.adding together all past deficits; $3 trillion. B. 1.automatic spending reductions. 2.not much—the deficit has actually grown since the passage of Gramm-Rudman. C. 1.moving expenditures to prior years. 2.treating Social Security taxes as income instead of loans. 3.making overly optimistic revenue forecasts (Gramm-Rudman targets are based on **projected**, not actual, deficits). D. 1.It is politically difficult to reduce constituents' benefit programs (and there isn't that much in the budget that can be cut, anyway!). 2.It is politically difficult to raise taxes. E. Most states have constitutional restrictions that prohibit deficit financing. F. income; borrowed funds.

13-2. A. 1.about 33%. 2.about 20%. B. 1.defense. 2.transfer payments. C. federal; state and local. D. 1.roughly constant. 2.nearly doubled.

13-3. A. 1.defense. 2.Social Security. 3.interest payments. B. 1.allocation of income. 2.Transfer payments are a bigger part of the budget than direct payments. C. 1.CN. 2.CN. 3.CN. 4.C. 5.C. 6.CN. 7.C. 8.C. D. 1. 4, 5. 2. 7, 8. 3. 1, 2, 3. E. 5%. F. 1–3. Answers will vary but could include defense, grants to local governments for transit, sewage, or water projects, subsidies for education, and any transfers that a household may receive.

13-4. A. education. B. finance capital projects. C. 1.prisons. 2.health care. D. 1.SL. 2.SL. 3.SL. 4.SL. 5.F. 6.F. 7.F. 8.F. E. 1–3. Answers may vary, but just about every state is having serious problems as of 1991. Areas may include transportation (potholes, fuel for buses), education (low teacher salaries, understaffing, poor facilities), public safety (rising crime, inadequate number of prison cells), and underfunding of social service programs (health care, day care).

Case Application: **Renovating America**

1. Federal spending on the renewal of the nation's public facilities would increase the pie slice in Figure 3 on page 362 of the textbook labeled "Other direct." That slice shows federal spending on nondefense goods and services.

2. The state and local government spending in Figure 4 on page 363 of the textbook that will be affected by the need to renovate the infrastructure is "transportation" and "utilities."

3. Open answer. It could be argued that renewing America's infrastructure should have one of the highest priorities in government spending because continued deterioration of the nation's transportation system and other public facilities would lead to a decrease in economic efficiency and a slowdown of GNP growth, not to mention the dangers and inconveniences to the public. Those who oppose massive spending on the infrastructure might argue that we cannot afford the high cost it would entail because of more pressing needs such as an adequate national defense and adequate human services such as education, food programs for malnourished children, and medical care.

Where Do Governments Get the Money to Spend?

Review of the Learning Objectives

13-5. A. 1.F. 2.S. 3.F(&S). 4.S&L. 5.F. 6.L. 7.F. B. The federal tax system is more **progressive** than state and local tax systems. Therefore collecting taxes at the federal level results in more vertical equity. C. 1.income and payroll taxes. 2.sales taxes, excise taxes. 3.income taxes on earned interest and dividends, and corporate income taxes on a corporation *before* it pays the dividends. 4.property taxes. D. 1.The supply of land would not change—it can't! 2.Taxes are a cost of production that must be paid, and removing the tax on buildings would make them less expensive to build. More (and bigger) buildings would therefore be built.

Case Application: Should the United States Have a Value-Added Tax?

1. If a value-added tax were imposed in the United States as a substitute for the existing Social Security taxes, approximately 36% of federal government revenues would have to be collected by the VAT. This can be seen from Figure 5 on page 367 of the textbook, which shows the percentage of federal government revenues collected from payroll taxes.

2. Income taxes, payroll taxes, and corporate profit taxes are said to discourage people and businesses from maximizing the amount of work and capital that they put into production because of the reduction in net returns after taxes. Those taxes are alleged to discourage risk-taking because they cannot be passed on, while value-added taxes can be passed on in the form of higher prices.

3. Open answer. Those who favor a value-added tax claim it is superior because it does not reduce incentives as other taxes do, is easy to collect and difficult to evade, and would help our international trade situation. Those who oppose VAT do so largely because it is a regressive tax and because it would have a direct inflationary effect on the prices of goods and services. The taxes which are most often proposed for elimination in favor of VAT are the payroll tax, which is itself a highly regressive tax, or a portion of income taxes because they are alleged to reduce incentives and be difficult and costly to collect.

Who Pays for Government Spending?

Review of the Learning Objectives

13-6. A. 1.horizontal equity. 2.vertical equity. B. 1.There would be less horizontal equity because two people with the same income could pay different taxes if one's income was from capital gains and the other's from wages. 2.There would be less vertical equity because wealthier households earning their incomes by buying and selling assets would pay a lower tax rate than lower-income wage earners. C. 1.Whoever uses that service. 2.Gasoline taxes are used to finance highway construction and maintenance. D. 1.collective goods (cannot exclude non-payers). 2.redistribution of income to the poor—if the poor could afford to pay for the services, they would not be poor! E. 1.E. 2.B. 3.B or E. 4.E. 5.E. 6.E. 7.B.

13-7. A. 1.taxes on things considered "sins"—drinking and smoking. 2.Smokers and drinkers affect their own health and the health of others through secondhand smoke and accidents. Also, they often require public health assistance paid for by taxpayers. By paying extra taxes, they pay for some of these costs. B. 1.People may work less. 2.fewer new buildings. 3.fewer people investing in corporate stocks. 4.more people buying and selling financial assets. 5.People will switch to blue pencils. 6.People will give less to charity.

13-8. A. If the demand is inelastic, the incidence will fall on the buyer. If demand is elastic, the incidence will fall on the seller, who must lower the price to keep people from switching to substitutes. B. 1.regressive. 2.progressive. 3.proportional. C. regressive. D. 1.P. 2.R. 3.R. 4.R. 5.Pr. 6.R. 7.R.

Case Application: A Look at the Flat-Rate Tax

1. A flat-rate income tax would eliminate the progressivity of the income tax structure and thereby change the vertical equity so that larger income earners would not pay higher percentages of their income in taxes.

2. A flat-rate tax could increase the efficiency of the tax system by eliminating the great complexity of income tax laws and regulations, thereby saving the

enormous funds spent in the private sector to avoid taxes and the government expenditures on enforcing their collection. It might also reduce the degree to which income tax laws distort the pattern of capital and other resource allocations.

3. Open answer. Whether you favor a pure flat-rate tax, the modified flat-rate tax, or the progressive income tax system depends on your attitudes toward vertical equity in the tax system and your beliefs concerning the degree to which the progressive income tax system is more or less fair and efficient than a pure flat-rate tax system, or whether a compromise modified flat-rate system accomplishes the efficiency and equity objectives better.

Answers to Practice Test

1.b. 2.e. 3.b. 4.a. 5.c. 6.c. 7.d. 8.c. 9.b. 10.a. 11.d. 12.d. 13.d. 14.a. 15.d. 16.F. 17.F. 18.T. 19.F. 20.T.

Chapter 14

What Can the Government Do About Unemployment and Inflation?

Review of the Learning Objectives

14-1. A. 1.economic growth. 2.low unemployment. 3.low inflation. B. 1.record budget deficits. 2.growing inequality of income. 3.international trade deficits (among others). C. 1.supply-side. 2.save; investment. 3.spent. D. Like the United States, if you borrowed a great deal you could have a good time living beyond your means **for a while**. Eventually, the bills would come due and you would need to reduce your future standard of living as more of your resources went to pay off old debts.

14-2. A. 1.by decreasing personal taxes. 2.by decreasing business taxes. 3.by reducing interest rates. B. 1.d. 2.c. 3.a. 4.b. C. Increased military expenditures would require an increase in government expenditures. D. Expecting higher inflation, lenders would raise the **nominal** interest rate. E. People might save their extra disposable income in order to pay future taxes, thus demand would not increase. F. 1.F, Down. 2.M, Up. 3.M, Up. 4.F, Up. 5.F, Down.

14-3. A. 1.Balancing the budget would require tax increases, less spending, or both. Either would reduce aggregate demand and make the recession worse. 2.Balancing the budget would require tax cuts, spending increases, or both. Either would increase aggregate demand and could be inflationary. B. surplus during expansions; deficit during recessions. C. Surpluses require either less spending on things that constituents want, higher taxes, or both. These are unpopular with voters. D. 1.C. 2.F. 3.A. 4.A. 5.C.

Case Application: **The Balanced Budget Amendment**

1. Congress could circumvent the requirement for a balanced budget by a vote of three-fifths of the whole number of both houses of Congress.

2. Passage of the Balanced Budget Amendment would virtually eliminate expansionary fiscal policy. If the government could not incur deficits when demand in the private sector was insufficient for full employment, there would be little it could do to combat recession or depression, since monetary policy may be ineffective at the bottom of a business cycle.

3. Open answer. Those in favor of the Balanced Budget Amendment believe that Congress and the administration do not have enough self-discipline to avoid budget deficits. They contend the political temptations to overspend are too great and, therefore, a balanced budget amendment to the Constitution is necessary. Those who oppose the Balanced Budget Amendment believe it would handcuff the federal government and prevent it from serving the needs of the country, including the need to stabilize the economy and achieve full employment, or, if the restrictions of the amendment proved too hampering, Congress would simply override them.

How Does Fiscal Policy Help Stabilize the Economy?

Review of the Learning Objectives

14-4. A. 1.S. 2.K. 3.S. 4.K. 5.S. 6.S. 7.K. B. Supply-side takes longer because it takes more time to increase the supply of productive resources than it does to increase spending. C. 1.Keynesian. 2.Supply-side.

14-5. A. 1. 10; $1,000. 2. 5; $500. 3. 3; $300. 4. 2; $200. 5. 1, $100. B. It would approach infinity. C. 1.inverse. 2.Spending increases aggregate demand and increased consumption rates increase the size of the multiplier. 3.It would cause it to increase. D. 1.$200,000,000. 2.$250,000,000. 3.$100,000,000.

14-6. A. "cushion" downturns and upturns. B. 1.increase aggregate demand. 2.decrease aggregate demand. C. consumption (C). D. 1, 2, and 4 should be checked.

310 / Working With The Study of Economics, 4/E

Case Application: What Happens to Tax-Cut Dollars?

1. The discretionary fiscal policy measure discussed in the application is the reduction of federal taxes in order to stimulate output, investment, income, and employment.

2. The multiplier effect works on tax-cut dollars as well as on government expenditure dollars. When taxpayers have additional after-tax income, they spend most of it on goods and services. The amounts they spend become income to other people, who in turn spend most of their new income on goods and services. The result is a multiplier effect, which increases the total income generated by some multiple of the initial amount of tax reduction.

3. Open answer. The tax legislation passed in the 1980s was wise and effective fiscal policy to the extent that it helped the economy recover from the 1981–82 recession. It was not wise and effective to the extent that it resulted in increased federal government deficits and a more unequal distribution of income.

How Can Monetary Policy Help Stabilize the Economy?

Review of the Learning Objectives

14-7. A. 1.MS up, r down, I up, AD up. 2.MS up, r down, I up, AD up. 3.MS down, r up, I down, AD down. B. 1.control interest rates. 2.timing. C. 1.supply of money. 2.velocity of money. 3.demand; saving.

D. 1.

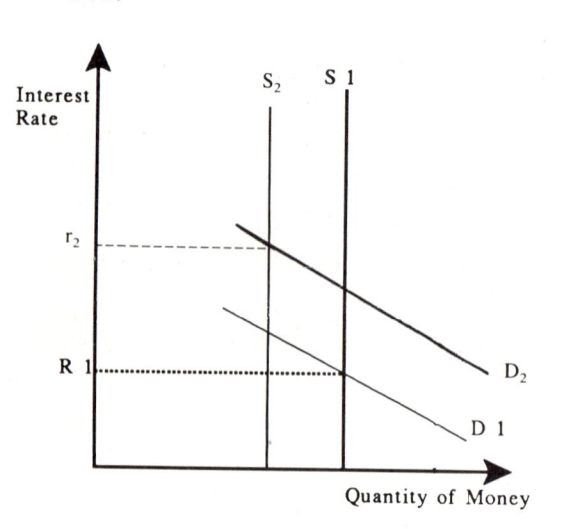

2.a. rise b. fall c. fall. 3.Hinder.

E. 1.

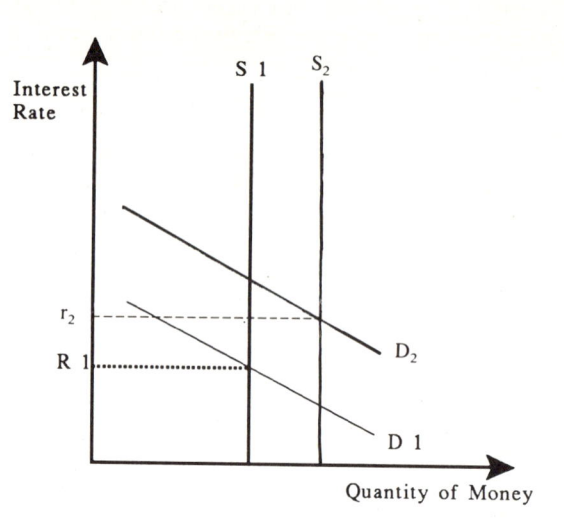

2.They would increase. 3.They would be lower. 4.It might be inflationary. F. 1.A constant velocity of money. 2.No.

Case Application: The Interest Rate Yo-Yo

1. When the Federal Reserve sells government securities in the open market, it "sops up" excess bank reserves. This restricts the banks' ability to expand credit to borrowers, which causes interest rates to rise.

2. The consequences of wide fluctuations in interest rates are to increase the amount of uncertainty for business firms, which may have formulated their plans on the basis of one interest rate and then find their plans defeated by large changes in the interest rates. This may lead to bankruptcy of the firms.

3. Open answer. Those who say that controlling the money supply necessitates wide swings in interest rates base their reasoning on the overriding importance of macroeconomic stability. They believe that the money supply is the key to putting an end to inflation, and interest rates are a secondary consideration. Those who are opposed to this policy believe that price stabilization can be achieved without the extreme swings in interest rates and that the costs that the policy imposes on individuals and businesses are too high to justify it.

How Can Economic Growth Be Increased?

Review of the Learning Objectives

14-8. A. 1.Current consumption. 2.A higher standard of living in the future. B. decrease. C. 1.quantity. 2.quality. D. 1.C. 2.I. 3.C. 4.C. 5.I. 6.I. 7.C. 8.C. E. (answers will vary) 1.highway improvements. 2.water projects. 3.human capital investment (education).

14-9. A. 1.quantity. 2.quality. B. 1."baby boomers" entering the labor force. 2.more women working outside the home. 3.more workers working longer years (retiring later). C. 1.formal education. 2.on-the-job training. D. 1.foregone wages while in school or lower wages during on-the-job training. 2.the older someone is, the fewer remaining work years available to get the returns. E. 1.1. 2.2. 3.4. 4.3.

Case Application: **How to Grow**

1. The factors discussed in this application that affect economic growth are expenditures on research and development and the number of years of education completed.

2. Spending on R&D would tend to increase in periods of rapid economic growth both because of rising demand for goods and services, causing producers to seek ways of increasing output to satisfy the market, and because of more revenues available to producers, enabling them to pay for increased R&D.

3. Open answer. Measures that might be taken to increase the rate of growth of GNP include encouraging research and development (for example, by government-sponsored research and development programs and subsidies) and encouraging youth to obtain more education (for example, by student loans).

Answers to Practice Test

1.c. 2.b. 3.a. 4.b. 5.b. 6.b. 7.d. 8.b. 9.b. 10.b. 11.b. 12.d. 13.d. 14.a. 15.c. 16.F. 17.T. 18.F. 19.T. 20.F.

Crossword Puzzle for Chapters 10–14

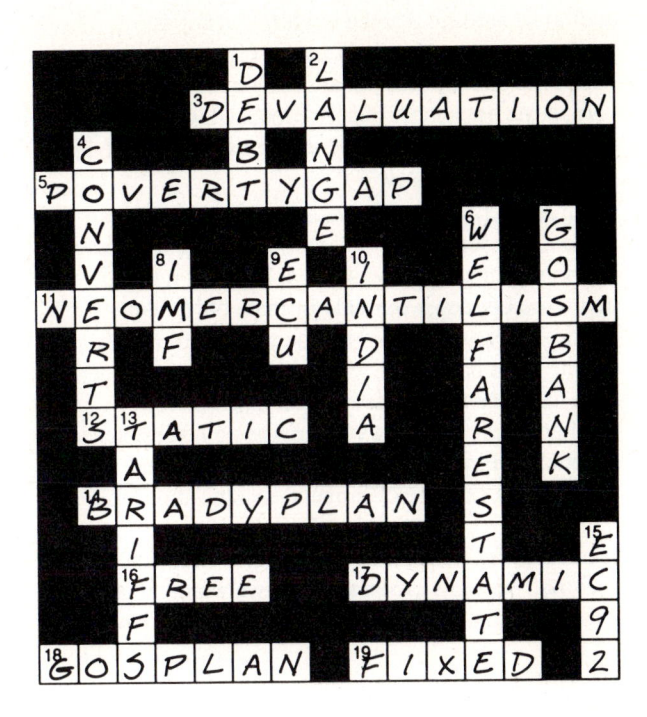

Across: 3.DEVALUATION, 5.POVERTYGAP, 11.NEOMERCANTILISM, 12.STATIC, 14.BRADYPLAN, 16.FREE, 17.DYNAMIC, 18.GOSPLAN, 19.FIXED

Down: 1.DEBT, 2.LDC, 4.CONVERTIBLE, 6.WEED, 7.GO, 8.IMF, 9.EUIDA, 10.J, 13.TA, 15.ECZ, etc.

Chapter 15

Why Do We Trade With Other Countries?

Review of the Learning Objectives

15-1. A. 1.absolute. 2.2. 3.4. 4.Mexico. 5.1/2. 6.1/4. 7.Nigeria. 8.Nigeria. 9.Mexico. 10. Mexico should trade textiles for Nigerian oil.

15-2. A. Only when each country produces a good that is not produced in the other. B. 1.A straight-line PPF implies that costs are constant. 2.increase as the output of a specific good increases. 3.perfectly adaptable (mobile) to all uses. 4.expensive. 5.limited.

15-3. A. 1.I. 2.I. 3.E. 4.I. 5.E. 6.E. B. from American purchases (imports) of their products. C. capital (technology); labor.

Case Application: **U.S. Farmers Selling Overseas**

1. Judging from the data on U.S. exports as a percentage of world exports, the United States apparently had the largest efficiency advantage over the rest of the world in the production of corn, followed closely by soybeans. U.S. corn exports accounted for 78.2% of world exports of the crop, while U.S. soybean exports accounted for 72.5% of world exports.

2. The United States does not completely specialize in corn production because of increasing costs. If additional acreage planted in corn was not as productive or was located in areas of the country where the climate was not as suitable for growing corn, costs per bushel of corn produced would rise and the United States would not be as competitive in the world corn market.

3. Open answer. Adding world demand to the domestic demand for our agricultural output does tend to raise the prices for some food items at home. If holding down food prices is our only or main objective, restricting exports would be one way of doing that. On the other hand, policies in this country for some time have been aimed at supporting the prices of farm products, frequently by government subsidies. Restricting farm exports would hold down food prices at the expense of farmers' income and would hurt the sales of other industries to the farm communities. The cost of living might be lower, but so would people's incomes. Also, we would not be able to purchase much from other countries.

Who Benefits and Who Is Hurt By Foreign Trade?

Review of the Learning Objectives

15-4. A. 1. 1/2 unit of textiles. 2. 2 units of oil. 3. 1/4 unit of oil. 4. 4 units of oil.

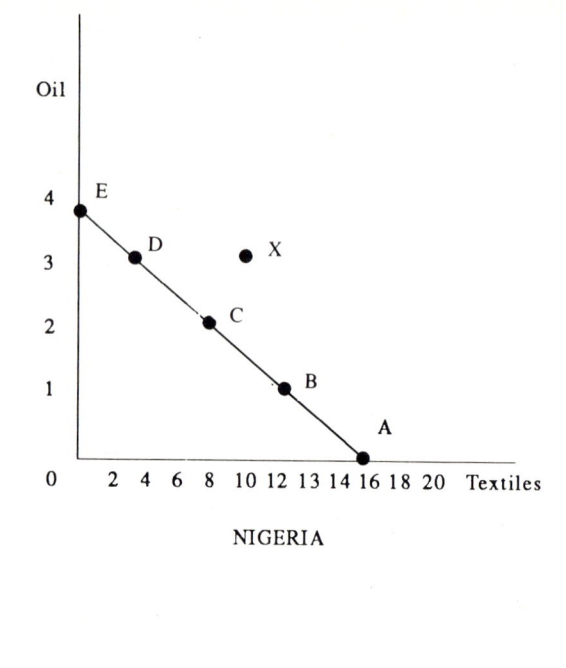

6.(a) 5 units of oil and 6 units of textiles. (b) 3 units of oil and 10 units of textiles. (c) Both countries now have more of each good—they are better off after specialization and trade.

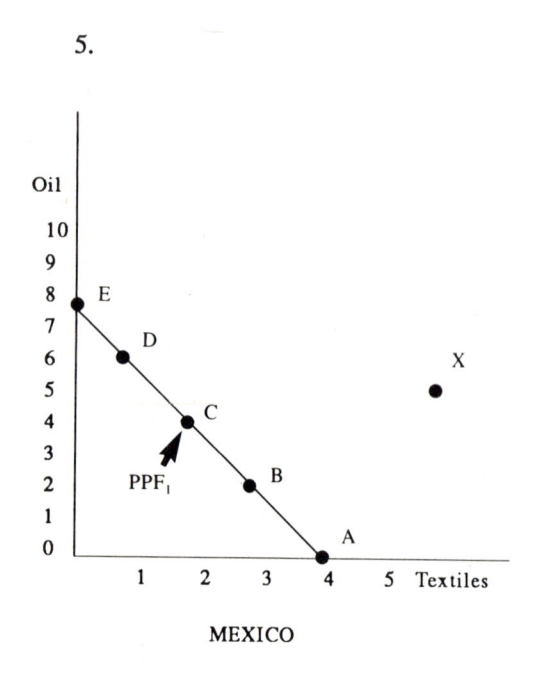

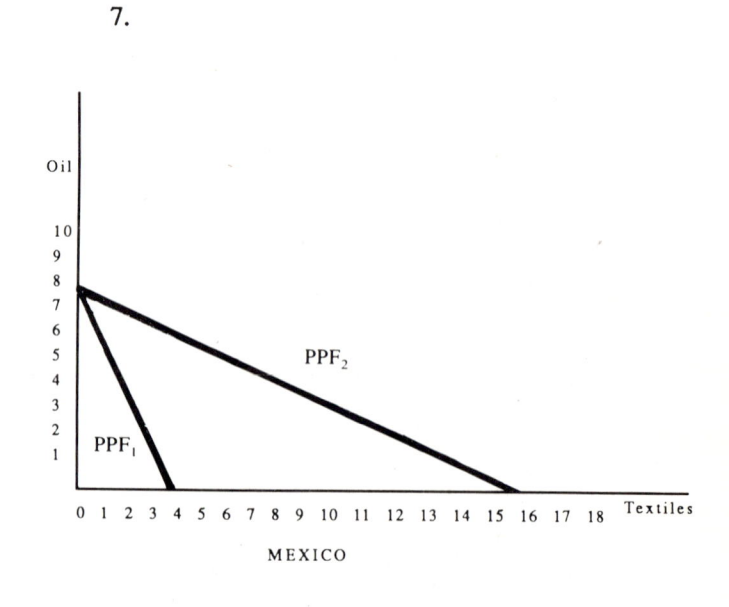

5.

7.

8.

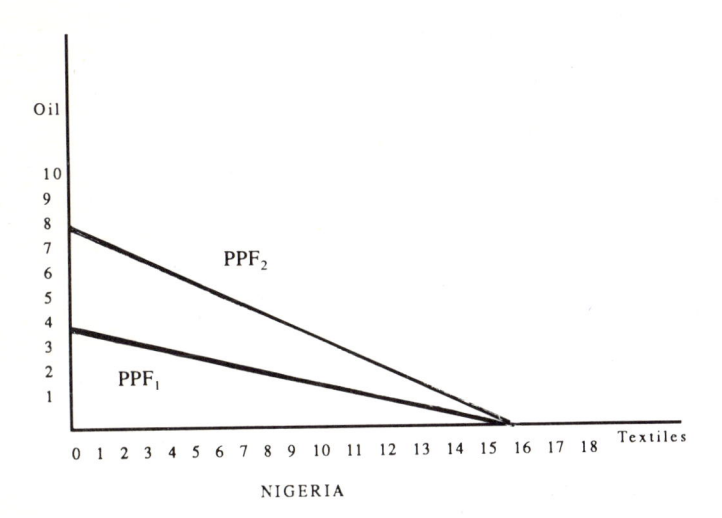

[Graph: Nigeria PPF, Oil vs Textiles, showing PPF₁ (from 4 oil to 16 textiles) and PPF₂ (from 8 oil to 16 textiles)]

9. Trade moves the PPF to the right for both countries, allowing them to attain previously unattainable combinations of both goods.

15-5. A, B, & C. Answers will vary. D. consumers. E. 1. American consumers; American auto workers. 2. American farmers; American bread consumers. 3. American shoe producers; American shoe buyers. 4. American energy companies; American consumers. F. structural. G. Answers will vary but might include 1. autos. 2. steel. 3. textiles.

Case Application: **The Top U.S. Exporters**

1. Among the top 10 exporters, the automobile industry accounted for the largest amount of export sales, with General Motors, Ford, and Chrysler exporting over $23 billion worth of vehicles and parts. In total exports, however, the major export industry is not automobiles—or aircraft or chemicals or food, although these are all important exports—but the largest export category is diverse types of machinery.

2. A number of industries that do not export much or any of their production but nevertheless benefit from international trade are those that use imported raw materials or semi-finished products. They benefit because the production inputs might not be available domestically, or, if available, would be more expensive. An example is the construction industry, which uses a large amount of imported construction materials and exports virtually none of its output.

3. Open answer. One explanation for the success of the U.S. aircraft, auto, and other industries, both in domestic and foreign sales, is that they have economies of scale in production that enable them to mass-produce at lower costs than most countries. Another advantage is the pool of skilled and trained labor available in this country. A third advantage is the large amount of capital available to develop and acquire advanced technological equipment.

How Do We Restrict Foreign Trade?

Review of the Learning Objectives

15-6. A.

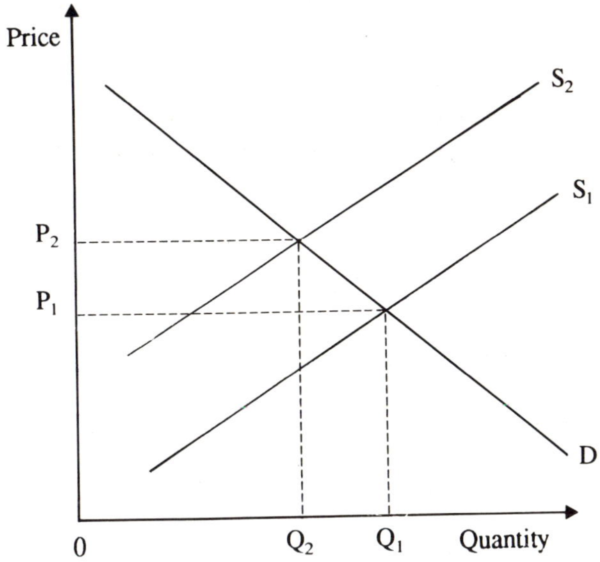

[Graph: Supply and demand with S₁ shifting to S₂, price rising from P₁ to P₂, quantity falling from Q₁ to Q₂]

B.

[Graph: Supply and demand with vertical quota supply Sq, price rising from P₁ to Pq, quantity falling from Q₁ to Qq]

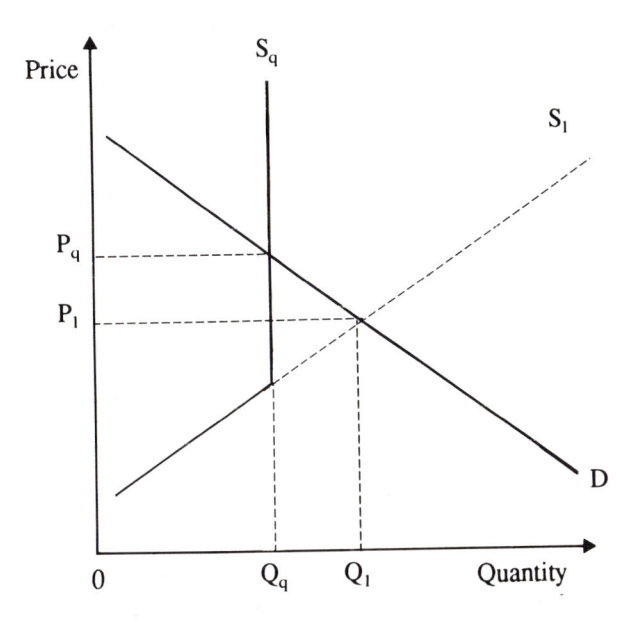

C. With quotas, because the supply curve will be vertical (perfectly inelastic), and the quantity supplied will be unable to increase to absorb some of the increased demand. D. 1.politics (punishment). 2.to protect technological advantages (neomercantilism). 3.national security. E. Answers will vary.

15-7. A. multilateral. B. 1.Smoot-Hawley. 2.It reduced international trade. C. 1.confusion resulting from different tariff rates with different countries on the same product. 2.most-favored nation clauses. 3.They give the "favored" nation all tariff reductions that are negotiated with any other country.

Case Application: Made-in-America Japanese Cars

1. A local content law is more like a quota because it limits the quantity of a commodity that can be imported, no matter how great the differential between foreign and domestic prices.
2. The effect of a local content law would be to nullify comparative advantage. American resources would be used to produce automobile components even if they were relatively inefficient in that production. They would not shift to industries in which they were relatively more efficient.
3. Open answer. A local content law for the automobile industry would have the same results in Mexico and the United States in the sense that it would create more jobs and profits in the industry. It would have different effects because Mexico would benefit from developing new skills in its labor force and reducing industrial production costs, while for the United States a local content law would increase production costs and monopoly pricing in the industry.

Should Foreign Trade Be Restricted?

Review of the Learning Objectives

15-8. A. 1.increase; decrease. 2.increase; decrease. B. 1.They have more and better capital to work with. 2.It would prevent the exporting of the technology that allows them to earn higher wages than some foreign workers. C. No. The infant industry argument applies to newly developing industries in an economy. The American steel and auto industries are hardly infants.

Case Application: Politics and Trade

1. The U.S. embargo on equipment for the Soviet gas pipeline resembled the neomercantilist position because it blocked the export of advanced technology and capital equipment.
2. The infant industry argument is more justified for developing countries than for developed countries because small new industries in developing countries have high production costs due to low volume and cannot compete with the mass production efficiencies of the industries in developed countries. Developed countries have adequate capital and market size to support a large-volume industry without restrictions on imports. In any country, however, the infant industry argument can be a smoke screen to protect inefficient producers, and the political influence of vested interests can be used to perpetuate protectionist tariffs and quotas indefinitely into the future, whether justified or not.
3. Open answer. Foreign trade has often been used in the past as a weapon of diplomacy. It could be argued that a country has the right to control its trade in order to achieve its international political objectives. On the other hand, using trade sanctions as a diplomatic weapon is costly to the country imposing the sanctions as well as to the country against which they are directed and may have an adverse effect on third parties as well. Furthermore, trade sanctions may not have their intended effects because of alternate sources of supply, evasion, or retaliation.

Answers to Practice Test

1.d. 2.b. 3.b. 4.b. 5.c. 6.a. 7.a. 8.d. 9.d. 10.c. 11.d. 12.c. 13.c. 14.b. 15.c. 16.F. 17.T. 18.T. 19.F. 20.F.

Chapter 16

How Do We Pay for Imports?

Review of the Learning Objectives

16-1. A. foreign-exchange. B. 1. 0.20 or 1/5 (20 cents). 2. 0.25 or 1/4 (25 cents). 3. 0.10 or 1/10 (10 cents). C. 1. 5 francs. 2.$20. 3.$24. 4.$25. D. 1.$0.20. 2. 75f. 3. 90f. 4. 60f. E. 1.more expensive. 2.less expensive. 3.more expensive. F. 1.less expensive. 2.more expensive. 3.less expensive.

Answers to Chapter Questions / 315

16-2. A. 1.supply of dollars. 2.supply of pounds.

B.

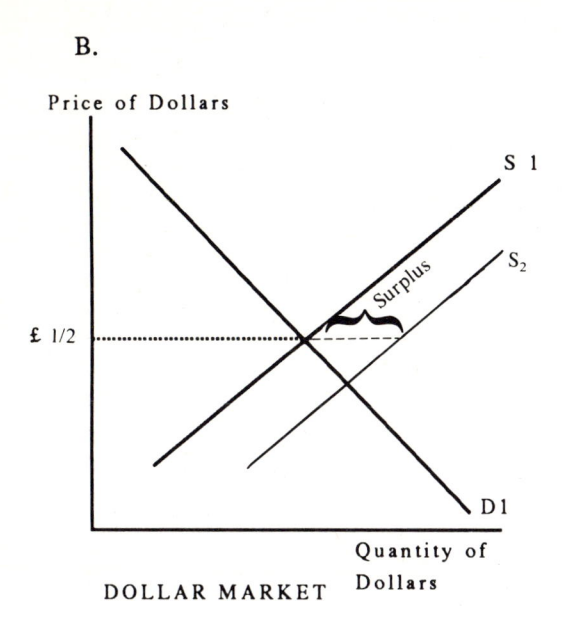

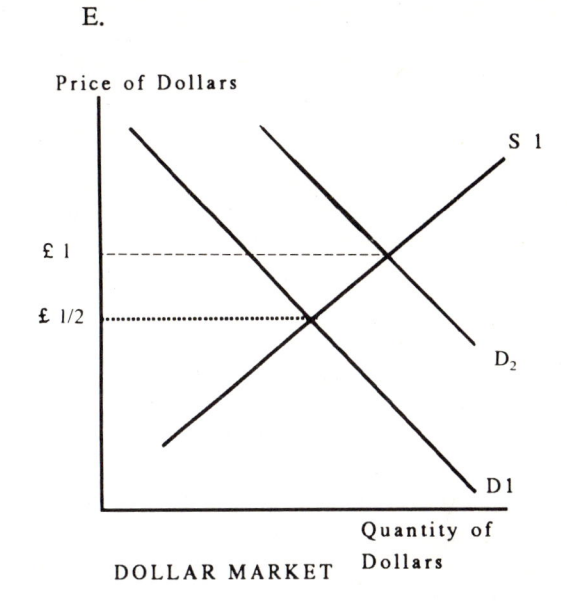

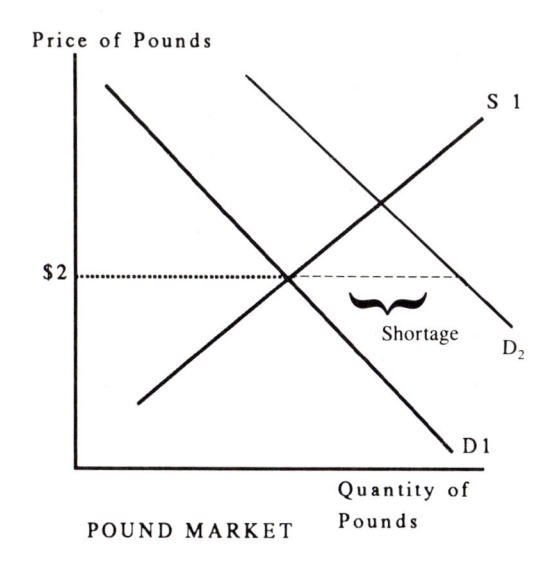

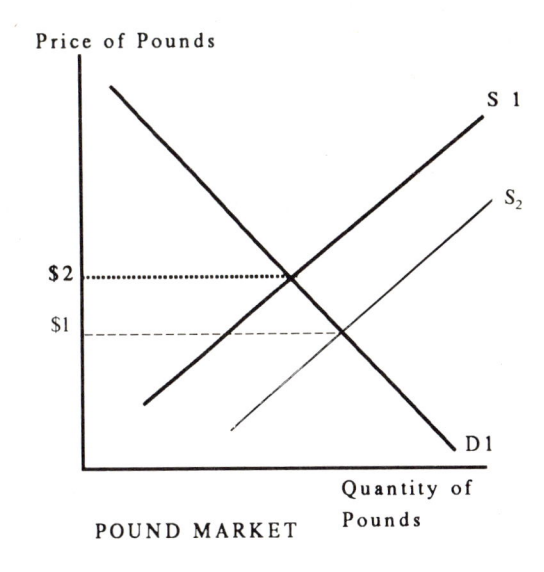

[Dollar Market diagram: S1, S2, D1; price £1/2 shown with Surplus]

[Pound Market diagram: S1, D1, D2; price $2 shown with Shortage]

C. 1.shortage. 2.The British government or central bank would need to provide pounds to the market at a rate of $2 = 1 pound. D. 1.surplus. 2.The U.S. government or Federal Reserve would need to buy up the excess dollars with pounds that they keep in reserve.

E.

[Dollar Market diagram: S1, D1, D2; prices £1 and £1/2 shown]

[Pound Market diagram: S1, S2, D1; prices $2 and $1 shown]

16-3. A. 1.revalued. 2.devalued. B. 1.appreciates. 2.depreciates. C. 1.devaluing. 2.exports. 3.employment and GNP. 4.Citizens of the country would be able to buy fewer imported goods. D. 1.Yes. A country can cause the value of its currency to appreciate by buying its own currency in exchange markets with foreign currencies that it has in reserve. It can cause its currency to depreciate by flooding the exchange markets with it. E. 1.D. 2.A. 3.A. 4.D. 5.A.

Case Application: **The End of the World Credit Binge**

1. Mexico was employing a fixed exchange rate system. The peso was officially devalued to 70 pesos to the dollar by government action rather than depreciating to that level as the result of demand and supply in the foreign-exchange market.

2. When oil exporters receive payment for the petroleum they sell, they leave a large amount of their receipts on deposit in New York and other Western nation banks because the stability in those countries provides security for their funds. Those funds thus become available for lending by the banks.

3. Open answer. The Mexican government believes it must pursue the domestic policies that maximize the welfare of its citizens. It is committed to a high economic growth rate in order to improve its low living standards. The IMF and its industrialized members, however, believe that since it is largely their funds and those of their private banking institutions that are at stake, the IMF must require Mexico to adopt austerity measures to ensure that the loans can be repaid.

What Happens When Exports and Imports Do Not Balance?

Review of the Learning Objectives

16-4. A. 1.I,C. 2.I,LT. 3.E,ST. 4.E,LT. 5.E,C. 6.E,ST. 7.I,C.

16-5. A. 1.exports exceed imports. 2.exporters and export workers. 3.consumers. 4.appreciate. B. 1.imports exceed exports. 2.exporters and export workers. 3.consumers. 4.depreciate. C. 1.increasing. 2.increase. 3.decrease. 4.increase. 5.increase. 6.decrease. 7.disappear. D. 1.decreasing. 2.decrease. 3.increase. 4.decrease. 5.decrease. 6.increase. 7. disappear. E. Freely fluctuating exchange rates act to remove trade surpluses and deficits. If a surplus exists, the currency will appreciate and increase imports while decreasing exports. The surplus will disappear. In the case of deficits, the currency will depreciate, leading to fewer imports and more exports.

16-6. A. 1.outflows of gold or similar internationally accepted assets. 2.borrowing funds from the IMF. 3.it can sell its assets to other countries (or 4.it can allow its currency to depreciate). B. 1.Basic deficits are less likely to remain if rates can fluctuate because currency depreciation and/or appreciation automatically eliminate deficits and surpluses (see 16.5E, above). C. 1.residual accounts. 2.gold or similar assets.

Case Application: **U.S. International Trade Position Takes a Nosedive**

1. The balance of payments transactions not included in the data shown in the chart are long-term and short-term capital transactions and monetary gold transactions.

2. As a result of the drastic fall in the U.S. current account position, you would expect the international value of the dollar to depreciate. The reason is that there were much larger numbers of dollars being supplied to the foreign currency markets in payment for U.S. imports than demand for dollars by foreigners to pay for U.S. exports of goods and services.

3. Open answer. One reason could be the decline in the competitiveness of U.S. producers both in the domestic and in world markets, as discussed in chapter 7. Another reason cited is the high consumption rate of U.S. consumers in the 1980s. A related reason is the large federal government deficits in the decade, inviting capital imports and postponing the normal adjustment mechanism to bring trade back into balance.

What Is the Relationship Between International Finance and the National Economy?

Review of the Learning Objectives

16-7. A. $G + I + X = T + S + M$.

B. 1.T,S,M. 2.inversely. C. 1.G,I,X. 2.directly.

D.

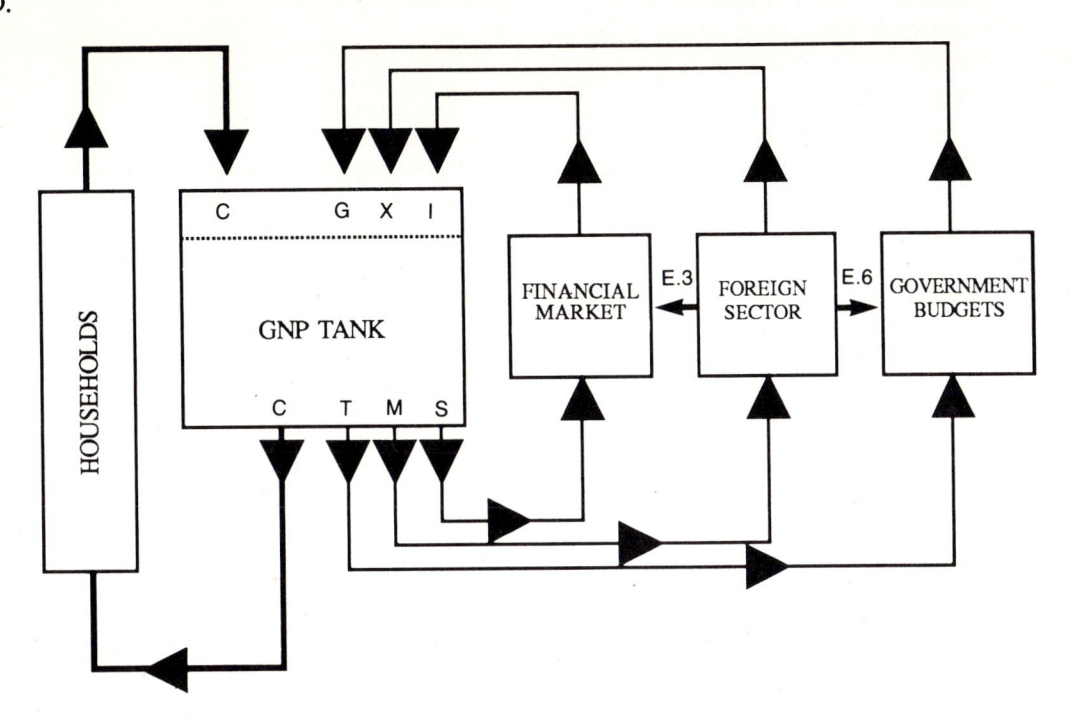

E. 1. More was flowing out of the financial markets. 2. They came from foreign lenders.

3. [See Figure above.]

4. More was flowing out of the government.
5. They came from foreign lenders.

6. [See Figure above.]

F. 1.

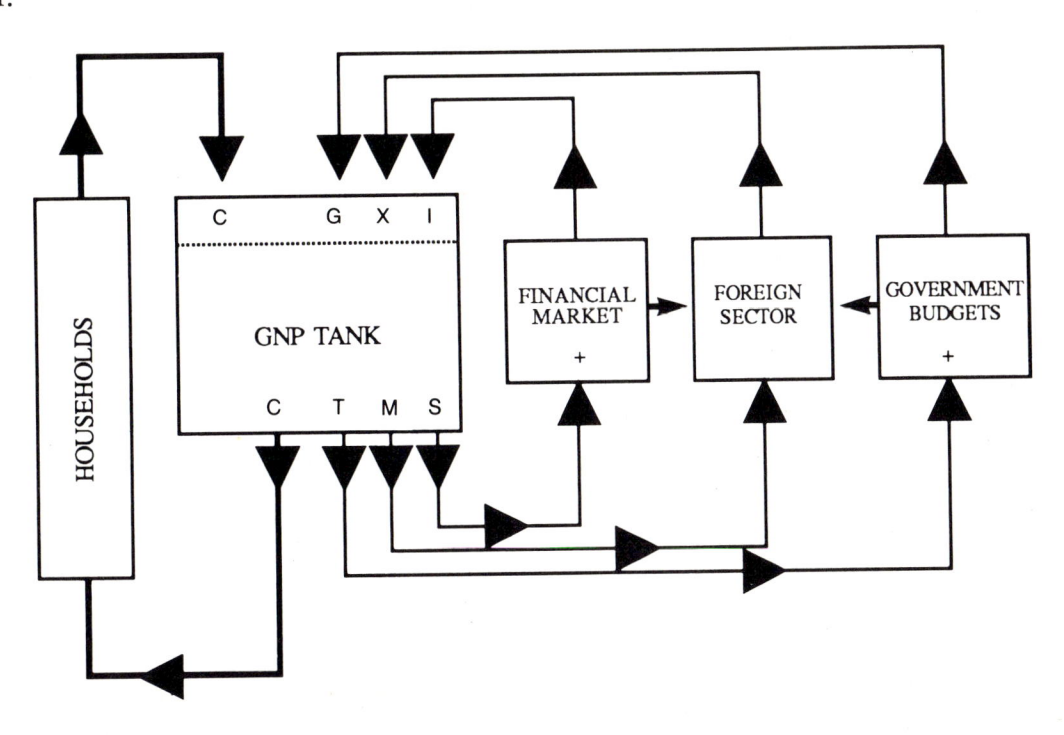

2. Lenders: government and financial markets; Borrowers: foreign sector. 3. It must be exporting more than it imports. 4. Japan.

16-8. A. In the short run, Americans have increased their standard of living because they were able to consume more than they produced. B. To buy American real estate, businesses, and government bonds (to finance the government budget deficit). C. Eventually we will need to pay others back by consuming less than we produce—the balance will be exported for others to enjoy. Our standard of living will decrease. Post–1980s Americans will be the ones to pay this price.

16-9. A. 1. It would find it difficult to borrow and would need to cut back on spending or raise taxes. 2. It would decrease as G decreased (or T increased), and aggregate demand decreased. 3. The same as in the government sector, investment would fall. 4. The same—GNP would decrease as I decreased. 5. There would be less money available for consumers to spend. B. 1. exports. 2. imports.

Case Application: **A Penny Saved Is a Rare Occurrence**

1. If the U.S. savings rate were greater, the consumption of domestic goods (C) and imported goods (I) would be less.
2. The low national savings rate in the United States contributes to an import surplus and balance of payments deficit, a fall in the dollar exchange rate, federal deficits that are partly financed by foreign capital, and a net debtor position in the world economy.
3. Open answer. It could be argued that the savings rate is the result of choices made by individuals and their representatives and that in a free-enterprise economy there should not be any interference with those choices. On the other side, it could be argued that when individual and national choices result in weakening the economy and reducing future standards of living, measures should be taken to change behaviors. Those measures might consist of tax incentives to increase personal and business savings and discourage consumption, reductions in federal deficits by cutting spending or raising taxes, and a campaign by the national leadership to change public attitudes.

Answers to Practice Test

1.b. 2.d. 3.d. 4.b. 5.a. 6.c. 7.b. 8.c. 9.a. 10.a. 11.e. 12.c. 13.b. 14.b. 15.d. 16.T. 17.F. 18.T. 19.F. 20.T.

Chapter 17

What Are the Alternatives to Capitalism?

Review of the Learning Objectives

17-1. A. 1.MS,SS. 2.SS. 3.MS,SS. 4.C,WS. 5.C,WS. 6.MS,SS. 7.WS. 8.WS. 9.C,WS. 10.C,WS. B. 1.SS. 2.MS. 3.WS. 4.C. C. 1.MS (or SS). 2.MS. 3.SS. 4.C. 5.C. 6.C. 7.WS. 8.SS. 9.MS. 10.WS. D. 1.SS. 2.MS. 3.MS. 4.C. 5.MS. 6.SS. 7.C (or WS or MS). 8.C.

Case Application: **Down Argentina Way**

1. The economic system that is characterized by powerful labor unions is the welfare state.
2. The system adopted by Perón was similar to state socialism in the nationalization of industry and services. It was also similar in redistributing income, taking it away from property owners. It was different in that there was not comprehensive economic planning, prices were not controlled, and strong labor unions were allowed.
3. Open answer. It was justified in the sense that he redistributed income more equally and provided social services for the poor. It was not justified in the deterioration of the economy that resulted from his policies.

How Do Alternative Economic Systems Resolve the Basic Economic Questions?

Review of the Learning Objectives

17-2. A. 1.five-year plans. 2.priority sectors. 3.Gosplan. 4.control figures. 5.economic ministries. 6.economic ministries. 7.Gosplan. 8.Gosbank. B. 1.entrepreneurs. 2.market prices. 3.factor markets. 4.market prices. 5.profits. 6.financial markets. C. 1.planners. 2.society. 3.consumer demand (markets). 4.the consumer. D. 1.planners. 2.employers.

Case Application: **Food Production in the Soviet Union**

1. No. Agriculture was not one of the priority sectors. The priority sectors were investment in heavy industry and military production.
2. Difficulties and deficiencies in the resolution of the "how to produce" food question in the Soviet Union include the failure of the bureaucratic planning hierarchy, the lack of an incentive system, and the lack of research facilities and organization.

3. If you were a member of the Council of Ministers, you might or might not vote to privatize agriculture. If you were committed to moving the system to a market economy, you would vote in favor. But if you feared the changes privatization would bring and wanted to preserve the status quo, you would vote against. If you were a farmer, you would probably vote in favor in order to have a higher income, although many farmers are not willing to put in the work and take the risks that would be entailed. If you were a consumer, you might vote against privatization, preferring food shortages under government-controlled pricing to high prices under privatization.

How Does the Performance of Alternative Economic Systems Compare?

Review of the Learning Objectives

17-3. A. 1.dynamic. 2.static. B. 1.flexible prices. 2.profit incentives. C. 1.public transportation. 2.No. Western European welfare states and capitalist economies have excellent public transit systems. D. 1.large savings balances. 2.long lines at stores. E. 1.they help maintain stable prices (no inflation). 2.prices cannot contribute to economic efficiency by rising to eliminate shortages. F. 1.high labor-force participation rates. 2.investment in human capital. G. 1.it helps achieve the goal of full employment. 2.labor (workers) is not allocated to its most efficient use.

17-4. A. 1.SS. 2.M. 3.SS. 4.SS. 5.SS. 6.M. 7.M (or neither). 8.SS. B. No owners of air and water with an incentive and/or the property rights with which to protect them. C. 1.Lake Baikal has been polluted by paper mills. 2.The Volga has been polluted with raw sewage. 3.Radioactive fallout from the Chernobyl nuclear plant. 4.Draining the Aral Sea. 5.One cannot drink the tap water in Leningrad.

Case Application: **Business Cycle Hits Eastern Europe**

1. The two primary economic goals that the Soviet Union succeeded in achieving much better than the West in the 1930s were full employment and economic growth.

2. An increase in petroleum prices might create more problems for command economies than for market economies because it is not as easy for them to adapt allocation and production to changed resource costs. In a command system, a change in one important variable, such as energy costs, requires conscious adjustment of countless allocation and production decisions throughout the system. In a market system, on the other hand, the changes automatically come about as a result of the operation of the price mechanism in marketplaces.

3. Open answer. It could be argued that if it were not for the increased trade relationships with the West, the communist bloc countries would not have suffered from the 1979 oil price shock and the slump of the early 1980s. On the other hand, without the imports of high-technology capital goods, food and industrial raw materials, and modern consumer products from the West, the communist bloc would likely have had lower standards of living and a slower long-term growth rate.

Answers to Practice Test

1.d. 2.d. 3.c. 4.d. 5.b. 6.a. 7.d. 8.c. 9.b. 10.a. 11.c. 12.c. 13.a. 14.a. 15.b. 16.F. 17.T. 18.F. 19.F. 20.F.

Chapter 18

How Do Standards of Living Compare?

Review of the Learning Objectives

18-1. A. 1.GNP. 2.per capita GNP. 3.growth of GNP. B. 1.adult illiteracy. 2.life expectancy. 3.infant mortality. C. 1.GNP growth. 2.literacy rates. 3.life expectancy. 4.infant mortality rates. D. 1.per capita GNP. E. (answers will vary) 1.a telephone. 2.indoor plumbing. 3.electricity.

18-2. A. 1.South Asia. 2.East Asia. 3.sub-Saharan Africa. B. (answers will vary) 1.India. 2.Bangladesh. 3.Afghanistan. 4.Sri Lanka. C. (answers will vary) 1.Indonesia. 2.China. 3.Thailand. 4.Laos. D. (answers will vary) 1.Nigeria. 2.Kenya. 3.Tanzania. 4.Zambia.

Case Application: **Report on Africa**

1. Nigeria has the second lowest per capita income among the five largest low-income countries. It also has the second lowest growth rate in per capita income.
2. The low life expectancy and high infant mortality rate in Nigeria could in part be due to malnutrition because of inadequate food supplies. Mothers that are malnourished give birth to babies with low birth weights, which tend to have high mortality rates.
3. Open answer. African governments have adopted policies of keeping food prices low in order to hold down the cost of living for their urban populations. This policy is designed to help the politically powerful urban residents. However, it results in greater poverty in the agricultural areas, discourages farmers from increasing output, and deprives the agricultural sector of revenues for increasing capital investment and productivity.

What Makes Countries Poor?

Review of the Learning Objectives

18-3. A. The economic surplus is anything left over after the people in a country take care of their basic needs. It is from this surplus that a country finances its investment spending. B. 1.overpopulation. 2.low initial investment (the vicious circle of poverty). 3.little human capital (4.the external exploitation, which may have taken away any surplus to other countries). C. 1.increased investment/GNP ratios. 2.low capital/output ratios. 3.investment in human capital. D. the welfare state because of the powerful labor unions and the emphasis on redistribution of income. E. 1.producers and labor unions. 2.The people in the LDC must rely on high-cost, low-quality import substitutes.

Case Application: **Do You Like Company? How About 10 Billion?**

1. Yes, Table 1 does show that, overall, poverty is associated with illiteracy. This is indicated by the fact that the adult illiteracy rate for the low-income countries as a whole is 44%, while that for the lower-middle-income countries is only 27% and that for higher-income countries even less.

2. They are related because they are both part of the poverty syndrome—they occur together in the LDCs and each reinforces the other. They are different in that the vicious circle of poverty deals with the relationship between poverty and economic productivity and growth while the population-education vicious circle deals with the relationship between literacy, birth rates, and the perpetuation of poverty.
3. Open answer. Those who are concerned about the negative effects of high population growth rates in the LDCs on the world economy and environment might support the restoration of funding. Those who oppose organizations that support abortion to control population growth would be against the restoration of funding.

What are the Prospects for World Economic Development?

Review of the Learning Objectives

18-4. A. 1.geometric rate. 2.arithmetic rate.

B.

Population	Ears of Corn	Ears per Person
100	1,000	10.00
200	2,000	10.00
400	3,000	7.50
800	4,000	5.00
1,600	5,000	3.12

C. an inverse relationship. D. 1.energy resources. 2.the environment. E. 1.starvation. 2.high infant mortality rates. (3.low life expectancy rates).

18-6. A. (answers will vary) 1.pollution control devices on cars. 2."scrubbers" on manufacturers' smokestacks. 3.the construction of municipal sewage treatment plants. B. 1.more expensive cars and lower mileage. 2.having scrubbers instead of more products. 3.having fewer local schools, roads, and clinics. C. 1.It is an inverse relationship: reducing pollution means sacrificing goods and services. 2.the developed (industrialized) countries. D. 1.Western European countries would benefit from helping Eastern European countries reduce the pollution that is killing Western European lakes and forests. 2.Everyone would benefit by helping to preserve the world's rain forests and thus reducing global warming.

Case Application: Growth Prospects for the LDCs

1. The reason why per capita growth is expected to be less while total growth is larger is because of the higher population growth rate.
2. The forecast for per capita growth in Latin America depends in part on the success of population programs because unless population growth is slowed the increase in GDP will all be absorbed in providing subsistence for the larger numbers of people. It also depends in part on the success of the Brady Plan because unless the Latin American countries with high levels of foreign debt are able both to bring fiscal discipline to their economies and to regain their international credit they will not be able to invest and increase their productivity.
3. Open answer. If you assume, as does the World Bank, that the LDCs as a whole will have higher rates of per capita GDP in the 1990s than will the industrial countries, then the gap in living standards will diminish. However, for the poorest countries, particularly those in sub-Saharan Africa, the gap will get larger. Even the optimistic projections for the LDCs as a whole depend on their successfully solving the population, debt, and environmental problems.

Answers to Practice Test

1.a. 2.a. 3.c. 4.b. 5.d. 6.b. 7.c. 8.d. 9.b. 10.d. 11.c. 12.d. 13.c. 14.d. 15.b. 16.F. 17.F. 18.T. 19.T. 20.F.

Crossword Puzzle for Chapters 15-18

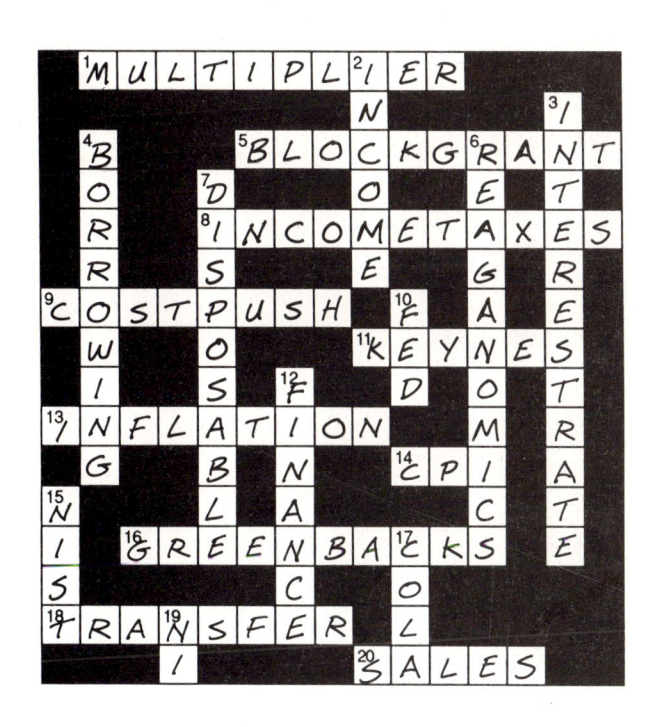